MAR 0 2 2011

The New Science
of Dreaming

The New Science of Dreaming

Volume 1
Biological Aspects

EDITED BY DEIRDRE BARRETT
AND PATRICK McNAMARA

Praeger Perspectives

Westport, Connecticut
London

Library of Congress Cataloging-in-Publication Data

The new science of dreaming / edited by Deirdre Barrett and Patrick McNamara.

    p. cm.

    Includes bibliographical references and index.

    ISBN 978-0-275-99045-9 (set : alk. paper) — ISBN 978-0-275-99046-6 (v. 1 : alk. paper) — ISBN 978-0-275-99047-3 (v. 2 : alk. paper) — ISBN 978-0-275-99048-0 (v. 3 : alk. paper) 1. Dreams. I. Barrett, Deirdre. II. McNamara, Patrick, 1956–

    BF1078.N454 2007

    154.6′3—dc22   2007008458

British Library Cataloguing in Publication Data is available.

Library of Congress Catalog Card Number: 2007008458
ISBN-13: 978-0-275-99045-9 (set)
ISBN-10: 0-275-99045-1
ISBN-13: 978-0-275-99046-6 (vol 1)
ISBN-10: 0-275-99046-X
ISBN-13: 978-0-275-99047-3 (vol 2)
ISBN-10: 0-275-99047-8
ISBN-13: 978-0-275-99048-0 (vol 3)
ISBN-10: 0-275-99048-6

First published in 2007

Praeger Publishers, 88 Post Road West, Westport, CT 06881
An imprint of Greenwood Publishing Group, Inc.
www.praeger.com

Printed in the United States of America

(∞)™

The paper used in this book complies with the Permanent Paper Standard issued by the National Information Standards Organization (Z39.48-1984).

10 9 8 7 6 5 4 3 2 1

Contents

Acknowledgments

We would like to thank Debora Carvalko from Greenwood Press for her advocacy of this project, for her help at every step of the way, and for her advice and encouragement at critical junctures of the project.

We would also like to thank our advisory board members John S. Antrobus, G. William Domhoff, Ernest Hartmann, J. Allan Hobson, and Charles Stewart. In addition to their help in identifying topics to be covered, they also helped us to find the best authors to cover them! These advisers have immeasurably increased the quality of these volumes.

We would also like to thank the International Association for the Study of Dreams, www.asdreams.org, whose conference, Web site, and publications have connected us with many of the authors in these volumes.

We would also like to thank Emily Abrams, Chris Dallas-Koziol, Jessica George, Anna Kookoolis, and Sarah Varghese for their help with editing and formatting the references for all the chapters in the series—a thankless task at best, but these assistants did it both conscientiously and carefully.

Finally, we would like to thank Erica Harris, who helped out on all aspects of this project. Her organizational help has meant all the difference throughout. She kept track of correspondence with authors, helped edit the chapters, and generally kept the project running smoothly and on schedule.

Introduction

"What are dreams?" has been a perennial question for philosophers and for ordinary dreamers throughout history. Over the last century, it has also become a focus of scientific inquiry. In 1985, Tore Nielsen surveyed scholarly dream articles published over the previous one hundred years and found that they contained two large waves of activity (Nielsen, 1985). The first began immediately after the publication of Freud's *The Interpretation of Dreams* (1900/ 1965). This surge consisted of clinical articles. Though Freud's ideas about dreams are often said to be "discredited," he actually introduced the characterization that dreams are predominately visual, metaphoric thought often linked to mental processes outside conscious awareness. This is now widely accepted and not thought of as "Freudian." It was Freud's emphasis on "wish fulfillment" of primitive sexual and aggressive urges as the overriding motivations in dreams that psychology has discarded. Freud also believed that dreams occurred only when a conflict arose, whereas research has come to show that we dream regularly through the night and recall only a fraction of this. Research showing the average dream is the negative side of neutral (Hall & Van de Castle, 1966) similarly made a central role for wish fulfillment more vulnerable to Occam's razor. The more extreme and obviously erroneous psychoanalytic assertions are often cited as having discouraged scientific researchers from exploring dream content and clinical issues.

The next wave of publications came as a physiologic one when rapid eye movement (REM) sleep was discovered. Aserinsky and Kleitman (1953) observed that the brain, cardiovascular, and respiratory systems became more active at approximately 90-minute intervals through the night. This corresponded with the timing of awakenings likeliest to result in a dream report. There were high hopes that this discovery might shed light not only on dreaming but on personality and mind/brain controversies in general. Though subsequent studies added much detail to the portrait of REM and its cycling with other stages of sleep, initially they did not impact clinical or cognitive knowledge of dreaming, much less other aspects of psychology. The physiologic researchers didn't combine their research with the type of detailed content studies in which clinicians are interested. The tone of their articles often implied that all interesting questions about dreams had been solved by describing the physiological processes of REM. In 1979, dream researcher Harry Fiss observed:

> The fact that sleep researchers have thus emphasized the biological substratum of dreaming and by and large neglected the psychological experience of dreaming has given rise to a curious paradox: despite the monumental achievements in sleep research in recent years, our prevalent notions of dreaming continue to be derived principally from clinical practice and psychoanalysis—as if REM had never been discovered. In brief, the technological breakthrough of the fifties and sixties has had relatively little impact on our understanding of dreaming. (Fiss, 1979, p. 41)

Over the last two decades, however, there has been more cross-fertilization of content and physiologic studies of dreaming. The technology has advanced so that researchers can identify the biochemistry and neuroimaging of the dreaming brain in enough detail to relate it to what is known about the psychological functions of these specific areas. Clinical and cognitive researchers have also begun comprehensive studies that tie into physiological findings. The subjective and physiologic data on dreaming are finally beginning to inform each other. New dream research has become relevant to helping clinicians treat posttraumatic stress and anxiety disorders. It is becoming a tool for cognitive psychologists studying the orienting response and memory. Dream studies are beginning to tell us more about brain development—both across species and across the human lifetime.

The New Science of Dreaming brings together this exciting new body of research. The volumes are organized around three broad themes: neurophysiological research, dream content and clinical approaches, and theoretical and cultural perspectives.

Volume 1 presents the recent physiological studies of dreaming—mostly characterizing REM sleep but also including non-REM (NREM) dreams and the differential aspects of REM most linked to dream characteristics. In Chapter 1, Claude Gottesmann surveys the history of research on the physiology of dreaming sleep. He begins with researchers some two centuries ago who noted isolated signs of REM without fully identifying it and follows this through the latest discoveries on biological characteristics of the state.

In Chapter 2, Patrick McNamara, Charles Nunn, Robert Barton, Erica Harris, and Isabella Capellini describe the phylogeny of REM and NREM and at what point in evolution a process analogous to dreaming may have arisen. Using REM sleep as a proxy for the dreaming brain/mind, McNamara et al. find that REM is most prominent in terrestrial, placental mammals and only occurs bihemispherically. NREM, on the other hand, can occur in a single hemisphere. Thus, the evolution of REM sleep may be tied to the evolution of brain structures like the corpus collosum that facilitate interhemispheric transfer of information. In Chapter 3, J. Allan Hobson discusses cellular and molecular models of dreaming and how they account for such formal dream features as sensorimotor hallucinosis, delusional errors of state identification, emotional intensification, and memory loss. In Chapter 4, Hobson explores how drugs alter these to affect dreaming.

In Chapter 5, Thien Thanh Dang-Vu, Manuel Schabus, Martin Desseilles, Sophie Schwartz, and Pierre Maquet review neuroimaging studies of REM sleep. The emerging picture reveals activation of the pons, the thalamus, temporo-occipital and limbic/paralimbic areas (including the amygdala), along with a relative quiescence of dorsolateral prefrontal and inferior parietal cortices. The authors note that these correlate well with observed cognition during dreaming. In Chapter 6, Edward F. Pace-Schott focuses in more detail on one of these findings—the frontal lobes' diminished activation during REM—to account for many dream characteristics. In Chapter 7, Erin J. Wamsley and John S. Antrobus describe their "Dual Rhythm" model of dreaming, which suggests that both the REM-NREM cycle and changes in cortical activation across the 24-hour cycle are sources of nonspecific brain activation supporting mentation during sleep. Maria Livia Fantini and Luigi Ferini-Strambi's Chapter 8 describes REM Behavior Disorder and other REM parasomnias in which movement is disinhibited during REM and people often thrash around—apparently acting out dreams. They discuss how the dream content interacts with the disorder. In Chapter 9, Patrick McNamara, Deirdre McLaren, Sara Kowalczyk, and Edward F. Pace-Schott describe the contrasting physiologies of REM and NREM sleep states and then report new data on dreams associated with these two sleep states. They find that while attributions of mental states to dream characters by the dreamer occurs in both sleep states, these "theory of mind" abilities are much more robust in REM than in NREM sleep. In Chapter 10, Sanford Auerbach reviews changes in dream recall and dream content in association with various neurologic disorders. Finally, in Chapter 11, David Kahn discusses how biochemical differences during REM decrease access to episodic memory and diminish the tendency to reflect on implausibility, incongruity, discontinuity, and illogical thinking.

Volume 2 presents cognitive, personality, and clinical research on dreams. In Chapter 1, G. William Domhoff reviews content studies and finds they do not support the common stereotype of dreams as highly emotional, bizarre, or similar in structure or content to schizophrenia or delirium. He concludes that most dreams are reasonable simulations of waking life containing occasional rare features, such as distorted settings and objects, unusual characters, inexplicable activities, strange images and metamorphoses, and sudden scene shifts. In Chapter 2, Michael Schredl examines the literature on gender differences in dreaming, summarizing the major findings: women recall dreams more often than men, men's dreams have more physical aggression and work settings, and women's dreams contain more people and household objects. He discusses how these findings map onto differences between gender roles in waking life and suggests this is supportive of the continuity hypothesis of dreaming.

In Chapter 3, Roar Fosse and G. William Domhoff present a model of dreams as "non-executive orienting"—suggesting that dynamic oscillations of the dreaming networks cause them to self-organize into narrow but spatially extended corridors of attention that reach conscious awareness. In Chapter 4, Michael Schredl reviews the literature on dream recall and proposes a model by which major correlates—stress, personality, attitudes toward dreams, sleep arousal and retrieval effects, and memory (especially visual memory)—all interact to produce the variations we observe in dream recall. In Chapter 5, Mark Blagrove looks in more detail at the effects of personality on recall and dream content differences. In Chapter 6, Clara E. Hill and Patricia Spangler review the history of dreams in psychotherapy and modern empirical evidence on outcomes of dream work, including differential predictors of who benefits most. They conclude that there is strong evidence that working with dreams in therapy is beneficial but that more research is needed to determine the effective components. The next few chapters explore nightmares. In Chapter 7, Mehmet Yücel Agargün describes these as terrifying REM dreams. He distinguishes between spontaneous nightmares, as opposed to posttraumatic ones, and explores a possible relationship between suicidality and nightmares. In Chapter 8, Raija-Leena Punamäki reviews the effects of trauma on dreaming. She describes posttraumatic nightmares and discusses how other dream parameters—frequency of recall, tendency toward recurring dreams, dreaming about the trauma or not—can predict who will recover better from trauma versus who goes on to experience long-lasting posttraumatic stress disorder (PTSD). In Chapter 9, Tore Nielsen and Jessica Lara-Carrasco suggest that dreaming serves an emotional regulation function and that nightmares are expressions of this function. They propose several possible mechanisms that may be central to emotion regulation during dreaming, especially during nightmares, including desomatization, contextualization, progressive emotional problem-solving, and fear memory extinction.

The last two chapters of Volume 2 are devoted to special types of dreams. In Chapter 10, Stanley Krippner describes reports of strange, extraordinary, and unexplained experiences related to dreams, which have fascinated people throughout the millennia. He gives examples of beliefs in dream precognition and divine guidance in Ancient Egypt Assyrian, Babylonian, and Sumerian cultures, follows these beliefs through Tibetan Buddhist, Hindu, and Native American traditions, and then reviews modern parapsychology research on dreaming. In Chapter 11, Stephen LaBerge reviews the research on "lucid dreaming"—dreams in which the dreamer realizes that they are dreaming. He describes the first volitional signaling by eye movements from a lucid dream, which established that they were indeed occurring in REM, and he reviews the research on characteristics of REM that make lucidity more or less likely, as well as intentional strategies to elicit the state.

Volume 3 presents cultural and theoretical perspectives on dreaming. This includes the perspectives of disciplines quite distinct from psychology. It also covers new psychological theories—many of which arise from the new field of evolutionary psychology. It begins with a look at the perspectives of ethnography, religion, and literature. In Chapter 1, Carol Schreier Rupprecht suggests that dreaming is the earliest form of human creativity and that literature made its first appearance when dreams went from being narrated orally to being written down. In Chapter 2, Roger Ivar Lohmann describes how ethnography views dream content, interpretation, and use in terms of cultural values, categories, expectations, and social conventions. In Chapter 3, Kelly Bulkeley surveys the role of dreams in Christianity, Islam, Buddhism, Judaism, Hinduism, and the local spiritualities of Africa, Oceania, and the Americas. He then presents his own research on dreams that the dreamer identifies as a mystical or religious experience. He concludes that mystical dreams may serve as "spirit simulations," provoking greater awareness of nonhuman beings and powers with whom humans may form beneficial relationships.

The next several chapters present different functional and evolutionary theories of dreaming. In Chapter 4, Katja Valli and Antti Revonsuo suggest that the function of dreams is "threat simulation" and perhaps simulation of other categories of events linked to survival. In Chapter 5, Patrick McNamara, Erica Harris, and Anna Kookoolis propose that REM and dreaming are best explained by the evolutionary concept of "costly signaling." While most characteristics and behaviors are adaptive, some are ironically selected exactly because they handicap the individual—indicating a robustness of all other survival mechanisms. Dreams and the sharing of dreams with others may involve emotional signaling. Chapter 6 by Deirdre Barrett posits that dreams are thinking or problem solving in a different biochemical state from that of waking. She reviews research on dreams and problem solving and proposes that specific characteristics of dream mentation are determined by which sensory modalities we must monitor (the need to remain still and quiet during sleep, she suggests), but other aspects of the state seems to be fine-tuned to certain psychological purposes.

In Chapter 7, Robert G. Kunzendorf proposes an alternative to Freud's position that dreams represent wish fulfillment to account for the same symbolic phenomena of dream imagery that Freud described. Kunzendorf's model is a continuum of decreasing symbolism from nocturnal dreaming to normal daydreaming to wakeful self-talk, and also a continuum of decreasing symbolism across individual development as people mature. In Chapter 8, Ernest Hartmann characterizes dreams as hyperconnective compared to waking thought. He says these connections are guided by emotions, which can be identified by identifying the "Central Image" of the dream. In Chapter 9, Jennifer Michelle Windt and Thomas Metzinger trace philosophical perspectives on dream consciousness from Aristotle's *On Dreams* through Descartes' first *Meditation*, Bertrand Russell's *Human Knowledge*, and finally Daniel Dennett's modern musings on dreams. They assert that philosophers' skepticism about dream awareness is more than an armchair exercise of theoretical doubt—that dreaming is a paradigm for questions about consciousness, truth, and reality. In Chapter 10, Alan T. Lloyd critically reviews several evolutionary theories of dreaming and then integrates insights from evolutionary theory with psychoanalytic theory into a fresh and clinically relevant approach to dreams. In Chapter 11, Richard Schweickert applies new mathematical techniques from complexity theory and network theory to social interconnections of characters in and among dreams. He reports that many dreams can be described formally as "small world networks," which are networks that are connected in such a way as to facilitate transfer of optimal amounts of information between nodes in the network. Interestingly, the famous "engine man's dreams" may be an exception to this rule.

Altogether, these essays provide a summary of the contemporary knowledge of dreaming. They integrate cognitive, personality, and clinical issues with physiology and prioritize questions about dreams that we want to answer over the next couple of decades.

We believe that a real science of dreams is now on the agenda and that the essays in these books support this belief.

REFERENCES

Aserinsky, E., & Kleitman, N. (1953). Regularly occurring periods of eye motility, and concomitant phenomena during sleep. *Science, 118*, 273–274.

Fiss, H. (1979). Current dream research: A psychobiological perspective. In B. Wolman (Ed.), *Handbook of dreams* (pp. 20–75). New York: Van Nostrand Reinhold.

Freud, S. (1965). *The interpretation of dreams* (J. Strachey, Trans.). London: Oxford University Press. (Original work published 1900)

Hall, C., & Van de Castle, R. (1966). *The content analysis of dreams*. New York: Appleton-Century-Crofts.

Nielsen, T. (1985). One century of dream research. *ASD Newsletter, 2*(3), 1 and 3.

One

A Neurobiological History of Dreaming

Claude Gottesmann

Dreaming has probably existed since the appearance of rapid eye movement (REM; or paradoxical) sleep. Incomplete (Siegel, Manger, Nienhuis, Fahringer, & Pettigrew, 1996, 1999) or complete (Nicol, Andersen, Phillis, & Berger, 2000) criteria of this sleep stage are already present in primitive mammals, and dreaming (or active hallucinatory behavior during sleep for the remaining skeptics!) is already clearly observed in rats (Mirmiran, 1983; Mouret & Delorme, 1967; Sanford et al., 2001) and cats (Henley & Morrison, 1974; Jouvet & Delorme, 1965; Jouvet & Mounier, 1960; Sastre & Jouvet, 1979) when the usual atonia has been experimentally suppressed. In fact, it seems probable that true dreaming appeared in species with the phylogenetic occurrence of fully activated cortex during REM sleep, which indicates a functional forebrain. Therefore, we will first analyze the results leading to the demonstration of activation of the peripheral and central activities related to the dreaming sleep stage. Then, we will present the concomitantly antagonist and complementary central inhibitory processes before the general discussion.

ACTIVATING PROCESSES

Behavior and Electrophysiology

Already in classical times, Lucretius (circa 98–55 BC) in "De rerum natura" (Lucrece & Xi, 1900) gave a wonderfully detailed description of dreaming and its behavioral activation correlates in animals as well as in humans.

> In truth you will see strong horses when their limbs lie at rest, yet sweat in their sleep, and go on panting, and strain every nerve as though for victory, or else as though the barriers were opened (struggle to start). And hunters' dogs often in their soft sleep yet suddenly toss their legs, and all at once give tongue, and again and again sniff the air with their nostrils, as if they had found and were following the tracks of wild beasts, yea, roused from slumber they often pursue empty images of stags, as though they saw them in eager flight, until they shake off the delusion and return to themselves. But the fawning brood of pups brought up in the house, in a moment shake their body and lift it from the ground, just as if they beheld unknown forms and faces. And the wilder any breed may be, the more must it needs rage in its sleep. But the diverse tribes of birds fly off, and on a sudden in the night time trouble the peace of the groves of the gods with the whirr of wings, as if in their gentle sleep they have seen hawks, flying in pursuit, offer fight and battle. Moreover, the minds of men, which with mighty movements bring forth mighty deeds, often in sleep do and dare just the same; they storm kings, are captured, join battle, raise a loud cry, as though being murdered—all without moving. Many men fight hard, and utter groans through their pain, and, as though the teeth of a panther or savage lion bit them, fill all around them with loud cries. Many in their sleep discourse of high affairs, and very often have been witness to their own guilt. Many meet death; many as though they were falling headlong with all their body from high mountains to the earth, are beside themselves with fear, and, as though bereft of reason, scarcely recover themselves from sleep, quivering with the turmoil of their body. Likewise, a thirsty man sits down beside a stream or a pleasant spring, and gulps almost the whole river down his throat. Cleanly persons often, if bound fast in slumber they think they are lifting their dress at a latrine or a shallow pot, pour forth the filtered liquid from their whole body, and the Babylonian coverlets of rich beauty are soaked. Later on those, into the channel of whose life the vital seed is passing for the first time, when the ripeness of time has created it in their limbs, there come from without idols from every body, heralding a glorious face or beautiful colouring, which stir and rouse their members swelling with much seed, and often, as though all were over, they pour forth huge floods of moisture and soil their clothes. (lines 987–1036)

Many centuries later, Fontana (1765), as quoted by numerous authors (Berlucchi, Moruzzi, Salvi, & Strata, 1964; Moruzzi, 1963; Piéron, 1912; Raehlmann & Witkowski, 1878), observed that shortly after sleep onset a cat "begins to tremble as though it were in convulsion. I have observed this phenomenon more than once in heavily sleeping animals, and more especially in dogs" (p. 22). Moreover, the pupils were restricted during sleep.

More recently, in the century before last, Hervey de Saint-Denys (1964) wrote, "If dreaming is related to sexuality, the external organs act under its dependency. The functions of external organs that passion usually stirs up are modified; respiration becomes panting, interrupted by sighs, the heart palpitates" (p. 156): nothing very different from Lucretius. However, Hervey de Saint-Denys also noticed that sensations, like pain, can induce dreams and nightmares (p. 141). Taking into account another author's remark, he wrote this premonitory observation that, as shown later by the corresponding slow wave sleep, "the first period following sleep onset is almost always free of dreaming" (p. 163). Finally, he also announced what was to be confirmed later, "there is no sleep of mind. Consciousness ignores sleep" (p. 165) (see Foulkes, 1962; Bosinelli, 1995). The nineteenth century provided other important results, particularly related to ocular phenomena. First, Raehlmann and Witkowski (1877) described eye movements during sleep in humans, and a year later Raehlmann and Witkowski (1878) observed that the pupils are restricted. Some years later, Gernet (1989) found that the pupils are insensitive to light, while Ladd (1892) became the first to insist on a retina "eigentlicht" (self-lighting) phenomena in addition to brain visual centers to explain dream images (p. 301). He wrote

> I am inclined . . . to believe that, in somewhat vivid dreams, the eyeballs move gently in their sockets, taking various positions induced by the retinal phantasms as they control the dreams. As we look down the street of a strange city, for example, in a dream we probably focus our eyes somewhat as we would do in making the same observation when awake, though with a complete lack of that determined teleological fixness which waking life carries with it. (p. 304)

Finally, the last of our findings in the nineteenth century, Weed and Hallam (1896) noted some interesting premonitory observations in a study devoted to dreaming: "The dreams occurring from 5 to 6:30 are the most frequent, most interesting, most vivid and most varied . . . These dreams are those best recalled" (p. 405). They also observed that only "20 dreams (out of 150) were caused by external stimuli" (p. 406) and that "more than the half (57.2 percent) of the 381 dreams . . . are said by the subject to contain 'disagreeable' emotions . . . with perplexity and hurry, discomfort and helplessness, fear and anger, disappointment and shame" (pp. 48–49), a finding nearly in accordance with the recent observations of Revonsuo (2000).

Although Piéron (1912) wrote a remarkable thesis on sleep comprising an extraordinary anticipatory study of cerebrospinal fluid transfer in sleep-deprived dogs, later developed for REM sleep in cats (Sallanon, Buda, Janin, & Jouvet, 1982), it was not until 1930 that experimental findings related to dreaming were published. Jacobson (1930) recorded eye movements, and, as quoted by Kleitman (1965, p. 94), he later wrote: "when a person dreams ... most often his eyes are active. When the sleeper whose eyes move under his closed lids ... awakes ... you are likely to find ... that he had seen something in a dream" (Jacobson, 1938). This was the first objective result related to dreaming obtained by using modern methodology.

Spontaneous and induced electrical brain activity was discovered in 1875 by Caton (1875) in monkeys and rabbits by means of a galvanometer. Caton observed potential variations of "the grey matter (which) appear to have a relation to its function. When any part of the grey matter is in a state of functional activity, its electrical current usually exhibits negative variation" (p. 278). This finding constituted an extraordinary discovery given the methodology then available. The history of the electroencephalogram (EEG) truly began with Berger (1929), who recorded brain activity directly on the patient's cortex (electrocorticogram) and scalp (electroencephalogram) in this case performed ... on his own son! He was later persecuted before the war, and he committed suicide in 1941. The electrical brain activity of REM sleep was first identified in 1936 when Derbyshire, Rempel, Forbes, and Lambert supplied the first indication of low-voltage cortical activity during sleep: "In two of the three cats ... we found during sleep occasional groups of (cortical) large waves, larger than those recorded in the waking state. At other times when sleep was apparently less tranquil judging by twitching of the vibrissae, there were only small rapid waves as in the alert waking state" (p. 582). Three other highly interesting papers appeared the following year. Blake and Gerard (1937) reported that "in the last third part of the night ... (the EEG showed) very feeble and irregular potentials like those present in the middle portion" of the night (p. 694). "Especially (when) feeble irregular potentials may be present ... yet the test sound (auditory threshold study with a 1,000 Hz stimulus) evokes no response" (p. 696). This was the first indication of increased threshold for awakening before Dement's similar finding in cats (Dement, 1958). The next crucial paper was written by Loomis, Harvey, and Hobart (1937). For the first time this paper showed hypnograms, and it clearly demonstrated that dreams appear on low-voltage EEG occurring during sleep. In animals, Klaue (1937) clearly identified in cats a "tiefer Schlaf" (deep sleep) stage characterized by "Beruhigung in Strombilde" (quiet electrical current), thus low-amplitude EEG, "eine völlige Entspannung der Muskulatur ... und häufige Zunkungen in einzelne Extremitäten" (complete muscular relaxation ... and numerous jerks of single extremities) (p. 514).

Before the integration of Aserinsky and Kleitman's (1953) well-known finding in the currently acknowledged history of REM sleep, Blake, Gerard, and Kleitman (1939) confirmed the appearance of low "null" voltage EEG during sleep (rapidly integrated by Gibbs and Gibbs [1950] in an EEG atlas). Shortly afterwards, McGlade (1942) observed an association of large body movements and dreams. Finally, Ohlmeyer's team, in two papers published during (Ohlmeyer, Brilmayer, & Hüllstrung, 1944) and shortly after (Ohlmeyer & Brilmayer, 1947) the war, described in detail recordings of periodic penile erection occurring during night sleep.

To conclude, it is of particular interest in the context of this chapter to mention the clinical observations of Humphrey and Zangwill (1951) on brain-damaged soldiers from the second World War. A lesion at the occipito-parietal level suppressed dreaming. In three cases, the lesion was located on the right hemisphere, and in one case it was bilateral but predominantly on the left side. The authors mentioned Penfield's observations of ecmnesia phenomena induced by temporal cortex stimulation. "Depression of dreaming was associated with impaired visual imagination and memory in the waking state" (p. 325). The abolition of dreaming after posterolateral lesions has been confirmed by several studies (Solms, 2000).

As already mentioned, the modern neurobiological history of REM sleep began in 1953, all the previous results having been discarded in the contemporary perspective. Thus, Aserinsky and Kleitman (1953) described "rapid, jerky and symmetrical (eye) movements" (p. 273) occurring periodically during the night. When awakened, in 20 of 27 observations the subjects reported dream recall. In contrast, in 19 of 23 awakenings outside the eye movements there was no dream recall. The first period of eye movements occurred between 1 hour, 40 minutes and 4 hours, 50 minutes (mean 3 hours) after sleep onset. The EEG from frontal and occipital level was described as "invariably of low amplitude (5–30 μV) and irregular frequency (15–25 and 5–8 c/s predominating)" (p. 274). "The respiratory rate had a mean of 16.9/min during eye mobility in contrast with 13.4/min during quiescence ($p < .001$) . . . In every case, the eye mobility periods were associated with peaks of overt bodily activity although the latter were frequently present in the absence of eye movements" (p. 274). As already described (Gottesmann, 2001), Lufkin (1968) explained that Aserinsky learned the eye recording method from Jacobson at the request of Kleitman. In addition, Aserinsky informed the present author that, at the defense of his PhD at Chicago University in 1953, the examiners told him that doctorates are awarded not for obtained results but in the hope of future discoveries!

However, in those days, the authors did not explicitly mention cortical activation during REM sleep. It was Dement (1958) who first wrote about "activated" sleep, although Aserinsky and Kleitman (1955), Dement (1955), and Dement and Kleitman (1957a, 1957b) had definitively established low-voltage activity during REM sleep. In fact, since Bremer (1936) and, above all, Moruzzi and Magoun (1949), it was admitted that cortical rapid and low amplitude activity is related to wakefulness and corresponds to an activated state. The next important step towards characterization of the cortical functional state during REM sleep was performed by Evarts (1962), who observed that the neurons of the primary visual cortex were more activated during REM sleep, especially during the eye movements, than during slow wave sleep. He defined this stage as the "deepest stage of sleep" in accordance with Klaue (1937) and Benoit and Bloch (1960), because of the high threshold of awakening by peripheral or brainstem reticular stimulation. The maximal increase of basal skin resistance in the last hours of the night in humans led Hawkins, Puryear, Wallace, Deal, and Thomas (1962) to the same conclusion. In two subsequent papers, Evarts (1964, 1965) showed that during REM sleep, the visual cortex neurons fire at a rate similar to active waking, with visual stimulation when the monkey was "looking about at its surroundings" (Figure 1.1). Cortical neuron activation during REM sleep was confirmed by Pisano, Rosadini, and Rossi (1962) through antidromic stimulation of the pyramidal tract, and by Arduini, Berlucchi, and Strata (1963) who found an increase in the integrated activity of the pyramidal tract when compared to slow wave sleep. Also, in recordings of cortical activity via the pyramidal tract, Morrison and Pompeiano (1965) found activation during REM sleep, especially during the eye movements.

Another criterion of cortical activation during REM sleep was provided during those same years by responsiveness studies. Cordeau, Walsh, and Mahut (1965); Demetrescu and Demetrescu (1964); Favale, Loeb, Manfredi, and Sacco (1965); Okuma and Fujimori (1963); Palestini, Pisano, Rosadini, and Rossi (1964); and later on, Gandolfo, Arnaud, and Gottesmann (1980) and Steriade (1970) showed that thalamocortical responsiveness is highest during REM sleep, while cortical responsiveness is still higher than during waking (Arnaud, Gandolfo, & Gottesmann, 1979; Cordeau et al., 1965; Rossi, Palestini, Pisano, & Rosadini, 1965). However, in spite of this high central excitability, humans (Williams, Tepas, & Morlock, 1962) as well as animals (Weitzman, Fishbein, & Graziani, 1965) are disconnected from the periphery as most often shown by the quasi-suppression of the peripheral auditory-induced evoked potentials.

Yet another criterion of cortical activation during REM sleep, as well as during waking, was the definitive confirmation by Wurtz in rats (1965) and cats (1966) of a common negative steady potential as already described by Kawamura and Sawyer (1964) in rabbits. In humans, the maximal oxygen consumption during REM sleep (Brebbia & Altshuler, 1965) was also an indication of central activation since the body is relaxed on account of muscular atonia (Jouvet, Michel, & Courjon, 1959; Berger, 1961).

FIGURE 1.1

First historical physiological explanations of dreaming mentation support. Top: Evarts (1964) showed in monkeys that cortical pyramidal neurons fire regularly and at a high rate during waking. During slow-wave sleep they fire more slowly and more irregularly. The high-rate irregular firing in bursts during REM sleep resulted from both intense activating influences and the disappearance of a frequency-limiting control process involving inhibitory influences. Bottom: Demetrescu et al. (1966) recorded in cats the recovery cycle of thalamocortical responsiveness. The results showed intense activating and inhibitory influences acting at cortical level during active waking, both decreasing during quiet waking and more importantly during slow-wave sleep. Prior to REM sleep both kinds of influence were at their lowest level. During REM sleep the activating influences reappeared while the strong disinhibition persisted.

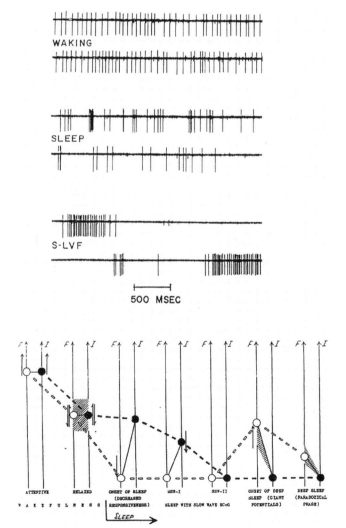

One main criterion of REM sleep was the discovery of ponto-geniculo-occipital (PGO) waves (Hobson, 1964; Jouvet et al., 1959; Michel, Jeannerod, Mouret, Rechtschaffen, & Jouvet, 1964; Mikiten, Niebyl, & Hendley, 1961). It is not the aim of this chapter to analyze the evidence for this activity (Callaway, Lydic, Bagdoyan, & Hobson, 1987; Datta, 1997, 2006; Datta, Siwek, Patterson, & Cipolloni, 1998; Gottesmann, 1997), but it should be highlighted that these spikes correspond to a phasic central activation, which was evidenced by the increase of thalamic (Steriade, Paré, Bouhassira, Deschènes, & Oakson, 1989) as well as cortical (Kiyono & Iwama, 1965; Satoh, 1971) responsiveness. Similar phasic waves were identified in humans (McCarley, Winkelman, & Duffy, 1983; Miyauchi, Takino, Fukuda, & Torii, 1987) and already previously supposed to be involved in generating REM sleep dreams (Hobson & McCarley, 1977; McCarley et al., 1983; Miyauchi et al., 1987), a theory which was already discarded (Vogel, 1978). Indeed, although the spikes end mainly in the visual cortex, this would suggest direct visual activation of dream generation. Steriade et al. (1989) even stated that, since there are very high amplitude isolated spikes (without occurring eye movements) before REM sleep entrance (during the so-called intermediate stage of rats (Gottesmann, 1964), cats (Gottesmann, Gandolfo, & Zernichi, 1984), and mice (Glin et al., 1991) (see Gottesmann, 1996) and the intermediate phase in humans (Lairy, Barros Fereira, & Golsteinas, 1968) vivid imagery may occur during these short periods. Nevertheless, as already described (Gottesmann, 2002), verbal reports obtained after awakening from this period do not reveal visual contents but "a feeling of indefinable discomfort, anxious perplexity and harrowing worry" (Lairy et al., 1968, p. 279). Also Larson and Foulkes (1969) showed that mental contents during this stage of sleep "are inconsistent with the hypothesis of an intensification of mental activity or cerebral vigilance" (p. 552). Moreover, in addition to these old data, which are the only ones available, the time scale of dreaming is ill-matched to PGO wave lengths, with a maximum of 100 milliseconds (McCarley et al., 1983; Miyauchi et al., 1987; see Gottesmann, 2000a) unless we accept as general rule the instantaneousness of dreams like that famous dream described by Maury (1861):

> I am dreaming about the (revolutionary) Terror. I witness scenes of carnage. I appear before the revolutionary tribunal. I see Robespierre, Marat, Fouquier-Tinville, all the ugly figures of that terrible epoch; I debate with them; finally, after numerous events, I remember imperfectly, I am convicted, sentenced to death, driven off in a cart, amidst a countless throng, to the revolution square; I mount the scaffold, the hangman attaches me to the fatal board, operates it, the blade falls; I feel that my head is separated from my trunk. I awake in the

most violent anguish, and I feel the bedpost which has come loose and fallen on my cervical vertebrae like the blade of the guillotine. (p. 161)

The narration was recorded 40 years after dream occurrence. Maury remembered to have been then unwell, his mother being at his bedside. Thus, even this spectacular dream has to be treated with caution, and such phenomena would imply that the successive spikes are responsible for rapid changes of dream content, a hypothesis that currently seems unlikely (Gottesmann, 1999). The only probable consequence of PGO spikes is to induce a very transient activation of the primary visual cortex, perhaps to teleologically maintain a background of activity in this deactivated area during REM sleep (Braun et al., 1998; see later paragraph).

In fact, there are several kinds of electrophysiological phasic activity. The second one, and the best known, comprises the eye movement potentials (EMPs) correlated to the eye movements as shown by the electrooculogram. These already appear in cats, mainly in the lateral geniculate nucleus; for example; in the figure in Michel et al.'s (1964) paper where they are clearly dissociated from the PGO waves. The EMPs were more clearly demonstrated a decade later (Sakai & Cespuglio, 1976). In rats, there are neither PGO waves nor EMPs in the lateral geniculate and cortex (Cespuglio, Calvo, Musolino, & Valatx, 1977; Gottesmann, 1967a, 1967b, 1969; Stern, Forbes, & Morgane, 1974) because of the absence of direct pontine-geniculate relations in this rodent (Datta et al., 1998). However, EMPs appear to be associated with the eye movements in the pons and even more clearly in the third nerve nucleus (Gottesmann, 1966a, 1967a, 1967b, 1969). However, later, PGO waves were identified in the pons (Bergmann, Winters, Rosenberg, & Rechschaffen, 1987; Farber, Marks, & Roffwarg, 1980; Kaufman & Morrison, 1981; Marks, Farber, & Roffwarg, 1980; Marks, Farber, Rubinstein, & Roffwarg, 1980). Datta (2006) prefers to speak of P-waves because they are absent in upper-situated structures. Finally, nonreplicated spike activity occurring mainly during REM sleep, then during waking and greatly reduced during slow wave sleep, was recorded in the interpeduncular nucleus not during but after central activations, their number being proportional to the intensity of central or behavioral activations (Gottesmann, 1966a, 1966b, 1967a, 1967b, 1969). From all these results on EMP and probably PGO waves, the important fact is that like the phasic integrated potentials (PIPS; Rechtschaffen, Molinari, Wabon, & Wincor, 1970), all available results reflect the occurrence of eye movements that were related to dream content. Indeed, Roffwarg's team (Herman et al., 1984; Roffwarg, Dement, Muzio, & Fisher, 1962) upon careful examination repeatedly found a strong correlation in contrast to other teams (Jacobs, Feldman, & Bender 1972; Moskowitz & Berger, 1969). The fact that the eye movements related to EMPs (and PGOs), which once again converge on a deactivated cortical area (Braun et al., 1998), occur in the mesencephalic and even pontine animal (Jouvet, 1962) suggests a feeble relation with dream content, especially because congenitally blind persons manifest eye movements during REM sleep in spite of the absence of corneo-retinal potential (Amadeo & Gomez, 1966; Gross, Byrne, & Fisher, 1965).

Finally, in more recent years, a new EEG criterion of cortical activation during REM sleep appeared with the discovery of gamma range activity. Bouyer, Montaron, and Rougeul (1981) were the first to describe in cats a 35- to 45-c/sec rhythm consisting of bursts of synchronized waves occurring during attentive behavioral arrest. This activity was recorded on the cortex and in the thalamus. This finding was confirmed and extended in the following years in monkeys (Freeman & Van Dijk, 1987), cats (Ferster, 1988; Gray & Singer, 1989; Munk, Roelfsema, König, Engel, & Singer, 1996; Steriade, Amzica, & Contreras, 1996; Steriade, Contreras, Amzica & Timofeev, 1996; Steriade, Curro dossi, Paré, & Oakson, 1991) and guinea pigs (Llinas, Grace, & Yarom, 1991). However, in humans, Ribary et al. (1991) observed that gamma rhythm can be observed during waking in all cortical areas, that it can be induced by any kind of sensory stimulation and, very importantly, that "it was clearly phase-locked over cortical areas" (p. 11039). This activity was observed to be disturbed in Alzheimer's disease, where it has a low amplitude and the wave form is distorted. The next major result was, of course, the discovery of gamma rhythm during REM sleep by Llinas and Ribary (1993). The latter described "the presence of well-defined 40 Hz oscillations during wakefulness and dreaming and a marked reduction during delta sleep" (p. 2079).

> While the awake and REM sleep states are similar electrically with the presence of 40 Hz oscillations, the central difference between these states is the lack of sensory reset of the REM sleep 40 Hz activity. By contrast, during delta sleep, the amplitude of these oscillations differs from that of wakefulness and REM sleep, it is much lower (also confirmed later (Gross & Gotman, 1999)). However, as in REM sleep there are no 40 Hz sensory responses. (Llinas and Ribary, 1993, p. 2080)

The absence of reset "indicates that we do not perceive the external world during REM sleep ... We may consider the dreaming condition a state of hyper attentiveness in which sensory input cannot address the machinery that generates conscious experience" (Llinas & Ribary, 1993, p. 2081). Pommier (1970) used the following metaphor "the mind is protected from distractions, in an office in which the sensory telephone has been unplugged." Because the gamma rhythm is also recorded in the thalamus, the authors suggested that its "specific system (relay nuclei) would provide the content and the nonspecific system would provide the temporal binding of such content into a single cognitive experience evoked either by external stimuli or, intrinsically, during dreaming" (Llinas and Ribary, 1993, p. 2081). The same team (Llinas & Paré, 1991) stated, "It is the dialogue between the thalamus and the cortex that generates subjectivity" (p. 532). It was later shown that during REM sleep, the gamma rhythm becomes uncoupled between receptive and frontal cortical areas (Perez-Garci, del Rio-Portilla, Guevara, Arce, & Corsi-Cabrera, 2001). The same absence of cross-talk was observed by other authors (Cantero, Atienza, Madsen, & Stickgold, 2004; Massimini et al., 2005). This gamma rhythm was also observed in animals (Franken, Djik, Tobler, & Borbely, 1994; Maloney, Cape, Gotman, & Jones, 1997), and it is particularly present during waking and REM sleep–related occurrence of the strong hippocampal theta rhythm (Maloney et al., 1997). It is increased by noradrenaline and decreased by serotonin infusion in the nucleus basalis, whereas REM sleep is dose-dependently reduced (Cape & Jones, 1998). The later observation in rats of gamma rhythm occurrence under anesthesia, but necessarily in the presence of cortical low-voltage activity, triggered a debate regarding its relation to consciousness (Vanderwolf, 2000).

Positron Emission Tomography

The study of cerebral blood flow and glucose utilization added numerous crucial findings to the knowledge regarding cerebral structures involved in mentation. In 1991, Madsen et al. (1991) observed during REM sleep an activation of visual associative areas, which could explain the complex processing of visual dream experiences. Shortly afterwards, Maquet et al. (1996) noticed an increase of cerebral blood flow "in the anterior cingulate cortex, the posterior part of the right operculum, the right amygdala and surrounding entorhinal cortex . . . local maxima of blood flow were located in the left amygdala, left thalamus" (p. 164). "The amygdalo cingulate coactivation could account for the emotional and affective aspects of dreams" (p. 165). Similar activation of neo- and paleocortex was observed by Braun et al. (1997, 1998). More precisely related to REM sleep eye movements, Hong, Gillin, Dow, Wu, and Buschbaum (1995) observed that the eye saccades of REM sleep are associated with activation of the right hemisphere in the saccadic eye movement area (frontal eye field). The authors suggested that REM sleep eye movements could be "saccadic scans of targets in the dream scene" (p. 570). Once again, this was a new and interesting hypothesis since, in addition to the correspondence between dream content and eye movement direction (Roffwarg et al., 1962; Herman et al., 1984), some results had shown that the fact the cortex could at least modulate the occurrence of eye movements because they are decreased by occipital lesions while being increased by frontal ones (Jeannerod, Mouret, & Jouvet, 1965; Mouret, Jeannerod, & Jouvet, 1965), and that pontine-induced eye movements (Pompeiano & Morrison, 1965; Vanni-Mercier & Debilly, 1998) resemble reflex-induced activities related to local neuron activations, because they persist in brainstem transected animals (Jouvet, 1962).

Neurochemistry

There are three main activating neurotransmitters: acetylcholine, glutamate, and aspartate.

Previous studies had already shown that acetylcholine was active at the cortical level. Bremer and Chatonnet (1949) demonstrated that prostigmine and eserine (two inhibitors of transmitter destruction) induced EEG activation, while atropine (a muscarinic receptor blocker) had the opposite effect, slowing down the EEG. Wikler (1952) observed that an atropine subcutaneous injection induced slow wave sleep EEG patterns in the behavioral awakened dog. Cortical neuron activation by acetylcholine was later confirmed by Vanderwolf (1988) and Szymusiak, McGinty, Shepard, Shouse, and Sterman (1990). However, previously several authors had shown that acetylcholine cortical release was increased during cortical and peripheral (Mitchell, 1963) or mesencephalic (Kinai & Szerb, 1965) reticular stimulation. This finding definitively correlated cortical activation with brainstem structures involved in waking processes (Moruzzi, 1963; Moruzzi & Magoun, 1949; Steriade, 1996). All these data related to cortical acetylcholine release during waking, which is higher than during slow wave sleep patterns, were confirmed again and again during these years (Celesia & Jasper, 1966; Cuculic & Himwich, 1968; Pepeu & Bartholini, 1968; Phillis & Chong, 1965; Szerb, 1967). It later transpired that acetylcholine acts at a cellular level on specific receptors that control ion channel permeability. More precisely, it decreases K^+ currents and blocks both a Ca^{2+}-dependent component of the slow hyperpolarization that follows the action potential, as well as a late component, that is a Ca^{2+}-independent K^+ current. In addition, this transmitter blocks the M current, a nonactivating current that is minimally active at resting potentials and turns on slowly with depolarization (it acts as a brake on repetitive firing) (Nicoll, Malenka, & Kauer, 1990). However, the main result related to the topic of this chapter was the quantification of acetylcholine release during REM sleep. Jasper and Tessier

(1971) showed a slight nonsignificant increase when compared to waking. However, Marrosu et al. (1995) found, also in cats, maximal release during active waking, a similar significant decrease during quiet waking and REM sleep and a minimal level during slow-wave sleep. It is of interest that cortical acetylcholine, in addition to cortical neurons' own release, is heavily dependent on the nucleus basalis cholinergic afferents (Buzsaki et al., 1988; Buzsaki & Gage, 1989) because lesion of this nucleus induces slow waves and reduces cortical choline acetyltransferase activity (Ray & Jackson, 1991), an effect that can be inverted by intracortical grafts of fetal nucleus accumbens neurons (Vanderwolf, Fine, & Cooley, 1990). This nucleus, again under activating control by noradrenaline and inhibitory by serotonin (Cape & Jones, 1998), interestingly shows a higher acetylcholine release during REM sleep than during waking (Vasquez & Baghdoyan, 2001). One major functional point that deserves to be highlighted is that acetylcholine mainly acts as a neuromodulator rather than as a true neurotransmitter. Indeed, very few cholinergic cortical terminals give rise to synaptic junctions; this is the case for only 14 percent of terminals, thus 3 percent of the total surface of varicosities (Descarries, Gisinger, & Steriade, 1997). This means that acetylcholine release is essentially diffuse with rather long duration "tonic" influences on a large neuron population. A full discussion of transmitter functioning can be found in McCormick's review (1992).

The glutamate and aspartate levels during sleep-waking stages were recently determined in the prefrontal cortex and nucleus accumbens of rats (Léna et al., 2005). In the cortex, their level was unchanged throughout the behavioral stages. The concentration of glutamate, probably the most important transmitter for our topic, is of various origins: subcortical (thalamocortical neurons [Wang, Ai, Hampson, & Snead III, 2005]), cortical (collateral of pyramidal cells [Levy, Reves, & Aoki, 2006]), and even astrocytes (Ye, Wyeth, Baltan-Tekkok, & Ransom, 2003). In contrast, in the nucleus accumbens, the maximal concentration of glutamate (aspartate remained unchanged) was observed during waking, and it decreased significantly during slow wave sleep and was minimal during REM sleep (Figure 1.2). In this structure, the glutamate level is dependent on prefrontal-, hippocampus-, and amygdala-issued release (Grace, 2000).

However, serotonin (5-HT) is also able in some cases to activate cortical neurons. 5-HT neurons of ascending dorsal (McGinty & Harper, 1976; McGinty, Harper, & Fairbanks, 1974) and medial (Rasmussen, Heym, & Jacobs, 1984) raphe nuclei fire at maximal but low frequency during waking, they decrease their firing rate during slow wave sleep, and they become silent during REM sleep. Cortical serotonin is released diffusely at thin varicosities level (Nelson, Hoffer, Chu, & Bloom, 1973; Descarries, Beaudet, &

Watkins, 1975). This means the so-called "neuromodulators" spread on numerous neurons and have a rather tonic, long-lasting influence since they are not rapidly eliminated, contrary to "neurotransmitters" that act at the synaptic level where there are rapid reuptake processes by the presynaptic neuron and/or enzyme destruction. The depolarizing (*activating*) effects are related to 5-HT$_2$ receptor activation (Araneda & Andrade, 1991; McCormick, 1992). In fact, it seems that this activation partly acts on gamma-aminobutyric acid (GABA)-ergic interneurons, resulting in hyperpolarization of pyramidal neurons (Sheldon & Aghajanian, 1990; see discussion later in this chapter). Serotonin has been shown to increase the signal-to-noise ratio of the neuron (McCormick, 1992), thus increasing its functional potential. Similarly, noradrenergic neurons of locus coeruleus (Aston-Jones & Bloom, 1981; Hobson, McCarley, & Wyzinski, 1975) fire maximally during active waking and become silent during REM sleep. This neuromodulator released at thin varicosities levels (Descarries, Watkins, & Lapierre, 1977; Fuxe, Hamberger, & Hökfelt, 1968) and increased the signal-to-noise ratio (Berlucchi, 1997; McCormick, 1992) but seldom activated cortical neurons (5 of 77) (Nelson et al., 1973) by α_1 postsynaptic receptors, which decrease K$^+$ conductance and

---

FIGURE 1.2
Current results showing the common neurochemical background of REM sleep and schizophrenia. Top: In the rat prefrontal cortex the dopamine (Léna et al., 2005) and cholinergic (Marrosu et al., 1995) activity levels are decreased during REM sleep as is the case in schizophrenia (Abi-Dargham & Moore, 2003; Collerton et al., 2005). The level of noradrenaline is significantly reduced during REM sleep (Léna et al., 2005) and there is a noradrenergic deficit in schizophrenia (Linner et al., 2002). The glutamate level during REM sleep is unchanged when compared to waking (Léna et al., 2005). In schizophrenic patients, the glutamate transporters mRNA expression is identical to normal subjects (Lauriat et al., 2005). The dopaminergic afferents are produced by the mesocortical tract. The cholinergic afferents mainly originate from nucleus basalis which is innervated by mesopontine cholinergic nuclei. The noradrenergic neurons emanate from the locus coeruleus. Bottom: In nucleus accumbens during REM sleep (Léna et al., 2005) as well as in schizophrenia (MacKay et al., 1982) there is a high level of dopamine concentration. The release of noradrenaline is greatly reduced during REM sleep (Léna et al., 2005) and there is also a deficit of this neuromodulator in schizophrenia (Linner et al., 2002). The level of glutamate is markedly reduced during REM sleep in rats (Léna et al., 2005), as is the case in schizophrenia (Grace, 2000). The glutamate level is dependent on hippocampal, prefrontal, and amygdala afferents. Noradrenaline mainly comes from the medulla oblongata, and secondarily from the locus coeruleus.

PREFRONTAL CORTEX

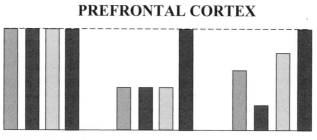

DA NA Ach GLU

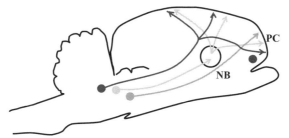

NUCLEUS ACCUMBENS

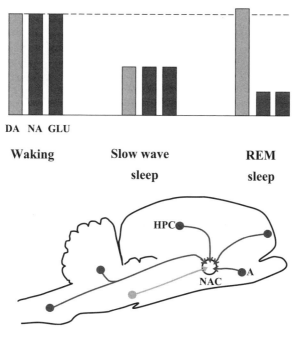

DA NA GLU

Waking   **Slow wave**   **REM**
                       sleep   **sleep**

α_1 receptors positively coupled to adenylate cyclase (Nicoll, Malenka, & Kauer, 1990).

The above-described data show that during REM sleep, the brain is strongly activated and is thus able to generate mental activity. However, concomitant inhibitory processes rapidly appeared to contribute to brain functioning.

INHIBITORY PROCESSES

Behavior and Electrophysiology

As already noted by Creutzfeldt, Baumgartner, and Schoen (1956) and Krnjevic, Randic, and Straughan (1966), the first demonstration of cortical inhibitory proceeses was performed in the nineteenth century. Bubnoff and Heidenhain (1881) showed in dogs that low-intensity peripheral and cortical stimulations inhibit cortical-induced motor activities. Anticipating later findings, they hypothesized that cortical inhibitory influences coexist with activating ones (p. 190). Pavlov (1962) (Nobel Prize 1904 for his studies on digestive processes) first considered the cortex as the exclusive site for the establishment of "temporary bindings," which are crucial to the production of conditioned reflexes. The connection between conditioned and unconditioned stimuli arose from activation of their respective cortical receptive fields, which are surrounded by inhibition of adjacent areas. The differentiation processes involved concentration of activating processes also surrounded by cortical inhibitory ones. However, the first author to speak about inhibition in the context of sleep-inducing processes was Hess (1931): "The essential mechanism of sleep cannot be explained differently as by active inhibition of some functions of the organism" (p. 1553).

In the specific context of REM sleep, Evarts, Fleming, and Huttenlocher (1960) made a premonitory finding when they showed that the recovery cycle of cortical responsiveness tested by stimulating radiations is shorter during slow wave sleep than during waking, thus pointing to a disinhibitory process. However, Evarts (1964, 1965) was the first to clearly identify cortical inhibitory processes that disappear during REM sleep (Figure 1.1). As we previously mentioned, he studied pyramidal neurons fired regularly and at a high rate during waking. The firing decreased and began to become irregular during slow wave sleep, while during REM sleep he observed high-frequency discharges but in large bursts of spikes separated by long silences. Evarts postulated the disappearance of inhibitory cortical control-regulating neuron activity by means of a "frequency-limiting" process. The most detailed study to reach the same conclusion was the findings of Demetrescu's (Demetrescu,

Demetrescu, & Iosif, 1966) team. By using a complex paradigm of four consecutive thalamocortical-evoked stimuli delivered at different intervals, these authors were able to show, through the different recoveries of responsiveness, that during active waking the cortex is under the influence of both high rate activating and inhibitory influences, both of which decreases during quiet waking and further during slow wave sleep and both of which are almost absent just before REM sleep. During the dreaming sleep stage, activating influences reappeared whereas the inhibitory influences remained at their lowest level (Figure 1.1). It is noteworthy that Rossi et al. (1965) and Allison (1965, 1968) confirmed the shortening of the recovery cycle of cortical-evoked potentials during REM sleep when compared to waking, strongly supporting the hypothesis of the influence of disinhibitory processes during this sleep stage.

A recent electrophysiological result confirmed the presence of such a disinhibitory process during REM sleep. Today, the so-called "prepulse inhibition" reproduces the old study of recovery cycle of responsiveness. Kisley et al. (2003) observed in humans a "sensory gating impairment" by studying the recovery cycle of auditory-evoked potentials. The N_{100} component of the second evoked potential at 500-ms latency was reduced during waking, but its inhibition disappeared during REM sleep, simply reproducing old animal results.

Another particulary new finding points to a disturbance occurring during REM sleep and related to a kind of responsiveness regulated by central structures. It is established that self-produced tactile stimulation feels less tickly than a stimulation with the same characteristics produced externally. Blagrove, Blakemore, and Thayer, (in press) have shown that at emergence from REM sleep dreaming, the attenuation of self-stimulation was nearly suppressed. The authors underlined that this indicates "a deficit in self-monitoring and a confusion between self- and external-stimulation." This result gives an indication of yet another function that is disturbed during REM sleep.

Tomography

Although we have emphasized the structures that show an increase of blood flow and oxygen consumption during REM sleep, several authors showed that other structures are deactivated, which certainly leads to a loss of functioning, a kind of inhibition. This is particularly the case of the frontal cortex, more precisely the dorsolateral prefrontal cortex, a part of the basal parietal and posterior cingulate cortex (Braun et al., 1997; Lövblad et al., 1999; Madsen et al., 1991; Maquet, 2000; Maquet et al., 1996, 2004). In addition, while the associative visual areas and the ventral processing stream are activated, the primary visual cortex is deactivated (Braun et al.,

1998; Madsen et al., 1991), which could account for the results of Llinas and Ribary (1993) who observed a lack of gamma rhythm reset during REM sleep. In addition, this apparent separation from the periphery is increased by thalamic processes. Indeed, although the postsynaptic responsiveness in relay nuclei is high during REM sleep (Albe-Fessard, Massion, Hall, & Rosenblith, 1964; Favale et al., 1965; Gandolfo et al., 1980; Rossi et al., 1965; Steriade, 1970), the presynaptic depolarization of thalamic afferents, particularly during the eye movements bursts (Dagnino, Favale, Loeb, Manfredi, & Seitun, 1969; Ghelarducci, Pisa, & Pompeiano, 1970; Iwama, Kawamoto, Sakkakura, & Kasamatsu, 1966) more importantly associated with dreams, points to the inhibition of sensory inputs. The origin of this presynaptic inhibition could be either a presynaptic target of GABAergic neurons from the thalamic reticular nucleus (Steriade, Domich, Oakson, & Deschenes, 1987) or be induced by the vestibular nuclei (Morrison & Pompeiano, 1966; Ghelarducci et al., 1970).

Neurochemistry

The first results were related to the silence of 5-HT and noradrenergic (NA) neurons. They decrease their firing during slow wave sleep and become silent during REM sleep (Aston-Jones & Bloom, 1981; Hobson et al., 1975; McGinty et al., 1974; McGinty & Harper, 1976; Rasmussen et al., 1984). Serotonin inhibits most cortical neurons (Krnjevic & Phillis, 1963; Reader, Ferron, Descarries, & Jasper, 1979), once again by diffuse release at varicosities level (Descarries, 1975; Nelson et al., 1973). More recently, Araneda and Andrade (1991) again confirmed the "very high prevalent" hyperpolarization of pyramidal neurons induced by this neuromodulator. The hyperpolarization is mainly consecutive to neuron exit of K^+ ions, entrance of Cl^- ions, or Ca^{2+} channel blockade. This induced inhibition was related to 5-HT_{1A} receptors, which increase K^+ conductance whereas the less frequent depolarizing effects were once again consecutive to 5-HT_2 receptor activation. These two kinds of receptors could be situated on the same pyramidal neurons and be impinged upon different serotonergic axon terminals (dorsal and medial raphe nuclei). Their respective activations depends on the increase in the signal-to-noise ratio of neuron functioning (McCormick, 1992). Noradrenaline mainly inhibits cortical neurons (Foote, Freedman, & Oliver, 1975; Frederickson, Jordan, & Phillis, 1971; Krnjevic & Phillis, 1963; Manunta & Edeline, 1999; Nelson et al., 1973) by acting on α_2 receptors that block Ca^{2+} channels or open K^+ channels. An interesting point for further discussion is that these neurons begin to fire again a few seconds before arousal from REM sleep (Aston-Jones & Bloom, 1981).

Consequently, the silence of 5-HT and NA neurons during REM sleep potentially deteriorates forebrain functioning because of the general cortical disinhibition possibly responsible for disturbances of the signal-to-noise ratio, which results in a loss of cortical control processes.

In a recent study involving microdialysis and capillary electrophoresis performed in rats, our laboratory also quantified the extracellular concentration of noradrenaline in the medial prefrontal cortex and nucleus accumbens. In the cortex, the noradrenaline is produced only by the ipsilateral locus coeruleus neurons (see Figure 1.2, top), which mainly innervate the molecular layer (Levit & Moore, 1978). The noradrenaline concentration was highest during waking and significantly diminished during both slow wave sleep and REM sleep (Figure 1.2). This result is in general agreement with the silence of corresponding neurons. The maintenance of a given concentration of noradrenaline is certainly the consequence of its diffuse release at the varicosities level without synaptic rapid reuptake and/or destruction by the catechol-O-methyl transferase. In nucleus accumbens, the noradrenergic afferents are only produced in part by the locus coeruleus but principally by the medulla oblongata A_2 area and then the A_1 area (Delfs, Zhu, Druhan, & Aston-Jones, 1998), the silence of which during REM sleep has still not been determined. However, another noradrenergic area, A_5, is silent during carbachol-induced REM-like sleep (Fenik, Marchenko, Janssen, Davies, & Kubin, 2002). Noradrenaline has certainly an important function in nucleus accumbens because in humans, the concentration is as great as for dopamine (Tong, Hornykiewicz, & Kish, 2006). The marked decrease during REM sleep cannot be without functional significance. For example, there is a dopamine reuptake by noradrenergic neurons in nucleus accumbens (Carboni & Silvagni, 2004). This should be decreased or suppressed during REM sleep noradrenergic silence.

The dopaminergic neurons of the ventral tegmental area projecting to the cortex and limbic system (see Figure 1.2) are the only monoaminergic neurons that continue firing during REM sleep (Miller, Farber, Gatz, Roffwarg, & German, 1983; Trulson & Preussler, 1984) since histaminergic neurons become silent already with the occurrence of light slow wave sleep (Vanni-Mercier, Gigout, Debilly, & Lin, 2003; Vanni-Mercier, Sakai & Jouvet, 1984). The neurons of the mesocortical tract mainly inhibit target neurons (Krnjevic & Phillis, 1963; Reader et al., 1979) by increasing GABA release from interneurons by influencing D_2 receptors and also by directly inhibiting pyramidal neuron apical dendrites through D_1 receptors (Abi-Dargham & Moore, 2003; Grobin & Deutch, 1998; Pirot et al., 1992; Rétaux, Besson, & Penit-Soria, 1991). In the prefrontal cortex, dopamine transforms the long-term potentiation (long duration facilitation) induced by glutamate into long-term depression (inhibition) but can increase neuron firing when glutamate input occurs simultaneously with postsynaptic depolarization (Otani, Blond, Desce, & Crepel, 1998). Consequently, dopamine, mediated by D_1 receptors, is able to increase the responsiveness of prefrontal cortex neurons (Lavin & Grace, 2001). Finally, in respect to higher integrated functions, dopamine has also been shown to increase the neurons signal-to-noise ratio (Luciana, Collins, & Depue, 1998).

The present author also recently studied dopamine release in the medial prefrontal cortex and nucleus accumbens of rats (Léna et al., 2005). In the prefrontal cortex the concentration was highest during waking, minimal during slow wave sleep and intermediate during REM sleep. The decrease during REM sleep when compared to waking was highly significant ($p < .01$), whereas the increase when compared to slow wave sleep was close to significance ($p < .07$) in our small sample of animals (six rats) (Figure 1.2). This significant decrease during REM sleep could be related to prefrontal deactivation (Braun et al., 1997, 1998; Lövblad et al., 1999; Madsen et al., 1991; Maquet et al., 1996; Maquet, 2000) since glutamatergic influences on the tegmental ventral area A_{10} increases dopamine release in the prefrontal cortex (Takahata & Moghaddam, 2000, 2003). Since dopamine associated with glutamate α-amino-3-hydroxy-5-methylisoazol-4-propionic acid (AMPA) receptor activation favors GABA release in the cortex (see also Arco del & Mora, 2005), the dopamine decrease in the prefrontal cortex during REM sleep should decrease GABA local release, inducing GABAergic disinhibitory processes similar to those encountered in schizophrenia (Lewis, 2000; Lewis, Hashimoto, & Volk, 2005). Moreover, dopamine acting at the D_2 receptor level in the prefontal cortex decreases dopamine and acetylcholine release in the nucleus accumbens (Arco del & Mora, 2005). Consequently, the decrease in prefrontal dopamine release during REM sleep observed in our experiments (Léna et al., 2005) could contribute to the abundant release of dopamine in nucleus accumbens during this sleep stage. It could be accompanied by an increase of local acetylcholine activating (by nicotinic receptors) and inhibitory (by muscarinic receptors) influences (Mansvelder, Rover de, McGehee, & Brussaard, 2003).

In the nucleus accumbens, the highest dopamine concentration we observed during REM sleep was not significantly different from waking. The concentration during both stages was significantly higher ($p < .05$) than the lowest level during slow wave sleep. The high-level concentration during REM sleep at least could be explained by different mechanisms. There could be a burst firing mode of ventral tegmental A_{10} neurons (Miller et al., 1983), which then release more dopamine (Chergui, Suaud-Chagny, & Gonon, 1994; Gonon, 1988; Grace, 1991). Indeed, Miller et al. (1983) have shown a greater variability of dopaminergic neuron firing during REM sleep compared to slow wave sleep, which assumes at least some bursting of the firing. This irregular firing, as already emphasized (Evarts, 1964, 1965; Wang & McCormick, 1993), results from the loss or decrease of a frequency-limiting process involving active inhibitory control of neuron functioning. Thus, this maximal release of dopamine could be the result of the prefrontal deactivation (Braun et al., 1997, 1998; Lövblad et al., 1999; Madsen et al., 1991; Maquet, 2000; Maquet et al., 1996), which increases dopamine release in the nucleus accumbens (Brake et al., 2000; Jackson, Frost, & Moghaddam, 2001) by a glutamate-induced deficit in the dopaminergic ventral tegmental area (Takahata & Moghaddam, 2000, 2003). Moreover, dopamine acting at the D_2-receptor level in the prefontal cortex decreases dopamine and acetylcholine release in the nucleus accumbens (Arco del & Mora, 2005). Consequently, the decrease of prefrontal dopamine release during REM sleep observed in our experiments (Léna et al., 2005) could contribute to the significant release of dopamine in the nucleus accumbens during this sleep stage. (It could be accompanied by an increase of local acetylcholine activating influences—by nicotinic receptors—on feed-forward GABAergic output processes [Mansvelder et al., 2003].) It could be related to the activation of the basolateral amygdala (Maquet & Franck, 1997) through its action on dopaminergic terminals (Howland, Taepavarapruk, & Phillips, 2002). Mesopontine activation of REM sleep could directly activate the ventral tegmental area neurons (Miller & Blaha, 2005). The silence of serotonergic and noradrenergic neurons might contribute to this high concentration of dopamine. Indeed, serotonergic 5-HT_{1B} knock-out mice (with elimination of the receptor at birth) show an enhanced dopamine level (Shippenberg, Hen, & He, 2000) and an activated turn-over (Ase, Reader, Hen, Riad, & Descarries, 2000) in the nucleus accumbens. Moreover, noradrenergic α_2 receptor agonists (Pothos, Rada, Mark, & Hoebel, 1991), as well as β receptor antagonists (Harris, Hedaya, Pan, & Kalivas, 1996), increase local dopamine release. Finally, since the dopamine train spikes induce inhibition of GABA release (Hjemstad, 2004), probably during both waking and REM sleep, the crucial factor characterizing REM sleep in the nucleus accumbens could be the decrease of glutamate, which should be the first consequence of the decrease of output from both the prefrontal cortex and hippocampus (Grace, 2000) and, second, from the decrease of the glutamate colocalized in the dopaminergic axon terminals (Chuhma et al., 2004). In contrast, the amgdala glutamatergic influences on the nucleus accumbens are increased (Grace, 2000) since this structure is strongly activated during REM sleep (Maquet & Franck, 1997). Thus, this could explain the emotionality encountered in dreams as already stated by Freud

(1955): "it is much more on account of its emotional rather than its representational content that dreaming impresses itself upon us as a psychological experience" (pp. 462–463).

In addition, acetylcholine is able to exert cortical inhibitory influences. Early results have already shown that its "inhibitory responses ... (had) shorter latency and faster recovery than the excitatory ones ... The thresholds of both inhibitory and excitatory responses were almost the same. (In some cases) responses to acetylcholine reversed from excitatory to inhibitory with increasing dose" (Nelson et al., 1973, p. 123). Recent findings have confirmed on pyramidal neurons inhibitory influences of this kind (Giulledge & Stuart, 2005; Levy et al., 2006) in addition to the excitatory ones (Mednikova, Karnup, & Loseva, 1998).

DISCUSSION

Certainly, the physiological support of dreaming went unnoticed during several millenia. However, this was but one of the reasons why attention was first long focused on the psychological significance of this fascinating activity. This was already the case in the very ancient hindu philosophy (sixteenth through eleventh centuries BC), which described a specific state of consciousness called "Taijasa" corresponding to the dreaming sleep stage (Datta, 2006). Already, nearly two thousand years ago, one of the first written interpretations suggested that dreams convey a message, often of symbolic nature. The Talmud (Fromm, 1953, p. 1) stated: "an uninterpreted dream is like an unread letter." However, around 1900, the most developed theory of the meaning of dreams was elaborated by Freud mainly in his masterly work: *The Interpretation of Dreams* (1955). It is not possible, and not the aim, to here develop Freud's extraordinary structured model in which he stated above all, that dreams are a means of realizing unconscious wishes. The (latent) content of dreams, he wrote, is unable to obtain access to the sleeper's consciousness as a result of repression and is therefore disguised by a censorship process into (manifest) content acceptable to the ego (Boarg, 2006). Recently, it was hypothesized that the bizarreness of dreams could be the consequence of the regression of dreaming content to primary-process mentation (Solms & Turnbull, 2002). All these concepts suggest that the brain is able to generate mentation during sleep with specific properties.

Mentation occurs during REM sleep since specific brainstem activating processes discovered already some time ago activate the forebrain structures generating dreaming (Gottesmann, 1967a, 1967b, 1969; Huttenlocher, 1961; McCarley & Hobson, 1971a; McGinty et al., 1974; Moroz, Foutz, & Gottesmann, 1977; Strumwasser, 1958; Vertes, 1977). Indeed, lesions to these structures suppress REM sleep (Carli & Zanchetti, 1965; Deurveilher & Hennevin, 2001; Jouvet, 1962; Jouvet & Michel, 1960a; Jouvet & Mounier, 1960; Webster & Jones, 1988). It has been long well established that cholinergic processes (George, Haslett, & Jenden, 1964; Jia, Yamuy, Sampogna, Morales, & Chase, 2003; Jouvet & Michel, 1960b; Pal & Mallick, 2004; Vazquez & Baghdoyan, 2004; see reviews (Baghdoyan, 1997; Jones, 1991, 2004; Jouvet, 1975) support this forebrain activation, particularly by influencing the also cholinergic basal forebrain nucleus (Buzsaki et al., 1988; Buzsaki & Gage, 1989; Steriade & Buzsaki, 1990; Steriade & McCarley, 1990), which releases more acetylcholine during REM sleep than during waking (Vasquez & Baghdoyan, 2001), although the cortical high release (Jasper & Tessier, 1971) is lower than during active waking (Marrosu et al., 1995). New results have shown that the two active pontine areas involved in REM sleep-generating processes, the peri-locus coeruleus α (Sakai, 1985, 1988; Sakai & Crochet, 2003) and the pedunculopontine and dorsolateral tegmental nucleus (Datta & Siwek, 1997, 2002) are in fact activated by glutamate, which constitutes the more advanced step in REM sleep-generating processes (Datta, Spoley, Mavanji, & Patterson, 2002; Datta, Spoley, & Patterson, 2001; Onoe & Sakai, 1995; Sakai & Crochet, 2003), since even in the atropinized animal, REM sleep can be induced by glutamate that passes the cholinergic link (Onoe & Sakai, 1995; Sakai & Crochet, 2003). This cortical activation during REM sleep was first evidenced in humans by the low amplitude EEG (Aserinsky & Kleitman, 1953; Dement, 1955; Dement & Kleitman, 1957a, 1957b; Loomis et al., 1937) and in animals by neuron firing (Evarts, 1964, 1965; McCarley & Hobson, 1971b). The more recent identification of PGO waves equivalents (McCarley et al., 1983, Miyauchi et al., 1987) and γ rhythm (Gross & Gotman, 1999; Llinas & Ribary, 1993), as well as the results of the tomographic approach (Braun et al., 1997, 1998; Lövblad et al., 1999; Madsen et al., 1991; Maquet, 2000; Maquet et al., 1996, 2004) strongly confirmed the role of these cortical-activating aspects in supporting mental processes.

However, in an earlier past, it appeared that alongside these activating processes there also existed inhibitory influences in the cortex that had to be taken into account. These inhibitory influences were identified early on during waking (Bubnoff & Heidenhain, 1881; Creutzfeldt, Baumgartner, & Schoen, 1956) and showed major variations during REM sleep. These antagonist but necessarily complementary influences decrease significantly during REM sleep (Demetrescu et al., 1966; Evarts, 1964, 1965). During these years, the present author already pointed out (Gottesmann, 1967a, 1970, 1971) that the contemporaneously activated and inhibited (controlled) cortex during waking could explain the logical thinking of waking, that the decrease of both during slow wave sleep may support the observed rather poor thinking-like mentation (Foulkes, 1962), and that the lowest level of both kinds of influence may explain the rather anxious nonvisual mental activity of the intermediate phase (Lairy et al., 1968a, 1968b). Finally, during REM sleep the activated but strongly disinhibited cortex could generate the rich but illogical mentation characteristic of this sleep stage. In addition, the loss of cortical control could possibly enable the occurrence of recurrent dreams because of the higher excitability of memory traces related to mainly painful memories. On emergence from REM sleep, the reappearance of waking both kinds of influence were thought to induce the forgetting of dreams (Gottesmann, 1967a, 1970, 1971). Later, these speculations were reinforced by the silence of serotonergic (McGinty et al., 1974; McGinty and Harper, 1976; Rasmussen et al., 1984) and noradrenergic (Aston-Jones & Bloom, 1981; Hobson et al., 1975) neurons that innervate the cerebral cortex and exert mainly inhibitory influences (Foote et al., 1975; Frederickson et al., 1971; Krnjevic & Phillis, 1963; Manunta & Edeline, 1999; Nelson et al., 1973; Phillis, Lake, & Yarbrough, 1973; Reader et al., 1979; Warren & Dykes, 1996). Interestingly, as already mentioned, these neuromodulators are released at the varicosities level, therefore, with a rather tonic, durable influence, thus explaining their continuous although much decreased influence during REM sleep. Finally, the decrease of prefrontal (mostly dorsolateral) activation during REM sleep probably contributes to the characteristic loss of reflectiveness occuring during this sleep stage (Braun et al., 1997; Madsen et al., 1991; Maquet, 2000; Maquet et al., 1996, 2004).

At first glance, two peripheral activities seem to be related to mentation during REM sleep. The first activity is eye movement, which can be related to pontine and/or cortical activations as evidenced by the pontine-generated PGO and EMP waves (for recent findings, see Datta, 1997; Datta & Hobson, 1994; Datta, Mavanji, Patterson, & Ulloor, 2003; Datta et al., 1998; for history, see Gottesmann, 1997). Since some eye movements are recorded in neodecorticated humans (Jouvet, Michel, & Mounier, 1960) as well as in brainstem transected animals (Jouvet, 1962; Mouret, 1964), even if they are most often isolated and restricted to lateral directions and controlled by cortical areas (Jeannerod et al., 1965; Mouret et al., 1965), appear to be rather reflex-generated. In contrast, the activation of the saccadic eye movement area (Hong et al., 1995) could explain the relation sometimes observed between dream content and eye movements (Herman et al., 1984; Roffwarg et al., 1962). The eye movements observed in life-long blind persons (Gross et al., 1965) could be preferentially related to pontine activations. The second peripheral activity is penile erection (Fisher, Gross, & Zuch, 1965; Karacan, Goodenough, Shapiro, & Starker, 1966; Ohlmeyer et al., 1944;

Ohlmeyer & Brilmayer, 1947). The mechanism of this function during REM sleep has been largely elucidated: the silence of the locus coeruleus, by noradrenergic disinhibition, induces the filling of cavernous tissue (Giuliano & Rampin, 2000). However, this activity is regulated by anterior brain processes (Schmidt, Sakai, Valatx, & Jouvet, 1999; Schmidt, Valatx, Sakai, Fort, & Jouvet, 2000), particularly by its dopaminergic influence (D'aquila, Panin, Cossu, Peana, & Serra, 2003). Since this phenomenon occurs during all REM sleep stages and in animals (Schmidt, Valatx, Schmidt, Wauquier, & Jouvet, 1994), its hypothesized connection to dream content has now been discarded. From the history of science standpoint, it is interesting that, as already mentioned (Gottesmann, 2001), although incorporations of memories, recent diurnal residues, and peripheral and visceral stimuli were described by Freud (1955) as the origin of dreams, there is no mention of peripheral activities related to dreaming. Freud merely writes repeatedly that the dreamer can awake with a specific feeling. However, his model of the psychic apparatus (Chapter 7) extends from perception to muscular output. It has to be underscored that although sexuality and sexual symbols are rather overrepresented in his dream interpretations, there is no indication that erection is always observed on emergence from REM sleep. This is more unexpected because Freud's theory encountered strong resistance from the scientific community, and erection as a biological characteristic of the dreaming sleep stage could have been of great help to the author. The most surprising thing is that Freud, who had extensive knowledge of classical literature (see his wonderful Chapter 1), mentioned Hervey de Saint Denys (1964), who described such peripheral activities during dreaming and was certainly aware of Lucretius. Was a form of psychological censorship at work?

Another observation related to Freud, the founder of psychoanalysis, claimed that dreams are not only constructed out of recent waking events (day-time residues), but that they can also originate in prehistoric "Urphantasien." Recently, Revonsuo (2000) gave new weight to this theory (Gottesmann, 2000a).

However, the main development in recent years has been the foregrounding of new results that update former oft-repeated claims. Indeed, as early as three centuries ago, Kant (1724–1804) pinpointed the abnormal kind of mentation characteristic of dreams: "the madman is a waking dreamer." Some time later, Schopenhauer (1788–1860) stated "dreams are brief madness" (1955, p. 85). Approximately at the same time in his well-known study on sleep, Maury (1817–1892) wrote "the dream is a kind of delirium" (1861, p. 26), while the distinguished neurophysiopathologist John Hughlings Jackson (1835–1911) announced with foresight: "Find out about dreams and you will find out about insanity" (Nahum, 1965). Finally, some decades ago, the neuropsychiatrist Henri Ey wrote: "it is obvious, it cannot be but obvious, that dream and madness spurt out from the same source" (1967, p. 575). Why this new consideration given to past observations? The fact is that there are strong convergent electrophysiological, tomographic, pharmacological, and neurochemical arguments showing a relationship between REM and schizophrenia (Gottesmann, 1999, 2000b, 2002, 2004a, 2004b, 2005, 2006).

The first electrophysiological argument is that the classical EEG of REM sleep (0.5–25 c/s) is similar to that of waking. It is rapid and of low amplitude, as during active waking. However, during REM sleep, as in schizophrenia during waking, there are very few α-waves, which are relaxed EEG rhythms that are severely diminished in schizophrenia since there is a deficit of habituation processes in this mental disease (as shown by the decreased P_{50} and P_{100} prepulse inhibition [Kisley et al., 2003] see discussion later in this chapter). A second powerful argument is that the γ rhythm during REM sleep becomes uncoupled in cortical areas, particularly between the perceptual and frontal areas (Perez-Garci et al., 2001; Yeragani, Cashmere, Miewald, Tancer, & Keshavan, 2006), as well as between the cortex and hippocampus (Cantero et al., 2004). Uncoupling is the index of intracortical disconnections. In schizophrenia, one of the most advanced theories and findings involves the intracerebral disconnection processes. This is particularly the case for cortex relations (Meyer-Lindenberg et al., 2001; Meyer-Lindenberg et al., 2005; Peled et al., 2000; Spencer et al., 2003; Yeragani et al., 2006) and intrahippocampus and hippocampo-entorhinal connections (Young, Beach, Falkai, & Honer, 1998). Tononi and Edelman (2000) also highlighted the "discontinuities in the interactions among brain regions" as an explaination of schizophrenic troubles. The third argument, in fact triple in nature, is related to brain excitability. Indeed, during REM sleep, the brain is as if it is disconnected from the periphery. The primary visual cortex is deactivated (Braun et al., 1998), and the presynaptic inhibition of sensory afferents at thalamic level (Dagnino et al., 1969; Gandolfo et al., 1980; Ghelarducci et al., 1970; Iwama et al., 1966; Steriade, 1970) contributes to isolating the cortex. Here also, the main hypotheses related to hallucination occurrence involves a reduction of sensory constraints (Behrendt & Young, 2005). In addition, we already described that the prepulse inhibition of the N_{100} component of the auditory-evoked potential is suppressed during REM sleep. The same phenomenon is also characteristic of schizophrenia (Kisley et al., 2003). Finally, a recent result shows that at emergence from REM sleep dreaming, contrary to waking, there is a confusion between self- and external stimulation, as is the case in schizophrenia (Blagrove et al., in press). It could be related to a disconnection between the prefrontal cortex and the areas involved in self-other distinction (Jeannerod, 2003, 2004).

The strong tomographic arguments are, first, the deactivation of the dorsolateral prefrontal (Braun et al., 1997; Maquet et al., 1996) or other frontal areas (Lövblad et al., 1999; Madsen et al., 1991) occurring during REM sleep. This is certainly at the origin of cognitive disturbances, among them the loss of reflectiveness during this sleep stage. The same dorsolateral deactivation is specifically observed in schizophrenia, particularly when the cognitive tasks are impaired (Bunney & Bunney, 2000; Fletcher et al., 1998; Weinberger, Berman, & Zec, 1986). In addition, there is deactivation of the posterior cingulate cortex (Braun et al., 1997; Maquet et al., 1996; Nofzinger, Mintun, Wiseman, & Kupfer, 1997), which is not part of the limbic system unlike the anterior cingulate cortex, which is activated (Braun et al., 1997; Maquet et al., 1996; Nofzinger et al., 1997) and which "could account for the emotional and affective aspects of dreams" (Maquet et al., 1996, p. 166). Although the function of the posterior cingulate cortex in relation to REM sleep cognitive potentialities is open to discussion, it has to be mentioned that the specific association of dorsolateral prefrontal and posterior cingulate cortex deactivation is also observed in the particular case of piano playing, particularly when the artists "lose themselves" during peak musical performances (Parsons, Sergent, Hodges, & Fox, 2005). Is it iconoclastic to think of Glenn Gould playing J.S. Bach? This behavior shows a resemblance with dreaming and schizophrenia where loss of reality consciousness and activations take place in other brain areas, particularly in the motor cortex (Evarts, 1964) and limbic system (Braun et al., 1997; Maquet, 2000; Maquet et al., 1996; Maquet & Franck, 1997, Nofzinger et al., 1997).

The increase of amygdala activation during REM sleep (Maquet & Franck, 1997) and its role in the emotional components of dreaming has to be related to schizophrenia. Today, glutamate disturbance constitutes one of the most important hypotheses towards an explanation of the disorders caused by this disease. It is now acknowledged that a decrease of nucleus accumbens glutamatergic afferents from the hippocampus and prefrontal cortex favors the appearance of hallucinations, delusions, and bizarre thought processes. In addition, it is thought to disinhibit the influences of amygdala glutamatergic afferents and could contribute to the affective disorders in schizophrenia (Grace, 2000). It is of great interest that during REM sleep, we found in rats a strong decrease of glutamate concentration in nucleus accumbens compared to waking (Léna et al., 2005). This is in close concordance with the fact that glutamate (N-methyl-D-aspartic acid; NMDA) antagonists induce psychotic troubles (Grace, 2000; Heresco-Levy, 2000) and, at the same time, vivid dreaming (Reeves, Lindholm, Myles, Fletcher, & Hunt, 2001). It is also of major interest that we did not observe any glutamate-level differences in the medial prefrontal cortex during sleep-waking stages—particularly between waking and REM sleep—since in schizophrenia there is no change of glutamate transporter mRNA expression in the prefrontal and primary visual cortex (Lauriat et al., 2005).

The functioning of dopamine also shows highly significant similarities during REM sleep and in schizophrenia. Already, pharmacology has shown that the increase of the central dopamine level induces psychotic symptoms, as well as vivid dreaming (Arnulf et al., 2000; Buffenstein, Heaster, & Ko, 1999; Larsen & Tandberg, 2001; Levin & Daly, 1998; Thompson & Pierce, 1999). On the other hand, neuroleptics decrease both (Remington & Chong, 1999; Solms, 2000). Neurochemistry has long shown a disturbance (increase) of dopamine functioning in schizophrenia (MacKay et al., 1982). We first confirmed this result in rats because the maximal release of dopamine in the nucleus accumbens occurs during REM sleep (Léna et al., 2005), as is the case in this mental disease. The difference with waking in our study was not significant, but there is parallel variation in schizophrenia. In contrast, our results showed a very significant dopamine decrease when compared to waking in the prefrontal cortex. This data shows a strong similarity with schizophrenia, in which this decrease is acknowledged to be responsible for the cognitive disorders (Okubo et al., 1997), particularly the decrease or loss of reflectiveness also observed during REM sleep. Dopamine increases the signal-to-noise ratio of brain information (Luciana et al., 1998) and exerts a state-dependent modulatory effect via D_1 receptors (Lavin & Grace, 2001). The decrease of prefrontal dopamine during REM sleep, as well as in schizophrenia, could situate this neuromodulator level outside the "optimal stimulation window" of D_1-receptor functioning (Abi-Dargham & Moore, 2003).

Serotonergic and noradrenergic neuron silence during REM sleep has also to be placed in parallel with findings in schizophrenia. First, it is well known that the rapid inhibition of raphe serotonergic neurons by lysergic acid diethylamide (LSD) (in rats, 1 to 2 minute latency after intravenous injection; Aghajanian, Foot, & Sheard, 1968), induces an increase of REM sleep in humans at 25 µg (Toyoda, 1964) and even lower doses (7–22 µg; Muzio, Roffwarg, & Kaufman, 1966), as well as psychotic symptoms. Recent results show that serotonergic agonists (reuptake inhibitors) are interesting adjuvants in newly designed neuroleptics (Silver, Barash, Aharon, Kaplan, & Poyurovsky, 2000; Van Hes et al., 2003). Noradrenaline is also involved in normal mental functioning since its decrease is, like serotonin, already a source of depression, and the rare locus coeruleus stimulations performed in humans induced "well being and improved clarity of . . . thinking" (Libet, 1994). A deficit of noradrenaline is also involved in schizophrenic disturbances, and new neuroleptics also comprise reuptake inhibitor properties

(Friedman, Adler, & Davis, 1999; Linner, Wiker, Wadenberg, Schalling, & Svensson, 2002). Finally, this deficit of noradrenaline could prevent this neuromodulator reappearance at normal level in the few seconds before emerging from REM sleep (Aston-Jones & Bloom, 1981). In subjects predisposed to schizophrenia, it could favor the onset of dreaming hallucinatory activity in the waking consciousness with belief of reality (Kelly, 1998).

Acetylcholine, a highly important neurotransmitter for normal mind functioning (Perry, Walker, Grace, & Perry, 1999; Sarter & Bruno, 2000), is also involved in schizophrenic symptoms because a central decrease of this transmitter is recognized to be at the origin of hallucinatory activity during waking (Collerton, Perry, & McKeith, 2005). The same phenomenon is observed during REM sleep (Marrosu et al., 1995) in which the concentration, lower as compared to active waking, only reaches the level of relaxed waking (Figure 1.2).

Finally, the very recent discovery of orexin/hypocretin has be considered as possibly related to schizophrenia. This neuropeptide deficit is responsible for the occurrence of the narcoleptic syndrome (Nishino, Ripley, Overheem, Lammers, & Mignot, 2000; Overeem, Scammell, & Lammers, 2002; Thannickal et al., 2000), which is characterized not only by the classical bouts of sleeping during the day but by the rapid entrance into REM sleep (Hishikawa & Kaneko, 1965; Rechtschaffen, Wolpert, Dement, Mitchell, & Fisher, 1963; Suzuki, 1966) not clearly detailed in the first study devoted to the psychological characteristics of narcolepsy (Vogel, 1960). This peptide, synthesized in the hypothalamus, activates locus coeruleus neurons, hence inhibiting REM sleep occurrence (Bourgin et al., 2000). The corresponding neurons, most active during active waking, become silent during REM sleep, except sometimes during its phasic activities (Mileykovskiy, Kiyashchenko, & Siegel, 2005). The hypnagogic hallucinations often encountered in this disease point to a severe schizoaffective disorder (Douglass, 2003), and a positive correlation can be found between orexin/hypocretin concentration in the cerebrospinal fluid and the usual sleep disturbances observed in schizophrenia (Nishino, Ripley, Mignot, Benson, & Zarcone, 2002). However, its infusion in the ventral tegmental A_{10} dopaminergic area induces an increase of dopamine release in the prefrontal cortex, which could on the contrary improve the negative symptoms of schizophrenia, whereas the release in nucleus accumbens remains unchanged (Vittoz & Berridge, 2005).

CONCLUSION

The fascinating history of REM sleep first showed that unexpected intense brain activation supported the intense psychological activity of dreaming. The explanation of dreaming illogical mental characteristics began to appear with the identification of forebrain inhibitory control processes. Both activating and inhibitory influences supplied highly important information to a better understanding of the waking functioning of the brain. Today, disconcerting psychological as well as neurobiological resemblances with schizophrenia are laying the foundation of a new approach to this sleep stage as a psychobiological model of this disease, without any experimental intervention such as central electrical or pharmacological stimulation or central lesions (Gottesmann, 2005, 2006, in press). Most characteristics of this sleep stage constitute endophenotypes (Gottesman & Gould, 2003; Gottesman & Shields, 1973) of schizophrenia. Also, in order to identify the genetic disturbances of this polygenic illness (Gottesman & Shields, 1967) and promote future specific therapies, the genic background of REM sleep characteristics seems to be a good target (Gottesmann & Gottesman, in press).

Acknowledgments. I gratefully thank Marc Rodi for the iconography and Professor George Morgan for improving the English of the manuscript.

REFERENCES

Abi-Dargham, A., & Moore, H. (2003). Prefrontal DA transmission at D1 receptors and the pathology of schizophrenia. *Neuroscientist, 9,* 404–416.

Aghajanian, G. K., Foot, W., & Sheard, M. (1968). Lysergic acid diethylamide: Sensitive neuronal units in the midbrain raphe. *Science, 161,* 706–708.

Albe-Fessard, D., Massion, J., Hall, R., & Rosenblith, W. (1964). Modifications au cours de la veille et du sommeil des valeurs moyennes de réponses nerveuses centrales induites par des stimulations somatiques chez le Chat libre [Modifications during waking and sleep of the mean value of central nervous responses induced by sensory stimmulations in the free moving cat]. *Comptes Rendus Hebdomadaires des Séances de l'Académie des Sciences, 258,* 353–356.

Allison, T. (1965). Cortical and subcortical evoked responses to central stimuli during wakefulness and sleep. *Electroencephalography & Clinical Neurophysiology, 18,* 131–139.

Allison, T. (1968). Recovery cycles of primary evoked potentials in cats sensorimotor cortex. *Experentia, 24,* 240–241.

Amadeo, M., & Gomez, A. (1966). Eye movements, attention and dreaming in the congenetically blind. *Canadian Psychiatric Association Journal, 11,* 501–507.

Araneda, R., & Andrade, R. (1991). 5-hydroxytryptamine2 and 5-hydroxytryptamine 1A receptors mediate opposing responses on membrane excitability in the association cortex. *Neuroscience, 40,* 399–412.

Arco del, A., & Mora, F. (2005). Glutamate-dopamine in vivo interaction in the prefrontal cortex modulates the release of dopamine and acetylcholine in the nucleus accumbens of the awake rat. *Journal of Neural Transmission, 112,* 97–109.

Arduini, A., Berlucchi, G., & Strata, P. (1963). Pyramidal activity during sleep and wakefulness. *Archives Italiennes de Biologie, 101,* 530–544.

Arnaud, C., Gandolfo, G. & Gottesmann, C. (1979). The reactivity of the somesthetic S1 cortex during sleep and waking in the rat. *Brain Research Bulletin, 4*, 735–740.

Arnulf, I., Bonnet, A. M., Damier, P., Bejjani, B. P., Seilhean, D., Derenne, J. P., et al. (2000). Hallucinations, REM sleep and Parkinson's disease: A medical hypothesis. *Neurology, 55*, 281–288.

Ase, A. R., Reader, T. A., Hen, R., Riad, M., & Descarries, L. (2000). Altered serotonin and dopamine metabolism in the CNS of serotonin 5-HT(1A) or 5-HT(1B) receptor knockout mice. *Journal of Neurochemistry, 75*, 2415–2426.

Aserinsky, E., & Kleitman, N. (1953). Regularly occurring periods of eye motility, and concomitant phenomena during sleep. *Science, 118*, 273–274.

Aserinsky, E., & Kleitman, N. (1955). Two types of ocular motility occurring during sleep. *Journal of Applied Physiology, 8*, 1–10.

Aston-Jones, G., & Bloom, F. E. (1981). Activity of norepinephrine-containing neurons in behaving rats anticipates fluctuations in the sleep-waking cycle. *Journal of Neuroscience, 1*, 876–886.

Baghdoyan, H. A. (1997). Cholinergic mechanisms regulating REM sleep. In *Sleep science. Basic research and clinical practice*, Schwartz, W. J. ed. *Monogr. Clin. Neurosci., 15*, M. Fisher, ed. (Karger, Basel), 88–116.

Behrendt, R. P., & Young, C. (2005). Hallucinations in schizophrenia, sensori impairment and brain disease: An unified model. *The Behavioral and Brain Sciences, 27*, 771–787.

Benoit, O., & Bloch, V. (1960). Seuil d'excitabilité réticulaire et sommeil profond chez le Chat [Reticular responsiveness threshold and deep sleep in the cat]. *Journal de Physiologie (Paris), 52*, 17–18.

Berger, H. (1929). Ueber das electroenkephalogram des menschen [On the electroencephalogram of humans]. *Arch Psychiat Nervenkrank. 87*, 527–570.

Berger, R. (1961). Tonus of extrinsic laryngeal muscles during sleep and dreaming. *Science, 134*, 840.

Bergmann, B. M., Winters, W. D., Rosenberg, R. S., & Rechschaffen, A. (1987). NREM sleep with low-voltage EEG in the rat. *Sleep, 10*, 1–11.

Berlucchi, G. (1997). One or many arousal system? Reflections on some of Guiseppe Moruzzi's foresights and insights about intrinsic regulation of brain activity. *Archives Italiennes de Biologie, 135*, 5–14.

Berlucchi, G., Moruzzi, G., Salvi, G., & Strata, P. (1964). Pupil behavior and ocular movements during desynchronized and synchronized sleep. *Archives Italiennes de Biologie, 102*, 230–244.

Blagrove, M., Blakemore, S. J., & Thayer, B. R. J. (2006). The ability to self-tickle following rapid eye movement sleep dreaming. *Consciousness & Cognition, 15*, 285–294.

Blake, H., & Gerard, R. W. (1937). Brain potentials during sleep. *American Journal of Physiology, 119*, 692–703.

Blake, H., Gerard, R. W., & Kleitman, N. (1939). Factors influencing brain potentials during sleep. *Journal of Neurophysiology, 2*, 48–60.

Boarg, S. (2006). Freudian dream theory, dream bizareness, and the disguise-censor controversy. *Neuro-Psychoanalysis, 8*, 5–17.

Bosinelli, M. (1995). Mind and consciousness during sleep. *Brain Research, 69*, 195–201.

Bourgin, P., Huitron-Resendiz, S., Spier, A. D., Fabre, V., Morte, B., Criado, J. R., et al. (2000). Hypocretin-I modulates rapid eye movement sleep through activation of locus coeruleus neurons. *Journal of Neuroscience, 20*, 7760–7765.

Bouyer, J. J., Montaron, M. F., & Rougeul, A. (1981). Fast fronto-parieta rhythms during combined focused attentive behavior and immobility in cat: Cortical and thalamic localizations. *Electroencephalography & Clinical Neurophysiology, 51*, 244–252.

Brake, W. G., Flores, G., Francis, D., Meaney, M. J., Srivastava, L. K., & Gratton, A. (2000). Enhanced nucleus accumbens dopamine and plasma corticosterone stress responses in adult rats with neonatal excitotoxic lesions to the medial prefrontal cortex. *Neuroscience, 96*, 687–695.

Braun, A. R., Balkin, T. J., Wesensten, N. J., Carson, R. E., Varga, M., Baldwin, P., et al. (1997). Regional cerebral blood flow throughout the sleep-wake cycle: An ^{15}0 PET study. *Brain, 120*, 1173–1197.

Braun, A. R., Balkin, T. J., Wesensten, N. J., Gwardry, F., Carson, R. E., Varga, M., et al. (1998). Dissociated pattern of activity in visual cortices and their projections during human rapid eye movement sleep. *Science, 279*, 91–95.

Brebbia, D. R. & Altshuler, K.Z. (1965). Oxygen consumption and electroencephalographic stage of sleep. *Science, 150*, 1621–1623.

Bremer, F. (1936). Nouvelles recherches sur le mécanisme du sommeil [New research on sleep mechanism]. *Comptes Rendus des Séances de la Société de Biologie et de Ses Filiales, 122*, 460–464.

Bremer, F., & Chatonnet, J. (1949). Acetylcholine et cortex cérébral [Acetylcholine and cerebral cortex]. *Archives internationales de physiologie et de biochimie, 57*(1), 106–109.

Bubnoff, N., & Heidenhain, R. (1881). Ueber Erregungs-Hemmungsvorgänge innerhalb der motorischen Hirncentren [On excitation and inhibition processes in the motor brain centers]. In EFW Pflüger (Ed). *Arch. Gesam. Physiol.*, pp 137–202.

Buffenstein, A., Heaster, J., & Ko, P. (1999). Chronic psychotic illness from amphetamine. *American Journal of Psychiatry, 156*, 662.

Bunney, W. E., & Bunney, B. G. (2000). Evidence for a compromised dorsolateral prefrontal cortical parallel circuit in schizophrenia. *Brain Research. Brain Research Reviews, 31*, 138–146.

Buzsaki, G., & Gage, F. H. (1989). The nucleus basalis: A key structure in neocortical arousal. In M. Froescher, & U. Misgeld (Eds.), *Central cholinergic synaptic transmission* (pp. 159–171). Basel: Kirhäuser Verlag.

Buzsaki, G., Bickford, R. G, Ponomareff, G., Thal, L. J., Mandel, R., & Cage F. H. (1988). Nucleus basalis and thalamic control of neocartical activity in the freely moving rat. *Journal of Neuroscience, 8*, 4007–4026.

Callaway, C. W., Lydic, R., Bagdoyan, H. A., & Hobson, J. A. (1987). Pontogeniculooccipital waves: Spontaneous visual system activity during rapid eye movement sleep. *Cellular & Molecular Neurobiology, 7*, 105–149.

Cantero, J. L., Atienza, M., Madsen, J. R., & Stickgold, R. (2004). Gamma EEG dynamics in neocortex and hippocampus during human wakefulness and sleep. *NeuroImage, 22*, 1271–1280.

Cape, E. G., & Jones, B. (1998). Differential modulation of high-frequency gamma-electroencephalogram activity and slee-wake state by noradrenaline and serotonin into the region of cholinergic basalis neurons. *Journal of Neuroscience, 18*, 2653–2666.

Carboni, E., & Silvagni, A. (2004). Dopamine reuptake by norepinephrine neurons: Exception or rule? *Critical Reviews in Neurobiology, 16,* 121–128.

Carli, G., & Zanchetti, A. (1965). A study of pontine lesions suppressing deep sleep in the cat. *Archives Italiennes de Biologie, 103,* 751–788.

Caton, R. (1875). The electrical currents of the brain. *British Medical Journal, 2,* 278.

Celesia, G. G., & Jasper, H. H. (1966). Acetylcholine released from cerebral cortex in relation to sate of activation. *Neurology, 16,* 1053–1063.

Cespuglio, R., Calvo, J. M., Musolino, R., & Valatx, J. L. (1977). Activité phasique chez le rat [Phasic activity in the rat]. *Physiology & Behavior, 19,* 589–596.

Chergui, K., Suaud-Chagny, M. F., & Gonon, F. (1994). Non-linear relationship between impulse flow. Dopamine release and dopamine elimination in the rat in vivo. *Neuroscience, 62,* 641–645.

Chuhma, N., Zhang. H., Masson, J., Zhuang, X., Sulzer, D., Hen, R., & Rayport, S. (2004). Dopamine neurons mediate a fast excitatory signal via their glutamatergic synapses. *Journal of Neuroscience, 24,* 972–981.

Collerton, D., Perry, E., & McKeith, I. (2005). Why people see things that are not there: A novel perception and attention deficit model for recurrent visual hallucinations. *Bahavioral & Brain Sciences, 28(6),* 737–757.

Cordeau, J. P., Walsh, J., & Mahut, H. (1965). Variations dans la transmission des messages sensoriels en fonction des différents états d'éveil et de sommeil [Variations in the transmission of sensory messages in relation to the different waking and sleep states]. In M. Jouvet (Ed.), *Aspects anatomo-fonctionnels de la physiologie du sommeil, A symposium* (pp. 477–507). CNRS: Paris.

Creutzfeldt, O., Baumgartner, G., & Schoen, L. (1956). Reaktionen einzelner Neurons des senso-motorischen cortex nach elektrischen Reizen. I Hemmung und Erregung nach direkten und contralateralen Einzelreizen [Reaction of single newrons of the sensory motor cortex following electrical stimulations I. Inhibition and activation following homolateral and contralateral stimulation]. *Archiv für Psychiatrie und Nervenkrankheiten, vereinigt mit Zeitschrift für die gesamte Neurologie und Psychiatrie, 194,* 597–619.

Cuculic, Z. & Himwich, H. E. (1968). An examination of a possible cortical cholinergic link in the EEG arousal reaction. *Progress in Brain Research, 28,* 27–39.

D'aquila, P. S., Panin, F., Cossu, M., Peana, A. T., & Serra, G. (2003). Dopamine D1 receptor agonists induce penile erection in rats. *European Journal of Neuroscience, 460,* 71–74.

Dagnino, N., Favale, E., Loeb, C., Manfredi, M., & Seitun, A. (1969). Presynaptic and postsynaptic changes in specific thalamic nuclei during deep sleep. *Archives Italiennes de Biologie, 107,* 668–684.

Datla, K., Spoley, E. E., Mavanji, V., & Patterson, E. H. (2002). A novel role of pedunculopontine tegmental kainate receptors: A mechanism of rapid eye movement sleep generation in the rat. *Neuroscience, 114,* 157–164.

Datta, S. (1997). Cellular basis of ponto-geniculo-occipital wave generation and modulation. *Cellular and Molecular Neurobiology, 17,* 341–365.

Datta, S. (2006). Activation of phasic pontine-wave generator: A mechanism for sleep-dependent memory processing. *Sleep and Biological Rhythms, 4,* 16–26.

Datta, S. & Hobson, J. A. (1994). Neuronal activity in the caudolateral peribrachial pons: relationship to PGO waves and rapid eye movements. *Journal of Neurophysiology, 71,* 95–109.

Datta, S., Mavanji, V., Patterson, E. H., & Ulloor, J. (2003). Regulation of rapid eye movement sleep in the freely moving rat: Local microinjection of serotonin, norepinephrine, and adenosine into the brainstem. *Sleep, 26,* 513–520.

Datta, S., & Siwek, D. F. (1997). Excitation of the brainstem pedunculopontine tegmentum cells induces wakefulness and REM sleep. *Journal of Neurophysiology, 77,* 2975–2988.

Datta, S., & Siwek, D. F., (2002). Single cell activity patterns of pedunculopontine tegmentum neurons across the sleep-wake cycle in freely moving rats. *Journal of Neuroscience Research, 70,* 611–621.

Datta, S., Siwek, D. F., Patterson, E. H., & Cipolloni, P.B. (1998). Localization of pontine PGO wave generation sites and their anatomical projections in the rat. *Synapse, 30,* 409–423.

Datta, S., Spoley, E. E., & Patterson, E. H. (2001). Microinjection of glutamate into the pedunculopontine tegmentum induces REM sleep and wakefulness in the rat. *American Journal of Physiology, 280,* R752–R759.

Delfs, J. M., Zhu, Y., Druhan, J. P., & Aston-Jones, G. S. (1998). Origin of noradrenergic afferents to the shell subregion of the nucleus accumbens: Anterograde and retrograde tract-tracing studies in the rat. *Brain Research, 806,* 127–140.

Dement, W. (1955). Dream recall and eye movements during sleep in schizophrenic and normals. *Journal of Nervous and Mental Disease, 122,* 263–269.

Dement, W., & Kleitman, N. (1957a). Cyclic variations in EEG during sleep and their relation to eye movements, body motility, and dreaming. *Electroencephalography and Clinical Neurophysiology, 9,* 673–690.

Dement, W., & Kleitman, N. (1957b). The relation of eye movements during sleep to dream activity: An objective method for the study of dreaming. *Journal of experimental psychology, 53,* 339–346.

Dement, W. C. (1958). The occurrence of low voltage fast electroencephalogram patterns during behavioral sleep in the cat. *Electroencephalography and Clinical Neurophysiology, 10,* 291–296.

Demetrescu, M., Demetrescu, M. (1964). Alterations of visual cortical responsivesness during wakefulness and sleep. *Review of Roumania Physiology, 4,* 357–362.

Demetrescu, M., Demetrescu, M., & Iosif, G. (1966). Diffuse regulation of visual thalamo-cortical responsiveness during sleep and wakefulness. *Electroencephalography and Clinical Neurophysiology, 20,* 450–469.

Derbyshire, A. J., Rempel, B., Forbes, A., & Lambert, E. F. (1936). The effects of anesthetics on action potentials in the cerebral cortex of the cat. *American Journal of Physiology, 116,* 577–596.

Descarries, L., Beaudet, A., & Watkins, K. C. (1975). Serotonin nerve terminals in the adult rat neocortex. *Brain Research, 100*(3), 563–588.

Descarries, L., Gisinger, V., & Steriade, M. (1997). Diffuse transmission by acetylcholine in the CNS. *Progress in Neurobiology, 53,* 603–625.

Descarries, L., Watkins, K. C., & Lapierre, Y. (1977). Noradrenergic axon terminals in the cerebral cortex of rats. III. Topometric ultrastructural analysis. *Brain Research, 133,* 197–222.

Deurveilher, S., & Hennevin, E. (2001). Lesions of the pedunculopontine tegmental nucleus reduce paradoxical sleep (PS) propensy: Evidence from a short-term PS deprivation study in rats. *European Journal of Neuroscience, 13,* 1963–1976.

Douglass, A. B. (2003). Narcolepsy: Differential diagnosis or etiology in some cases of bipolar disorder and schizophrenia. *CNS Spectrums, 8,* 120–126.

Evarts, E. V. (1962). Activity of neurons in visual cortex of the cat during sleep with low voltage EEG activity. *Journal of Neurophysiology, 25,* 812–816.

Evarts, E. V. (1964). Temporal patterns of discharge of pyramidal tract neurons during sleep and waking in the monkey. *Journal of Neurophysiology, 27,* 152–171.

Evarts, E. V. (1965). Neuronal activity in visual and motor cortex during sleep and waking. In *Aspects anatomo-fonctionnels de la physiologie du sommeil [Atatomo-functional aspects of the physiology of sleep]* (pp. 189–212). Paris: CNRS.

Evarts, E. V., Fleming, T. C., & Huttenlocher, P. R. (1960). Recovery cycle of visual cortex of the awake and sleeping cat. *American Journal of Physiology, 199,* 373–376.

Ey, H. (1967). La dissolution du champ de la conscience dans le phénomène sommeil-veille et ses rapports avec la psychopathologie [Abolition of consciousness in sleep-waking phenomenon and its relation with psychopathology]. *Presse Médicale 75,* 575–578.

Farber, J., Marks, G. A., & Roffwarg, H. P. (1980). REM sleep PGO-type waves are present in the dorsal pons of the albino rat. *Science, 209,* 615–617.

Favale, E., Loeb, C., Manfredi, M., & Sacco, G. (1965). Somatic afferent transmission and cortical responsiveness during natural sleep and arousal in the cat. *Electroencephalography & Clinical Neurophysiology, 18,* 354–368.

Fenik, V., Marchenko, V., Janssen, P., Davies, R. O., & Kubin, L. (2002). A5 cells are silenced when REM sleep-like signs are elicited by pontine carbachol. *Journal of Applied Physiology, 93,* 1448–1456.

Ferster, D. (1988). Spatially opposed excitation and inhibition in simple cells of the cat visual cortex. *Journal of Neuroscience, 8,* 1172–1180.

Fisher, C., Gross, J., & Zuch, J. (1965). Cycle of penile erection synchronous with dreaming (REM) sleep. *Archives of General Psychiatry, 12,* 29–45.

Fletcher, P. C., McKenna, P. J., Frith, C. D., Grasby, P. M., Friston, K. J., & Dolan, R. J. (1998). Brain activation in schizophrenia during a graded memory task studied with functional neuroimaging. *Archives of General Psychiatry, 55,* 1001–1008.

Fontana, F. (1765). Dei moti dell'iride [On the eye movements]. Stamperia Jacopo Giusti Lucca.

Foote, S. L., Freedman, R., & Oliver, A. P. (1975). Effects of putative neurotransmitters on neuronal activity on monkey auditory cortex. *Brain Research, 86,* 229–242.

Foulkes, W. D. (1962). Dream reports from different stages of sleep. *Journal of Abnormal Social Psychology, 65,* 14–25.

Franken, P., Djik, D. J., Tobler, I., & Borbely, A. A. (1994). High-frequency components of the rat electrocorticogram are modulated by the vigilance states. *Neuroscience Letters, 167,* 89–92.

Frederickson, R. C. A., Jordan, L. M., & Phillis, J. W. (1971). The action of noradrenaline on cortical neurons: Effects of pH. *Brain Research, 35,* 556–560.

Freeman, W. J., & Van Dijk, B. W. (1987). Spatial patterns of visual fast EEG during conditioned reflex in a rhesus monkey. *Brain Research, 422,* 267–276.

Freud, S. (1955). *The interpretation of dreams.* (J. Strachey, Trans.) London: Hogarth Press. (Original work published 1900)

Freud, S. (1900–1961). *Die Traumdeutung [The interpretation of dreams].* Hamberg: Fischer, S. Verlag.

Friedman, J. I., Adler, D. N., & Davis, K. L. (1999). The role of norepinephrine in the physiopathology of cognitive disorders: Potential applications to the treatment of cognitive dysfunction in schizophrenia and Alzheimer's disease. *Biological Psychiatry, 46*, 1243–1252.

Fromm, E. (1953). *Le langage oublié* [*The forgotten language*]. Paris: Payot.

Fuxe, K., Hamberger, B., & Hökfelt, T. (1968). Distribution of noradrenaline nerve terminals in cortical areas of the rat. *Brain Research, 8*, 125–131.

Gandolfo, G., Arnaud, C., & Gottesmann, C. (1980). Transmission in the ventrobasal complex of rat during the sleep-waking cycle. *Brain Research Bulletin, 5*, 921–927.

George, R., Haslett, W. L., & Jenden, D. J. (1964). A cholinergic mechanism in the brainstem reticular formation: Induction of paradoxical sleep. *International Journal of Neuropharmacology, 3*, 541–552.

Gernet, R. (1989). *Das Verhalten der Augen im Schlaf* [*The behavior of eyes during sleep*]. Berlin: Gustav Shade.

Ghelarducci, B., Pisa, M., & Pompeiano, M. (1970). Transformation of somatic afferent volleys across the prethalamic and thalamic components of the lemniscal sytem during the rapid eye movements of sleep. *Electroencephalography & Clinical Neurophysiology, 29*, 348–357.

Gibbs, F. A., & Gibbs, E. L. (1950). *Atlas of electroencephalography*. Cambridge: Addison-Wesley Press.

Giuliano, F., & Rampin, O. (2000). Central noradrenergic control of penile erection. *International Journal of Impotence Research, 12*, S13–S19.

Giulledge, A. T., & Stuart, G. J. (2005). Cholinergic inhibition of neocortical pyramidal neurons. *Journal of Neuroscience, 25*, 10308–10320.

Glin, L., Arnaud, C., Berracochéa, D., Galey, D., Jaffard, R., & Gottesmann, C. (1991). The intermediate stage of sleep in mice. *Physiology & Behavior, 50*, 951–953.

Gonon, F. G. (1988). Nonlinear relationship between impulse flow and dopamine released by rat midbrain dopaminergic neurons as studied by in vivo electrochemistry. *Neuroscience, 24*, 19–28.

Gottesmann, C. (1964). Données sur l'activité corticale au cours du sommeil profond chez le rat [Results on the cortical activity during deep sleep in the rat]. *Comptes Rendus des Séances de la Société de Biologie et de ses Filiales, 158*, 1829–1834.

Gottesmann, C. (1965). Phase paradoxale et activité réticulaire chez le rat [Paradoxical phase and reticular activity in the rat]. *Comptes Rendus des Séances de la Société de Biologie et de ses Filiales, 159*, 2182–2184.

Gottesmann, C. (1966a). Identification d'une activité électrophysiologique phasique indépendante de la phase paradoxale du sommeil chez le rat [Identification of a phasic electrophysiological activity independent of the paradoxical phase of sleep in the rat]. *Comptes Rendus des Séances de la Société de Biologie et de ses Filiales, 160*, 528–534.

Gottesmann, C. (1966b). Données complémentaires sur l'activité électrophysiologique phasique indépendante de la phase paradoxale du sommeil chez le rat [Complementary data on the phasic electrophysiological activity independent from the paradoxical phase of sleep in the rat]. *Comptes Rendus des Séances de la Société de Biologie et de ses Filiales, 160*, 1390–1396.

Gottesmann, C. (1967a). *Recherche sur la psychophysiologie du sommeil chez le rat* [*Research on the psychophysiology of sleep in the rat*]. Paris: Presses du Palais Royal. [Still available. Discussion and summary in English]

Gottesmann, C. (1967b). Données récentes sur les activités électrophysiologiques phasiques [Recent data on the phasic electrophysiological activities]. *Psychol Franç., 12*, 1–14.

Gottesmann, C. (1969). Etude sur les activités électrophysiologiques phasiques chez le rat [Study on the phasic electrophysiological activities in the rat]. *Physiology & Behavior, 4*, 495–504.

Gottesmann, C. (1970). La psychophysiologie du sommeil [The psychology of sleep]. *Bulletin of Psychology, 24*, 520–528.

Gottesmann, C. (1971). Psychophysiologie du sommeil. *Année Psychologique, 71*, 451–488.

Gottesmann, C. (1996). The transition from slow wave sleep to paradoxical sleep: Evolving facts and concepts of the neurophysiological processes underlying the intermediate stage of sleep. *Neuroscience & Biobehavioral Reviews, 20*, 367–387.

Gottesmann, C. (1997). Introduction to the neurophysiological study of sleep: Central regulation of skeletal and ocular activities. *Archives Italiennes de Biologie, 135*, 279–314.

Gottesmann, C. (1999). Neurophysiological support of consciousness during waking and sleep. *Progress in Neurobiology, 59*, 469–508.

Gottesmann, C. (2000a). Each different type of mentation is supported by specific brain functioning. *Behavioral & Brain Sciences, 23*, 941–943.

Gottesmann, C. (2000b). Hypothesis for the neurophysiology of dreaming. *Sleep Research Online, 3*, 1–4.

Gottesmann, C. (2001). The golden age of rapid eye movement sleep discoveries. I. Lucretius-1964. *Progress in Neurobiology, 65*, 211–287.

Gottesmann, C. (2002). The neurochemistry of waking and sleeping mental activity. The disinhibition-dopamine hypothesis. *Psychiatry & Clinical Neurosciences, 56*, 345–354.

Gottesmann, C. (2004a). Brain inhibitory mechanisms involved in basic and higher integrated sleep processes. *Brain Research. Brain Research Reviews, 45*, 230–249.

Gottesmann, C. (2004b). Find out about dreams and you will find out about insanity (Hughlings Jackson). In J. E. Pletson (Ed.), *Progress in schizophrenia research* (pp. 23–43). Hauppage: Nova Science Publications Inc.

Gottesmann, C. (2005). Dreaming and schizophrenia. A common neurobiological background. *Sleep & Biological Rhythms, 3*, 64–74.

Gottesmann, C. (2006). The dreaming sleep stage: A new neurobiological model of schizophrenia. *Neuroscience, 140*, 1105–1115.

Gottesmann, C. (2006). Rêve et schizophrénie: Un même support neurobiologique? [*Dreaming and schizophrenia: The same neurobiological support?*] *Médecine Sciences, 22*(2), 201–205.

Gottesmann, C., Gandolfo, G., & Zernicki, B. (1984). Intermediate stage of sleep in the cat. *Journal de Physiologie (Paris), 79*, 359–372.

Gottesmann, C., & Gottesmann, I. I. (in press). The neurobiological characteristics of rapid eye movement (REM) sleep are candidate endophenotypes of depression, schizophrenia, mental retardation, and dementia. *Progress in Neurobiology*.

Gottesman, I. I., & Gould, T. D. (2003). The endophenotype concept in psychiatry: Etymology and strategic intentions. *American Journal of Psychiatry, 160,* 636–645.

Gottesman, I. I., & Shields, J. (1967). A polygenic theory of schizophrenia. *Proceedings of the National Academy of Sciences of the United States of America, 58,* 199–205.

Gottesman, I. I., & Shields, J. (1973). Genetic theorizing and schizophrenia. *British Journal of Psychiatry, 122,* 15–36.

Grace, A. A. (1991). Phasic versus tonic dopamine release and the modulation of dopamine system responsivity: a hypothesis for the etiology of schizophrenia. *Neuroscience, 41,* 1–24.

Grace, A. A. (2000). Gating information flow within the limbic system and the pathophysiology of schizophrenia. *Brain Research. Brain Research Reviews, 31,* 330–341.

Gray, C. M., & Singer, W. (1989). Stimulus-specific neuronal oscillations in orientation columns of cat visual cortex. *Proceedings of the National Academy of Sciences of the United States of America, 86,* 1698–1702.

Grobin, A. C., & Deutch, A. Y. (1998). Dopaminergic regulation of extracellular g-aminobutyric acid levels in the prefrontal cortex of the rat. *Journal of Pharmacology & Experimental Therapeutics, 285,* 350–357.

Gross, D. W., & Gotman, J. (1999). Correlation of high-frequency oscillations with the sleep-wake cycle and cognitive activity in humans. *Neuroscience, 94,* 1005–1018.

Gross, J., Byrne, J., & Fisher, C. (1965). Eye movements during emergent stage 1 EEG in subjects with lifelong blindness. *Journal of Nervous & Mental Disease, 141,* 365–370.

Harris, G. C., Hedaya, M. A., Pan, W. J., & Kalivas, P. W. (1996). Beta-adrenergic antagonism alters the behavioral and neurochemical response to cocaine. *Neuropsychopharmacology, 14,* 195–204.

Hawkins, D. R., Puryear, H. B., Wallace, C. D., Deal, W. B., & Thomas, E. S. (1962). Basal skin resistance during sleep and "dreaming." *Science, 136,* 321–322.

Henley, K., & Morrison, A. R. (1974). A re-evaluation of the effects of lesions of the pontine tegmentum and locus coeruleus on phenomena of paradoxical sleep in the cat. *Acta Neurobiologiae Experimentalis, 34,* 215–232.

Heresco-Levy, U. (2000). N-methyl-D-aspartate (NMDA) receptor-based treatment approaches in schizophrenia: The first decade. *International Journal of Neuropharmacology, 3,* 243–258.

Herman, J. H., Erman, M., Boys, R., Peiser, L., Taylor, M. E., & Roffwarg, H. (1984). Evidence for a directional correspondence between eye movements and dream imagery in REM sleep. *Sleep, 7,* 52–63.

Hervey de Saint Denys, M. J. L. (1964). *Les rêves et les moyens de les diriger* [*The dreams and the means to manage them*]. Paris: Tchou. (Original work published 1887, Paris: Amyot)

Hess, W. R. (1931). Le sommeil [Sleep]. *Comptes Rendus des Séances de la Société de Biologie et de ses Filiales, 107,* 1333–1364.

Hishikawa, Y., & Kaneko, Z. (1965). Electroencephalographic study of narcolepsy. *Electroencephalography & Clinical Neurophysiology, 18,* 249–259.

Hjemstad, G. O. (2004). Dopamine excites nucleus accumbens neurons through the differential modulation of glutamate and GABA release. *Journal of Neuroscience, 24,* 8621–8628.

Hobson, J. A. (1964). L'activité électrique phasique du cortex et du thalamus au cours du sommeil désynchronisé chez le chat [The phasic electrical activity of the cortex and thalamus during desynchronized sleep in the cat]. *Comptes Rendus des Séances de la Société de Biologie et de ses Filiales, 158,* 2131–2135.

Hobson, J. A., & McCarley, R. W. (1977). The brain as a dream state generator: An activation-synthesis hypothesis of the dream process. *American Journal of Psychiatry, 134,* 1335–1348.

Hobson, J. A., McCarley, R. W., & Wyzinski, P. W. (1975). Sleep cycle oscillation: Reciprocal discharge by two brainstem neuronal groups. *Science, 189,* 55–58.

Hong, C. C. H., Gillin, J. C., Dow, B. C., Wu, J., & Buschbaum, M. S. (1995). Localized and lateralized cerebral glucose metabolism associated with eye movements during REM sleep and wakefulness: A positron emission tomography (PET) study. *Sleep, 18,* 570–580.

Howland, J. G., Taepavarapruk, P., & Phillips, A. G. (2002). Glutamate receptor-dependent modulation of dopamine efflux in the nucleus accumbens by basolateral but not central, nucleus of the amygdala. *Journal of Neuroscience, 22,* 1137–1145.

Humphrey, M. E., & Zangwill, O. L. (1951). Cessation of dreaming after brain injury. *Journal of Neurology, Neurosurgery, & Psychiatry, 14,* 322–325.

Huttenlocher, P. R. (1961). Evoked and spontaneous activity in single units of medial brain stem during natural sleep and waking. *Journal of Neurophysiology, 24,* 451–468.

Iwama, K., Kawamoto, T., Sakkakura, H., & Kasamatsu, T. (1966). Responsiveness of cat lateral geniculate at pre- and postsynaptic levels during natural sleep. *Physiology & Behavior, 1,* 45–53.

Jackson, M. E., Frost, A. S., & Moghaddam, B. (2001). Stimulation of prefrontal cortex at physiologically relevant frequencies inhibits dopamine release in nucleus accumbens. *Journal of Neurochemistry, 78,* 920–923.

Jacobs, B. L., Feldman, M., & Bender, M. B. (1972). Are the eye movements of dreaming sleep related to the visual images of the dreams. *Psychophysiology, 9,* 393–401.

Jacobson, A. (1930). Electrical measurements of neuromuscular states during mental activities. III. Visual imagination and recollection. *American Journal of Physiology, 95,* 694–702.

Jacobson, A. (1938). *You can sleep well: The ABC's of restful sleep for the average person.* New York: Whittley House.

Jasper, H. H., & Tessier, J. (1971). Acetylcholine liberation from cerebral cortex during paradoxical (REM sleep). *Science, 172,* 601–602.

Jeannerod, M. (2003). The mechanism of self-recognition in humans. *Behavioural Brain Research, 142,* 1–15.

Jeannerod, M. (2004). Visual and action cues contribute to the self-other distinction. *Nature Neuroscience, 7,* 1–2.

Jeannerod, M., Mouret, J., & Jouvet, M. (1965). Etude de la motricité oculaire au cours de la phase paradoxale du sommeil chez le chat [Study of ocular motricity during the paradoxical phase of sleep in the cat]. *Electroencephalography & Clinical Neurophysiology, 18,* 554–566.

Jia, H. G., Yamuy, J., Sampogna, S., Morales, F. R., & Chase, M. H. (2003). Colocalization of g-aminobutyric acid and acetylcholine in neurons of the laterodorsal and pedunculopontine tegmental nuclei in the cat: A light and electron microscopic study. *Brain Research, 992*, 205–219.

Jones, B. E. (1991). Paradoxical sleep and its chemical/structural substrates in the brain. *Neuroscience, 40*, 637–656.

Jones, B. E. (2004). Paradoxical sleep promoting and permitting networks. *Archives Italiennes de Biologie, 142*, 379–396.

Jouvet, M. (1962). Recherches sur les structures nerveuses et les mécanismes responsables des différentes phases du sommeil physiologique [Researches on the central structures and mechanisms responsible for the different phases of physiological sleep]. *Archives Italiennes de Biologie, 100*, 125–206.

Jouvet, M. (1975). Cholinergic mechanisms and sleep. In P. G. Waser (Ed.), *Cholinergic mechanisms* (pp. 455–476). New York: Raven Press.

Jouvet, M., & Delorme, F. (1965). Locus coeruleus et sommeil paradoxal [Focus coeruleus and paradoxical sleep]. *Comptes Rendus des Séances de la Société de Biologie et de ses Filiales, 159*, 895–899.

Jouvet, M., & Michel, F. (1960a). Mise en évidence d'un "centre hypnique" au niveau du rhombencéphale chez le chat [Identification of a hypnic center at the level of hindbrain in the cat]. *Comptes Rendus Hebdomadaires des Séances de l'Académie des Sciences, 251*, 1188–1190.

Jouvet, M., & Michel, F. (1960b). Nouvelles recherches sur les structures responsables de la "phase paradoxale" du sommeil [New researches on the structures responsible for the paradoxical phase of sleep]. *Journal de physiologie, 52*, 130–131.

Jouvet, M., Michel, F., & Courjon, J. (1959). Sur la mise en jeu de deux mécanismes à expression électro-encéphalographique différente au cours du sommeil physiologique chez le chat [Involvement of two mechanisms with different electroencephalographic expression during physiological sleep in the cat]. *Comptes Rendus Hebdomadaires des Séances de l'Académie des Sciences, 248*, 3043–3045.

Jouvet, M., Michel, F., & Mounier, D. (1960). Analyse électroencéphalographique comparée du sommeil physiologique chez le chat et chez l'homme [Compared electroencephalographic analysis of physiological sleep in the cat and humans]. *Revue Neurologique, 103*, 189–205.

Jouvet, M., & Mounier, D. (1960). Effets des lésions de la formation réticulaire pontique sur le sommeil du chat [Influence of pontine reticular formation lesions on sleep of cats]. *Comptes Rendus des Séances de la Société de Biologie et de ses Filiales, 154*, 2301–2305.

Karacan, I., Goodenough, D. R., Shapiro, A., & Starker, S. (1966). Erection cycle during sleep in relation to dream anxiety. *Archives of General Psychiatry, 15*, 183–189.

Kaufman, L. S., & Morrison, A. R. (1981). Spontaneous and elicited PGO spikes in rats. *Brain Research, 214*, 61–72.

Kawamura, H., & Sawyer, C. H. (1964). D-C potential changes in rabbit brain during slow-wave and paradoxical sleep. *American Journal of Physiology, 207*, 1379–1386.

Kelly, P. H. (1998). Defective inhibition of dream event memory formation: A hypothesized mechanism in the onset and progression of symptoms of schizophrenia. *Brain Research Bulletin, 46*, 189–197.

Kinai, T., & Szerb, J. C. (1965). Mesencephalic reticular activating system and cortical acetylcholine output. *Nature, 205*, 80–82.

Kisley, M. A., Olincy A., Robbins E., Polk S. D., Adler L. E., Waldo M. C., et al. (2003). Sensory gating impairment associated with schizophrenia persists into REM sleep. *Psychophysiology, 40,* 29–38.

Kiyono, S., & Iwama, K. (1965). Phasic activity of cat's cerebral cortex during paradoxical sleep. *Medical Journal of Osaka University, 16,* 149–159.

Klaue, R. (1937). Die bioelektrische Tätigkeit der Grosshirnrinde im normalen Schlaf und in der Narkose durch Schlafmittel [Bioelectrical activity of the cortex during natural sleep and under narcosis]. *J Psychol Neurol. 47,* 510–531.

Kleitman, N. (1965). *Sleep and wakefulness.* Chicago: University Chicago Press.

Krnjevic, K., Randic, M., & Straughan, D. W. (1966). Pharmacology of cortical inhibition. *Journal of Physiology (London), 184,* 78–105.

Krnjevic, K., & Phillis, J. W. (1963). Actions of certain amines on cerebral cortex neurons. *Brit J Pharmacol, 20,* 471–490.

Ladd, G. T., 1892. Contribution to the psychology of visual dreams. *Mind, 1,* 299–304.

Lairy, G. C., Barros Fereira, M., & Golsteinas, L. (1968). Les phases intermédiaires du sommeil [The intermediate phases of sleep]. In H. Gastaut, E. Lugaresi, G. Berti Ceroni, & G. Coccagna (Eds.), *The abnormalities of sleep in man* (pp. 275–283). Bologna, Italy: Aulo Gaggi

Larsen, J. P., & Tandberg, E. (2001). Sleep disorders with Parkinson's disease: Epidemiology and management. *CNS Drugs, 15,* 267–275.

Lauriat, T. L., Dracheva, S., Chin, B., Schmeidler, J., McInnes, L. A., & Haroutunian, V. (2005). Quantitative analysis of glutamate transporter mRNA expression in prefrontal and primary visual cortex in normal and schizophrenic brain. *Neuroscience, 37,* 843–851.

Lavin, A., & Grace, A. A. (2001). Stimulation of D_1-type dopamine receptors enhances excitability in prefrontal cortical pyramidal neurons in a state-dependent manner. *Neuroscience, 104,* 335–346.

Léna, I., Parrot, S., Deschaux, O., Muffat, S., Sauvinet, V., Renaud, B., et al. (2005). Variations in the extracellular levels of dopamine, noradrenaline, glutamate and aspartate across the sleep-wake cycle in the medial prefrontal cortex and nucleus accumbens of freely moving rats. *Journal of Neuroscience Research, 81,* 891–899.

Levin, R., & Daly, R. S. (1998). Nightmares and psychotic decompensation: A case study. *Psychiatry, 61,* 217–222.

Levit, P., & Moore, R. Y. (1978). Noradrenaline neuron innervation on the neocortex in the cat. *Brain Research, 139,* 219–232.

Levy, R. B., Reves, A. D., & Aoki, C. (2006). Nicotinic and muscarinic reduction of unitary excitatory post synaptic potentials in sensory cortex: Dual intracellular recording in vitro. *Journal of Neurophysiology, 95,* 2155–2166.

Lewis, D. A. (2000). GABAergic local circuit neurons and prefrontal cortical dysfunction in schizophrenia. *Brain Research. Brain Research Reviews, 31,* 270–276.

Lewis, D. A., Hashimoto, T., & Volk, D. W. (2005). Cortical inhibitory neurons in schizophrenia. *Nature Reviews Neuroscience, 6,* 312–324.

Linner, L., Wiker, C., Wadenberg, M. L., Schalling, M., & Svensson, T. H. (2002). Noradrenaline reuptake inhibition enhances the antipsychotic-like effect of raclopride and potentiates D2-blockade-induced dopamine release in the medial prefrontal cortex of the rat. *Neuropsychpharmacology, 27,* 691–698.

Llinas, R., Grace, A. A., & Yarom, Y. (1991). In vitro neurons in mammalian cortical layer 4 exhibits intrinsic oscillatory activity in the 10- to 50-Hz frequency range. *Proceedings of the National Academy of Sciences of the United States of America, 88*, 897–901.

Llinas, R., & Paré, D. (1991). Of dreaming and wakefulness. *Neuroscience, 44*, 521–535.

Llinas, R., & Ribary, U. (1993). Coherent 40 Hz oscillation characterizes dream state in humans. *Proceedings of the National Academy of Sciences of the United States of America, 90*, 2078–2081.

Loomis, A. L., Harvey, E. N., & Hobart, G. A. I. (1937). Cerebral states during sleep, as studied by human brain potentials. *Journal of Experimental Psychology, 21*, 127–144.

Lövblad, K. O., Thomas, R., Jakob, P. M., Scammel, T., Bassetti, C., Griswold, M., et al. (1999). Silent functional magnetic resonance imaging demonstrates focal activation in rapid eye movement sleep. *Neurology, 53*, 2193–2195.

Luciana, M., Collins, P. F., & Depue, R. A. (1998). Opposing role for dopamine and serotonin in the modulation of human spatial working memory functions. *Cerebral Cortex, 8(3)*, 218–226.

Lucrece, T. L. C., & Xi, M. C. (1900). De rerum natura OXONII. (C. Baily, Trans.) Topographeo Clarendoniano, 178 pp.

Lufkin, B. (1968). Letter to the editor. *Psychophysiology, 5*, 449–450.

MacKay, A. V., Iversen, L. L., Rossor, M., Spokes, E., Bird, E., Arregui, A., et al. (1982). Increased brain dopamine and dopamine receptors in schizophrenia. *Archives of General Psychiatry, 39*, 991–997.

Madsen, P. L., Holm, S., Vorstrup, S., Friberg, L., Lassen, N. A., & Wildschiodtz, G. (1991). Human regional cerebral blood flow during rapid-eye-movement sleep. *Journal of Cerebral Blood Flow & Metabolism, 11*, 502–507.

Maloney, K. J., Cape, E. G., Gotman, J., & Jones, B. E. (1997). High-frequency-electroencephalogram activity in association with sleep-wake states and spontaneous behaviors in the rat. *Neuroscience, 76*, 541–555.

Mansvelder, H. D., Rover de, M., McGehee, D. S., & Brussaard, A. B. (2003). Cholinergic modulation of dopaminergic reward areas: Upstream and downstream targets of nicotine addiction. *European Journal of Pharmacology, 480*, 117–123.

Manunta, Y., & Edeline, J. M. (1999). Effects of noradrenaline on frequency tuning of auditory cortex neurons during wakefulness and slow wave sleep. *European Journal of Neuroscience, 11*, 2134–2150.

Maquet, P. (2000). Functional neuroimaging of normal sleep by positon emission tomography. *Journal of Sleep Research, 9*, 207–231.

Maquet, P., & Franck, G. (1997). REM sleep and amygdala. *Molecular Psychiatry, 2*, 195–196.

Maquet, P., Peters, J. M., Aerts, J., Delfiore, G., Degueldre, C., Luxen, A., et al. (1996). Functional neuroanatomy of human rapid-eye-movement sleep and dreaming. *Nature, 383*, 163–166.

Maquet, P., Ruby, P., Schwartz, S., Laurey, S., Albouy, T., Dang-Vu, T., et al. (2004). Regional organisation of brain activity during paradoxical sleep. *Archives Italiennes de Biologie, 142*, 413–419.

Marks, G. A., Farber, G., & Roffwarg, H. (1980). Metencephalic localization of ponto-geniculo-occipital waves in the albino rat. *Experimental Neurology, 69*, 667–677.

Marks, G. A., Farber, G., Rubinstein, M., & Roffwarg, H. (1980). Demonstration of ponto-geniculo-occipital waves in the albino rat. *Experimental Neurology, 69*, 648–666.

Marrosu, F., Portas, C., Mascia, M. F., Casu, M. A., Fa, M., Giagheddu, M., et al. (1995). Microdialysis measurement of cortical and hippocampal acetylcholine release during sleep-wake cycle in freely moving cats. *Brain Research, 671*, 329–332.

Massimini, M., Ferrarelli, F., Huber, R., Esser, S. K., Singh, H., & Tononi, G. (2005). Breakdown of cortical effective connectivity during sleep. *Science, 309*, 2228–2232.

Maury, F. (1861). *Le sommeil et les rêves* [*Sleep and dreams*]. Didier (Ed). 156.

McCarley, R. W., & Hobson, J. A. (1971a). Single neuron activity in gigantocellular tegmental field: Selectivity of discharge in desynchronized sleep. *Science, 174*, 1250–1252.

McCarley, R. W., & Hobson, J. A. (1971b). Single neuron activity in desynchronized sleep. *Science, 167*, 901–903.

McCarley, R. W., Winkelman, J. W., & Duffy, F. H. (1983). Human cerebral potentials associated with REM sleep rapid eye movements: Links to PGO waves and waking potentials. *Brain Research, 274*, 359–364.

McCormick, D. A. (1992). Neurotransmitter actions in the thalamus and cerebral cortex and their role in neuromodulation of thalamocortical activity. *Progress in Neurobiology, 39*, 337–388.

McGinty, D. J., & Harper, R. M. (1976). Dorsal raphe neurons: Depression of firing during sleep in cats. *Brain Research, 101*, 569–575.

McGinty, D. J., Harper, R. M., & Fairbanks, M. K. (1974). Neuronal unit activity and the control of sleep states. In: Weitzman, E. D. (Ed.), *Advances in sleep research* (Vol. 1, pp. 173–216). New York: Spectrum.

McGlade, H. B. (1942). The relationship between gastric motility, muscular twitching during sleep and dreaming. *American Journal of Digestive Diseases, 9*, 137–140.

Mednikova, Y. S., Karnup, S. V., & Loseva, E. V. (1998). Cholinergic excitation of dendrites in neocortical neurons. *Neuroscience, 87*, 783–796.

Meyer-Lindenberg, A., Olsen, R. K., Kohn, P. D., Brown, T., Egan, M. F., Weinberber, D. R., et al. (2005). Regionally specific disturbance of dorsolateral prefrontal-hippocampal function connectivity in schizophrenia. *Archives of General Psychiatry, 62*, 379–386.

Meyer-Lindenberg, A., Poline, J. B., Kohn, P. D., Holt, J. L., Egan, M. F., Weinberger, D. R., et al. (2001). Evidence for abnormal cortical functional connectivity during working memory in schizophrenia. *American Journal of Psychiatry, 158*, 1809–1817.

Michel, F., Jeannerod, M., Mouret, J., Rechtschaffen, A., & Jouvet, M. (1964). Sur les mécanismes de l'activité de pointes au niveau du système visuel au cours de la phase paradoxale du sommeil [On the mechanisms of spike activity at the level of the visual system during paradoxical phase of sleep]. *Comptes Rendus des Séances de la Société de Biologie et de ses Filiales, 158*, 103–106.

Mikiten, T. M., Niebyl, P. H., & Hendley, C. D. (1961). EEG desynchronization during behavioral sleep associated with spike discharges from the thalamus of the cat. *Federation Proceedings, 20*, 327.

Mileykovskiy, B. Y., Kiyashchenko, L. I., & Siegel, J. M. (2005). Behavioral correlates of activity in identified hypocretin/orexin neurons. *Neuron, 46*, 696–698.

Miller, A. D., & Blaha, C. D. (2005). Midbrain muscarinic receptor mechanisms underlying regulation of mesoaccumbens and nigrostriatal dopaminergic transmission in the rat. *European Journal of Neuroscience, 21*, 1837–1846.

Miller, J. D., Farber, J., Gatz, P., Roffwarg, H., & German, D. (1983). Activity of mesencephalic dopamine and non-dopamine neurons across stages of sleep and waking in the rat. *Brain Research, 273*, 133–141.

Mirmiran, M. (1983). "Oneiric" behavior during active sleep induced by bilateral lesions of the pontine tegmentum in juvenile rats. In W. P. Koella (Ed.), *Sleep* (pp. 236–239). Basel, Switzerland: Karger.

Mitchell, J. F. (1963). The spontaneous and evoked release of acetylcholine from the cerebral cortex. *Journal of Physiology (London), 165*, 98–116.

Miyauchi, S., Takino, R., Fukuda, H., & Torii, S. (1987). Electrophysiological evidence for dreaming: Human cerebral potentials associated with rapid eye movements during REM sleep. *Electroencephalography and Clinical Neurophysiology, 66*, 383–390.

Moroz, G., Foutz, A. S., & Gottesmann, C. (1977). Paradoxical sleep and pontine activation in the rat. In W. P. Koella, & P. Levin (Eds.), *Sleep 1976* (pp. 186–188). Basel, Switzerland: Karger.

Morrison, A. R., & Pompeiano, O. (1965). Pyramidal discharge from somatosensory cortex and cortical control of primary afferents during sleep. *Archives Italiennes de Biologie, 103*, 538–568.

Morrison, A. R. & Pompeiano, O. (1966). Vestibular influences during sleep. IV. Functional relations between vestibular nuclei and lateral geniculate nucleus during desynchronized sleep. *Archives Italiennes de Biologie, 104*, 425–458.

Moruzzi, G. (1963). Active processes in the brain stem during sleep. In *The Harvey lectures* (Vol. 58, pp. 233–297). New York: Academic Press.

Moruzzi, G., & Magoun, H. W. (1949). Brain stem reticular formation and activation of the EEG. *Electroencephalography & Clinical Neurophysiology, 1*, 455–473.

Moskowitz, E., & Berger, R. J. (1969). Rapid eye movements and dream imagery: Are they related. *Nature, 244*, 613–614.

Mouret, J. (1964). *Les mouvements oculaires au cours du sommeil paradoxal [The eye movements during paradoxical sleep]*. Lyon, France: Imprimerie des Beaux Arts.

Mouret, J., & Delorme, F. (1967). Lesions du tegmentum pontique et sommeil chez le rat [Pontine tegmentum lesions and sleep in the rat]. *Comptes Rendus des Séances de la Société de Biologie et de ses Filiales, 161*, 1603–1606.

Mouret, J., Jeannerod, M., & Jouvet, M. (1965). Mise en jeu du système oculomoteur pendant le sommeil [Involvement of the oculomotor system during sleep]. *Confinia Neurologica, 25*, 291–299.

Munk, M. H., Roelfsema, P. R., König, P., Engel, A. K., & Singer, W. (1996). Role of reticular activation in the production of intracortical synchronization. *Science, 272*, 271–274.

Muzio, J. N., Roffwarg, H. P., & Kaufman,E. K. (1966). Alterations in the nocturnal sleep cycle resulting from LSD. *Electroencephalography & Clinical Neurophysiology, 21*, 313–324.

Nahum, L. H. (1965). The functions of dream cycles. *Connecticut Medicine, 29*, 701–705.

Nelson, C. N., Hoffer, B. J., Chu, N. S., & Bloom, F. E. (1973). Cytochemical and pharmacological studies on polysensory neurons in the primate frontal cortex. *Brain Research, 62*, 115–133.

Nicol, S. C., Andersen, N. A., Phillis, N. H., & Berger, R. J. (2000). The echidna manifests typical characteristics of rapid eye movement sleep. *Neuroscience Letters, 283,* 49–52.

Nicoll, R. A., Malenka, R. C., & Kauer, J. A. (1990). Functional comparison of neurotransmitter receptor subtypes in mammalian central nervous system. *Physiological Reviews, 70,* 513–566.

Nishino, S., Ripley, B., Mignot, E., Benson, K. L., & Zarcone, V. P. (2002). CSF hypocretin-1 levels in schizophrenics and control: Relationship to sleep architecture. *Psychiatric Research, 110,* 1–7.

Nishino, S., Ripley, B., Overheem, S., Lammers, G. L., & Mignot, E. (2000). Hypocretin (orexin) deficiency in human narcolepsy. *Lancet, 355,* 39–40.

Nofzinger, E. A., Mintun, M. A., Wiseman, M. B., & Kupfer, J. (1997). Forebrain activation during REM sleep: An FDG PET study. *Brain Research, 770,* 192–201.

Ohlmeyer, P., & Brilmayer, B. (1947). Periodische Vörgange im Schlaf. II Mitteilung [Periodic erections during sleep]. *Pflügers Archiv, 249,* 50–55.

Ohlmeyer, P., Brilmayer, H., & Hüllstrung, H. (1944). Periodische Vorgänge im Schlaf. *Pflügers Archiv, 248,* 559–560.

Okubo, Y., Suhara, T., Kobahashi, K., Inoue, O., Terasaki, O., Someya, Y., Sassa, T., et al. (1997). Decreased prefrontal dopamine D1 receptors in schizophrenia revealed by PET. *Nature, 385,* 634–636.

Okuma, T., & Fujimori, M. (1963). Electrographic and evoked potential studies during sleep in the cat (The study of sleep I). *Folia Psychiatrica et Neurologica Japonica, 17,* 25–50.

Onoe, H., & Sakai, K. (1995). Kainate receptors: A novel mechanism in paradoxical (REM) sleep generation. *NeuroReport, 6,* 353–356.

Otani, S., Blond, O., Desce, J. M., & Crepel, F. (1998). Dopamine facilitates long-term depression of glutaminergic transmission in the prefrontal cortex. *Neuroscience, 85,* 669–676.

Overeem, S., Scammell, T. E., & Lammers, G. J. (2002). Hypocretin/orexin and sleep: Implications for the pathophysiology and diagnosis of narcolepsy. *Current Opinion in Neurology, 15,* 739–745.

Pal, D., & Mallick, B. N. (2004). GABA in pedunculo pontine tegmentum regulate spontaneous rapid eye movement sleep by acting on GABAA receptors in freely moving rats. *Neuroscience Letters, 29,* 200–2004.

Palestini, M., Pisano, M., Rosadini, G., & Rossi, G. F. (1964). Visual cortical responses evoked by stimulating lateral geniculate body and optic radiations in awake and sleeping cats. *Experimental Neurology, 9,* 17–30.

Parsons, L. M., Sergent, J., Hodges, D. A., & Fox, P. T., 2005. The brain basis of piano performance. *Neuropsychologia, 43,* 199–215.

Pavlov, I. (1962). *Les réflexes conditionnés [Conditioned reflexes].* Paris: Masson.

Peled, A., Geva, A. B., Kremen, W. S., Blankfeld, H. M., Esfandiarfard, R., & Nordahl, T. E., (2000). Functional connectivity and working memory in schizophrenia: An EEG study. *International Journal of Neuroscience, 106,* 47–61.

Pepeu, G., & Bartholini, A. (1968). Effect of psychoactive drugs on the output of acetylcholine from the cerebral cortex of the cat. *European Journal of Pharmacology, 4,* 254–263.

Perez-Garci, E., del Rio-Portilla, Y., Guevara, M. A., Arce, C., & Corsi-Cabrera, M. (2001). Paradoxical sleep is characterized by uncoupled gamma activity between frontal and perceptual cortical regions. *Sleep, 24*, 118–126.

Perry, E., Walker, M., Grace, J., & Perry, R. (1999). Acetylcholine in mind: A neurotransmitter of consciousness? *Trends in Neuroscience, 22*, 273–280.

Phillis, J. W., & Chong, G. C. (1965). Acetylcholine release from the cerebral and cebellar cortices: Its role in cortical arousal. *Nature, 207*, 1253–1255.

Phillis, J. W., Lake, N., & Yarbrough, G. (1973). Calcium mediation of the inhibitory effects of biogenic amines on cerebral coritical neurons. *Brain Research, 53*, 465–469.

Piéron, H. (1912). *Le problème physiologique du sommeil [The physiological problem of sleep]*. Paris: Masson.

Pirot, S., Godbout, R., Mantz, J., Tassin, J. P., Glowinski, J., & Thierry, A. M. (1992). Inhibitory effects of ventral tegmental area stimulation on the activity of the prefrontal cortex neurons: Evidence for the involvement of both dopaminergic and GABAergic components. *Neuroscience, 49*, 857–865.

Pisano, M., Rosadini, G., & Rossi, G. F. (1962). Riposte corticali evocate da stimoli dromici ed antidromici durante il sonno e la veglia [Orthodromic and antidromic cortical responses induced during sleep and waking]. *Rivista di Neurobiologia, 8*, 414–426.

Pommier, J. (1970). *Le langage intérieur [The inner language]*. Paris: Denoel.

Pompeiano, O., & Morrison, A. R. (1965). Vestibular influences during sleep. I. Abolition of the rapid eye movements of desynchronized sleep following vestibular lesions. *Archives Italiennes de Biologie, 103*, 569–595.

Pothos, E., Rada, P., Mark, G. P., & Hoebel, B. G. (1991). Dopamine microdialysis in the nucleus accumbens during acute and chronic morphine, naloxone-precipited withdrawal and clonidine treatment. *Brain Research, 566*, 348–350.

Raehlmann, E., & Witkowski, L. (1877). Ueber atypische Augenbewegungen [On atypic eye movements]. *Archiv für Anatomie und Physiologie, S*, 454–471.

Raehlmann, E., & Witkowski, L. (1878). Ueber das Verhalten der pupilen während des Schlafes nebst Bemerkungen zur innervation der Iris [On the behavior of pupils during sleep and comments on the innervation of the iris]. *Archiv für Anatomie und Physiologie, S*, 109–121.

Rasmussen, K., Heym, J., & Jacobs, B. L. (1984). Activity of serotonin-containing neurons in nucleus centralis superior of freely moving cats. *Experimental Neurology, 83*, 302–317.

Ray, P. G., & Jackson, W. J. (1991). Lesions of nucleus basalis alter ChAT activity and EEG in rat frontal neocortex. *Electroencephalography & Clinical Neurophysiology, 79*, 62–68.

Reader, T. A., Ferron, A., Descarries, L., & Jasper, H. H. (1979). Modulatory role for biogenic amines in the cerebral cortex. Microiontopheric studies. *Brain Research, 160*, 219–229.

Rechtschaffen, A., Molinari, S., Wabon, R., & Wincor, M. Z. (1970). Extraocular potentials: Possible indicator of PGO activity in the human. *Psychophysiology, 7*, 336.

Rechtschaffen, A., Wolpert, E. A., Dement, W. C., Mitchell, S. A., & Fisher, C. (1963). Nocturnal sleep in narcoleptics. *Electroencephalography & Clinical Neurophysiology, 15*, 599–609.

Reeves, M., Lindholm, D. E., Myles, P. S., Fletcher, H., & Hunt, J. O. (2001). Adding ketamine to morphine for patient-controlled analgesia after major abdominal surgery: A double-blind, randomized trial. *Anesthesia & Analgesia, 93,* 116–120.

Remington, G., & Chong, S. A. (1999). Conventional versus novel antipsychotics: changing concepts and clinical implications. *Journal of Psychiatry & Neuroscience, 24,* 431–441.

Rétaux, R., Besson, M. J., & Penit-Soria, J. (1991). Opposing effects of dopamine D2 receptor stimulation on the spontaneous and electrically-evoked release of 3H GABA on rat prefrontal cortex slices. *Neuroscience, 42,* 61–72.

Revonsuo, A. (2000). The reinterpretation of dreams: An evolutionary hypothesis of the function of dreaming. *Behavioral & Brain Sciences, 23,* 877–901.

Ribary, U., Ionnides, A. A., Singh, K. D., Hasson, R., Bolton, J., Lado, F., et al. (1991). Magnetic field tomography of coherent thalamocortical 40 Hz oscillations in humans. *Proceedings of the National Academy of Sciences of the USA, 88,* 11037–11041.

Roffwarg, H. P., Dement, W. C., Muzio, J. N., & Fisher, C. (1962). Dream imagery: Relationship to rapid eye movements of sleep. *Archives of General Psychiatry, 7,* 235–258.

Rossi, G. F., Palestini, M., Pisano, M., & Rosadini, G. (1965). An experimental study of the cortical reactivity during sleep and wakefulness. In *Aspects anatomo-fonctionnels de la physiologie du sommeil* [Anatomo-functional aspects of the physiology of sleep] (pp. 509–532). CNRS: Paris.

Sakai, K. (1985). Anatomical and physiological basis of paradoxical sleep. In R. Drucker-Colin, A. R. Morrison, & P. L. Parmeggiani (Eds.), *Brain mechanisms of sleep* (pp. 111–137). New York: Raven Press.

Sakai, K. (1988). Executive mechanisms of paradoxical sleep. *Archives Italiennes de Biologie, 126,* 239–257.

Sakai, K., & Cespuglio, R. (1976). Evidence for the presence of eye movement potentials during paradoxical sleep in cats. *Electroencephalography & Clinical Neurophysiology, 41,* 37–48.

Sakai, K., & Crochet, S. (2003). A neural mechanism of sleep and wakefulness. *Sleep and Biological Rhythms, 1,* 29–42.

Sallanon, M., Buda, C., Janin, M., & Jouvet, M. (1982). Restoration of paradoxical sleep by cerebrospinal fluid transfer to PCPA pretreated insomniac cats. *Brain Research, 251,* 137–147.

Sanford, L. D., Cheng, C. S., Silvestri, A. J., Tang, X., Mann, G. L., Ross, R. J., et al. (2001). Sleep and behavior in rats with pontine lesions producing REM without atonia. *Sleep Research Online, 14,* 1–5.

Sarter, M., & Bruno, J. P. (2000). Cortical cholinergic inputs mediating arousal, attentional processing and dreaming: Differential afferent regulation of the basal forebrain by telencephalic and brainstem afferents. *Neuroscience, 95,* 933–952.

Sastre, J. P., & Jouvet, M. (1979). Oneiric behavior in cats. *Physiology & Behavior, 22,* 979–989.

Satoh, T. (1971). Direct cortical response and PGO spike during paradoxical sleep of the cat. *Brain Research, 28,* 576–578.

Schmidt, M. H., Sakai, K., Valatx, J. L., & Jouvet, M. (1999). The effects of spinal or mesencephalic transections on sleep-related erections and ex-copula penile reflexes in the rat. *Sleep, 22,* 409–418.

Schmidt, M. H., Valatx, J. L., Sakai, K., Fort, P., & Jouvet, M. (2000). Role of the lateral preoptic area in sleep-related erectile mechanisms and sleep generation in the rat. *Journal of Neuroscience, 20*, 6640–6647.

Schmidt, M. H., Valatx, J. L., Schmidt, H. S., Wauquier, A., & Jouvet, M. (1994). Experimental evidence of penile erections during paradoxical sleep in the rat. *NeuroReport, 5*, 561–564.

Sheldon, P. W., & Aghajanian, G. K. (1990). Serotonin (5-HT) induces IPSPs in pyramidal layer cells of rat piriform cortex: Evidence for the involvement of a 5-HT$_2$-activated interneuron. *Brain Research, 506*, 62–69.

Shippenberg, T. S., Hen, R., & He, M. (2000). Region-specific enhancement of basal extracellular and cocaine-evoked dopamine levels following constitutive deletion of the serotonin (B1) receptor. *Journal of Neurochemistry, 75*, 258–265.

Siegel, J. M., Manger, P. R., Nienhuis, R., Fahringer, H. M., & Pettigrew, J. D. (1996). The echidna Tachyglossus aculeatus combines REM and non-REM aspects in single sleep state: Implications for the evolution of sleep. *Journal of Neuroscience, 16*, 3500–3506.

Siegel, J. M., Manger, P. R., Nienhuis, R., Fahringer, S. T., & Pettigrew, J. D. (1999). Sleep in the platypus. *Neuroscience, 91*, 391–400.

Silver, H., Barash, I., Aharon, N., Kaplan, A., & Poyurovsky, M. (2000). Fluvoxamine augmentation of antipsychotics improves negative symptoms in psychotic chronic schizophrenic patients: A placebo-controlled study. *International Clinical Psychopharmacology, 15*, 257–261.

Solms, M. (2000). Dreaming and REM sleep are controlled by different brain mechanisms. *Behavioral and Brain Sciences, 23*, 843–850.

Solms, M., & Turnbull, O. (2002). *The brain and the inner world: An introduction to the neuroscience of subjective experience.* New York: Other Press.

Spencer, K. M., Nestor, P. G., Niznikiewicz, A., Salisbury, D. F., Shenton, M. E., & McCarley, R. W. (2003). Abnormal neural synchrony in schizophrenia. *Journal of Neuroscience, 23*, 7407–7411.

Steriade, M. (1970). Ascending control of thalamic and cortical responsiveness. *International Review of Neurobiology, 12*, 87–144.

Steriade, M. (1996). Arousal: Revisiting the reticular system. *Science, 272*, 225–226.

Steriade, M., Amzica, F., & Contreras, D. (1996). Synchronization of fast (30–40 Hz) spontaneous cortical rhythms during brain activation. *Journal of Neuroscience, 16*, 392–417.

Steriade, M., & Buzsaki, G. (1990). Parallel activation of thalamic and cortical neurons by brainstem and basal forebrain cholinergic systems. In M. Steriade, & D. Biesold (Eds.), *Brain cholinergic systems* (pp. 3–62). Oxford: Oxford Science.

Steriade, M., Contreras, D., Amzica, F., & Timofeev, I. (1996). Synchronization of fast (30–40 Hz) spontaneous oscillations in the intrathalamic and thalamocortical networks. *Journal of Neuroscience, 16*, 2788–2808.

Steriade, M., Curro dossi, R., Paré, D., & Oakson, G. (1991). Fast oscillations (20–40 Hz) in thalamocortical systems and their potentiation by mesopontine cholinergic nuclei in the cat. *Proceedings of the National Academy of Sciences of the United States of America, 88*, 4396–4400.

Steriade, M., Domich, L., Oakson, G., & Deschenes, M. (1987). The deafferented reticular thalamic nucleus generates spindle rhythmicity. *Journal of Neurophysiology, 57*, 260–273.

Steriade, M., & McCarley, R. W. (1990). *Brainstem control of wakefulness and sleep*. New York: Plenum Press.

Steriade, M., Paré, D., Bouhassira, D., Deschènes, M., & Oakson, G. (1989). Phasic activation of lateral geniculate and perigeniculate thalamic neurons during sleep with ponto-geniculate-occipital waves. *Journal of Neuroscience, 9*, 2215–2229.

Stern, W. C., Forbes, A., & Morgane, P. J. (1974). Absence of ponto-geniculo-occipital (PGO) spikes in rats. *Physiology & Behavior, 12*, 293–296.

Strumwasser, F. (1958). Long-term recording from single neurons in brain of unrestrained mammals. *Science, 127*, 469–470.

Suzuki, J. (1966). Narcoleptic syndrome and paradoxical sleep. *Folia Psychiatrica et Neurologica Japonica, 20*, 123–149.

Szymusiak, R., McGinty, D., Shepard, D., Shouse, M. N., & Sterman, M. (1990). Effects of systemic atropine sulfate administration on the frequency content of the cat sensorimotor EEG during sleep and waking. *Behavioral Neuroscience, 104*, 217–225.

Takahata, R., & Moghaddam, B. (2000). Target-specific glutamatergic regulation of dopamine neurons in the ventral tegmental area. *Journal of Neurochemistry, 75*, 1775–1778.

Takahata, R., & Moghaddam, B. (2003). Activation of glutamate neurotransmission in the prefrontal cortex sustains the motoric and dopaminergic effects of phencyclidine. *Neuropsychopharmacology, 28*, 117–1124.

Thannickal, T. C., Moore, R.Y., Nienhuis, R., Ramanathan, L., Gulyani, S., Aldrich, M., et al. (2000). Reduced number of hypocretin neurons in human narcolepsy. *Neuron, 27*, 464–474.

Thompson, D. F., & Pierce, D. R. (1999). Drug-induced nightmares. *Annals of Pharmacotherapy, 33*, 93–98.

Tong, J., Hornykiewicz, O., & Kish, S. J. (2006). Identification of a noradrenaline-rich subdivision of the human nucleus accumbens. *Journal of Neurochemistry, 96*, 349–354.

Tononi, G., & Edelman, G. M. (2000). Schizophrenia and the mechanism of conscious integration. *Brain Research. Brain Research Reviews, 31*, 391–400.

Toyoda, J. (1964). The effects of chlorpromazine and imipramine on the human nocturnal sleep electroencephalogram. *Folia Psychiatrica et Neurologia, 18*, 198–221.

Trulson, M. E., & Preussler, D. W. (1984). Dopamine-containing ventral tegmental area neurons in freely moving cats: Activity during the sleep-waking cycle and effects of stress. *Experimental Neurology, 83*, 367–377.

Van Hes, R., Smid, P., Stroomer, C. N., Tipker, K., Tulp, M. T., Van der Heyden, J. A., et al. (2003). SL V310, a novel, potential antipsychotic, combining potent dopamine d2 receptor antagonism with serotonin reuptake inhibition. *Bioorganic & Medicinal Chemistry Letters, 13*, 405–408.

Vanderwolf, C. H. (1988). Cerebral activity and behavior control by central cholinergic and serotonergic systems. *International Review of Neurobiology, 30*, 225–340.

Vanderwolf, C. H. (2000). Are neocortical gamma waves related to consciousness. *Brain Research, 855*, 217–224.

Vanderwolf, C. H., Fine, A., & Cooley, R. K. (1990). Intracortical grafts of embryogenic basal forebrain tissue restore low voltage fast activity in rats with basal forebrain lesions. *Experimental Brain Research, 81*, 426–432.

Vanni-Mercier, G., & Debilly, G., (1998). A key role for the caudoventral pontine tegmentum in the simultaneous generation of eye saccades in bursts and associated ponto-geniculo-occipital waves during paradoxical sleep in the cat. *Neuroscience, 86,* 57–585.

Vanni-Mercier, G., Gigout, S., Debilly, G., & Lin, J. S. (2003). Waking selective neurons in the posterior hypothalamus and their response to histamine H_3-receptor ligands: An electrophysiological study in freely moving cats. *Behavioural Brain Research, 144,* 227–241.

Vanni-Mercier, G., Sakai, K., & Jouvet, M. (1984). Neurones spécifiques de l'éveil dans l'hypothalamus postérieur [Specific neurons of waking in the posterior hypothalamus]. *Comptes Rendus Hebdomadaires des Séances de l'Académie des Sciences, 298,* 195–200.

Vasquez, J., & Baghdoyan, H. A. (2001). Basal forebrain acetylcholine release during REM sleep is significantly greater than during waking. *American Journal of Physiology, 280,* R598–R601.

Vazquez, J., & Baghdoyan, H. A. (2004). $GABA_A$ receptors inhibit acetylcholine release in cat pontine reticular formation: Implications for REM sleep regulation. *Journal of Neurophysiology, 92,* 2198–2206.

Vertes, R. P. (1977). Selective firing of rat pontine gigantocellular neurons during movement and REM sleep. *Brain Research, 128,* 146–152.

Vittoz, N. M., & Berridge, C. W. (2005). Hypocretin/orexin selectively increases dopamine efflux within the prefrontal cortex: Involvement of the ventral tegmental area. *Neuropsychopharmacology, 31,* 384–395.

Vogel, G. (1960). Studies in psychophysiology of dreams. III. The dream of narcolepsy. *Archives of General Psychiatry, 3,* 421–428.

Vogel, G. (1978). An alternative view of the neurobiology of dreaming. *American Journal of Psychiatry, 135,* 1531–1535.

Wang, X., Ai, J., Hampson, D. R., & Snead III, O. C. (2005). Altered glutamate and GABA release within thalamocortical circuitry in metabotropic glutamate receptor 4 knockout mice. *Neuroscience, 134,* 1195–1203.

Wang, Z., & McCormick, D. A. (1993). Control of firing mode of corticotectal and corticopontine layer V burst-generating neurons by norepinephrine, acetylcholine and 1S, 3R-ACPD. *Journal of Neuroscience, 13,* 2199–2216.

Warren, R. A., & Dykes, R. W. (1996). Transient and long-lasting effects of iontophoretically administered norepinephrine on somatosensory cortical neurons in halothane-anesthetized cats. *Canadian Journal of Physiology & Pharmacology, 74,* 38–57.

Webster, H. H., & Jones, B. (1988). Neurotoxic lesions of the dorsolateral pontomesencephalic tegmentum-cholinergic cell area in the cat. II. Effect upon sleep-waking states. *Brain Research, 458,* 285–302.

Weed, S. C., & Hallam, F. M. (1896). A study of the dream-consciousness. *American Journal of Psychology, 7,* 405–411.

Weinberger, D. R., Berman, K. F., & Zec, R. F. (1986). Physiological dysfunction of dorsolateral prefrontal cortex in schizophrenia. 1. Regional cerebral blood flow evidence. *Archives of General Psychiatry, 43,* 114–124.

Weitzman, E. D., Fishbein, W., & Graziani, L. (1965). Auditory evoked responses obtained from the scalp electroencephalogram of the full-term human neonate during sleep. *Pediatrics, 35,* 458–462.

Wikler, A. (1952). Pharmacological dissociation of behavior and EEG "sleep patterns" in dogs: Morphine, N-allylmorphine, and atropine. *Proceedings of the Society for Experimental Biology and Medicine. Society for Experimental Biology and Medicine, 79,* 261–265.

Williams, H. L., Tepas, D. I., & Morlock, J. H. C. (1962). Evoked responses to clicks and electroencephalographic stages of sleep in man. *Science, 138,* 685–686.

Wurtz, R. H. (1965). Steady potential shifts in the rat during desynchronized sleep. *Electroencephalography & Clinical Neurophysiology, 19,* 521–523.

Wurtz, R. H. (1966). Steady potential fields during sleep and wakefulness in the cat. *Experimental Neurology, 15,* 274–292.

Ye, Z., Wyeth, M. S., Baltan-Tekkok, S., & Ransom, B. R. (2003). Functional hemichannels in astrocytes: A novel mechanim of glutamate release. *Journal of Neuroscience, 23,* 3588–3596.

Yeragani, V. K., Cashmere, D., Miewald, J., Tancer, M., & Keshavan, M. S. (2006). Decreased coherence in higher frequency ranges (beta and gamma) between central and frontal EEG in patients with schizophrenia: A preliminary report. *Psychiatric Research, 141,* 53–60.

Young, C. E., Beach, T. G., Falkai, P., & Honer, W. G. (1998). SNAP-25 deficit and hippocampal connectivity in schizophrenia. *Cerebral Cortex, 8,* 261–268.

Two

Phylogeny of Sleep and Dreams

Patrick McNamara, Charles Nunn, Robert Barton, Erica Harris, and Isabella Capellini

Sleep is a need. Whether we like it or not, we eventually succumb to sleep. It is an involuntary physiologic function. Like many other involuntary functions, sleep appears to be maintained around a homeostatic set point. Following sleep deprivation in many animals, there is a compensatory rebound in the amount of sleep engaged in, such that the lost sleep is "made-up," and a relatively constant daily amount of sleep is maintained over the long-term. The manifestations of sleep rebound phenomena vary across amniotes (that is, birds, reptiles, and mammals, the three classes of animals we will be considering in this chapter).

In mammals, the deprivation of NREM sleep leads to a remarkable increase in both the amount and intensity of NREM slow wave activity (SWA; or sleep stage IV in primates). This effect is well-known and has been demonstrated in a diverse array of species including humans, squirrel monkeys, rats, mice, Syrian and djungarian hamsters, cats, and ground squirrels (Tobler, 2005). REM sleep is also homeostatically regulated in mammals (as REM amounts are increased after REM deprivation), but it is unclear whether an intensity dimension exists for REM sleep. Outside of the order mammalia, the manifestations of sleep rebound vary. Some reptiles (crocodiles, for example) exhibit sleep-associated sharp slow waves and then rebound effects in the amount of these waves after rest deprivation. In birds, there is little physiologic evidence for sleep rebound effects after sleep deprivation, but behavioral signs of unihemispheric sleep (for example, increased duration of unilateral eye closures) are increased in some birds after sleep deprivation.

Returning to mammals, the phenomenon of post-deprivation sleep rebound points to a potential homeostatic function of sleep, meaning some physiologic process that is indexed by sleep duration (and intensity) and maintained at an optimal level. This homeostatic component of sleep raises the question of biologically imposed constraints on sleep and even potential adaptive functions of sleep. If sleep serves some primary homeostatic physiologic function, it operates under specific biologic constraints that in turn are likely to have an evolutionary history. Investigation of that history may reveal important information about sleep's functional correlates.

SLEEP-RELATED MENTATION (SRM)

SRM refers to any perceptual or mental state that occurs in temporal relation to some sleep process or state. In humans we call some forms of SRM "dreams," where "dreams" refer to extended experiences of emotion-laden imagery structured into story-like action episodes typically concerning the dreamer and his/her socially significant others. Many SRMs, however, are not dreams. Instead, they may be classified as hypnagogic images or fleeting and isolated thought fragments, ongoing ruminations, verbalizations, or all manner of other types of mentation. Whether or not REM or NREM sleep processes "cause" associated perceptual or mentation experiences is an empirical question that needs to be decided after appropriate investigation. There is little doubt, however, that each of the two major sleep states influences the SRM experience in humans.

REM dreams, for example, tend to be more vivid, story-like, emotional, and action-oriented than their NREM counterparts even after controlling for length of report, time of night, and other variables (Nielsen, 2000). On the assumption that brain activation patterns produce all forms of mentation, the most salient candidate for the production of REM dreams is the characteristic pattern of brain activation known to occur during a REM episode, namely intense amygdalar, limbic, temporal, and occipital activation along with prefrontal deactivation (Hobson, Pace-Schott, & Stickgold, 2000). This pattern of REM-associated brain activation suggests that memorable REM dreams (that is, dreams that are remembered upon awakening) should on average contain a greater number of unpleasant (fear, anger, rage, and so on) than pleasant emotions. Content analyses of hundreds of dreams have generally, though not invariably, supported this supposition (Domhoff, 2003; Revonsuo, 2000).

Clinical evidence also supports the supposition that REM-associated brain activity produces a tendency towards unpleasant emotional content in dreams. One can see clear evidence of negatively toned dream content in the dreams of patients who have lost the ability to inhibit the motor execution of internally experienced dreams (that is, the normal REM-associated inhibition of the spinal motor neurons is destroyed). Patients with so-called REM Behavior Disorder (RBD) may physically react to events transpiring in their dreams (Mahowald & Schenck, 2000). Up to 89 percent of the dreams reported by RBD patients involve the dreamer being attacked by an animal or a violent person. Patients react to the hallucinated attack in myriad and dangerous ways. Some individuals have been observed to jump out of bed and run wildly out of the room. Or individuals may attempt to jump out of windows or fire unloaded guns. In bed, they may punch, kick, or even attempt to strangle their bed partners (Olson, Boeve, & Silber, 2000). EEG measurements verify that patients are typically in REM sleep when these violent behaviors take place. The lack of spinal motor inhibition normally associated with REM is confirmed via similar neurophysiologic measurement. When the patient awakens, he is relatively lucid and has no difficulty providing a detailed verbal report of what was happening in the dream. The report typically involves threats of various kinds to the dreamer and closely matches the dreamer's violent bed behaviors.

Taken together, the hundreds of studies of dream content along with the evidence from RBD patients in the clinic strongly suggest that SRM in humans is real, measurable, and emotionally consequential. What about for nonhuman animals? We, of course, do not know for sure whether SRM occurs in other animals. Although nonhuman animals may not experience "dreaming" as defined above (and that is an open empirical question), they very likely experience some types of emotional, perceptual, or imagistic SRMs in tandem with the two major sleep states. If, as happens in REM sleep, selected networks of the brain were activated to levels high enough to support mentation in humans, we would expect some sort of mental processes to engage after such activation in nonhuman animals that have REM sleep.

But how can we verify whether SRM experiences occur in nonverbal animals? The experiences of patients with RBD suggest one strategy. In the case of patients with RBD, we observed overt dream enactment behaviors occurring in tandem with REM sleep when the normal REM-associated spinal motor inhibition process was abolished by disease. What if that spinal motor inhibition process was experimentally abolished in animals? Would we see "dream" enactment behaviors in these animals?

Very early in the modern study of REM sleep physiology (in the 1960s), Jouvet and colleagues (Jouvet, Vimont, Delorme, & Jouvet, 1964; described in Jouvet, 1999) managed to selectively lesion REM sleep-related spinal motor inhibition neurons in the brainstem of cats, thereby abolishing the normal REM sleep-associated muscle atonia in these animals. When the cats were observed to enter an episode of REM sleep, they began to enact their dreams. The cats hissed and arched their backs as if they were preparing to fight an imaginary enemy. Often they would act as if they were stalking an imaginary prey. These data indicate that other animals may experience something like dreams. At a minimum, the data suggests that there is a marked similarity in reactions at the behavioral level when REM biology is disinhibited.

Most of us have observed sleeping dogs yelp, bark, or growl in their sleep. Similar anecdotal reports of other animals of all kinds suggest that most animals experience hallucinatory and "emotional" imagery during sleep that is analogous to dreaming in humans. Even birds and reptiles emit vocalizations during sleep. As is the case with human beings, these sleep-related vocalizations may be functionally correlated with both SRM experiences and with the underlying sleep state the animal is in when it vocalizes.

The case of birds may be particularly instructive. Recent data on cellular activity levels in avian brain nuclei devoted to song shows that these cells are reactivated and perhaps resculpted during sleep. A form of apparent song replay may occur in selected sleep states in some birds. Dave and Margoliash (2000; see also Deregnacourt, Mitra, Feher, Pytte, & Tchernichovski, 2005), for example, showed that "spontaneous" activity of certain neurons known to be associated with song production during waking life are reactivated during sleep in a form that reproduces the sensorimotor activation patterns normally associated with song produced in waking life. In addition, the timing and structure of neuronal activity elicited in the bird's motor "cortex" by the playback of song during sleep matches neuronal activity during daytime singing. The authors concluded that, "these data suggest a model whereby sensorimotor correspondences are stored during singing but do not modify behavior, and off-line comparison (e.g., during sleep) of rehearsed motor output and predicted sensory feedback is used to adaptively shape motor output" (p. 812).

Is the bird "practicing" its song during sleep? Is the bird "hearing" or dreaming its song during sleep? How can we answer such questions? Some birds exhibit the typical mammalian pattern of muscle atonia during REM. If the REM-associated motor inhibition was experimentally abolished in one of these birds, would we see any form of dream enactment behavior? As far as we know, researchers have never investigated this possibility in birds. Complicating the picture is the fact that REM episodes in birds are quite short, typically lasting on the order of seconds. Moreover, song replay in birds is often associated with a non-REM form of sleep in these animals. Finally, most birds exhibit what is called "unihemispheric sleep," in which one hemisphere sleeps at a time (more about this later). Given this type of complexity regarding sleep processes in birds and in various types of other animals, investigation of SRMs in nonverbal animals is likely to be an arduous and complicated process.

Although investigation of SRM processes in nonhuman animals will certainly be difficult, such information can help us to better understand potential functions of sleep and dreams. If it turns out, for example, that other animals dream solely of potential predators or solely of potential mates or solely of potential prey, then that fact is one more clue that can be used to construct a theory of the functions of sleep itself. Data on existence and content of SRM in other animals might also throw some light on the vexed question of the origins and functions of thought and consciousness itself.

Thus, we are at an early stage in our understanding of whether other animals dream. Knowing the details of what they dream about is likely to be even further in the future. There are, however, data on the amount of REM sleep found in other animals, and this information can give us some clues as to the evolutionary history of at least one form of dreaming—REM dreaming, and of brain activation patterns during REM sleep. In humans, mentation can occur in tandem with both REM and NREM sleep states, but it is clear that REM-related mentation is more vivid and memorable. We will, therefore, focus this review on the phylogeny of *REM sleep*. We will return to the issue of SRM in nonhuman animals after reviewing the available data on comparative REM sleep. First, we consider how broad evolutionary patterns in sleep can be investigated by using the comparative method. Next, we examine broad patterns of sleep across vertebrates, with a special focus on mammals. Finally, we integrate these details on the distribution of sleep to formulate hypotheses for the origin of REM sleep and its links to dreaming. Our goals are to give an overview of interesting questions related to REM sleep and dreams and to provide this overview in a synthetic framework that allows for progress in answering questions about the phylogeny of SRM.

USING THE COMPARATIVE METHOD TO UNCOVER THE FUNCTION OF SLEEP

The study of variation in sleep patterns across species is an important method for studying potential adaptive functions of sleep. It is the only method we have for inferring the evolutionary history of sleep and the factors that have influenced variation in sleep patterns among animals. It is important, however, to keep in mind several points when considering the evolutionary history of something as complex as the mental functions associated with REM. Rattenborg and Amlaner (2002) point out that think-ing on the evolution of sleep has to some extent been distorted by an assumption that mammals are more advanced than nonmammals. Yet in some respects, birds have developed innovations in cortical laminar structure not observed in mammals. Similarly, reptiles have developed quite complex neural systems specialized to transduce light information into neural impulses that regulate rest-activity cycles (e.g., a parietal eye, a complex pin-eal system, and a brain site homologous to the suprachiasmatic nucleus or SCN). Clearly, we should not be seduced by evolutionary stories that inevi-tably lead to big-brained species sitting at the top of "a great chain of being" as the most fit or successful. Nor should we deny the possibility that certain evolutionary transitions could have been crucial for development of big brains, resulting in the highly differentiated REM and NREM sleep states characteristic of primates. One can identify such transitions and innovations without necessarily assuming that earlier steps in the pathway represent evo-lutionary dead ends in the taxa in which those transitions occurred. Rather, it is likely that sleep traits in those taxa continued to evolve, sometimes slowly, sometimes rapidly, depending on selective pressures faced by the spe-cies. Thus, differences in sleep traits across different species may, as Ratten-borg and Amlaner (2002) point out, "actually reflect alternative means of fulfilling similar functions, rather than indicating different levels of sleep evolution" (p. 7).

On the other hand, when one or more of the behavioral, physiologic, electrophysiologic, or functional components of, for example, primate sleep are identified in taxa whose divergence from primates can be accurately esti-mated (by using molecular phylogenies and comparative methods—see below), then we can make some reasonable estimates concerning when selected traits of REM and NREM emerged in the line leading to the pri-mates. Furthermore, when selected sleep traits are found to be associated with significant ecologic, life history, or physiologic traits across taxa with similar biological characteristics, including brain structure, then it is reasonable to investigate those associations in hopes of revealing functional relationships.

In short, if we use appropriate methods—namely the comparative phyloge-netic methods to be discussed next, then analyses of sleep variation can help us discern when a trait evolved, in how many lineages, how long it survived over evolutionary time, and what its consistent functional relationships are.

We need to discuss one final methodological point before summarizing the phylogenetic approach to comparative sleep analyses. Analyses of any kind are only as good as the input data they work with. So, we need to say something about the data used in these analyses. Phylogenetic comparative analyses are typically carried out on large-scale databases that contain data points on dozens of variables, including both sleep variables and variables hypothesized to be related to sleep, such as body size, metabolic rates, brain size, and so on. Previously constructed comparative databases suffered from a number of shortcomings related to the reliability and validity of the data contained in the databases. Campbell and Tobler (1984) published a dataset of total sleep durations for 168 species, but there were no values for REM and NREM. Zepelin (1989) constructed the largest published dataset on REM and NREM (rather than just total sleep) values (containing 84 species). Elgar, Pagel, and Harvey (1988) analyzed a dataset comprising 69 species. To control for phylogenetic associations, Elgar et al. (1988) calculated correlations across taxonomic families (by computing means for species within genera and then genera within families). This taxonomic approach reduced sample sizes to between 20 and 34. They found correlations between sleep quotas and body weight, metabolic rate, mode of development (altricial versus precocial), and latitude. Subsequently, Berger (1990) criticized this study on the grounds that a number of the species estimates were highly questionable. Elgar, Pagel, and Harvey (1990) responded correctly that comparative analysis is the only way to derive general conclusions about sleep, and largely replicated their original findings using a substantially reduced sample that omitted data not satisfying Berger's criteria for reliability (42 species, giving actual sample sizes of up to 30 families). Nevertheless, analyses on these comparative datasets have been stymied by inconsistent data collation and modest sample sizes.

Recent developments in comparative analytical methods can help address these methodologic problems concerning comparative sleep datasets. For example, use of the technique of phylogenetically controlled "independent contrasts" (Harvey & Pagel, 1991) obviates the need to exclude attention to variance below the level of the taxonomic family. Thus, we can avoid the problem of reduced sample sizes arising from a focus only at family-level analyses. In addition, a large proportion of the variance in comparative biological variables is commonly associated with two factors: body size (allometry) and, as mentioned previously, phylogeny. Allometry is the study of how a trait scales with body size. Previous studies of sleep quotas have found negative correlations between sleep durations and body size (Zepelin, 1994), but little attention has been paid to establishing quantitative scaling relationships, despite the fact that regularities in these relationships may be important for understanding sleep variation in general. For example, metabolic rate and body mass scale with an exponent of 0.75 predict similar scaling patterns for sleep traits under hypotheses involving metabolic functions.

With regard to the issue of phylogeny, problems arose in previous comparative analyses because it was not clear (using only standard multiple regression techniques) whether similarities/associations in sleep expression obtained between animals was because of common functional relationships or common phylogenetic ancestry. Animals that were related phylogenetically were all too often treated as wholly independent data points. Given that most statistical tests of sleep variables in the databases (implicitly) assumed independence of the species data, some of the results of these early analyses are likely to be invalid. One needs to take phylogeny into account to identify true functional relationships between sleep properties and some other non-sleep-related trait. Indeed, in order to properly describe even the allometric scaling of a sleep trait, it is necessary to take phylogenetic information into account (Harvey & Pagel, 1991; Nunn & Barton, 2000, 2001), yet this is rarely done in studies of sleep.

Properly conducted phylogenetic and allometric analyses can help us answer four fundamental questions about the evolution of REM sleep. First, do phylogenetically close species share similar REM properties (e.g., durations)? In other words, do sleep-related traits exhibit what Blomberg and Garland (2002) call "phylogenetic signal"? Second, which sleep-related traits are evolutionarily primitive for mammals and birds, which are derived, and which similarities have arisen through convergent evolution? Third, do groups of taxa exhibit different scaling relationships? A deeper understanding of allometric patterns can be accomplished through understanding such "grade shifts" (Nunn & Barton, 2000). Fourth, what general evolutionary relationships exist (a) between sleep traits and (b) between sleep traits and other aspects of behavioral biology and ecology? Have particular taxa evolved distinctively different patterns of sleep, and, if so, how do these patterns relate to other features of their biology?

We cannot yet answer these fascinating questions about the phylogeny of sleep states because no such phylogenetically controlled studies of comparative sleep values have yet been conducted. We mention the questions here to highlight these promising areas for future study.

THE PHYLOGENY OF SLEEP

We turn now to a survey of comparative sleep patterns, focusing mainly on mammals, but with a short excursus on reptiles and birds. Our aim is to reconstruct the basic picture of what is currently known about comparative patterns of sleep, particularly REM sleep. It will be necessary to keep this basic picture of the variability in expression of REM and NREM sleep patterns in mind so that we can ground our discussion of the evolutionary history of sleep related mentation firmly in the context of comparative sleep biology.

Reptiles

Electrophysiologic signs of active/REM sleep appear to be absent in most and perhaps all reptiles (Frank, 1999; but see Rial, Nicolau, Lopez-Garcia, & Almirall, 1993). Although behavioral signs of sleep are clearly observable in reptiles, correlations between these behavioral signs of sleep and selected EEG indices are difficult to evaluate given the complexities of recording sleep EEGs from the reptilian scalp and brain. Early studies by Flanigan and others (Flanigan, 1973; see review in Rial et al., 1993) reported an association between behavioral sleep and intermittent high-voltage spikes and sharp waves recorded from various brain structures in crocodilians, lizards, and turtles. Other investigations found no such association between behavioral sleep and high-amplitude spikes and sharp waves in the same animals. Hartse (1994) argued that high-amplitude spikes and sharp waves define a reptilian sleep state homologous with mammalian slow wave sleep (SWS).

High-voltage slow waves superimposed on the waking and sleeping EEG in reptiles has been proposed as a precursor of SWA found in the sleep of mammals. The equation of reptilian high-voltage slow waves (HVSW) with mammalian SWA is supported by findings (Flanigan, 1973) of compensatory rebound of sleep-related processes, including EEG spikes after sleep deprivation in reptiles. The latency to behavioral sleep was increased and the duration of behavioral sleep was increased as well after sleep deprivation in reptiles.

With respect to REM, the consensus at this point is that reptiles do not exhibit REM sleep. When Frank (1999) reviewed the literature on reptilian sleep, he concluded that no convincing evidence had yet been produced of REM-like states in reptiles. Rattenborg and Amlanar (2002) also called the evidence for REM in reptiles "equivocal." Even when investigators claim to have found signs of REM in a reptile, they have hitherto failed to report whether those signs were observed while the animal was unresponsive to the environment (that is, whether arousal thresholds were elevated) or other crucial signs of behavioral sleep. Thus, it may be that putative REM-like episodes in reptiles were actually brief arousals into waking or some form of waking. On the other hand, crocodilian sharp waves and spike activity in the context of HVSW may be a kind of indeterminate or mixed form of what is called in mammalian species REM and NREM, thus these reptiles may exhibit protoforms of REM.

Avian Sleep

As is the case with mammals, birds can be either monophasic (with one consolidated period of sleep per day) or polyphasic sleepers (with several short episodes of sleep per day). Birds appear to exhibit a special form of SWA and very little REM-like sleep. SWA in birds does not appear to be homeostatically regulated. SWA in NREM sleep in pigeons does not decline in the course of the dark period, suggesting that SWA in these animals is not building up chemicals that are depleted during waking. Moreover, SWA does not appear to increase after sleep deprivation. Unlike mammals, sleep spindles are absent during NREM in birds. In addition to this unusual form of SWA, birds also display sleep states that simultaneously combine features of both wakefulness and SWA. As in aquatic mammals, unilateral eye closure and unihemispheric SWA also occur in birds (reviewed in Rattenborg, Amlaner, & Lima, 2000a, 2000b).

Avian REM-like sleep states are associated with desynchronized EEG, impaired thermoregulation, and higher arousal thresholds, but they last only seconds and are cumulatively only one-quarter the amount typically reported for mammalian species. Moreover, there appears to be no REM rebound following REM sleep deprivation.

Mammals

Monotremes

Composed of three extant species (two species of echidna and the duck-billed platypus), monotremes are thought to have diverged from the main mammalian line before the divergence of marsupials and placental mammals. Allison, Van Twyver, and Goff's (1972) original polysomnographic study of the short-beaked echidna (*Tachyglossus aculeatus*) revealed unequivocal SWA but no EEG evidence for REM. Siegel, Manger, Nienhuis, Fahringer, and Pettigrew (1996) investigated activity of brain stem reticular neurons in the same species. Patterned reticular neuronal activity varies consistently in REM and NREM states. Discharge rate is high and irregular during REM and low and regular during SWA. Siegel et al. (1996) found irregular reticular discharge patterns during SWA in the short-beaked echidna (that is, a mixture of REM and NREM signs). REMs were also later recorded in the duck-billed platypus despite no overt EEG signs of REM. Thus, the monotremes appear to exhibit a mixed, indeterminate form of sleep containing elements of both REM and NREM mammalian sleep states. Siegel and others have suggested that mammalian sleep states emerged out of this primordial hybrid state of indeterminate sleep with SWS and REM segregating into independent brain states dependent on the central nervous system organization of the animal. Therefore, they assume that monotremes are primitive in their sleep pattern.

Nicol, Andersen, Phillips, and Berger (2000) reported REM characteristics in short-beaked echidnas. This conclusion was based on evidence for concurrent cortical activation, reduced tonic electromyogram (EMG) activity, and REMs under low, thermo-neutral, and high-ambient temperatures. Some investigators have suggested that the REM sleep episodes reported by Nicol et al. (2000) actually reflect a quiet waking state in these animals. These studies of REM in monotremes have led some researchers to acknowledge that some REM-like electrophysiologic activity occurs in these animals, but the work also confirms previous impressions that REM without signs of SWA does not occur in monotremes.

Marsupials

Marsupials show more definite signs of REM sleep. Affani, Vaccarezza, and Abellone (1967) and Van Twyver and Allison (1970) were the first to document abundant signs of REM in a marsupial—the opossum. Cicala, Albert, and Ulmer (1970) found evidence for REM in the red kangaroo. Walker and Berger (1980) obtained sleep and wakefulness recordings from infant opossums, aged 48 to 79 days, while they were in their mothers' pouches. The ontogenesis of sleep in this marsupial was similar to that of placental mammals: quiet sleep increased from 13 percent sleep time at 48 days to 55 percent at 79 days; conversely, active sleep decreased from 87 percent to 45 percent, respectively. The amplitude of the EEG during quiet sleep increased with age and quiet sleep could be categorized as SWA at 75 days. Active sleep could be identified as REM sleep at the same age.

Aquatic Mammals

Members of three different orders that contain aquatic mammals—cetaceans (dolphins, porpoises, and whales), carnivores (seals, sea lions, and otters), and sirenians (manatees)—typically engage in unihemispheric sleep (Manger, 2006; Rattenborg, Amlaner, & Lima, 2000b). Cetaceans exhibit a clear form of unihemispheric slow wave sleep (USWS) or SWS. EEG signs of REM are absent, but cetaceans show other behavioral signs of REM, including REMs, penile erections, and muscle twitching. The two main families of pinnipeds, Otariidae (sea lions and fur seals) and Phocidae (true seals), show both unihemispheric and bihemispheric forms of sleep. Phocids sleep underwater (obviously holding their breath) while both hemispheres exhibit either REM or SWS. Amazonian manatees (*Trichechus inunguis*) also sleep underwater, exhibiting three sleep states: bihemispheric REM, bihemispheric SWS, and USWS. Both hemispheres awaken to surface and breathe.

In addition, when REM occurs in marine mammals, it is always bihemispheric. The bilateral nature of REM may be considered one of its distinctive features, and the brain structure of certain marine mammals apparently cannot mediate this feature. Interestingly, even when REM occurs in aquatic mammals, it never occurs unihemispherically.

Explanations of the loss of EEG signs of REM and the emergence of unihemisphericity of SWS in some aquatic mammals tend to reference the supposed incompatibility of REM-related muscle atonia and breathing while underwater. Yet, as just described, other marine mammals with similar ecologic constraints (e.g., Phocidae) evidence bihemispheric REM sleep even while underwater. Given the alternative means of sleeping and breathing in water observed in pinnipeds, one would expect manatees (order Sirenia) to display either of these strategies. As noted, however, Amazonian manatees (*T. inunguis*) exhibit REM sleep, bihemispheric SWS, and USWS. Thus, unlike that in dolphins and Otariidae, USWS in manatees is not clearly linked to surfacing to breathe. Nor does the relatively advanced nature of the cetacean brain help explain the absence of REM in cetaceans. Other mammals with equally developed brains (such as primates) express abundant REM.

As in birds, unihemispheric sleep in aquatic mammals is associated with keeping one eye open during sleep, which is typically the eye contralateral to the hemisphere that is asleep. Goley (1999; quoted in Rattenborg & Amlaner, 2002) reported that when a group of sleeping Pacific white-sided dolphins (*Lagenorhynchus obliquidens*) swim slowly side-by-side in a group, they preferentially direct the open eye toward the other dolphins, as if watching to maintain contact with the group. Interestingly, when the sleeping dolphins switched, on an hourly basis, from one side of the group to the other, the side with the open eye switched accordingly, as if allowing each hemisphere a turn to sleep. Many male dolphins form coalitions to monopolize access to fertile females (Connor, Smolker, & Richards, 1992). Therefore, the open eye may be monitoring the herded female.

Placental Terrestrial Mammals

Behavioral measures of REM in placental mammals include a species-specific body posture and sleeping site, reduced physical activity (quiescence), reduced muscle tone, reduction in neck/nuchal muscle tone, paralysis of the antigravity muscles in some species, increased arousal threshold, and rapid reversibility to wakefulness. Physiologic indices of REM sleep include significant lability in the autonomic nervous system (ANS), cardiovascular, and respiratory systems, along with increases in metabolism. Electrophysiologic measures of REM include low-voltage fast waves, REMs, theta rhythms in the hippocampus, and pontine-geniculo-occipital (PGO) waves. Electrophysiologic measures of NREM include HVSW, spindles, and k-complexes. Functional indices of sleep include increased amounts of sleep after sleep deprivation, and increased sleep intensity after sleep deprivation.

REM sleep accounts for about 22 percent of total sleep time in adult humans. Humans are about average among placental mammals in the amount of REM sleep they engage in. Although the cortex is activated in REM, arousal thresholds are higher in REM than in the waking state (or in SWS for that matter). The phasic aspects of REM, such as intermittent muscle twitching, ANS discharges, and REM, occur in some mammals in association with bursts of PGO waves. Placental mammals (with the possible exception of humans) also exhibit a theta rhythm in the hippocampal formation during REM. Like NREM sleep, REM deprivation results in a rebound phenomenon, indicating that a certain amount of REM is required and must be made up if lost.

Although REM of placental mammals engages both hemispheres, it respects a very selective pattern of brain activation. Certain brain sites are activated while others are deactivated. Recent positron emission tomography (PET) and functional magnetic resonance imaging (fMRI) studies of the sleeping brain in both humans and nonhuman animals have revealed that REM demonstrates high activation levels in pontine, midbrain tegmentum, portions of the cingulate gyrus, temporal-limbic, and amygdaloid sites, and orbitofrontal cortex. Conversely, other brain regions are deactivated in REM, including dorsolateral prefrontal areas, portions of the parietal cortex, and the cingulate (Braun et al., 1997; Hobson, Stickgold, & Pace-Schott, 1998; Maquet & Franck, 1997; Maquet et al., 1996; Nofzinger, Mintun, Wiseman, Kupfer, & Moore, 1997).

Finally, when human subjects are awakened from REM, they generally report a narrative involving the dreamer, with vivid visual detail, unpleasant emotions, and occasional bizarre and improbable events (Domhoff, 2003; Hobson & Pace-Schott, 2002; Nielsen, 2000; Strauch & Meier, 1996). As mentioned above there is reason to believe that other placental mammals "dream."

The foregoing brief review of the phylogenetic distribution of the two major sleep states suggests that the emergence of distinct sleep states, and in particular of REM, began with the evolution of reptiles and reaches its most derived state in terrestrial placental mammals. Avian REM is peculiar in that it is brief and shows no rebound effects. Nor does Avian NREM show clear rebound effects. Avian NREM furthermore appears to be unihemispheric. Turning now to the reptiles, REM-like sleep states do not occur at all in reptiles. On the other hand, the presence of HVSWs, as well as sharp spikes in the EEG of reptilian sleep, suggests that what is now called SWA in mammals first appeared in reptiles. The fact that some aspects of EEG sleep in reptiles appear to exhibit rebound effects after sleep deprivation supports the argument that some form of SWA is present in reptiles. REM, however, does not occur in reptiles, with the possible exception of the crocodiles. Crocodiles themselves, however, seem to exhibit some behaviors of mammals (like play in the young and care for young). *It thus appears that REM-related mentation experiences—let's call them dreams for the rest of this chapter—appear to be evolutionary innovations of proto-mammalian and mammalian taxa.*

With the appearance of the monotremes, clear signs of REM begin to appear in the EEG, although they are mixed with signs of NREM. Following the evolution of marsupials, clear electrophysiologic signs of REM emerge but they are again partially mixed with NREM, and it is not clear whether one or both sleep states are uni- or bihemispherically expressed. Finally, with the emergence of placental mammals we get the derived state of bihemispheric REM sleep. Recall that our review of comparative patterns of REM expression revealed that REM never occurred in the unihemispheric state. Only NREM or SWA occurred when unihemispheric sleep was present in a species.

We, therefore, tentatively conclude that REM requires bihemispheric activation to occur, and this activation pattern must decisively influence the form of mentation that occurs in REM.

If REM is a uniquely bihemispheric phenomena, then REM sleep may also require a functioning corpus callosum in order to achieve its full expression. The corpus callosum connects the two hemispheres, thereby exponentially increasing brain connectivity and integration relative to unihemispheric functional states (Scamvougeras, Kigar, Jones, Weinberger, & Witelson, 2003). A functioning corpus callosum permits simultaneous bihemispheric activation and all manner of patterns of cross-hemispheric interactions. The corpus callosum is a unique feature of the brain of placental mammals (Aboitiz & Montiel, 2003). Although marsupials evidence enlarged anterior commissures, the corpus callosum is less developed in them than in placentals. Aquatic mammals without REM evidence unique and perhaps reduced (in size) forms of the corpus callosum (Gilissen, 2006). Avian REM, as far as we know, is not strictly analogous to mammalian REM. Nor does avian REM exhibit sleep rebound effects after sleep deprivation (as is the case with mammalian REM). Thus, while bird song appears to be a partially sleep dependent process, it is related to unihemispheric NREM forms of sleep and thus may not be like REM-related forms of mentation at all. The hemispheres in birds are not as densely connected as are the hemispheres in mammals. In birds, for example, there is no structure corresponding to the mammalian corpus callosum. If REM does indeed require bihemispheric activation to occur, it is not surprising then that REM sleep in birds is fleeting. On the other hand, very little is known about this area of research, thus the relation between mammalian REM/dreams to avian unihemispheric NREM mentation processes remains a question for future research.

Bihemispheric REM produces a very special form of mentation or consciousness. Indeed, REM sleep itself has been associated with increased gamma wave frequencies (30–80 Hz)—an index of binding during waking life (Kahn, Pace-Schott, & Hobson, 1997; Llinas & Ribary, 1993). However, while bihemispheric binding appears to be enhanced in REM, anterior-posterior connectivity is impaired in REM. Within REM sleep, gamma frequency oscillations become desynchronized between frontal and posterior perceptual areas (Corsi-Cabrera et al., 2003; Perez-Garci, del-Rio-Portilla, Guevara, Arce, & Corsi-Cabrera, 2001). The picture, therefore, is complex. While REM-related mentation appears to support integration of right-left contributions, REM does not allow for integration of anterior-posterior information sources.

Thus, REM-related mentation experiences are the expression of intense activation of the limbic and amygdalar centers as well as integration of right-left hemispheric sources, along with de-synchrony in frontal-parietal areas. The monotremes were the first to experiment with binding across the hemispheres, but the marsupials and terrestrial placental mammals developed it more fully. Bihemispheric integration of information is most fully expressed in the primate line and of course in humans. This bihemispheric integration of information processing resources yields additional computational power and new emergent forms of attentional capacities (Banich, 2003). When coupled with anterior-posterior de-synchrony or disconnection, bihemispheric cross-talk produces the new form of consciousness we call dreams. The purpose of this new form of consciousness is still unknown.

REFERENCES

Aboitiz, F., & Montiel, J. (2003). One hundred million years of interhemispheric communication: The history of the corpus callosum. *Brazilian Journal of Medical and Biological Research, 36,* 409–420.

Affanni, J. M., Vaccarezza, O. L., & Abellone, J. C. (1967). Difference in electrical activity during wakefulness and the phase of 'sleep with muscular twitches' as recorded from the cortex of the marsupial *Didelphis azarae* (South American opossum). *Experientia, 23,* 216–217.

Allison, T., Van Twyver, H., & Goff, W. R. (1972). Electrophysiological studies of the echidna, *Tachyglossus aculeatus*. I. Waking and Sleep. *Archives of Italian Biology, 110,* 145–184.

Banich, M. T. (2003). Interaction between the hemispheres and its implications for the processing capacity of the brain. In K. Hugdahl, & R. J. Davidson (Eds.), *The asymmetrical brain* (pp. 261–302). Cambridge: The MIT Press.

Berger, R. J. (1990). Relations between sleep duration, body-weight and metabolic rate in mammals. *Animal Behavior, 40,* 989–991.

Blomberg, S. P., & Garland, T. (2002). Tempo and mode in evolution: Phylogenetic inertia, adaptation and comparative methods. *Journal of Evolutionary Biology, 15,* 899–910.

Braun, A. R., Balkin, T. J., Wesenstein, N. J., Varga, M., Baldwin, P., Selbie, S., et al. (1997). Regional cerebral blood flow throughout the sleep-wake cycle. *Brain, 120,* 1173–1197.

Campbell, S. S., & Tobler, I. (1984). Animal sleep: A review of sleep duration across phylogeny. *Neuroscience & Biobehavioral Reviews, 8,* 269–300.

Cicala, G. A., Albert, I. B., & Ulmer, F. A., Jr. (1970). Sleep and other behaviors of the red kangaroo (*Megaleia rufa*). *Animal Behavior, 18,* 787–790.

Connor, R. C., Smolker, R. A., & Richards, A. F. (1992). Two levels of alliance formation among male bottlenose dolphins (*Tursiops* sp.). *Proceedings of the National Academy of Sciences, 89,* 987–990.

Corsi-Cabrera, M., Miro, E., del-Rio-Portilla, Y., Perez-Garci, E., Villanueva, Y., & Guevara, M. A. (2003). Rapid eye movement sleep dreaming is characterized by uncoupled EEG activity between frontal and perceptual cortical regions. *Brain & Cognition, 51,* 337–345.

Dave, A. S., & Margoliash, D. (2000). Song replay during sleep and computation rules for sensorimotor vocal learning. *Science, 290,* 812–816.

Deregnacourt, S., Mitra, P. P., Feher, O., Pytte, C., & Tchernichovski, O. (2005). How sleep affects the developmental learning of bird song. *Nature, 433,* 710–716.

Domhoff, G. W. (2003). *The scientific study of dreams: Neural networks, cognitive development, and content analysis.* Washington, DC: American Psychological Association.

Elgar, M. A., Pagel, M. D., & Harvey, P. H. (1988). Sleep in mammals. *Animal Behavior, 36,* 1407–1419.

Elgar, M. A., Pagel, M. D., & Harvey, P. H. (1990). Sources of variation in mammalian sleep. *Animal Behaviour, 40,* 991–995.

Flanigan, W. F. (1973). Sleep and wakefulness in iguanid lizards, *Ctenosaura pectina. Brain, Behavior & Evolution, 8,* 401–436.

Frank, M. G. (1999). Phylogeny and evolution of rapid eye movement (REM) sleep. In B. N. Mallick & S. Inoue (Eds.), *Rapid eye movement sleep* (pp. 15–38). New Delhi, India: Narosa Publishing House.

Gilissen, E. (2006). Scaling patterns of interhemispheric connectivity in eutherian mammals. *Behavioral & Brain Sciences, 29,* 16–18.

Goley, P. D. (1999). Behavioral aspects of sleep in Pacific whitesided dolphins (*Lagenorhynchus obliquidens*, Gill 1865). *Marine Mammal Science, 15,* 1054–1064.

Hartse, K. M. (1994). Sleep in insects and nonmammalian vertebrates. In M. H. Kryger, T. Roth, & W. C. Dement (Eds.), *Principles and practice of sleep medicine* (2nd ed., pp. 95–104). Philadelphia, PA: W. B. Saunders.

Harvey, P. H., & Pagel, M. D. (1991). *The comparative method in evolutionary biology.* Oxford: Oxford University Press.

Hobson, J. A., & Pace-Schott, E. F. (2002). The cognitive neuroscience of sleep: Neuronal systems, consciousness and learning. *Nature Reviews Neuroscience, 3,* 679–693.

Hobson, J. A., Pace-Schott, E. F., & Stickgold, R. (2000). Dreaming and the brain: Toward a cognitive neuroscience of conscious states. *Behavioral & Brain Sciences, 23,* 793–842.

Hobson, J. A., Stickgold, R., & Pace-Schott, E. F. (1998). The neuropsychology of REM sleep dreaming. *Neuroreport, 9,* R1–R14.

Jouvet, M. (1999). *The paradox of sleep: The story of dreaming.* Cambridge, MA: MIT Press.

Jouvet, D., Vimont, P., Delorme, F., & Jouvet, M. (1964). [Study of selective deprivation of the paradoxical sleep phase in the cat]. *Comptes Rendus des Seances de la Societe de Biology et de ses Filiales, 158,* 756–759.

Kahn, D., Pace-Schott, E. F., & Hobson, J. A. (1997). Consciousness in waking and dreaming: The roles of neuronal oscillation and neuromodulation in determining similarities and differences. *Neuroscience, 78,* 13–38.

Llinas, R., & Ribary, U. (1993). Coherent 40-Hz oscillation characterizes dream state in humans. *Proceedings of the National Academy of Sciences of the United States of America, 90,* 2078–2081.

Mahowald, M. W., & Schenck, C. H. (2000). REM sleep parasomnias. In M. H. Kryger, T. Roth, & W. C. Dement (Eds.), *Principles and practice of sleep medicine* (3rd ed., pp. 724–741). Philadelphia, PA: Saunders.

Manger, P. R. (2006). An examination of cetacean brain structure with a novel hypothesis correlating thermogenesis to the evolution of a big brain. *Biological Reviews, 81,* 293–338.

Maquet, P., & Franck, G. (1997). REM sleep and amygdala. *Molecular Psychiatry, 2,* 195–196.

Maquet, P., Peters, J. M., Aerts, J., Delfiore, G., Degueldre, C., Luxen, A., et al. (1996). Functional neuroanatomy of human rapid-eye-movement sleep and dreaming. *Nature, 383,* 163–166.

Nicol, S. C., Andersen, N. A., Phillips, N. H., & Berger, R. J. (2000). The echidna manifests typical characteristics of rapid eye movement sleep. *Neuroscience Letters, 283,* 49–52.

Nielsen, T. A. (2000). A review of mentation in REM and NREM sleep: "Covert" REM sleep as a possible reconciliation of two opposing models. *Behavioral & Brain Sciences, 23,* 851–866.

Nofzinger, E. A., Mintun, M. A., Wiseman, M. B., Kupfer, D. J., & Moore, R. Y. (1997). Forebrain activation in REM sleep: An FDG PET study. *Brain Research, 770,* 192–201.

Nunn, C. L., & Barton, R. A. (2000). Allometric slopes and independent contrasts: A comparative study of Kleiber's law in primate ranging patterns. *American Naturalist, 156,* 519–533.

Nunn, C. L., & Barton, R. A. (2001). Comparative methods for studying primate adaptation and allometry. *Evolutionary Anthropology, 10,* 81–98.

Olson, E. J., Boeve, B. F., & Silber, M. H. (2000). Rapid eye movement sleep behaviour disorder: Demographic, clinical and laboratory findings in 93 cases. *Brain, 123,* 331–339.

Perez-Garci, E., del-Rio-Portilla, Y., Guevara, M. A., Arce, C., & Corsi-Cabrera, M. (2001). Paradoxical sleep is characterized by uncoupled gamma activity between frontal and perceptual cortical regions. *Sleep, 24*, 118–126.

Rattenborg, N. C., & Amlaner, C. J. (2002). Phylogeny of sleep. In T. L. Lee-Chiong, M. J. Sateia, & M. A. Carskadon (Eds.), *Sleep medicine* (pp. 7–22). Philadelphia, PA: Hanley & Belfus.

Rattenborg, N. C., Amlaner, C. J., & Lima, S. L. (2000a). Unihemispheric slow-wave sleep and predator detection in the pigeon (*Columbia livia*). *Sleep, 23*(Suppl. 1), A43–A44.

Rattenborg, N. C., Amlaner, C. J., & Lima, S. L. (2000b). Behavioral, neurophysiological and evolutionary perspectives on unihemispheric sleep. *Neuroscience & Biobehavioral Reviews, 24*, 817–842.

Revonsuo, A. (2000). The reinterpretation of dreams: An evolutionary hypothesis of the function of dreaming. *Behavioral & Brain Sciences, 23*, 877–901.

Rial, R., Nicolau, M. C., Lopez-Garcia, J. A., & Almirall, H. (1993). On the evolution of waking and sleeping. *Comparative Biochemistry & Physiology. Comparative Physiology, 104*, 189–193.

Scamvougeras, A., Kigar, D. L., Jones, D., Weinberger, D. R., & Witelson, S. F. (2003). Size of the human corpus callosum is genetically determined: An MRI study in mono and dizygotic twins. *Neuroscience Letters, 338*, 91–94.

Siegel, J. M., Manger, P. R., Nienhuis, R., Fahringer, H. M., & Pettigrew, J. D. (1996). The echidna *Tachyglossus aculeatus* combines REM and non-REM aspects in a single sleep state: Implications for the evolution of sleep. *Journal of Neuroscience, 16*, 3500–3506.

Strauch, I., & Meier, B. (1996). *In search of dreams: Results of experimental dream research*. Albany, NY: State University of New York Press.

Tobler, I. (2005). Phylogeny of sleep regulation. In M. Kryger, T. Roth, & W. Dement (Eds.), *Principles and practice of sleep medicine* (pp. 77–90). Philadelphia, PA: Saunders.

Van Twyver, H., & Allison, T. (1970). Sleep in the opossum *Didelphis marsupialis*. *Electroencephalography & Clinical Neurophysiology, 29*, 181–189.

Walker, J. M., & Berger, R. J. (1980). Sleep as an adaptation for energy conservation functionally related to hibernation and shallow torpor. *Progress in Brain Research, 53*, 255–278.

Zepelin, H. (1989). Mammalian sleep. In M. H. Kryger, T. Roth, & W. C. Dement (Eds.), *Principles and practices of sleep medicine* (pp. 81–92). Philadelphia, PA: Saunders.

Zepelin, H. (1994). Mammalian sleep. In W. C. Dement (Ed.), *Principles and practice of sleep medicine*. (2nd ed., pp. 30–48). Philadelphia, PA: Saunders.

Three

Current Understanding of Cellular Models of REM Expression

J. Allan Hobson

In 1895, when Sigmund Freud first considered the prospects of a science of the mind, he hoped to base his theory upon the solid base of neurobiology (Freud, 1895). Because that base did not exist, he turned his attention to what he claimed was a purely psychological approach and developed his disguise-censorship theory of dreams, which became the cornerstone of psychoanalytic theory (Freud, 1900/1965). Throughout the rest of his life, Freud denied the usefulness of neurobiological data despite the fact that he explicitly predicted that ultimately all of his assertions would need to be tested at the level of brain science.

Now, over 100 years later, many of the neurobiological facts that Freud needed have become available, yet their interpretation is highly controversial. Writers like Mark Solms favor revision and retention of the psychoanalytic model (Solms, 1997, 2000, 2004). In this and the following chapter, I will argue for discarding the psychoanalytic model altogether. The point of this entry is not only to cast doubt on Freud's view, but to express skepticism about any and all interpretation schemes that view dream content as symbolic expression of deep personal conflict. I will also cast doubt on the idea that dream content is interpretable with anything approaching scientific validity.

My position is not that dreams are meaningless. I certainly do not deny that dreaming is characterized by content of emotional salience. But, in contrast to Freud's dream theory, I hold that emotional salience can easily be detected and understood by careful dream documentation (Hobson, 2004). This view, which I call the transparency tenet of the activation synthesis theory of dreaming (Hobson & McCarley, 1977), is so different from Freud's disguise-synthesis model as to force a choice. Instead of viewing dreaming as obscure and with disguised meaning as Freud maintained, I argue that dreams are undisguised and hence revelatory. I will review the cellular neurophysiology in those terms to make it clear to the reader why at least one contemporary dream scientist views the Freudian model as hopelessly outdated, misleading, and, therefore, dispensable.

SLEEP NEUROPHYSIOLOGY AND NEURONAL ACTIVITY

The pioneers of the single cell recording technique had a strong interest in sleep because, like Charles Sherrington, they did not appreciate that consciousness could be lost with only a 20 percent decrease in neuronal activity (in early night NREM sleep) and that subsequent reactivation of the brain brought the still sleeping brain back up to waking levels of activation (in late night REM sleep). Positron emission tomography (PET) studies have since clearly shown that the REM activation was selective, not universal: some forebrain and brainstem structures were more active than in waking while a few were less so (Braun et al. 1997; Maquet et al. 1996; Nofzinger, Mintum, Wiseman, Kupfer, & Moore, 1997).

When, at Herbert Jasper's instance, David Hubel first succeeded in recording single cells in the visual cortex of anaesthetized cats, he found that as many neurons became more active in sleep as became inactive (Hubel & Wiesel, 1959). Because the data required statistical analysis, Hubel turned his attention to the visual system of his cats when awake and with Torsten Wiesel showed how the signals from the retina were translated by the visual thalamus (the lateral geniculate body) and how those signals were in turn, translated by the visual cortex areas (V_1 and V_2). These findings, for which Hubel and Wiesel were awarded the Nobel Prize, are of great relevance to the study of the neuronal basis of dreaming. In our dreams, we see quite clearly despite the fact that our eyes are closed. This fact implies that the visual system must be internally activated in sleep.

The second assault on neuronal activity in sleep was mounted by Edward Evarts, who was primarily interested in the motor system (Evarts, 1962). En route to developing his famous trained-monkey single cell test system, Evarts solved the statistical problems that Hubel had side-stepped. Evarts also showed that some of his precentral cortical neurons could be identified as motoric by antidromic activation from the pyramidal tract in the medulla. Such neurons fired less actively and less regularly in NREM sleep than they did in waking. They then discharged in intense bursts during REM sleep. In proposing that his results could be explained as a product of neuronal reactivation via disinhibition, Evarts was the first to propose a cellular level theory of sleep.

NEURAL ACTIVITY OF THE SUBCORTICAL BRAIN

The EEG recording, ablation, and stimulation studies in cats performed by Michel Jouvet revealed several phenomena of interest to the neurobiology of sleep with special reference to REM sleep and dreaming (Jouvet, 1962). (1) The NREM–REM sleep cycle of the cat appeared to be programmed by a neuronal mechanism in the pontine brainstem. (2) The pontine brainstem activated the forebrain in REM sleep, and there was intermittent phasic activation of the visual thalamus and cortex associated with the REMs, in addition to the tonic activation that operated throughout REM sleep. (3) In REM sleep, both sensory input and motor output were suppressed. The sensory blockade was caused by presynaptic inhibition of the IA afferent fibers from sense organs in skin and muscle to the spinal cord, while the motor blockade was caused by strong postsynaptic inhibition of the anterior horn cells (Pompeiano, 1967).

After first focusing on the cholinergic system, Jouvet later postulated that the differential chemical modulation of the activated brain was effected by norepinephrine (from the locus coeruleus) and serotonin (from the raphe nuclei) (Jouvet, 1969). He also demonstrated that the decerebrated "pontine cat" was able to make eye movements and inhibit its muscle tone with a periodicity and duration similar to that of REM sleep. The stage was thus set for a neuronal analysis of the pontine brainstem itself.

THE RECIPROCAL INTERACTION MODEL

By modifying the Hubel-Evarts movable micromanipulation technique and by introducing a head restraint system, Allan Hobson and Robert McCarley were able to record from single neurons in the pontine brainstem of cats for several successive NREM–REM sleep cycles (see Figure 3.1).

Hobson and McCarley first reported that the large neurons of the pontine reticular formation discharged selectively in REM. They called those neurons REM-on cells and proposed that they were cholinergic. While characterizing the REM-on neurons, they discovered, by accident, that there were also REM-off cells in the pontine tegmentum (Hobson, McCarley, & Wyzinki, 1975). To their surprise, they were located in the locus coeruleus and dorsal raphe nucleus. They then proposed that the sleep cycle was caused by reciprocal interaction between the cholinergic REM-on cells of the paramedian pontine reticular formation and the aminergic REM-off cells in the locus coeruleus and raphe nuclei.

FIGURE 3.1

Location and discharge properties of D-off and D-on cells. The first four cells (D-off) were localized to the posterior pole of the LC (559, 560, 561) and the nucleus subcoeruleus (562). The last three cells (D-on) were localized to the FTG (563, 566, 567). The time course of discharge rate change at D onset (vertical line) is shown to be reciprocal for the negatively inflected cumulative histograms of the D-off cells and the positively inflected D-on data. Note that the behavior in the cells was consistent in repeated cycles for cells 559, 561, 562, and 566.

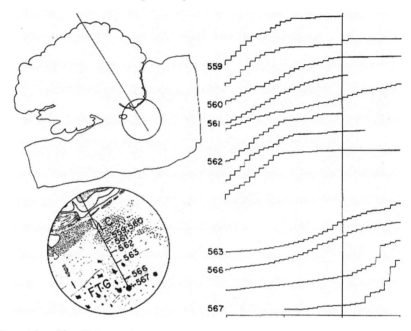

Source: Adapted from Hobson et al., 1975.

When activity of the aminergic REM-off cells was maximal, the animal was awake. After an epoch of NREM sleep, the REM generator was released from inhibition, and REM was produced (Hobson et al., 1975; McCarley & Hobson, 1975).

THE ACTIVATION-SYNTHESIS MODEL OF REM SLEEP DREAMING

Within two years of their enunciation of the reciprocal interaction model of sleep cycle control, Hobson and McCarley suggested that dreaming occurred when the brain was activated in sleep (Hobson & McCarley, 1977). The activation could be residual (as at sleep onset) or circadian (as in late night NREM sleep) but was most likely to occur in REM sleep when brain activation caused subjectively vivid dreams. They suggested that it was the motivationally neutral brain activation of sleep (and not Freud's repressed infantile wishes) that caused dreaming.

On the sensorimotor side, the hallucinoid percepts of dreams were attributed to endogenous activation of the deafferented visual system, while the perception of movement was attributed to endogenous activation of the output-blocked motor system. The strong and stereotyped emotions (anxiety, elation, and anger) were attributed to endogenous activation of the limbic system.

On the cognitive side, the loss of self-reflective awareness, the loss of memory, and the bizarre images of dreams were ascribed to the chaotic nature of the neuronal activation process and aminergic demodulation. Now we know from PET studies that there is also deactivation of the dorsolateral prefrontal cortex in REM sleep. The dorsolateral prefrontal cortex is the seat of executive ego functions. As described by neuropsychologists, those functions include self-reflective awareness, voluntary agency, and metacognition, all of which are diminished in dreaming. (For reviews, see Hobson, Stickgold, & Pace-Schott, 1998, and Hobson, Pace-Schott, & Stickgold, 2000.)

REVISIONS OF THE RECIPROCAL INTERACTION MODEL

The original attribution of cholinergic neuromodulation to the REM-on cells of the pontine reticular formation (PRF) was incorrect. Those neurons turned out to be glutamatergic. Furthermore, the apparent REM discharge selectivity of the large paramedion reticular cells was a function of the head restraint required to allow long-term recording. In free-moving cats, the putative REM-on cells fired in waking with movement. They are thus thought to play a nonspecific role in the REM activation process but contribute to the continuous sense of movement in dreams.

Selective tonic REM-on cells were described by Sakai in the subcoereleus region of the pontine reticular formation (Sakai & Koyama, 1996). This REM-specific discharge was strongly correlated with the muscle tone inhibition of REM. Selective REM-on neuronal firing was also found in the peribrachial region of the pons, where the neurons were mixed with the truly cholinergic neurons of that region. Because they fired in advance of ipsiversive eye movements and PGO waves, they were called PGO burst cells (Nelson, McCarley, & Hobson, 1983), and their encoding of eye movement direction was a feature of possible relevance to the activation-synthesis hypothesis that visual image production by the forebrain was, in part, a bottom-up process. The chaotic, quasi-random firing of the PGO burst cells could thus contribute to dream discontinuity and incongruity.

The revised model, shown in Figure 3.2, is complicated but formally similar to the original reciprocal interaction proposal. The neuropharmacological

FIGURE 3.2

The original reciprocal interaction model of NREM-REM alternation and the subsequent revision of this model to reflect the findings of self-inhibitory cholinergic autoreceptors in the mesopontine cholinergic nuclei, and excitatory interactions between mesopontine cholinergic and non-cholinergic neurons.

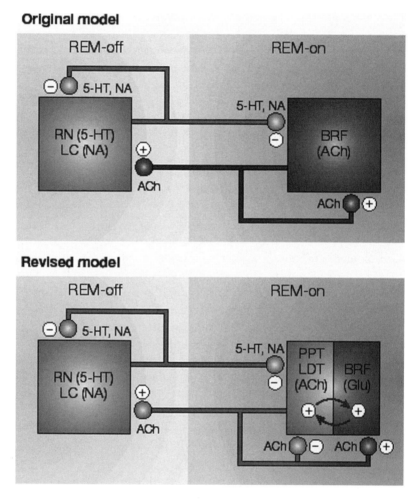

tests of the cholinergic tenet of the model, which are reviewed in more detail in Chapter 5, showed clearly that REM sleep, and the dreaming associated with it, could be experimentally controlled by artificial excitation. This goes a long way to affirming Freud's prediction that the instigation of dreaming might be chemically determined but raises questions about the role, if any, of unconscious infantile wishes in the process of dream production.

BRAIN-MIND ISOMORPHISM AND DREAMING

Similarity of form, or isomorphism, is an important philosophical assumption of Freud's early works and of our own research on REM sleep at the cellular level. Activation synthesis has made an important distinction between dream form and dream content. For example, such formal qualities of dreams as the hallucinatory percepts (and their sensory and motor properties) and the delusional beliefs (along with impairment of analytic thought), the bizarre cognition, the memory loss, and the confabulation of dreaming have been explained in neurobiological terms.

So far, so good—but what about the content? Isn't it possible that while the formal properties of dreams may be appreciated and correctly explained by neurobiology, the meaning of dream content may nonetheless be cognitively veiled justifying interpretive investigation using free association or some related method to uncover unconscious motivations in dreams?

Science can never conclusively prove a negative. It can only offer more attractive and concise alternatives. To that end, the activation synthesis of dreaming asserts that dreams are emotionally salient and are thus worthy of psychological attention, but that dreams do not require complex decoding to reveal their significance. As evidence for these claims, take the finding that dream emotion is never bizarre (Merritt, Stickgold, Pace-Schott, Williams, & Hobson, 1994). It always maps well on to dream cognition even when that cognition is in itself bizarre (Hobson, Hoffman, Helfand, & Kostner, 1987). To understand this paradox, consider the familiar anxiety dream when incongruous and discontinuous aspects of the plot all fit quite well with the emotion. One implication is that emotion, once triggered, is a driving force of dream plot construction and that the forebrain responds by pulling out all its cognitive associates despite the looseness of the associations that link those cognitive elements together.

The transparency tenet of the activation-synthesis dream theory says that yes, there is emotional salience in dreams but, no, the emotion is not concealed. Rather it is revealed and there for the taking. It is not just the "manifest" content as Freud assumed, it is the so-called "latent" content too. To discard, overlook, or otherwise devalue the emotionally salient cognition of dreams is perverse and counterproductive. Dreams are scenarios filled with anxiety, elation, and anger. These are among the robust facts of dream life that Freud's model cannot account for!

Having said that, I do not wish to imply that dreaming is uniquely qualified to reveal such concerns. They may be equally accessible in waking life. This is because all three of dreaming's most prevalent emotions are of the utmost importance to our survival and reproductive success. Following Darwin, it can be proposed that anxiety and aggression are both in the service of survival and that elation and aggression may be both in the service of procreation via mate-finding and mate-holding. That such scenarios should be played out in dreams, just as they are in waking life, is not altogether surprising because the brain, including the limbic system, is automatically activated in REM sleep.

RECENT DEVELOPMENTS IN CELLULAR LEVEL MODELING

Reciprocal interaction could not say why its expression was sleep dependent, because the way in which the pontine NREM–REM oscillator was linked to the circadian clock in the suprachiasmatic nucleus was unknown. The recent work of Clifford Saper and his colleagues (Saper, Chou, & Scammell, 2001) has filled this gap and also amplified the findings regarding REM-off cells. The hypothalamus, known to be the locus of the suprachiasmatic nucleus, and nearby areas of the diencephalon have frustrated previous workers because of the multiplicity of small, presumably specialized nuclei composed of small neurons that are difficult to identify and, record. By using a combination of innovative anatomical and physiological methods the existence of two flip-flop switches has been postulated. One constitutes a sleep-wake switch, the other a REM sleep switch.

As a first step, Sherin, Elmquist, Torrealba, and Saper (1998) showed that the histamine-containing cells of the tuberomammillary nucleus shared the REM-off pattern of locus coeruleus) norepinephrine (LC [NE]) and dorsal raphe nucleus (DRN) (serotonin; 5-HT) neurons. Since they project directly to the cortex, these monominergic neurons, together with the dopamine neurons of the substantia nigra, constitute a unified system of activation during waking. As far as dream theory is concerned, it is important to emphasize that the differences from waking are the cessation of firing in REM sleep of the LC (NE), DRN serotonin (SHT) and tubero-mammillary nucleus histamine (TMN [HA]) groups). The Ach and dopamine (DA) systems are both active in both waking and REM. Specific psychological features (such as the memory loss in dreaming) must therefore be attributable to the demodulation of monocinergic, serotonergic, and histaminergic systems and not to dopamine or acetylcholine.

THE FLIP-FLOP SWITCH

In Saper's model, waking is mediated by the LC, the raphe nucleus (RN), and TMN, whereas sleep is mediated by the ventrolateral preoptic nucleus

(VLPO). Because they are mutually inhibitory, either the one is on while the other is off, or the one is off while the other is on. Stabilization of the switch is provided by a newly discovered group of cells in the lateral hypothalamus (LHA) that secrete orexin. They activate the monoaminergic neurons that mediate waking. It has been shown by Mignot and Nishino (1999) that patients with narcolepsy have a genetic defect in this switch-stabilizing system. Diagnostic of narcolepsy are the sleep onset REM periods with intense dreaming and hypnogogic hallucinations. These findings further reinforce the hypothesis that it is the change in brain activity from wake to REM that underlies hallucinoid dreaming.

THE NEW NEUROPSYCHOLOGY OF SLEEP

Although PET and MRI methods measure regional changes in neuronal activity even if the method cannot resolve single cells, the overall neuronal activity of most regions of the brain is relatively reduced in NREM sleep compared to waking or REM (Figure 3.3). And almost all brain regions show equally high levels of neuronal activation in wake and REM. Some are higher in REM (the pons, the amygdala, the parietal operculum, the deep frontal white matter, and the parahippocampal cortex). These areas are relevant to the activation-synthesis theory of dreams since they are compatible with (a) the pons as the source of REM sleep brain activation and (b) the limbic system as the source of dream emotion.

The one brain area that remains as inactive in REM as it is in NREM sleep is the dorsolateral prefrontal cortex (DLPFC). The DLPFC is thought to be the source of such executive ego functions as working memory, self-reflective awareness, and voluntary action. All of these functions are deficient in dreaming, possibly because their brain basis is disabled in REM sleep.

AIM—A THREE-DIMENSIONAL STATE SPACE MODEL

Building upon the cellular, molecular, and electrophysiological discoveries of basic sleep research, it is now possible to create a three-dimensional state space model of the brain-mind (see Figure 3.4, a and b). The x-axis of the model quantifies the level of activation A. The z-axis of the model measures the state of input-output gating of the system. When sensory inputs and motor outputs are maximal, axis I values are high. When they are blocked (and endogenous inputs supervene), axis I values are low. The y-axis carries values of modulation, M, given by the ratio or aminergic to cholinergic drive.

The waking domain is characterized by high values of A, I, and M. It is, therefore, located in the right, upper-rear corner of the state space.

FIGURE 3.3

Summary of PET study evidence of brain region activation in NREM and REM sleep. Compared to the blood flow distribution in waking (a), the global decreases observed in NREM sleep (b) suggest widespread deactivation consistent with the greatly diminished capacity of conscious experience early in the night. In REM sleep (c), many regions are activated about their levels in waking (solid black) while others are deactivated (shaded).

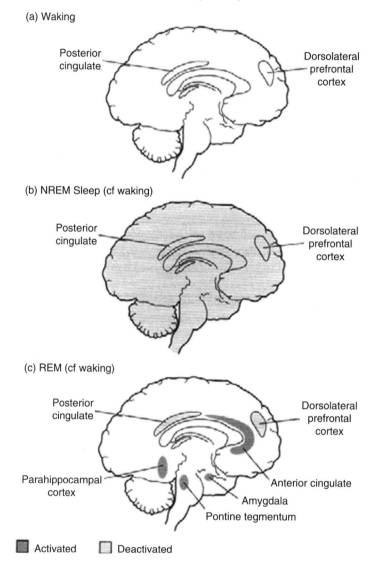

(a) Waking

Posterior cingulate

Dorsolateral prefrontal cortex

(b) NREM Sleep (cf waking)

Posterior cingulate

Dorsolateral prefrontal cortex

(c) REM (cf waking)

Posterior cingulate

Dorsolateral prefrontal cortex

Parahippocampal cortex

Anterior cingulate

Amygdala

Pontine tegmentum

■ Activated   ▨ Deactivated

FIGURE 3.4a
Three-dimensional representation of the model. Activation (A) varies from low to high on the x-axis. Input-output gates (I) run from closed to open along the z-axis. The modulatory (M) ratio runs from low to high aminergic on the y-axis.

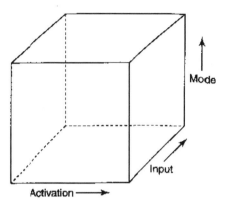

FIGURE 3.4b
Four-dimensional representation of the model. The domains of waking, NREM, and REM sleep are indicated and the elliptical cycle that links them is shown. The cycle repeats itself four to five times a night.

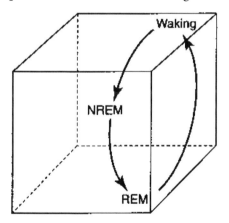

The NREM sleep domain is in the center of the state space because the values of A, I, and M have all declined to about 50 percent of the waking values.

In REM sleep, the value of A has gone back to wake state levels while both I and M are at their lowest points. As a consequence, the REM domain is like waking, to the right, but, in sharp contrast to waking, it is in the lower and front corner of the state space.

In normal sleep, the brain-mind follows an elliptical trajectory through the state space. Successive NREM-REM cycles (1,2,3, and 4) are displaced in the wake-REM direction as the circadian influence is more and more powerfully expressed. Dreaming is mostly like to occur at sleep onset (when residual activation is high and when I and M are falling) and in late night NREM (as activation level rises); dreaming is maximal in REM (when activation level is highest) and I and M are at their lowest values.

SUMMARY AND CONCLUSION

The cellular and molecular models of modern sleep research constitute the brain basis of a theory that ascribes such formal dream features as sensorimotor hallucinosis, delusional errors of state identification, emotional intensification, and memory loss to natural and universal changes in brain neurobiology. The new theory accounts for all of the dream features that Freud sought to explain with his disguise censorship model. It facilitates and simplifies the interpretive task by eliminating the distinction between manifest and latent content. By asserting that dream content is emotionally salient on its face and aligning that fact with Darwinian biology, the new theory also solves a problem that baffled Freud: that of explaining why the affect of many dreams is negative.

REFERENCES

Braun, A. R., Balkin, T. J., Wesensten, N. J., Carson, R. E., Varga, M., Baldwin, P., et al. (1997). Regional cerebral blood flow throughout the sleep-wake cycle. *Brain 120*, 1173–1197.

Evarts, E. V. (1962). Activity of neurons in visual cortex of the cat during sleep with low voltage fast EEG activity. *Journal of Neurophysiology, 25,* 812–816.

Freud, S. (1895). Project for a scientific psychology. In M. Bonaparte, A. Freud, & E. Kris (Eds.), *The origins of psychoanalysis. Letters to Wilhelm Fleiss, drafts and notes: 1887–1902.* Basic Books.

Freud, S. (1965). *The interpretation of dreams* (J. Strachey, Trans.). New York: Avon Books. (Original work published 1900)

Hobson, J. A. (2004). *13 dreams Freud never had.* New York: Pearson Press.

Hobson, J. A., Hoffman, E., Helfand, R., & Kostner, D. (1987). Dream bizarreness and the activation-synthesis hypothesis. *Human Neurobiology, 6,* 157–164.

Hobson, J. A., & McCarley, R. W. (1977). The brain as a dream-state generator: An activation-synthesis hypothesis of the dream process. *American Journal of Psychiatry, 134,* 1335–1348.

Hobson, J. A., McCarley, R. W., & Wyzinki, P. W. (1975). Sleep cycle oscillation: Reciprocal discharge by two brainstem neuronal groups. *Science, 189,* 55–58.

Hobson, J. A., Pace-Schott, E. F., & Stickgold, R. (2000). Dreaming and the brain: Toward a cognitive neuroscience of conscious states. *Behavioral & Brain Sciences, 23,* 793–842.

Hobson, J. A., Stickgold, R., & Pace-Schott, E. F. (1998). The neuropsychology of REM sleep dreaming. *NeuroReport, 9,* R1–R14.

Hubel, D. H., & Wiesel, T. N. (1959). Receptive fields of single neurones in the cat's striate cortex. *Journal of Physiology, 148,* 574–591.

Jouvet, M. (1962). Recherche sur les structures nerveuses et les mechanismes responsables des differentes phases du sommeil physiologique [Research on the brain structure and mechanisms responsible for the different phases of physiological sleep]. *Archives Italiennes de Biologie, 100,* 125–206.

Jouvet, M. (1969). Biogenic amines and the states of sleep. *Science, 163,* 32–41.

Maquet, P., Peters J. M., Aerts, J., Delfiore, G., Degueldre, C., Luxen, A., et al. (1996). Functional neuroanatomy of human rapid-eye-movement sleep and dreaming. *Nature, 383,* 163–166.

McCarley, R. W., & Hobson, J. A. (1975). Discharge patterns of cat pontine brain stem neurons during desynchronized sleep. *Journal of Neurophysiology, 38,* 751–766.

Merritt, J. M., Stickgold, R., Pace-Schott, E., Williams, J., & Hobson, J. A. (1994). Emotion profiles in the dreams of men and women. *Consciousness & Cognition, 3,* 46–60.

Mignot, E., & Nishino, S. (1999). Narcolepsy. In R. Lydic & H. A. Baghdoyan (Eds.), *Handbook of behavioral state control: Molecular and cellular mechanisms* (Section 2, pp. 129–142). Boca Raton, FL: CRC Press.

Nelson, J. P., McCarley, R. W., & Hobson, J. A. (1983). REM sleep burst neurons, PGO waves, and eye movement information. *Journal of Neurophysiology, 50,* 784–797.

Nofzinger, E. A., Mintun, M. A., Wiseman, M. B., Kupfer, D. J., & Moore, R. Y. (1997). Forebrain activation in REM sleep: An FDG PET study. *Brain Research, 770,* 192–201.

Pompeiano, O. (1967). The neurobiological mechanisms of the postural and motor events during desynchronized sleep. *Proceedings of the Association for Research of Nervous Mental Disorders, 45,* 351–423.

Sakai, K., & Koyama, Y. (1996). Are there cholinergic and non-cholinergic paradoxical sleep-on neurons in the pons? *NeuroReport, 7,* 2449–2453.

Saper, C. B., Chou, T. C., & Scammell, T. E. (2001). The sleep switch: Hypothalamic control of sleep and wakefulness. *Trends in Neurosciences, 24,* 726–731.

Sherin, J. E., Elmquist, J. K., Torrealba, F., & Saper, C. B. (1998). Innervation of histaminergic tuberomammillary neurons by GABAergic and galininergic neurons in the ventrolateral preoptic nucleus of the rat. *The Journal of Neuroscience, 18,* 4705–4721.

Solms, M. (1997). *The neuropsychology of dreams: A clinico-anatomical study.* Mahwah, NJ: Lawrence Erlbaum.

Solms, M. (2000). Dreaming and REM sleep are controlled by different brain mechanisms. *Behavioral & Brain Sciences, 23,* 843–850.

Solms, M. (2004). Reply to Domhoff: Dream research in the court of public opinion. *Dreaming: Journal of the Association for the Study of Dreams, 14,* 18–20.

Four

Drugs and Dreams

J. Allan Hobson

Most of the prescription and recreational drugs that effect dreaming act on the brainstem generators (or inhibitors) or REM sleep (Hobson, 2001, 2002). Instead of referring immediately to classes of drugs and discussing their effects on dreaming, I will first discuss the principles of brain state neuropharmacology so as to create a framework for understanding drug effects.

For details of the neurobiology, the reader is referred to Chapter 4, the entry on cellular and molecular mechanisms or REM sleep generators. An overriding assumption is that REM sleep is the principle physiological substrate of dreaming and that such dreaming, as does occur outside that state, is produced by REM-like brain mechanisms (Nielsen, 1999).

REM SLEEP AND DREAMING

Dreaming occurs in sleep whenever the cortex is sufficiently activated to generate internal perceptions and the input-output gates of the brain are sufficiently closed to preserve sleep in the face of internal brain activation. The most favorable state for dreaming is REM sleep when internal brain activation is strong and the input-output gates are closed. In REM sleep, the cortex is also aminergically demodulated (which reverses its activation state from that of waking). It is simultaneously cholinergically and dopaminergically modulated (just as it is in waking). Dreaming also occurs at sleep onset when residual cortical activation supports fleeting dream generation. At sleep onset the input-output gates are rapidly closing and aminergic modulation is declining. Dreaming is far less likely to occur in NREM Stages III and IV of the first two cycles of the night because of strong cortical deactivation. Later in the night, when the circadian clock raises the level of activation, dreaming occurs in NREM Stages II sleep but it is never as frequent, prolonged, or intense as in REM sleep regardless if time of night effects (Fosse, Stickgold, & Hobson, 2004).

THE NEUROPHARMACOLOGY OF REM SLEEP GENERATION

In animal experiments it has been conclusively demonstrated that drugs that mimic the action of acetylcholine (cholinergic agonists) and drugs that interfere with the breakdown of acetylcholine (anticholinesterase) produce a dramatic increase in REM sleep when they are microinjected into the pontine brainstem. The effects are most potent when the drug is placed in the pontine tegmentum at the level of the locus coeruleus (noradrenergic) between the dorsal raphe nucleus (serotonergic) and the peduculopontine nucleus (cholinergic). When atropine is microinjected into the pontine brainstem before the administration of cholinergic agonists or anticholinesterase agents, the REM sleep potentiation is also blocked, presumably because of localized occupation of acetylcholine receptors in the brainstem.

Drug microinjection experiments cannot be performed in humans. However, the parenteral administration of cholinergic blocking agents such as atropine may cause delirium. The mnemonic for atropine effects is hot (as a fire), red (as a beet), dry (as a bone), and mad (as a hatter). The differences between localized and diffuse effects are informative and create difficulties for the approach taken here, because the drugs used by humans have such widespread effects in the brain. They are not localized to the brainstem even if the sleep control systems are.

Nonetheless, even the diffuse effects may be explained via the brainstem neuropharmacological model. For example the delirium of atropine overdosage is from a formal point of view, not unlike that of dreaming: "Mad as a hatter" means (1) visually hallucinated, (2) disoriented, (3) amnesic, and (4) confabulatory. Normal dreaming is all of these things, but it occurs in sleep, not waking. We will come back to this argument when we consider the withdrawal effects of alcohol, barbiturates, and stimulant drugs.

When cholinergic agonists are microinjected into the far lateral pontine brainstem, the effects are quite different. Instead of acute, short-lived, and pronounced REM enhancement, one observes delayed, long-lasting, and more moderate REM enhancement. Acutely, there are ipsilateral PGO waves and ipsiversive eye movements. Only after 24 hours does the level of REM sleep go up, but it remains elevated for 6 to 7 days!

Besides indicating that the brain is complex and that the effects of drugs upon sleep are quite unpredictable, the results show that whereas some drug effects are short-lived, others endure for significantly long periods of time. The long-term effects are particularly significant for clinical psychiatry. When drugs are given repeatedly for days, weeks, months, or even years, the chronic drug use is likely to produce effects that are unforeseen in the short-term data available from the clinical trials mandated by the regulatory agencies. Tardive dyskinesia with prolonged phenothiazine use is a case in point, and we will come back to this issue when we discuss the selective serotonin reuptake inhibitor (SSRI) induction of REM sleep behavior disorder (RBD). The bottom line here is to realize that no drug affecting the brain's dream generator mechanisms can be considered safe until it may be too late.

Another important caveat is to notice the still large gap between the basic science data of cellular and molecular neurobiology and clinical neuropharmacology. When drugs are taken by mouth or even by parenteral routes of administration, their effects are infinitely more widespread than when they are microinjected, in small amounts, into precisely localized brain targets. Parenteral drug effects are hence unlocalizable and nonspecific. Given this gap, it is surprising that any of the clinical and basic science data fit together at all. More weight should be given to internally consistent findings while we await explanation of the inconsistent ones.

It is also important to point out that when we discuss drug effects on REM sleep, we are not directly assessing their effects on dreaming. So powerful has been the effect upon research of the REM sleep discovery that dreaming itself is rarely measured in drug studies (for an exception, see Pace-Schott et al., 1998, 2001). In fact, we know very little about how drugs alter our subjective experience in sleep. Since there can be considerable variation in subjective dream experience that is not detectable at the level of neurophysiology, we must be cautious about assuming that studies assessing polysomnographic variables are indicative of changes in dreaming. They may or may not be the case. Dreaming must be studied on its own or as a complement to laboratory studies of sleep.

ANXIOLYTICS AND SEDATIVES

The chemicals most commonly used (and abused) are those that are intended to overcome insomnia. At the outset, it should be said that none of these drugs produce normal sleep.

ALCOHOL

The easy availability of alcohol makes it the drug of choice for many people in treating a host of human ills inducing insomnia, anxiety, and depression. As a central nervous system (CNS) depressant, it is an effective knock-out drug. But because it so powerfully suppresses REM sleep (and presumably dreaming), its somnogenic effects are obtained at a very high price. Alcoholic REM suppression (or deprivation) incurs a REM debt, which must ultimately be paid back, with interest.

As all spree drinkers know, the first sign or impending hangover is early morning awakening. This is caused by the effect of rising titers of the aldehyde byproducts of alcohol catabolism by the liver. Hence, a night of sleep following acute alcohol excess is likely to be poor, and the second (or abstinent recovery) night is likely to be better because the alcohol effects are gone and the REM sleep debt is promptly paid back.

Should the drinker repeat his excess intake, his sleep will be even poorer on subsequent nights and his REM debt will increase. Chronic alcoholics, therefore, accumulate huge debts of REM. When they ultimately stop drinking, they suffer from the symptoms of delirium tremens, which include visual hallucinations (often of a stereotyped nature with insects and animals present), memory loss, confabulation, and heightened negative affect (especially anxiety).

Since many of the formal features of delirium tremens are also seen in normal dreams, it has been suggested that delirium tremens represents the breakthrough into waking of the alcohol suppressed REM sleep generator. The delirious patient is thus a waking dreamer. Conversely, normal dreaming has been likened to delirium because of the formal properties that they have in common and because their organic basis is partially shared.

That such theorizing is not far-fetched is suggested by the high percentages in REM sleep associated with alcohol withdrawal. On the third night of abstinence that figure may reach 100 percent (where 15 to 25 percent is normal). Furthermore, one potentially fatal sign of delirium tremens is temperature dyscontrol, an unexpected but fatal feature of experimental sleep deprivation. Together with evidence that REM sleep normally entails a temporary suppression of central thermoregulation, these surprising correlations conspire to suggest that a deep and significant function of REM sleep, not at all predictable from the experience of dreaming, may be to refurbish the temperature control mechanisms of the brain. Since mammals and birds thermoregulate and only these species have REM, this theory is biologically appealing.

SEDATIVES

For those subjects who seek medical relief of their insomnia (and excess anxiety), the story is not much better. In the 1960s and 1970s, the drugs of choice were the barbiturates, which, like alcohol, had a powerful REM suppressant effect (as well as a low margin of safety). They were replaced, with great fanfare and enthusiasm by the benzodiazapines (BDZs), which did not suppress REM. But it was not widely appreciated that the BDZs did suppress NREM sleep, eliminating the deep Stage IV almost entirely.

As with most other drugs, habituation was usual, requiring an increase in dose to obtain the desirable reduction in sleep onset latency. An unanticipated difficulty, called rebound insomnia, often complicated intentional withdrawal of BDZs. Rebound insomnia may prompt unwise continuation of the drug. Hence, an addiction-like syndrome can make drug suspension difficult.

When sleep is sustained, dream recall becomes less frequent, but this cannot be taken as evidence of dream suppression or dream reduction. Because our memory for dreams is so dependent upon awakening conditions, this effect may be simply because of enhanced sleep continuity.

ANTIDEPRESSANTS

Depression is characterized by a shortened latency to onset of the first REM period and a corresponding reduction in Stage IV. Depressed patients complain of less restful sleep and of an increase in the negative affect of their dreams. Most of the drugs that are used to fight depression increase the level of energy availability in waking by enhancing the aminergic modulatory systems, especially the norepinephrine and serotonin systems. It will be recalled that these two neuromodulators are selectively released in normal waking and selectively inhibited in normal sleep. Hence, it might be expected that enhancing their efficacy would produce insomnia. For reasons that are yet to be detailed, this is not the case. On the contrary, the tricyclic antidepressants are actually good sedatives.

The most immediate effect of antidepressant medication is a return to normal REM latency and a lengthening and intensification of the first REM period. This is seen especially in patients who will later enjoy a beneficial lifting of their mood. The delay between the early change in sleep architecture and the later lifting of mood is as yet inexplicable, but it is akin to they delay between PGO wave enhancement and REM sleep augmentation following cholinergic microinjection in the far-lateral pons. In this coupling of immediate synaptic effects with later metabolic effects, we may be glimpsing long-term effects involving second messengers, protein transport, and other slow neurobiological processes.

When an antidepressant tricyclic, like amitryptiline, causes, first, sedation, second, REM sleep latency correction, and third, mood elevation, the link between sleep and mood, already so phenomenologically obvious, invites analysis in search of cellular and molecular level commonalities. We can now understand the second of the three effects as aminergic REM suppression (which is predicted by the reciprocal interaction), and it makes intuitive sense that increased aminergic efficacy would lighten mood. But why is there initial sedation and why the delay between REM latency correction and mood improvement? And what happens to dreaming during the course of this phenomenon? We do not know the answers to either of these questions.

SSRIs

The antidepressants most widely prescribed today are the selective serotonin reuptake blockers. These and related drugs that also potentiate norepinephrine's synaptic efficacy are such reliable mood elevators as to rival the stimulants as cosmetic psychopharmacologicals. However, these drugs all raise havoc with sleep architecture by causing eye movements (and with them dreams) to escape the normal bounds of REM sleep. Indeed, patients often complain of dreaming all night long!

Following SSRI administration, one sees first REM suppression (as predicted by the reciprocal interaction model). But this initial effect is followed within 10 days by sleep fragmentation, REM explosion, and dream flooding. The switch from sleep enhancement to sleep fragmentation is particularly true of Paxil but is also seen with Prozac (Pace-Schott et al., 1998).

Another link to dreaming is the rare but disturbing occurrence of RBD. The symptoms tend to occur after several years of SSRI use and may persist after discontinuance of the drug. RBD patients literally act out their dreams, performing motor acts that correspond perfectly to their imagined dream behavior. This dream enactment occurs because the inhibitory gate, which normally opposes the motor commands of our dreams, is open (Schenck & Mahowald, 1996).

The spontaneous occurrence of RBD in humans is indirect proof that normal dreaming involves the activation of motor pattern generators in the brain creating the fictive movement of dreams. These fictive movements are normally experienced as the visuomotor hallucinations that are a hallmark formal feature of dreams and as such resuscitate the early suggestion of Roffwarg, Dement, Muzio, and Fisher (1962) that dream hallucinations bare a 1:1 relationship with the eye movements of REM. The RBD syndrome strongly supports the activation synthesis theory of dreaming by showing that dreamed motor acts are, in fact, commanded by automatic brain mechanisms. An analog state, REM sleep without atonia, is seen in cats following lesions of the subcerulean pontine brainstem (Jouvet, Vimont, & Delorme, 1965; Morrison, Sanford, & Ross, 1999). The movements that are released are described as stereotyped attack and defense postures, an observation that supports Revonsuo's theory of dreaming (2000) as evincing a simulated threat that serves a survival function.

MONOAMINE OXIDASE INHIBITORS (MAOIs)

One way to enhance aminergic neuromodulation and to relieve depression is to inhibit the enzyme, monoamine oxidase, which normally breaks down norepinephrine (NE) and serotonin (SHT) in the synaptic cleft. Patients given MAOIs may stop having REM sleep (and its associated dreaming) for months, raising questions about the survival theory (and any other functional theory of REM). It should be recognized, however, that as long as the MAOIs are in the brain, the supply of NE and 5-HT is guaranteed so that any function that depends upon the synaptic efficacy of those neuromodulators is artificially assured. Thus, the REM sleep mediation of those functions may no longer be necessary.

STIMULANTS

By administrating drugs like cocaine or amphetamine, it is possible to mimic the synaptic actions of NE and DA causing increased alertness and euphoria during waking. The fact that these drugs also suppress REM sleep dreaming may be tied to the problems of withdrawal from them. The occurrence of paranoid psychoses during withdrawal from amphetamine may share the REM rebound seen after alcohol withdrawal, although the clinical picture of amphetamine psychosis is quite different from that of delirium tremens. This difference could be because of the more dopaminergic effects of the stimulant drugs. In any case, the REM-dream suppression of the amphetamines and other stimulants (such as Ritalin) may ultimately counter the desired effects on alertness.

ANTIPSYCHOTICS

The analogy between dreaming and psychosis fits best with organic delirium. It fits less well with spontaneous mania and stimulant induced psychoses, and least well with schizophrenia. Thus, it is not surprising that effective antipsychotics, which block the D2 dopamine receptors, have little effect on REM sleep dreaming. An important implication of these findings is that schizophrenia psychosis and dreaming are produced by analogous but quite different mechanisms.

In schizophrenia, dreams are characterized by fewer characters and less animation than normal dreams, indicating that there is a state independent impoverishment of mental life in schizophrenia. When schizophrenic patients respond to Thematic Apperception Test (TAT) pictures (in waking), they show cognitive bizarreness that is equal in strength to that of their dreams.

Normal control subjects score equally high in reports of their dreams but do not make bizarre responses to TAT pictures. This means that normal and schizophrenic dreams, while differing in content, are equally bizarre and, in the patients (but not normals), waking cognition is equally bizarre (Scarone, Manzone, Gambini, & Hobson, personal communication, June 30, 2006).

PSYCHEDELICS

All recreational drugs that produce altered states of consciousness (such as LSD, mescaline, and ecstasy) interfere with neurotransmission via their interaction with the neuromodulators of the brainstem, especially serotonin (Hobson, 2001; Snyder, 1986). The visual hallucinations produced by these drugs are of dreamlike intensity, but the brain is still processing external data and distorting it, as well as creating the internal perceptions.

Thus, the altered states of consciousness induced by psychedelic drugs are best thought of as dissociative phenomena with some features of dreaming and some features of waking. For example, the visual illusions, distortions, and hallucinations of LSD may arise because the drug, via its interaction with serotonin, interferes with neurotransmission in the visual thalamus (lateral geniculate body, LGB) making normal vision impossible and dreamlike image production more probable.

SUMMARY AND CONCLUSION

The neurobiology of normal REM sleep is now well enough understood to allow an explanation of the formal features of dreaming and to explain some of the effects of drugs on dreaming. By extension, the models of REM sleep dream generation form a useful framework for understanding the effects of drugs on dreaming. It is now quite clear that dreaming and dream-like alterations of consciousness are natural phenomena with biological mechanisms that are beginning to be understood.

REFERENCES

Fosse, R., Stickgold, R., & Hobson, J. A. (2004). Thinking and hallucinating: Reciprocal changes in sleep. *Psychophysiology, 41,* 298–305.

Hobson, J. A. (2001). *The dream drug store.* Cambridge, MA: MIT Press.

Hobson, J. A. (2002). *Dreaming: An introduction to the science of sleep.* Oxford: Oxford University Press.

Jouvet, M., Vimont, P., & Delorme, F. (1965). Elective suppression of paradoxical sleep in the cat by monoamine oxidase inhibitors. *Comptes Rendus des Seances de la Societe de Biologie et de ses Filiales, 159,* 1595–1599.

Morrison, A. R., Sanford, L. D., & Ross, R. J. (1999). Initiation of rapid eye movement sleep: Beyond the brainstem. In B. N. Mallick & S. Inoue (Eds.), *Rapid eye movement sleep* (pp. 51–68). New York: Marcel Decker.

Nielsen, T. A. (1999). Mentation during sleep: The NREM/REM distinction. In R. Lydic & H. A. Baghdoyan (Eds.), *Handbook of behavioral state control: Molecular and cellular mechanisms* (pp. 101–128). Boca Raton: CRC Press.

Pace-Schott, E. F., Gersh, T., Silvestri, R., Stickgold, R., Salzman, C., & Hobson, J. A. (1998). The nightcap can detect sleep quality changes caused by selective serotonin reuptake inhibitor (SSRI) treatment in normal subjects. *Sleep, 21*, 102.

Pace-Schott, E. F., Gersh, T., Silvestri, R., Stickgold, R., Salzman, C., & Hobson, J. A. (2001). SSRI treatment suppresses dream recall frequency but increases subjective dream intensity in normal subjects. *Journal of Sleep Research, 10*, 129–142.

Revonsuo, A. (2000). The reinterpretation of dreams: An evolutionary hypothesis of the function of dreaming. *Behavioral & Brain Sciences, 23*, 877–901, 904–1121.

Roffwarg, H. P., Dement, W. C., Muzio, J. N., & Fisher, C. (1962). Dream imagery: Relationship to rapid eye movements of sleep. *Archives of General Psychiatry, 7*, 235–258.

Schenck, C. H., & Mahowald, M. W. (1996). REM sleep parasomnias. *Neurological Clinics, 14*, 697–720.

Snyder, S. (1986). *Drugs and the brain* (Scientific American Library Series). New York: W. H. Freeman & Company.

Five

Neuroimaging of REM Sleep and Dreaming

Thien Thanh Dang-Vu, Manuel Schabus,
Martin Desseilles, Sophie Schwartz, and Pierre Maquet

Dreams are sensory experiences occurring spontaneously during sleep. Their distribution during sleep is not homogeneous, as they are more frequent, vivid, and longer during rapid eye movement (REM) sleep. REM sleep might, therefore, constitute a permissive condition for the generation of dream experiences.

Over the last decade, functional brain imaging allowed us to characterize the distribution of regional cerebral activity during human REM sleep. The emerging picture reveals activation of the pons, the thalamus, temporo-occipital, and limbic/paralimbic areas (including amygdala), along with a relative quiescence of dorsolateral prefrontal and inferior parietal cortices. This pattern of activation offers new insights into the neural correlates of dreaming experience. For instance, amygdala activation is consistent with the predominance of negative emotions, anxiety, and fear in dream reports. Temporo-occipital activation is in keeping with a pervasiveness of visual dream content. Prefrontal deactivation might explain several cognitive impairments of the dreamer's mind relative to normal waking abilities, such as poor voluntary access to episodic memories, altered spatio-temporal orientation, deficient working memory, attention and self-awareness, altered reasoning and decision-making, including the usual lack of criticism toward bizarre elements in dreams. Prefrontal deactivation might also account for several characteristics of the dream scenario, such as spatio-temporal discontinuity associated with contextual misbinding.

INTRODUCTION

Dreaming is experienced every night by most humans as multisensory mental representations occurring spontaneously during sleep, often organized in a narrative manner. Dreams are characterized by their perceptual (mostly visual and auditory) and emotionally loaded content (including frequent threat-related content). They typically appear bizarre because of the incongruity, discontinuity, and instability of time, places, and persons (Hobson, Stickgold, & Pace-Schott, 1998; Schwartz & Maquet, 2002). Yet, they are usually taken as real by the dreamer. In a dream, it is, for example, not suspicious to us if we are suddenly able to fly or if a cat starts talking proper English. Indeed, the dream world is (mistakenly) experienced as real, very much like our waking perceptions and actions (Johnson, Kahan, & Raye, 1984). Some scientists even think of this illusory feeling of reality as a necessity for certain functions of the dream (Revonsuo, 2000; Valli et al., 2005). For example, Revonsuo (2000) and Valli (2005) have proposed that, by simulating threatening events, the biological function of dreaming is to afford the rehearsal of threat perception and avoidance, in a completely safe "virtual" environment and without any immediate damaging repercussion. Finally, the memory of the dream is generally quite poor and labile as compared to memory for waking events. As Pace-Schott, Stickgold, and Hobson (1997) suggested, the description of half an hour of waking life would be ten times longer than all the dream reports from one night.

The scientific study of dreaming constitutes a tough but fascinating challenge. Indeed, the dreamer is the unique observer of his dream and, as any subjective experience, dream content is not accessible to direct (third-person) observation. Consequently, information about a dream is obtained introspectively through memory recall. Several confounding factors may, therefore, affect the genuineness of dream reports such as forgetting, reconstruction mechanisms, verbal description difficulties, and censorship (Schwartz & Maquet, 2002). When studying dreams, one should always remain aware of these limitations and use appropriate strategies to prevent them from hindering valuable dream information.

The conception of dreams has slowly evolved through the centuries. In Greek antiquity, dreams were divine messages delivered to humans to warn them about upcoming disasters or misfortune. However, Aristotle challenged this common belief by bringing down any seemingly prophetic dream content to mere coincidence. He emphasized that dreams are endogenously generated and arise from the amplification of real external stimulation occurring during sleep. During the second half of the nineteenth century, several scientists conducted ingenious experimental studies on dreaming, focusing on the phenomenological descriptive features of dreams rather than their meaning. They proposed theories about the cerebral mechanisms underlying dreams that are strikingly close to some recent theories (Schwartz, 2000). This wave of dream studies was slowed down when the psychoanalytic interpretation of dreams emerged. Indeed, more than 100 years ago, Freud believed that dreams were the expression of hallucinatory satisfaction of repressed desires or the "royal road to the unconscious" (Freud, 1900/1955). Then it was only in the 1950s that a neurophysiological marker of dreaming was described, leading to a renewed interest for the scientific study of dreaming. In 1953, Aserinsky and Kleitman (1953) described for the first time recurrent periods of rapid eye movements during sleep. Since these periods were also characterized by high-frequency/low-amplitude electroencephalographic (EEG) activity and muscular atonia, they were identified as a specific sleep stage called "Rapid-Eye-Movement sleep" (REM sleep) or paradoxical sleep (Jouvet, 1962). Critically, awakenings from this sleep stage were associated with a high probability of vivid dream reports (Dement & Kleitman, 1957). This discovery shaped a new field of research for dreaming: sleep was no longer considered as a homogeneous resting state but included periods of enhanced neurophysiological activity underlying the production of dream experiences (Aserinsky & Kleitman, 1953). The generation of dreams was thus supposed to be restricted to REM sleep, but this concept has changed since then as dreaming also seems to occur during non-REM sleep (Antrobus, 1983; Cicogna, Cavallero, & Bosinelli, 1991; Mannim, 2005; Solms, 2000). It is still discussed whether dreaming mentation in REM and non-REM sleep depends on one common set of processes or rather on two separate generators (Foulkes, 1996; Nielsen, 2000).

Yet, the study of dreams and REM sleep physiology remain closely associated, because dreams during this sleep stage are reported much more frequently, are better recalled, longer, more emotionally charged and perceptually vivid, and they contain more bizarre features (Aserinsky & Kleitman, 1953; Hobson, Pace-Schott, & Stickgold, 2000). REM sleep neurophysiology is dominated by complex neuromodulatory changes (Hobson et al., 1998; Hobson et al., 2000). In cats and rodents, REM sleep is generated by cholinergic input arising from brainstem nuclei located in the pedunculopontine tegmentum (PPT) and laterodorsal tegmentum (LDT) (Baghdoyan, Lydic, Callaway, & Hobson, 1989; Capece, Efange, & Lydic, 1997; Datta, 1995; Hobson, Datta, Calvo, & Quattrochi, 1993; Kodama, Takahashi, & Honda, 1990; Velazquez-Moctezuma, Gillin, & Shiromani, 1989; Velazquez-Moctezuma, Shalauta, Gillin, & Shiromani, 1991; Yamamoto, Mamelak, Quattrochi, & Hobson, 1990). These cholinergic generators are mainly controlled by inhibition from aminergic neurotransmitters (noradrenalin [NA] and serotonin [5-HT]), which are repressed during REM sleep, leading to cholinergic firing increase (Gentili et al., 1996; Horner, Sanford, Annis, Pack, & Morrison, 1997; Imeri, De Simoni, Giglio, Clavenna, & Mancia, 1994; Leonard & Llinas, 1994; Nicholson & Pascoe, 1991; Portas & McCarley, 1994; Singh & Mallick, 1996). Other neuromodulatory systems might also participate in REM sleep modulation, such as gamma-aminobutyric acid (GABA) (Nitz & Siegel, 1997), nitric oxide (NO) (Leonard & Lydic, 1997), glutamate (Onoe & Sakai, 1995), glycine (Chase, Soja, & Morales, 1989), neuropeptides (Bourgin et al., 1997), as well as other non-pontine systems involving structures such as the basal forebrain (Szymusiak, 1995), hypothalamus (Lu et al., 2002), thalamus (Marini, Imeri, & Mancia, 1988; Marini, Gritti, & Mancia, 1992), amygdala (Sanford, Tejani-Butt, Ross, & Morrison, 1995), periaqueductal grey area (Sastre, Buda, Kitahama, & Jouvet, 1996), and medulla (Chase & Morales, 1990).

The function of dreaming is a source of intense debate and a fascinating topic in the field of cognitive neuroscience (for review see, Revonsuo, 2000). Although several theories claim that dreaming is simply a random by-product of REM physiology, others suggest it has quite important, if not vital, functional significance.

For example, Hobson and McCarley suggested that dreams merely result from the forebrain responding to (and trying to interpret) random activation initiated at the brainstem, or as a by-product related to "unlearning" in an otherwise overloaded brain (Crick & Mitchison, 1995; Hobson & McCarley, 1977).

Other researchers have proposed that dreams might reflect active functions like reprocessing and further consolidation of novel and (individually) relevant features encountered during previous waking experience. According to these authors (Cipolli, Fagioli, Mazzetti, & Tuozzi, 2004), the restructuring occurring during sleep and dreaming should be beneficial for long-term storage of freshly encoded information. By contrast, Jouvet proposed that dreaming involves the genetic reprogramming of cortical networks that might promote the maintenance of psychological individuality despite potentially adverse influences from the waking experiences (Jouvet, 1998).

More extreme views have suggested vital and adaptive functions to dreams in the course of brain development and evolution. Extending the evolutionary hypothesis of the function of dreaming (that is, "threat simulating theory") from Revonsuo and colleagues (2000), Franklin and Zyphur (2005) proposed that REM sleep may be so prominent early in life because it might function as a "virtual rehearsal mechanism." For optimizing brain development and connectivity, a young organism would benefit from adaptively experiencing rich and vivid environments during dreams.

Finally, following on psychoanalytical theories, others have argued that dreaming is a process of internal activation, arising from a person's affective and emotional history (Mancia, 2005).

Over the last decades, the development of neuroimaging techniques allowed researchers to investigate in a noninvasive way functional changes in brain activity across various experimental conditions. In the field of sleep research, positron emission tomography (PET) was the main technique used to assess the global and regional cerebral activity during the different sleep stages. When applied to brain imaging, PET technique allows an assessment of cerebral activity using compounds labeled with positron-emitting isotopes. In sleep studies, different probes can be used, such as $[^{18}F]$fluorodeoxyglucose (^{18}FDG), which is a marker of glucose metabolism, and oxygen-15-labeled water ($H_2^{15}O$), which is a marker of blood flow. The neuroimaging data confirmed and extended some sleep physiological theories raised from animal data. Below, we first review the available functional neuroimaging studies that describe the pattern of regional cerebral activity during normal human REM sleep, as well as the likely activating neurophysiological mechanisms underlying this pattern of activity. Then, we discuss how these results could also be interpreted in more cognitive terms based on common dream features. This integrated view contributes to the characterization of the neural correlates of dreaming and may provide important elements for the understanding of the organization and functions of dreaming.

REM SLEEP PHYSIOLOGY VIEWED FROM A NEUROIMAGING PERSPECTIVE

Electrophysiological data showed that REM sleep is characterized by sustained neuronal activity (Jones, 1991; Steriade & McCarley, 1990). Early neuroimaging results demonstrated that REM sleep also displays a *global* high-level of cerebral energy requirements (Maquet et al., 1990) and cerebral blood flow (Madsen et al., 1991; Madsen & Vorstrup, 1991), which are comparable to wakefulness values. Subsequent neuroimaging studies, mostly conducted with PET, described REM sleep *regional* patterns of activity compared to wakefulness and/or non-REM sleep (Braun et al., 1997; Maquet et al., 1996; Maquet et al., 2000; Maquet et al., 2005; Nofzinger, Mintun, Wiseman, Kupfer, & Moore, 1997) (see Figure 5.1). The resulting maps showed a distribution of brain areas that displayed a higher (activation) or

FIGURE 5.1

Schematic representation of the functional neuroanatomy of normal human REM sleep. Regions with dark shading are those in which there is a relative increase in neural activity associated with REM sleep; those with light shading show relative decreases in neural activity during REM sleep. Arrows show the proposed relationships between brain areas and several dreaming features, which may be accounted for by regional patterns of activity during REM sleep. (a) lateral view; (b) medial view; (c) ventral view. A: amygdala; B: basal forebrain; Ca: anterior cingulate gyrus; Cp: posterior cingulate gyrus and precuneus; F: dorsolateral prefrontal cortex (middle and inferior frontal gyri); H: hypothalamus; M: motor cortex; P: parietal cortex (inferior parietal lobule); PH: parahippocampical gyrus; O: occipital-lateral cortex; Th: thalamus; T-O: temporo-occipital extrastriate cortex; TP: pontine tegmentum.

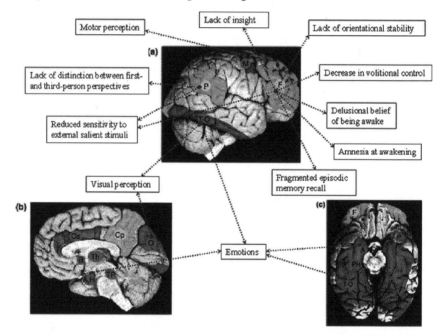

Source: Reprinted from *Trends in Cognitive Sciences*, volume 6:1, S. Schwartz and P. Maquet, "Sleep imaging and the neuro-psychological assessment of dreams," pp. 23–30. Copyright 2002, with permission from Elsevier.

lower (deactivation) regional cerebral blood flow (rCBF) during REM sleep in comparison to wakefulness and/or non-REM sleep. Regional activations were found in the pontine tegmentum, thalamus, basal forebrain, amygdala, hippocampus, anterior cingulate cortex, and temporo-occipital areas. Regional deactivations were found in the dorsolateral prefrontal cortex (DLPF), posterior cingulate gyrus, precuneus, and the inferior parietal cortex.

Reported activation of *pontine tegmentum, thalamic nuclei,* and *basal fore-brain* (Braun et al., 1997; Maquet et al., 1996) is in agreement with REM sleep-generation mechanisms in animals (Datta, 1995, 1997; Marini et al., 1992). Namely, REM sleep is believed to be generated by cholinergic processes arising from brainstem structures (PPT and LDT) that mediate widespread cortical activation via a dorsal pathway innervating the thalamus and a ventral pathway innervating the basal forebrain (Steriade & McCarley, 2005).

A major finding from PET studies is the demonstration that *limbic and paralimbic* structures, including amygdaloid complexes, hippocampal formation, and anterior cingulate cortex, were consistently activated during REM sleep in humans (Braun et al., 1997; Maquet et al., 1996; Nofzinger et al., 1997). This result is also in line with earlier studies in animals showing a high regional glucose metabolism in the limbic system of rats (Ramm & Frost, 1983) and cats (Lydic et al., 1991; Ramm & Frost, 1986). Amygdala is known to play a key role in REM sleep modulation. For instance, in cats the stimulation of the central nucleus of amygdaloid complexes, either by electrical stimulation (Calvo, Badillo, Morales-Ramirez, & Palacios-Salas, 1987) or by injections of a cholinergic agonist (Calvo, Simon-Arceo, & Fernandez-Mas, 1996) enhances REM sleep activity. Besides the amygdala, the hippocampal formation is also activated during REM sleep in some studies (Nofzinger et al., 1997), suggesting an activation of the whole limbic system rather than the amygdala alone. The activation of the amygdala and the hippocampus, which are both involved in memory processing (Bechara et al., 1995), also suggests memory consolidation processes during REM sleep. Numerous data support the involvement of sleep in memory (for review, see Dang-Vu, Desseilles, Peigneux, & Maquet, 2006; Maquet, 2001; Maquet, Smith, & Stickgold, 2003; Peigneux, Laureys, Delbeuck, & Maquet, 2001a; Rauchs, Desgranges, Foret, & Eustache, 2005), but the relationships with dream content remain to be demonstrated.

Activated cortical *temporo-occipital* areas encompass the inferior temporal cortex and the fusiform gyrus (Braun et al., 1997), which belong to visual association areas (extrastriate cortex), but they do not include the primary visual cortex (striate cortex). Furthermore, striate and extrastriate cortices were shown to be functionally dissociated during REM sleep (Braun et al., 1998): extrastriate cortex activation is significantly correlated with striate cortex deactivation during REM sleep, whereas their activities are usually positively correlated during wakefulness. This dissociation between visual association areas and primary visual areas seems to be a hallmark of REM sleep and has led Braun and colleagues to hypothesize that REM sleep allows internal information processing (between extrastriate areas and their paralimbic projections, both activated during REM sleep) in a closed system dissociated from interactions with the environment (via striate cortex and prefrontal cortex, both deactivated during REM sleep) (Braun et al., 1998).

Deactivated areas during REM sleep were first found in the *DLPF*, the *precuneus*, the *posterior cingulate* cortex, and the *parietal* cortex (Braun et al., 1997; Maquet et al., 1996). A recent PET study, however, showed that only parts of the parietal and DLPF cortices are hypoactive during REM sleep when compared to wakefulness (Maquet et al., 2005): the temporo-parietal region, the inferior parietal lobule, and the inferior and middle frontal gyrus of the DLPF. Conversely, activity in the superior parietal lobe and in the superior and medial prefrontal cortex is not different from waking level. The neurophysiological mechanisms underlying this functional segregation are still hypothetical. The amygdala might play a role in this cortical mapping: in monkeys, the amygdala sends abundant projections to the extrastriate and anterior cingulate cortices, which are activated during human REM sleep, but sends only sparse or indirect projections to the parietal cortex and DLPF, which are deactivated during REM sleep (Amaral & Price, 1984). These data suggest that the amygdala might "orchestrate" cortical activity during REM sleep. In line with this hypothesis, PET data also showed functional interactions between the amygdala and the temporal cortex, whereby amygdala activity was significantly and positively correlated with activity in the ipsilateral temporal cortex during REM sleep, but not during other states of vigilance (Maquet & Phillips, 1998). One proposed function for this amygdalo-cortical network may be the selective processing of emotionally-relevant memories during REM sleep (Maquet et al., 1996).

In animals, rapid eye movements during REM sleep are closely related to the occurrence of the so-called ponto-geniculo-occipital (PGO) waves. These *PGO waves* are bioelectrical phasic potentials occurring during the transition from non-REM sleep to REM sleep or during REM sleep itself (Callaway, Lydic, Baghdoyan, & Hobson, 1987). They are observed at many locations in the animal brain (Hobson, 1964), but most easily recorded in the pons (Jouvet, 1967), the lateral geniculate bodies of the thalamus (Mikiten, Niebyl, & Hendley, 1961) and the occipital cortex (Mouret, Jeannerod, & Jouvet, 1963). PGO waves might have important functional roles, such as the promotion of brain development and the facilitation of brain plasticity (Datta, 1999). There is also some evidence that PGO waves may exist in humans, as suggested by direct intracerebral recordings in epileptic patients (Salzarule et al., 1975), surface EEG (Salzarule et al., 1975), and magnetoencephalography (MEG) (Inoue, Saha, & Musha, 1999). A human PET study also found correlations during REM sleep, but not during wakefulness, between spontaneous eye movements and rCBF in the occipital cortex and the lateral geniculate bodies of the thalamus, giving further support for the existence of PGO-like activities during REM sleep in humans (Peigneux, et al., 2001b). This finding was recently corroborated by a functional magnetic resonance imaging (fMRI) study (Wehrle et al., 2005).

Overall, neuroimaging studies have shown that the functional neuroanatomy (Braun et al., 1997; Maquet et al., 1996; Maquet et al., 2005; Nofzinger et al., 1997) but also the functional interactions between brain areas (Braun et al., 1998; Maquet & Phillips, 1998) were significantly different during REM sleep compared to wakefulness and to other sleep stages. These patterns of activity contribute to build a model of REM sleep physiology integrating human and animal data: (1) REM sleep is generated by processes arising from the pons and projecting to the cortex via the thalamus and the basal forebrain. (2) The limbic/paralimbic structures, mostly the amygdala, may serve as important modulators of internally-generated cortical input. (3) The hallmark of this segregated cortical activity is the activation of temporo-occipital visual association areas, contrasting with DLPF and inferior parietal deactivations. (4) The resulting network may be shaped by PGO-like activities and could underlie important functions such as brain plasticity and memory.

DREAMING VIEWED FROM A NEUROIMAGING PERSPECTIVE: INTEGRATION OF REM SLEEP CEREBRAL MAPPING AND MAJOR DREAM FEATURES

The previous maps reflect some aspects of REM sleep physiology, but may also convey information about the neural basis of dreaming. Indeed, the functional patterns of cerebral activity during REM sleep can be interpreted in the light of common features of dream content, and therefore potentially account for the generation of oneiric activity (see Figure 5.1).

Dream reports usually include different sensory modalities, largely dominated by *visual* (close to 100 percent) and *auditory* (40 to 60 percent) percepts, whereas movement and tactile sensations (15 to 30 percent) or smell and taste (less than 1 percent) are much less frequent (Strauch, Meier, & Foulkes, 1996). The occipito-temporal activation during REM sleep may underpin these perceptual aspects of dreams, consistently dominated by visual and auditory elements (Braun et al., 1997). Accordingly, cessation of visual dream imagery was reported for patients with occipito-temporal lesions (Solms, 1997).

Dream content is also characterized by the prominence of *emotions*, and especially negative emotions such as fear and anxiety (Strauch et al., 1996). Responses to threatening stimuli or stressful situations are modulated by the amygdala during wakefulness (Sah, Faber, Lopez, & Power, 2003). The high limbic—and amygdalar—activity during REM sleep may thus underlie the emotional intensity occurring during dreams (Maquet et al., 1996). Moreover, PET data have shown positive functional interactions between amygdala and occipito-temporal cortices during REM sleep (Maquet & Phillips, 1998), while a recent fMRI study has found a positive relationship between the emotional load of visual stimuli and the functional activity in both amygdala and infero-temporal cortex (Sabatinelli, Bradley, Fitzsimmons, & Lang, 2005). Together, these data suggest that the emotional experience during dreams might involve specific brain networks encompassing the amygdala and the occipito-temporal cortex.

The regional hypoactivity patterns during REM sleep, and especially the deactivation of parts of the prefrontal and parietal cortex (Maquet et al., 2005), have been proposed to explain several other dreaming features such as the uncritical acceptance of bizarre dream content, the alteration in time perception, the delusional belief of being awake during dreams, and the amnesia at awakening (Hobson et al., 1998). As discussed below, these deactivations could also account for the discontinuity and incongruity of dream content, the lack of control on the dreaming scenario, the fragmented recall of dreaming episodic elements, the reduced sensitivity of the dreaming narrative to external information, and the lack of distinction between first- and third-person perspectives in mind representation during dreaming (Maquet et al., 2005).

The prefrontal cortex can be functionally divided in distinct subregions, each of them underlying the monitoring of specific *cognitive processes* during wakefulness (Koechlin, Ody, & Kouneiher, 2003). In this model, the DLPF areas deactivated during REM sleep (Maquet et al., 2005) correspond to the prefrontal subregions involved in the selection of stimulus-response associations according to contextual signals, past events, and internal goals. The decreased activity of these areas would, therefore, prevent the brain from supervising the meaningful integration and continuity of dream information with respect to waking routines, physical rules, and social conventions. It may also explain the dreamer's failure to organize his/her mental representation toward specific goals or to control the flow of dream events.

During wakefulness, the retrieval of *episodic memory*, which refers to the ability to recollect personally experienced events anchored within a particular spatio-temporal context (Tulving, 1983), has been shown to involve the activation of lateral and inferior prefrontal cortices (Buckner, Wheeler, & Sheridan, 2001; Cabeza & Nyberg, 2000; Fletcher & Henson, 2001; Rugg & Wilding, 2000; Rugg, Otten, & Henson, 2002), which are typically deactivated during REM sleep (Maquet et al., 2005). It is indeed believed that prefrontal areas participate in the processing of information retrieved from episodic memory; for instance, by checking its accuracy and completeness (Maquet et al., 2005). The hypoactivity of these regions during REM sleep is in line with the demonstration that, although 65 percent of dream reports contain residues of previous waking activity, only 1.4 percent of them are considered as representing the replay of full memory episodes (Fosse, Fosse, Hobson, & Stickgold, 2003). In other words, the dreamer reactivates episodic elements in a fragmented fashion (probably via the activation of the hippocampus and posterior cortical areas), but is unable to integrate the details of past events into an identifiable life episode because of the deactivation of the DLPF (Maquet et al., 2005; Schwartz, 2003).

The DLPF (inferior and middle frontal gyri) and the inferior parietal lobule, both deactivated during REM sleep, are included in the *ventral attentional network* (Corbetta & Shulman, 2002). This network acts as an alerting mechanism that is specialized in the detection of salient, unexpected, behaviorally relevant stimuli and helps to reorient the focus of attention toward the incoming stimulus (Corbetta, Kincade, Ollinger, McAvoy, & Shulman, 2000). A relative quiescence of the ventral attentional network during REM sleep might be induced by the decrease of noradrenergic tone, given that the locus coeruleus sends heavy projections to the inferior parietal cortex (Morrison & Foote, 1986) and also participates in selective attention, especially to salient and unexpected stimuli (Aston-Jones & Rajkowski, 2000). These functional patterns then predict that the dream narrative, reported after awakening from REM sleep, would hardly be modified by external stimulation, even if behaviorally relevant (Maquet et al., 2005). This view is supported by observations describing that external stimuli delivered during REM sleep are either ignored or automatically incorporated into the dream narrative, instead of interrupting the flow of the dream storyline (Burton, Harsh, & Badia, 1988; Foulkes, 1966).

The ability to attribute intentions, thoughts, and feelings to oneself and to others is commonly referred to as the "Theory of Mind." Instances of *mind representation* appear in dreams: the dreaming mind creates characters and attributes thoughts, emotions, and intentions to those characters (Kahn & Hobson, 2005). Neuroimaging studies of theory of mind tasks during wakefulness have demonstrated a consistent involvement of the medial prefrontal cortex (MPF) (Frith & Frith, 2003; Gallagher & Frith, 2003; Harris, Todorov, & Fiske, 2005). While the DLPF is deactivated during REM sleep, the MPF has been shown to remain as active during REM sleep as during wakefulness (Maquet et al., 2005). This stands in contrast with its significant deactivation during non-REM sleep (Dang-Vu et al., 2005; Maquet et al., 1997; Maquet et al., 2005). The similar level of activity in the MPF during REM sleep and wakefulness could therefore contribute to the persistence of the ability to represent others' mind during REM sleep dreaming. On the other hand, the inferior parietal lobule and temporo-parietal junction would be involved in the *distinction of first- versus third-person perspectives* in the representation of actions, thoughts, and emotions during wakefulness (Chaminade & Decety, 2002; Farrer et al., 2003; Ruby & Decety, 2001; Ruby & Decety, 2003, 2004). Contrasting with the MPF preserved activity, the hypoactivity of these parietal areas would predict a decrease of the ability to distinguish the perspective of others as compared to our own during REM sleep and dreaming. Accordingly, dream reports show that the self can participate to the dream scenario both in a first-person (the self sees and acts) and in a third-person perspective (the dreamer sees the self acting in the dream) (Maquet et al., 2005).

CONCLUSION

Over the last decade, neuroimaging studies have successfully described the distribution of brain activity across the sleep-wake cycle. When compared to non-REM sleep, REM sleep is characterized by an overall elevated level of activity, together with a specific pattern of regional brain activations and deactivations. This functional mapping of human REM sleep also allowed confirming theories of REM sleep neurophysiology derived from animal experiments. It has also been proposed that the cerebral correlates of REM sleep could underpin some important dreaming characteristics, including the predominance of threat-related emotions and visual percept, the loss of orientational stability and volitional control, the fragmented episodic memory recall, the reduced sensitivity to external relevant information, as well as the possibility of attributing feelings and goals to other characters in the dream.

To further improve the accuracy of the neural correlates of dreaming, future functional brain imaging studies should be combined with refined neuropsychological analysis of dream reports (Schwartz & Maquet, 2002). Dreams are indeed multifarious, often bizarre, and cannot be reduced to a list of broad and typical sensory or cognitive features. Some specific and bizarre but common dream features of normal human sleep resemble clinical signs of neuropsychological syndromes resulting from focal brain damages, thus potentially predicting the topography of the corresponding brain functional changes (Schwartz & Maquet, 2002). On the basis of these observations, it has been proposed to quantify and categorize the dream narrative in terms of different perceptual, emotional, or bizarre elements to provide useful constraints to the analysis and interpretation of future REM sleep data (Schwartz & Maquet, 2002). Perhaps a special type of dreaming during which the dreamer is conscious of being in a dream ("lucid dreaming") might provide an interesting test case for future neuroimaging studies (LaBerge & DeGracia, 2000). The fact that lucid dreamers can remember to perform predetermined actions during a dream might allow assessing the neural correlates of a large variety of dreaming features. Non-REM sleep dreaming should also be investigated in upcoming dedicated studies, and the differences (or similarities) between REM on non-REM dreaming mentation should be further clarified.

The reviewed neurophysiological and neuroimaging research on REM sleep offers an increasingly detailed picture of the cerebral correlates of dreaming, which may finally bring significant insight into dreaming mechanisms and possible functions.

ACKNOWLEDGMENTS

T.D., M.D., and P.M. are supported by the Fonds National de la Recherche Scientifique (FNRS) (Belgium). M.S. is supported by the Austrian Science Foundation (FWF Erwin-Schrödinger-grant J2470). S.S. is supported by the Swiss National Science Foundation (grants: 3100-AO-102133 and 3200B0-104100). Additional support for the work presented here comes from the University of Liege and the Queen Elisabeth Medical Foundation.

REFERENCES

Amaral, D. G., & Price, J. L. (1984). Amygdalo-cortical projections in the monkey (Macaca fascicularis). *Journal of Comparative Neurology, 230,* 465–496.

Antrobus, J. (1983). REM and NREM sleep reports: Comparison of word frequencies by cognitive classes. *Psychophysiology, 20,* 562–568.

Aserinsky, E., & Kleitman, N. (1953). Regularly occurring periods of eye motility, and concomitant phenomena, during sleep. *Science, 118,* 273–274.

Aston-Jones, G., Rajkowski, J., & Cohen, J. (2000). Locus coeruleus and regulation of behavioral flexibility and attention. *Progress in Brain Research, 126,* 165–182.

Baghdoyan, H. A., Lydic, R., Callaway, C. W., & Hobson, J.A. (1989). The carbachol-induced enhancement of desynchronized sleep signs is dose dependent and antagonized by centrally administered atropine. *Neuropsychopharmacology, 2,* 67–79.

Bechara, A., Tranel, D., Damasio, H., Adolphs, R., Rockland, C., & Damasio, A. R. (1995). Double dissociation of conditioning and declarative knowledge relative to the amygdala and hippocampus in humans. *Science, 269,* 1115–1118.

Bourgin, P., Lebrand, C., Escourrou, P., Gaultier, C., Franc, B., Hamon, M., et al. (1997). Vasoactive intestinal polypeptide microinjections into the oral pontine tegmentum enhance rapid eye movement sleep in the rat. *Neuroscience, 77,* 351–360.

Braun, A. R., Balkin, T. J., Wesenten, N. J., Carson, R. E., Varga, M., Baldwin, P., et al. (1997). Regional cerebral blood flow throughout the sleep-wake cycle. An H2(15)O PET study. *Brain, 120,* 1173–1197.

Braun, A. R., Balkin, T. J., Wesensten, N. J., Gwadry, F., Carson, R. E., Varga, M., et al. (1998). Dissociated pattern of activity in visual cortices and their projections during human rapid eye movement sleep. *Science, 279,* 91–95.

Buckner, R. L., Wheeler, M. E., & Sheridan, M. A. (2001). Encoding processes during retrieval tasks. *Journal of Cognitive Neuroscience, 13,* 406–415.

Burton, S. A., Harsh, J. R., & Badia, P. (1988). Cognitive activity in sleep and responsiveness to external stimuli. *Sleep, 11,* 61–68.

Cabeza, R., & Nyberg, L. (2000). Imaging cognition II: An empirical review of 275 PET and fMRI studies. *Journal of Cognitive Neuroscience, 12,* 1–47.

Callaway, C. W., Lydic, R., Baghdoyan, H. A., & Hobson, J. A. (1987). Pontogeniculooccipital waves: Spontaneous visual system activity during rapid eye movement sleep. *Cellular & Molecular Neurobiology, 7,* 105–149.

Calvo, J. M., Badillo, S., Morales-Ramirez, M., & Palacios-Salas, P. (1987). The role of the temporal lobe amygdala in ponto-geniculo-occipital activity and sleep organization in cats. *Brain Research, 40,* 22–30.

Calvo, J. M., Simon-Arceo, K., & Fernandez-Mas, R. (1996). Prolonged enhancement of REM sleep produced by carbachol microinjection into the amygdala. *NeuroReport, 7,* 577–580.

Capece, M. L., Efange, S. M., & Lydic, R. (1997). Vesicular acetylcholine transport inhibitor suppresses REM sleep. *NeuroReport, 8,* 481–484.

Chaminade, T., & Decety, J. (2002). Leader or follower? Involvement of the inferior parietal lobule in agency. *NeuroReport, 13,* 1975–1978.

Chase, M. H., & Morales, F. R. (1990). The atonia and myoclonia of active (REM) sleep. *Annual Review of Psychology, 41,* 557–584.

Chase, M. H., Soja, P. J., & Morales, F. R. (1989). Evidence that glycine mediates the postsynaptic potentials that inhibit lumbar motoneurons during the atonia of active sleep. *Journal of Neuroscience, 9,* 743–751.

Cicogna, P., Cavallero, C., & Bosinelli, M. (1991). Cognitive aspects of mental activity during sleep. *American Journal of Psychology, 104,* 413–425.

Cipolli, C., Fagioli, I., Mazzetti, M., & Tuozzi, G. (2004). Incorporation of presleep stimuli into dream contents: Evidence for a consolidation effect on declarative knowledge during REM sleep? *Journal of Sleep Research, 13,* 317–326.

Corbetta, M., Kincade, J. M., Ollinger, J. M., McAvoy, M. P., & Shulman, G. L. (2000). Voluntary orienting is dissociated from target detection in human posterior parietal cortex. *Nature Neuroscience, 3,* 292–297.

Corbetta, M., & Shulman, G. L. (2002). Control of goal-directed and stimulus-driven attention in the brain. *Nature Reviews Neuroscience, 3,* 201–215.

Crick, F., & Mitchison, G. (1995). REM sleep and neural nets. *Behavioral Brain Research, 69,* 147–155.

Dang-Vu, T. T., Desseilles, M., Laureys, S., Degueldre, C., Perrin, F., Phillips, C., et al. (2005). Cerebral correlates of delta waves during non-REM sleep revisited. *NeuroImage, 28,* 14–21.

Dang-Vu, T. T., Desseilles, M., Peigneux, P., & Maquet, P. (2006). A role for sleep in brain plasticity. *Pediatric Rehabilitation, 9,* 98–118.

Datta, S. (1995). Neuronal activity in the peribrachial area: Relationship to behavioral state control. *Neuroscience & Biobehavioral Reviews, 19,* 67–84.

Datta, S. (1997). Cellular basis of pontine ponto-geniculo-occipital wave generation and modulation. *Cellular & Molecular Neurobiology, 17,* 341–365.

Datta, S. (1999). PGO wave generation: Mechanism and functional significance. In B. N. Mallick & S. Inoue (Eds.), *Rapid eye movement sleep* (pp. 91–106). New Delhi: Narosa Publishing House.

Dement, W., & Kleitman, N. (1957). The relation of eye movements during sleep to dream activity: An objective method for the study of dreaming. *Journal of Experimental Psychology, 53,* 339–346.

Farrer, C., Franck, N., Georgieff, N., Frith, C. D., Decety, J., & Jeannerod, M. (2003). Modulating the experience of agency: A positron emission tomography study. *NeuroImage, 18,* 324–333.

Fletcher, P. C., & Henson, R. N. (2001). Frontal lobes and human memory: Insights from functional neuroimaging. *Brain, 124,* 849–881.

Fosse, M. J., Fosse, R., Hobson, J. A., & Stickgold, R. J. (2003). Dreaming and episodic memory: A functional dissociation? *Journal of Cognitive Neuroscience, 15,* 1–9.

Foulkes, D. (1966). *The psychology of sleep.* New York: Charles Scribner's Sons.

Foulkes, D. (1996). Dream research: 1953–1993. *Sleep, 19,* 609–624.

Franklin, M. S., & Zyphur, M. J. (2005). The role of dreams in the evolution of the human mind. *Evolutionary Psychology, 3,* 59–78.

Freud, S. (1955). *The interpretation of dreams* (J. Strachey, Trans.). New York: Basic Books. (Original work published 1900)

Frith, U., & Frith, C. D. (2003). Development and neurophysiology of mentalizing. *Philosophical Transactions of the Royal Society of London, Series B, Biological Sciences, 358,* 459–473.

Gallagher, H. L., & Frith, C. D. (2003). Functional imaging of "theory of mind." *Trends in Cognitive Sciences, 7,* 77–83.

Gentili, A., Godschalk, M. F., Gheorghiu, D., Nelson, K., Julius, D. A., & Mulligan, T. (1996). Effect of clonidine and yohimbine on sleep in healthy men: A double-blind, randomized, controlled trial. *European Journal of Clinical Pharmacology, 50,* 463–465.

Harris, L. T., Todorov, A., & Fiske, S. T. (2005). Attributions on the brain: Neuroimaging dispositional inferences, beyond theory of mind. *NeuroImage, 28,* 763–769.

Hobson, J. A. (1964). The phasic electrical activity of the cortex and thalamus during desynchronized sleep in cats. *Comptes Rendus des Seances de la Societe de Biologie et de ses Filiales, 158,* 2131–2135.

Hobson, J. A., Datta, S., Calvo, J. M., & Quattrochi, J. (1993). Acetylcholine as a brain state modulator: Triggering and long-term regulation of REM sleep. *Progress in Brain Research, 98,* 389–404.

Hobson, J. A., & McCarley, R. W. (1977). The brain as a dream state generator: An activation-synthesis hypothesis of the dream process. *American Journal of Psychiatry, 134,* 1335–1348.

Hobson, J. A., Pace-Schott, E. F., & Stickgold, R. (2000). Dreaming and the brain: Toward a cognitive neuroscience of conscious states. *The Behavioral & Brain Sciences, 23,* 793–842.

Hobson, J. A., Stickgold, R., & Pace-Schott, E. F. (1998). The neuropsychology of REM sleep dreaming. *NeuroReport, 9,* R1-R14.

Horner, R. L., Sanford, L. D., Annis, D., Pack, A. I., & Morrison, A. R. (1997). Serotonin at the laterodorsal tegmental nucleus suppresses rapid-eye-movement sleep in freely behaving rats. *Journal of Neuroscience, 17,* 7541–7552.

Imeri, L., De Simoni, M. G., Giglio, R., Clavenna, A., & Mancia, M. (1994). Changes in the serotonergic system during the sleep-wake cycle: Simultaneous polygraphic and voltammetric recordings in hypothalamus using a telemetry system. *Neuroscience, 58,* 353–358.

Inoue, S., Saha, U., & Musha, T. (1999). Spatio-temporal distribution of neuronal activities and REM sleep. In B. N. Mallick & S. Inoue (Eds.), *Rapid eye movement sleep* (pp. 214–230). New Delhi: Narosa Publishing House.

Johnson, M. K., Kahan, T. L., & Raye, C. L. (1984). Dreams and reality monitoring. *Journal of Experimental Psychology General, 113,* 329–344.

Jones, B. E. (1991). Paradoxical sleep and its chemical/structural substrates in the brain. *Neuroscience, 40,* 637–656.

Jouvet, M. (1962). Research on the neural structures and responsible mechanisms in different phases of physiological sleep. *Archives of Italian Biology, 100,* 125–206.

Jouvet, M. (1967). Neurophysiology of the states of sleep. *Physiological Reviews, 47,* 117–177.

Jouvet, M. (1998). Paradoxical sleep as a programming system. *Journal of Sleep Research, 7*(Suppl 1), 1–5.

Kahn, D., & Hobson, J. A. (2005). Theory of mind in dreaming: Awareness of feelings and thoughts of others in dreams. *Dreaming, 15,* 48–57.

Kodama, T., Takahashi, Y., & Honda, Y. (1990). Enhancement of acetylcholine release during paradoxical sleep in the dorsal tegmental field of the cat brain stem. *Neuroscience Letters, 114,* 277–282.

Koechlin, E., Ody, C., & Kouneiher, F. (2003). The architecture of cognitive control in the human prefrontal cortex. *Science, 302,* 1181–1185.

LaBerge, S., & DeGracia, D. J. (2000). Varieties of lucid dreaming experience. In R. G. Kunzendorf & B. Wallace (Eds.) *Individual differences in conscious experience* (pp. 269–307). Amsterdam: John Benjamins.

Leonard, C. S., & Llinas, R. (1994). Serotonergic and cholinergic inhibition of mesopontine cholinergic neurons controlling REM sleep: An in vitro electrophysiological study. *Neuroscience, 59,* 309–330.

Leonard, T. O., & Lydic, R. (1997). Pontine nitric oxide modulates acetylcholine release, rapid eye movement sleep generation, and respiratory rate. *Journal of Neuroscience, 17,* 774–785.

Lu, J., Bjorkum, A. A., Xu, M., Gaus, S. E., Shiromani, P. J., & Saper, C. B. (2002). Selective activation of the extended ventrolateral preoptic nucleus during rapid eye movement sleep. *Journal of Neuroscience, 22,* 4568–4576.

Lydic, R., Baghdoyan, H. A., Hibbard, L., Bonyak, E. V., DeJoseph, M. R., & Hawkins, R. A. (1991). Regional brain glucose metabolism is altered during rapid eye movement sleep in the cat: A preliminary study. *Journal of Comparative Neurology, 304,* 517–529.

Madsen, P. L., Holm, S., Vorstrup, S., Friberg, L., Lassen, N. A., & Wildschiodtz, G. (1991). Human regional cerebral blood flow during rapid-eye-movement sleep. *Journal of Cerebral Blood Flow & Metabolism, 11,* 502–507.

Madsen, P. L., & Vorstrup, S. (1991). Cerebral blood flow and metabolism during sleep. *Cerebrovascular & Brain Metabolism Reviews, 3,* 281–296.

Mancia, M. (2005). The dream between neuroscience and psychoanalysis. *Schweizer Archiv für Neurologie und Psychiatre, 156,* 471–479.

Mannim, R. (2005). Rapid eye movement sleep, non-rapid eye movement sleep, dreams, and hallucinations. *Current Psychiatry Reports, 7,* 196–200.

Maquet, P. (2001). The role of sleep in learning and memory. *Science, 294,* 1048–1052.

Maquet, P., Degueldre, C., Delfiore, G., Aerts, J., Peters, J. M., Luxen, A., et al. (1997). Functional neuroanatomy of human slow wave sleep. *Journal of Neuroscience, 17,* 2807–2812.

Maquet, P., Dive, D., Salmon, E., Sadzot, B., Franco, G., Poirrier, R., et al. (1990). Cerebral glucose utilization during sleep-wake cycle in man determined by positron emission tomography and [18F]2-fluoro-2-deoxy-D-glucose method. *Brain Research, 513,* 136–143.

Maquet, P., Laureys, S., Peigneux, P., Fuchs, S., Petiau, C., Phillips, C., et al. (2000). Experience-dependent changes in cerebral activation during human REM sleep. *Nature Neuroscience, 3,* 831–836.

Maquet, P., Peters, J., Aerts, J., Delfiore, G., Degueldre, C., Luxen, A., et al. (1996). Functional neuroanatomy of human rapid-eye-movement sleep and dreaming. *Nature, 383,* 163–166.

Maquet, P., & Phillips, C. (1998). Functional brain imaging of human sleep. *Journal of Sleep Research, 7*(Suppl 1), 42–47.

Maquet, P., Ruby, P., Maudoux, A., Albouy, G., Sterpenich, V., Dang-Vu, T., et al. (2005). Human cognition during REM sleep and the activity profile within frontal and parietal cortices: A reappraisal of functional neuroimaging data. *Progress in Brain Research, 150,* 219–227.

Maquet, P., Smith, C., & Stickgold, R. (2003). *Sleep and brain plasticity.* Oxford: Oxford University Press.

Marini, G., Gritti, I., & Mancia, M. (1992). Enhancement of tonic and phasic events of rapid eye movement sleep following bilateral ibotenic acid injections into centralis lateralis thalamic nucleus of cats. *Neuroscience, 48,* 877–888.

Marini, G., Imeri, L., & Mancia, M. (1988). Changes in sleep-waking cycle induced by lesions of medialis dorsalis thalamic nuclei in the cat. *Neuroscience Letters, 85,* 223–227.

Mikiten, T., Niebyl, P., & Hendley, C. (1961). EEG desynchronization during behavioural sleep associated with spike discharges from the thalamus of the cat. *Federation Proceedings, 20,* 327.

Morrison, J. H., & Foote, S. L. (1986). Noradrenergic and serotoninergic innervation of cortical, thalamic, and tectal visual structures in Old and New World monkeys. *Journal of Comparative Neurology, 243,* 117–138.

Mouret, J., Jeannerod, M., & Jouvet, M. (1963). L'activite électrique du systeme visuel au cours de la phase paradoxale du sommeil chez le chat [Electrical activity of the visual system during the paradoxical phase of sleep in the cat]. *Journal of Physiology (Paris), 55,* 305–306.

Nicholson, A. N., & Pascoe, P. A. (1991). Presynaptic alpha 2-adrenoceptor function and sleep in man: Studies with clonidine and idazoxan. *Neuropharmacology, 30,* 367–372.

Nielsen, T. A. (2000). A review of mentation in REM and NREM sleep: "Covert" REM sleep as a possible reconciliation of two opposing models. *The Behavioral & Brain Sciences, 23,* 851–866.

Nitz, D., & Siegel, J. M. (1997). GABA release in the locus coeruleus as a function of sleep/wake state. *Neuroscience, 78,* 795–801.

Nofzinger, E. A., Mintun, M. A., Wiseman, M., Kupfer, D. J., & Moore, R. Y. (1997). Forebrain activation in REM sleep: An FDG PET study. *Brain Research, 770,* 192–201.

Onoe, H., & Sakai, K. (1995). Kainate receptors: A novel mechanism in paradoxical (REM) sleep generation. *NeuroReport, 6,* 353–356.

Pace-Schott, E. F., Stickgold, R., & Hobson, J. A. (1997). Memory processes within dreaming: Methodological issues. *Sleep Research, 26,* 277.

Peigneux, P., Laureys, S., Delbeuck, X., & Maquet, P. (2001a). Sleeping brain, learning brain. The role of sleep for memory systems. *NeuroReport, 12,* A111–A124.

Peigneux, P., Laureys, S., Fuchs, S., Delbeuck, X., Degueldre, C., Aerts, J. et al. (2001b) Generation of rapid eye movements during paradoxical sleep in humans. *NeuroImage, 14,* 701–708.

Portas, C. M., & McCarley, R. W. (1994). Behavioral state-related changes of extracellular serotonin concentration in the dorsal raphe nucleus: A microdialysis study in the freely moving cat. *Brain Research, 648,* 306–312.

Ramm, P., & Frost, B. J. (1983). Regional metabolic activity in the rat brain during sleep-wake activity. *Sleep, 6,* 196–216.

Ramm, P., & Frost, B. J. (1986). Cerebral and local cerebral metabolism in the cat during slow wave and REM sleep. *Brain Research, 365,* 112–124.

Rauchs, G., Desgranges, B., Foret, J., & Eustache, F. (2005). The relationships between memory systems and sleep stages. *Journal of Sleep Research, 14,* 123–140.

Revonsuo, A. (2000). The reinterpretation of dreams: An evolutionary hypothesis of the function of dreaming. *The Behavioral & Brain Sciences, 23,* 877–901.

Ruby, P., & Decety, J. (2001). Effect of subjective perspective taking during simulation of action: A PET investigation of agency. *Nature Neuroscience, 4,* 546–550.

Ruby, P., & Decety, J. (2003). What you believe versus what you think they believe: A neuroimaging study of conceptual perspective-taking. *European Journal of Neuroscience, 17,* 2475–2480.

Ruby, P., & Decety, J. (2004). How would you feel versus how do you think she would feel? A neuroimaging study of perspective-taking with social emotions. *Journal of Cognitive Neuroscience, 16,* 988–999.

Rugg, M. D., Otten, L. J., & Henson, R. N. (2002). The neural basis of episodic memory: Evidence from functional neuroimaging. *Philosophical Transactions of the Royal Society of London, Series B, Biological Sciences, 357,* 1097–1110.

Rugg, M. D., & Wilding, E. L. (2000). Retrieval processing and episodic memory. *Trends in Cognitive Sciences, 4,* 108–115.

Sabatinelli, D., Bradley, M. M., Fitzsimmons, J. R., Lang, P. J. (2005). Parallel amygdala and inferotemporal activation reflect emotional intensity and fear relevance. *NeuroImage, 24,* 1265–1270.

Sah, P., Faber, E. S., Lopez, D.A., & Power, J. (2003). The amygdaloid complex: Anatomy and physiology. *Physiological Reviews, 83,* 803–834.

Salzarule, P., Liary, G. C., Bancaud, J., Munari, C., Barros-Ferreira, M. D., Chodkiewicz, J. P., et al. (1975). Direct depth recording of the striate cortex during REM sleep in man: Are there PGO potentials? *Electroencephalography & Clinical Neurophysiology, 38,* 199–202.

Sanford, L. D., Tejani-Butt, S. M., Ross, R. J., & Morrison, A. R. (1995). Amygdaloid control of alerting and behavioral arousal in rats: Involvement of serotonergic mechanisms. *Archives of Italian Biology, 134,* 81–99.

Sastre, J. P., Buda, C., Kitahama, K., & Jouvet, M. (1996). Importance of the ventrolateral region of the periaqueductal gray and adjacent tegmentum in the control of paradoxical sleep as studied by muscimol microinjections in the cat. *Neuroscience, 4,* 415–426.

Schwartz, S. (2000). A historical loop of one hundred years: Similarities between 19th century and contemporary dream research. *Dreaming, 10,* 55–66.

Schwartz, S. (2003). Are life episodes replayed during dreaming? *Trends in Cognitive Sciences, 7,* 325–327.

Schwartz, S., & Maquet, P. (2002). Sleep imaging and the neuro-psychological assessment of dreams. *Trends in Cognitive Sciences, 6,* 23–30.

Singh, S., & Mallick, B. N. (1996). Mild electrical stimulation of pontine tegmentum around locus coeruleus reduces rapid eye movement sleep in rats. *Neuroscience Research, 24,* 227–235.

Solms, M. (1997). *The neuropsychology of dreams: A clinico-anatomical study.* Mahwah, NJ: Lawrence Erlbaum Assoc.

Solms, M. (2000). Dreaming and REM sleep are controlled by different brain mechanisms. *The Behavioral & Brain Sciences, 23,* 843–850. (Discussion 904–1121)

Steriade, M., & McCarley, R. W. (1990). *Brainstem control of wakefulness and sleep.* New York: Plenum Press.

Steriade, M., & McCarley, R. W. (2005). *Brain control of wakefulness and sleep.* New York: Springer.

Strauch, I., Meier, B., & Foulkes, D. (1996). *In search of dreams: Results of experimental dream research.* Albany, NY: State University of New York Press.

Szymusiak, R. (1995). Magnocellular nuclei of the basal forebrain: Substrates of sleep and arousal regulation. *Sleep, 18,* 478–500.

Tulving, E. (1983). *Elements of episodic memory.* Oxford: Oxford University Press.

Valli, K., Revonsuo, A., Palkas, O., Ismail, K. H., Ali, K. J., & Punamaki, R. L. (2005). The threat simulation theory of the evolutionary function of dreaming: Evidence from dreams of traumatized children. *Consciousness & Cognition, 14,* 188–218.

Velazquez-Moctezuma, J., Gillin, J. C., & Shiromani, P. J. (1989). Effect of specific M1, M2 muscarinic receptor agonists on REM sleep generation. *Brain Research, 503,* 128–131.

Velazquez-Moctezuma, J., Shalauta, M., Gillin, J. C., & Shiromani, P. J. (1991). Cholinergic antagonists and REM sleep generation. *Brain Research, 543,* 175–179.

Wehrle, R., Czisch, M., Kaufmann, C., Wetter, T. C., Holsboer, F., Auer, D. P., et al. (2005). Rapid eye movement-related brain activation in human sleep: A functional magnetic resonance imaging study. *NeuroReport, 16,* 853–857.

Yamamoto, K., Mamelak, A. N., Quattrochi, J. J., & Hobson, J. A. (1990). A cholinoceptive desynchronized sleep induction zone in the anterodorsal pontine tegmentum: Spontaneous and drug-induced neuronal activity. *Neuroscience, 39,* 295–304.

Six

The Frontal Lobes and Dreaming

Edward F. Pace-Schott

WAKING CONSCIOUSNESS AS A WINDOW INTO DREAMING

As advances are made in the cognitive neuroscience, neurophysiology, and behavioral neurology of waking, study of the far less experimentally accessible dream state can greatly benefit from new discoveries and conceptual paradigms applied to waking consciousness. This is especially true when considering the role of frontal systems in dreams since such networks are the most complex, least modality-specific, and most highly evolved circuits in humans and other higher primates (Fuster, 1997; Goldberg, 2001). As such, concepts on the functions of frontal systems in waking are more diverse, controversial, and abstract than those dealing with the sensory and other cognitive functions of posterior cortices.

The current review examines frontal function in dreams in terms both of what is known about the cognitive neuroscience of sleep, as well as of related capabilities and pathologies in waking, about which much more is known. The focus will be on the roles of the frontal lobes' multimodal association and paralimbic and limbic regions (here, collectively termed prefrontal cortex, or PFC) rather than the motor cortices and, for brevity, limbic and paralimbic frontal cortex will be abbreviated here as "limbic" PFC (see Mesulam, 2002, for anatomical details). It will be suggested that changes in prefrontal function during sleep facilitate dreaming by a combination of changes in frontal lobe function, each of which have approximate analogues in the brain bases of normal and/or pathological waking experience. Specifically, it will be argued that the dream experience combines features of

(1) spontaneous confabulation and normal narrative, (2) ascending activation leading to complex hallucinosis, (3) limbic biases in top-down influence on posterior cortex, and (4) activity in frontal limbic circuits subserving emotion and social cognition.

A brief overview of frontal system function during waking will be followed by a summary of recent findings on physiological changes occurring in frontal systems between waking and sleep, as well as within sleep. Such changes include the deactivation of frontal areas in sleep, the selective reactivation of limbic regions in rapid eye movement (REM) sleep, neurochemical changes across the sleep-wake cycle, and changes in the ability of brain regions to interact during sleep. These physiological features of, as well as recent findings in, the cognitive neuroscience of waking consciousness will then be related to each of the above proposed physiological conditions favoring dreaming.

Although the following discussion bears specifically on frontal systems in sleep, modern theories on the function of the frontal lobes increasingly emphasize their regulatory role in the brain as a whole (for example, Duncan, 2001; Duncan & Miller, 2002; Miller, 1999, 2000; Miller & Cohen, 2001). Therefore, sleep-related changes in prefrontal influences on posterior perceptual and mnemonic systems are an important aspect of frontal function in dreams.

FRONTAL SYSTEMS, EXECUTIVE FUNCTION, AND EMOTION

Contemporary views on frontal system function stress the interaction between prefrontal cortices and other brain regions. For example, Miller and Cohen (2001) suggest that the essential function of the PFC is to maintain an on-line representation of a goal, the means to achieve it, and the ongoing context relevant to this goal in order to "bias" the functioning of networks elsewhere in the brain toward this particular outcome. Duncan and Miller (2002) describe this biasing in terms of an "adaptive coding" model, whereby prefrontal neurons and networks direct activity in more posterior systems by competitively strengthening goal-relevant activity while weakening competing alternatives. Mesulam (2002) has conceptualized this general function of the frontal cortex as allowing the organism to "transcend the default mode" of stimulus-bound behaviors, thereby allowing delay, inhibition of prepotent responses, and selection of the most adaptive alternatives. Similarly, Fuster (1997) conceives the function of frontal systems as those capacities that allow the temporal organization of behavior in the service of a particular goal. Supporting such prefrontal modulation of other regions are long-range association fiber bundles directly connecting the frontal cortex with occipital, parietal, and temporal sensory regions, as well as with cortical and subcortical limbic areas in the medial temporal lobe (Pandya & Schmahmann, 2006; Petrides & Pandya, 2002). Moreover, the different regions of the prefrontal cortex are themselves among the most extensively interconnected cortical areas of the brain (Barbas, 2000; Pandya & Yeterian, 1996; Petrides & Pandya, 2002).

The functions of prefrontal multimodal association regions have been closely linked historically to the concept of executive function (EF). EFs can be seen as those high-level cognitive processes that select, organize, and confer cognitive control over more autonomous cognitive functions in the service of a superordinate goal (Mesulam, 2002; Miller & Cohen, 2001). The PFC has traditionally been designated as the primary cerebral region subserving EF and the key cognitive processes that support EF, including working memory (WM), complex attention, and behavioral inhibition (Fuster, 1997; Goldberg, 2001; Mesulam, 2002). However, recent sophisticated technology and experimental designs in functional neuroimaging have increasingly qualified the exclusive importance of the PFC for EF and have identified parietal regions, such as Brodmann areas (BA) 7 and 40 that are also consistently activated by EF tasks (Collette & Van der Linden, 2003; Wager & Smith, 2003; Wager, Jonides, & Reading, 2004).

Based upon the clinical presentation of patients with lesions in different areas of the PFC, it has also been traditionally suggested that dorsal and lateral areas of the prefrontal cortex subserve EFs, such as planning, working, and temporal memory and cognitive flexibility, while ventral and medial regions subserve behavioral inhibition and emotional regulation (Fuster, 1997). However, like the frontal-posterior distinction, this dichotomy of EF capacities subserved by dorsolateral (DLPFC) and ventromedial (vmPFC) PFC regions has been qualified by recent neuroimaging studies (D'Esposito & Postle, 2002; Duncan & Miller, 2002; Duncan & Owen, 2000), as well as by analyses of large sets of lesional data (for example, Stuss et al., 2002). Control of WM in different regions of lateral prefrontal cortex had also been suggested to show considerable domain specificity, with spatial WM subserved more dorsally and object WM more ventrally as termini of dorsal and ventral visual processing streams respectively (Courtney, Petit, Haxbury, & Ungerleider, 1998; Goldman-Rakic, 1996; Levy & Goldman-Rakic, 2000). However, recent studies have provided more evidence for dorso-ventral and antero-posterior segregation of function in the lateral PFC, with ventrolateral regions subserving WM maintenance in multiple domains and dorsal and polar regions recruited as demands for manipulation of WM and its use in more complex EF increase (Christoff, Ream, Geddes, & Gabrieli, 2003; D'Esposito et al., 1998; D'Esposito, Postle, & Rypma, 2000; Fletcher

& Henson, 2001; Koechlin, Ody, & Kouneiher, 2003; Petrides, 2005; Wager & Smith, 2003).

Recent findings have also altered our understanding of the functional anatomy of ventral and medial PFC, regions that include the lateral and medial orbitofrontal cortex, anterior cingulated, and the more dorsal and anterior medial walls of the frontal cortex. For example, the role of the orbitofrontal cortex in behavioral inhibition (Fuster, 1997) has been shown to be shared by the inferior frontal junction (Derfuss, Brass, Neumann, & von Cramon, 2005; Duncan & Owen, 2000; Jonides, Badre, Curtis, Thompson-Schill, & Smith, 2002). Similarly, the role of the anterior cingulate in conflict monitoring (Botvinick, Cohen, & Carter, 2004) may be shared by more anterior medial regions, such as the presupplementary motor area or pre-SMA (Ridderinkhof, Ullsperger, Crone, & Nieuwenhuis, 2004; Wittfoth, Buck, Fahle, & Herrmann, 2006). The ventral orbitofrontal and medial PFC (vmPFC), is involved with emotion, visceral sensorimotor processing, salience attribution, and reward processes (Gusnard, Akbudak, Shulman, & Raichle, 2001; Kringlebach, 2005; Phan, Wager, Taylor, & Liberzon, 2002; Price, 1999). Within the vmPFC, more lateral orbital multimodal sensory areas integrate exteroceptive and interoceptive (viscerosensory) information and interact with medial visceromotor systems that are densely interconnected with subcortical limbic structures that can initiate autonomic and homeostatic responses (Price, 1999). Within the orbitofrontal cortex, more lateral areas have been shown to be involved with processing aversive stimuli, whereas more medial regions are associated with reward processing (Kringlebach, 2005; Kringlebach & Rolls, 2004).

Importantly, vmPFC functions can be somewhat differentiated from those of dorsal- and anterior-medial PFC (dmPFC), which is involved in self-referential, theory of mind (ToM), and social cognition processes (Amodio & Frith, 2006; Frith & Frith, 2006; Gallagher & Frith, 2003; Gusnard et al., 2001). For example, in a recent meta-analysis of studies on functional neuroimaging of the experience of self, Northoff et al. (2006) have distinguished a ventromedial region of the mPFC consisting of medial orbitofrontal, ventromedial polar regions, and sub- and perigenual anterior cingulated cortex (ACC), from a dorsomedial sector consisting of medial portions of BA 9 and the supragenual ACC. These authors associate the ventromedial region with a basic labeling of stimuli as self-related, while dorsomedial regions evaluate and appraise such stimuli in association with the lateral PFC. Northoff et al. (2006) hypothesized that such evaluative processes include the differentiation of self-related from other-related stimuli, processes involved in attribution of mental processes to others (theory of mind) and other forms of social cognition.

Ventromedial prefrontal areas have also been widely implicated in decision-making processes (Bechara, Damasio, & Damasio, 2000). As articulated in the somatic marker hypothesis (Damasio, 1996, 2003), the vmPFC associates bio-regulatory, autonomic responses that are detected (as well as potentially generated) by interoceptive brain structures (for example, insula, somatosensory cortices, and brainstem nuclei), with the particular classes of complex, salient events that previously elicited such somatic responses (Bechara et al., 2000). Association of interoceptive signals with general types of past experience (the mnemonic specifics of which are represented in other brain regions), creates preconscious biases that improve the speed and accuracy of decision-making (Bechara et al., 2000). Recent neuroimaging studies have further suggested that emotionally modulated, "hot" decision-making processes are subserved by orbitofrontal areas, whereas more purely cognitive, "cool" decision processes are associated more with dorsolateral PFC activity (Krain, Wilson, Arbuckle, Castellanos, & Milham, 2006).

Circuits interconnecting prefrontal and subcortical regions are also vitally important regulatory components of frontal system function. Fronto-striato-pallido-thalamo-frontal connections form semisegregated circuits, with more dorsal circuits modulating motor, working memory, and EF functions, while more ventral circuits are important components of emotion, reward, and motivational systems (Saint-Cyr, 2003; Saint-Cyr, Bronstein, & Cummings, 2002). Dysexecutive symptoms following cerebellar damage (the cerebellar cognitive affective syndrome) has also implicated fronto-ponto-cerebello-thalamo-frontal circuits in normal EF (Schmahmann, 2004). The amygdala and orbitofrontal cortex serve as an integrated unit in processing and regulation of emotion (Barbas, 2000) while direct connections from the ventromedial prefrontal cortex to the hypothalamus and amygdala allow these executive areas to directly influence autonomic output (Barbas, Saha, Rempel-Clower, & Ghashghaei, 2003).

HYPOFRONTALITY AND SLEEP

In recent years, converging evidence from functional neuroimaging, electrophysiology, and neuropsychology suggests that sleep, both REM and NREM, is accompanied by diminished neuronal activity in certain regions of the frontal lobes (reviewed in Dang-Vu et al., 2005a; Maquet, 2000; Maquet et al., 2005; Muzur, Pace-Schott, & Hobson, 2002; Pace-Schott, 2003, 2005a). These same technical advances reveal that sleep shares this general condition, often termed "hypofrontality," with many neuropsychiatric pathologies (reviewed in Dietrich, 2003; Pace-Schott, 2003; Schwartz & Maquet, 2002), as well as with altered states of waking consciousness in healthy individuals (reviewed in Dietrich, 2003; Pace-Schott, 2003). Hypo-frontality is often invoked as causal of psychological differences between mental activity in such states and normal waking, and these state-dependent differences relative to waking can be characterized as a decline of EF capacity (for example, Dietrich, 2003; Pace-Schott, 2003).

Three important points, however, qualify this linkage between hypofron-tal states (including sleep and dreaming) and lessened executive abilities. First, as noted above, EF is supported by neural circuits linking the frontal cortex with structures in the posterior cortex and subcortex and not by the PFC in isolation. Second, anatomic subregions of the frontal cortex are recruited to a greater or lesser degree depending a particular EF's type (for example, Moskovitch & Winocur, 2002), difficulty (for example, Duncan & Owen, 2000) or situational salience (Duncan & Miller, 2002). Third, and most importantly for the current discussion, only certain PFC areas and not others are inactive relative to waking in REM sleep (Dang-Vu et al., 2005a; Maquet et al., 2005; Pace-Schott, 2005a), the behavioral state that produces greatest recall and intensity of dreaming (Hobson, Pace-Schott, & Stickgold, 2000; Nielsen, 1999, 2000).

Deactivation of frontal cortices is one of the first physiological signs of human sleep whether measured by quantitative electroencephalography (EEG) (Borbely, 2001; Finelli, Borbely, & Achermann, 2001; Werth, Acher-mann, & Borbely, 1996, 1997), magnetoencephalography (MEG) (Simon, Kemp, Manshanden, & Lopes da Silva, 2003), oxygen utilization ($H_2{}^{15}O$), or glucose-metabolic (^{18}FDG) positron emission tomography (PET) (Braun et al., 1997, 1998; Kjaer, Law, Wiltschiotz, Paulson, & Madsen, 2002; Maquet et al., 1997; Nofzinger et al., 2002) or by functional magnetic resonance imaging (fMRI) (Kaufmann et al., 2006; Laufs et al., 2006). For example, right frontal deactivation is seen even in early light sleep (Kaufmann et al., 2006; Kjaer et al., 2002). This pattern of decreased blood flow in the frontal cortex with the onset and deepening of NREM sleep has now been widely replicated (for example, Andersson et al., 1998; Finelli et al. 2000; Kajimura et al., 1999). Additional evidence that frontal deactiva-tion is a general characteristic of sleep comes with the discovery that frontal reactivation lags behind that of the rest of the brain following awakening (Balkin et al., 2002).

A recent fMRI study provides details on changes in regional cerebral blood flow (rCBF) between waking and specific stages of NREM using measures of regional blood oxygen level-dependent (BOLD) signal response (Kaufmann et al., 2006). Most strikingly in regard to frontal deactivation was the finding that the most prominent and consistent deactivations from waking to NREM were seen in frontal areas including inferior, middle, and superior frontal gyri, as well as medial frontal and primary motor cortices. In addition to medial frontal areas, other limbic cortices such as the anterior and posterior cingulate were also less active in NREM compared to waking. Notably, wake-NREM comparisons revealed that these deactivations were considerably greater in the right hemisphere. These frontal deactivations in NREM relative to waking were also accompanied by deactivations in midline subcortical (hypothalamus, caudate), thalamic (anterior nucleus), as well as limbic (insula, hippocampal complex), parietal (for example, inferior parietal), and occipital (precuneus, cuneus) cortical structures.

Frontal areas may also display a greater need for recovery sleep than more posterior regions (Finelli et al., 2001). For example, in the first NREM episode of the night, there is relatively greater slow wave spectral power, termed "slow wave activity" (SWA), a marker of homeostatic sleep pressure, in frontal than in parietal and occipital regions (Finelli et al., 2001; Werth et al., 1996, 1997). At sleep onset, greater SWA, an electrophysiological feature associated with reduced rCBF (Dang-Vu et al., 2005b; Hofle et al., 1997), is seen in frontal versus more posterior scalp sites (Finelli et al., 2001; Werth et al., 1996, 1997). There is evidence that slow wave activity then spreads progressively to posterior regions (De Gennaro et al., 2004). Increasing sleep pressure by sleep or SWS deprivation has been shown to enhance the frontal predominance of SWA (Cajochen, Foy, & Dijk, 2000; De Gennaro et al., 2004; Finelli et al., 2001), especially in the left hemisphere (Achermann, Finelli, & Borberly, 2001).

Recent combined EEG and fMRI studies during sleep indicate that an increase in posterior cortical activation relative to frontal regions may accompany the shift of alpha EEG rhythms in quiet waking toward theta frequencies in Stage 1 NREM sleep (Laufs et al., 2006). Moreover, such studies suggest that additional processes exist that further synchronize the EEG (that is, increase delta power) in response to sensory stimulation (Born et al., 2002; Czisch et al., 2002; Czisch et al., 2004). Such increased EEG synchronization is accompanied by a widespread decrease in the fMRI BOLD signal. Such stimulus-induced deactivation occurs during light Stage 2 NREM but not in highly synchronized SWS, suggesting that this response may be a mechanism by which sleep is preserved in the face of external stimuli during light sleep (Czisch et al., 2004).

Both PET (Dang-Vu et al., 2005b; Hofle et al., 1997; Maquet, 1995) and fMRI (Czisch et al., 2004; Kaufmann et al., 2006) studies have shown that global cerebral activity, including that of frontal areas, continues to diminish with deepening NREM sleep. Although the transition from waking to NREM involves a prominent thalamic deactivation in addition to widespread cortical and subcortical deactivations (Dang-Vu, 2005b; Hofle et al.,

1997), once sleep is achieved further thalamic deactivation does not appear to characterize deepening NREM (Dang-Vu et al., 2005b). Instead, a PET study showed that progressive deactivation within NREM sleep is centered on regions in the medial prefrontal cortex including anterior medial areas in BA 9 and 10, orbitofrontal cortices (BA 11) including caudal orbital basal forebrain, anterior cingulate (BA24), bilateral anterior insula, basal fore-brain/anterior hypothalamus, bilateral putamen, and left precuneus (Dang-Vu et al., 2005a). Similarly, using fMRI, activity in cingulate and frontal areas progressively declined from Stage 1 to Stage 2 to SWS (Kaufmann et al., 2006).

Much of the lateral frontal cortex remains less active than during waking after the transition from NREM to REM, a phenomenon that has been demonstrated by using $H_2^{15}O$ PET (Braun et al. 1997; Braun et al., 1998; Maquet et al., 1996), single photon emission computed tomography (SPECT) (Madsen et al., 1991), and fMRI (Lovblad et al., 1999). In a recent meta-analysis of their many $H_2^{15}O$ PET studies of human sleep, Maquet and colleagues (2005) have shown that the regions most consistently hypoactive in REM sleep compared to waking include association cortices in the middle and inferior frontal gyri, as well as the inferior parietal and temporo-parietal junction (Dang-Vu et al., 2005a; Maquet et al., 2005).

Given the now abundant evidence of prefrontal deactivation in sleep relative to waking, any neurocognitive theory of dreaming must take this into account as a basic feature of the brain in sleep. Accordingly, hypofrontality is important whether dreaming is seen as state of consciousness expressed in its most qualitatively complete form during REM sleep (Gottesmann, 2006; Hobson et al., 2000; Nielsen, 2000; Pace-Schott, 2005a; Stickgold et al., 2001; Takeuchi et al., 2003) or as a mental state fully expressed in any stage of sleep (Antrobus, 1990; Domhoff, 2003; Foulkes, 1996; Solms, 1997). The consistent finding that lesions of the lateral prefrontal areas do not disrupt dreaming (Doricchi & Violani, 1992; Solms, 1997) provides additional evidence for a weak influence of the cognitive functions subserved by these regions, most notably WM, during dreams.

CORTICAL AND SUBCORTICAL LIMBIC REACTIVATION IN REM SLEEP

Selective regional activation in REM, relative to global deactivation in NREM and to waking activity patterns, allows us to better understand the brain basis of dreaming. This is because what is physiologically unique or enhanced during REM must be related to those psychological aspects of dreaming that are likewise enhanced during REM. Nonetheless, dream reports can be obtained from any stage of sleep (Cavallero, Cicogna, Natale,

Occhionero, & Zito, 1992; Foulkes, 1962; Foulkes & Vogel, 1965; reviewed in Nielsen, 1999, 2000). Therefore, to best address dream physiology, it is important to consider changes in regional activity that exist between sleep and waking, between different sleep stages and substages, as well as between short, transient (phasic) sleep events and more long-lasting (tonic) sleep conditions.

Unlike in lateral frontal association areas, during the transition from REM to NREM sleep rCBF increases to subcortical brain regions such as the pons, midbrain, and thalamus (Braun et al., 1997; Maquet et al., 1996); amygdala (Maquet et al., 1996); hypothalamus; and basal ganglia (Braun et al., 1997). Notably, rCBF also increases to anterior limbic-related cortices such as rostral and subcallosal anterior cingulate (Braun et al., 1997; Maquet et al., 1996), anterior insular and caudal orbitofrontal cortex, paracingulate area BA32, and anterior medial prefrontal BA10 (Braun et al., 1997). In the NREM-REM transition, rCBF to limbic cortices also increases more caudally in the parahippocampal gyrus and temporal pole (Braun et al., 1997).

As is the case for rCBF, a REM-related increase in regional glucose metabolism is also observed in a "bilateral confluent paramedian zone which extends from the septal area into ventral striatum, infralimbic, prelimbic, orbitofrontal and anterior cingulate cortex" (Nofzinger, Mintun, Wiseman, Kupfer, & Moore, 1997, p. 192). These authors have termed this region the "anterior paralimbic REM activation area," and characterize it further as including hypothalamus, ventral striatum and pallidum, hippocampus, and uncus, as well as supplementary motor and pre- and subgenual anterior cingulate and insular cortices (Nofzinger et al., 2004). Reactivation of this midline area, including the above paralimbic cortices, during REM has now been widely replicated (Braun et al., 1997; Maquet et al., 1996; Nofzinger et al., 1999, 2001, 2004; Smith et al., 1999; Wu et al., 1999; Wu, Buchsbaum, & Bunney, 2001).

NEUROMODULATION OF THE PFC IN WAKING AND SLEEP

During waking, ascending arousal systems of the brainstem, hypothalamus, and basal forebrain provide wake-promoting neuromodulatory input to the forebrain, including the PFC. Such alerting neuromodulators have maximal influence on the forebrain in the waking state and include the monoamines serotonin, norepinephrine, histamine, and dopamine, in addition to acetylcholine and the neuropeptide orexin. Their influence on the forebrain is attenuated at sleep and diminishes further with deepening of NREM sleep. During REM, the monoamines serotonin, norepinephrine, and histamine reach minimum levels, cholinergic neuromodulation returns to waking levels, and dopaminergic neuromodulation of the forebrain may also persist. Details of these state-dependent neuromodulatory changes can be found in Hobson et al. (2000); Pace-Schott and Hobson (2002a, 2002b); Saper, Chou, and Scammell (2001); Saper, Scammel, and Lu (2005); and Saper, Cano, and Scammell (2005); see also Gottesmann (2006).

Cognitive processing in the PFC during waking is known to be sensitive to levels of these same arousal-related neuromodulators, particularly dopamine, norepinephrine, and acetylcholine (Arnsten, 1997; Arnsten, & Robbins, 2002; Robbins, 2005). Dopamine and norepinephrine levels can strongly influence EFs such as WM, planning, and set shifting subserved by lateral regions of the PFC (Arnsten & Robbins, 2002). Activation of post-synaptic D1 dopamine receptors appears most important in mediating dopaminergic effects on prefrontal regions, while D1 and D2 receptors modulate functioning of direct and indirect striatal circuits respectively within fronto-striatal loops (Arnsten & Robbins, 2002; Ferre, Fredholm, Morelli, Popoli, & Fuxe, 1997). Unlike dopamine and norepinephrine's effects throughout the PFC including its lateral regions, the effects of serotonin in the PFC may specifically enhance cognitive functions subserved by orbitofrontal regions (Arnsten & Robbins, 2002; Rogers et al., 1999). Similarly, cholinergic innervation is especially dense in anterior subcortical and cortical limbic regions (Mesulam, Hersh, Mash, & Geula, 1992; Selden, Gitelman, Salamon-Murayama, Parrish, & Mesulam, 1998) and may most heavily influence ventral and medial areas of the frontal cortex (Arnsten & Robbins, 2002).

Since both neuromodulatory influences on the forebrain and the frequency and intensity of recalled dreaming change dramatically with transitions from wake to NREM to REM, theories of neuromodulatory effects on dreaming have been proposed. Activation-synthesis (AS) and activation-input-modulation (AIM) models suggest that the increase in cholinergic relative to noradrenergic and serotonergic contributions to forebrain activation during REM sleep favors non-wake-like aspects of dream consciousness (Hobson, 1988; Hobson & McCarley, 1977; Hobson et al., 2000). Another hypothesis suggests that dopaminergic stimulation of limbic reward and prefrontal structures generate motivational impulses that trigger dreaming throughout sleep (Solms, 1997, 2000, 2002). A third hypothesis suggests that dopaminergic stimulation of the cortex during REM, in the absence of the serotonergic and noradrenergic inhibition present in waking, favors emergence of a psychotomimetic (psychosis-like) dream state (Gottesmann, 2002a, 2002b, 2006). These theories are consistent with an attenuation of EFs in dreams resulting from a sleep-related, and, specifically, a REM sleep-related decrease in noradrenergic and serotonergic modulation of the PFC. For a more detailed discussion of neuromodulatory theories on dreaming, see Hobson et al. (2000), Pace-Schott (2005a) and Perry, Ashton, and Young (2002). The current chapter will focus specifically on dream effects of neuromodulators in the PFC.

CORTICAL CONNECTIVITY IN SLEEP

A frequent theme in recent imaging, electrophysiological, and theoretical studies of sleep and dreaming is of a functional disconnection, relative to waking, between frontal and posterior cortical regions or between left and right hemispheres. In waking, fast oscillatory rhythms in the gamma frequency range (30–80 Hz) have been associated with conscious cognitive effort and temporal binding of perceptual awareness (Engel, Fries, & Singer, 2001; Tallon-Baudry & Bertrand, 1999), and a similar role for such fast oscillations in the temporal binding of dream imagery has been postulated (Kahn et al., 1997). Gamma frequency oscillations are attenuated in NREM with the onset of intrinsic slow thalamocortical and cortico-cortical rhythms (Steriade, 2000, 2006), but return in REM sleep (Gross & Gottman, 1999; Llinas & Ribary, 1993).

However, in REM sleep compared to waking, gamma frequency oscillations become desynchronized between frontal and posterior perceptual areas (Corsi-Cabrera et al., 2003; Perez-Garci et al., 2001). Such REM-related oscillatory desynchrony has been suggested to reflect a functional disconnection of posterior perception related cortical areas from frontal executive control (Corsi-Cabrera et al., 2003; Perez-Garci et al. 2001). Moreover, intracranial EEG (iEEG) has demonstrated a similar sleep-related decline of coherence (the tendency for rhythms of the same frequency to be in phase) in gamma frequencies between cortico-cortical and cortico-hippocampal sites (Cantero, Atienza, Madsen, & Stickgold, 2004). These authors suggest that reduced gamma frequency coherence contributes to the hypofrontal features and bizarreness of REM sleep dreaming (Cantero et al., 2004; Corsi-Cabrera et al., 2003; Perez-Garci et al., 2001). (For an interesting review relating such disconnection phenomena in REM to those in psychosis, see Gottesmann, 2006.)

Because of the synchronizing influence of intrinsic, sleep-related thalamo-cortical and cortico-cortical oscillations (Steriade, 2000, 2006), interhemispheric coherence at slow EEG frequencies such as delta (1–3 Hz) and theta (4–7 Hz) are typically greater in sleep than in waking (for example, Guevara, Lorenzo, Arce, Ramos, & Corsi-Cabrera, 1995; Nielsen, 1999). Nonetheless, some studies have also shown reduced intrahemispheric or antero-posterior coupling in sleep versus waking (or in REM versus NREM) even at these slower frequencies. For example, a progressive decline in alpha frequency coherence has been demonstrated between fronto-frontal and fronto-occipital sites from waking through NREM to REM sleep (Cantero, Atienza, Salas, & Gomez, 1999; Cantero, Atienza, & Salas, 2000). Similarly, awakenings that yielded dream reports showed greater intrahemispheric coherence at 13 to 16, 21 to 23, and 25 to 32 Hz during the previous 10 minutes of sleep in Stage 2 NREM than in REM (Corsi-Cabrera et al., 2003). At still slower frequencies (5–8 Hz), antero-posterior coherence was significantly lower for REM than for NREM Stage 2 but significantly higher for REM than Stage 2 between different posterior sites, a finding that Corsi-Cabrera et al. (2003) link with reduced executive control but heightened perceptual intensity in REM versus NREM dreaming (Corsi-Cabrera et al., 2003).

Moving beyond correlative studies to experimental manipulations that can demonstrate causation, transcranial magnetic stimulation (TMS) studies have demonstrated reduced functional influence between different brain regions during REM sleep compared to waking (Bertini et al., 2004; Massimini et al., 2005). For example, Bertini et al. (2004) demonstrated that transcallosal inhibition of motor-evoked potentials (MEPs) by contralateral magnetic stimulation is greatly reduced immediately after awakening from REM sleep compared both to Stage 2 NREM awakenings and to waking. Interestingly, these authors found that during REM, unlike during waking, transcallosal inhibition of the contralateral MEP was greater for right compared to left hemisphere stimulation. These authors hypothesize that their results reflect reduced interhemispheric connectivity in REM sleep compared to waking.

Similarly, Massimini et al. (2005) have shown that, in waking, TMS stimulation of premotor cortex BA 6 leads to subsequent, high-frequency responses lasting as long as 300 milliseconds that were time locked to the initial stimulus and which propagated to contralateral and ipsilateral sites at distances from the site of stimulation as far away as the parietal cortex. In contrast, during NREM sleep, the localized response to TMS was of higher amplitude but failed to persist in time or propagate to other sites. TMS in Stage 1 NREM resulted in a response intermediate between that following stimulation in waking and in deeper stages of NREM. These authors suggest that such decline in cortical "effective connectivity" (the ability of information to propagate among distributed cortical regions subserving specific cognitive processes) may underlie the attenuation of consciousness in sleep and especially in deeper NREM.

DREAMS, SPONTANEOUS CONFABULATION, AND NARRATIVE

Dreaming can be seen to involve a particularly potent form of spontaneous confabulation in which imaginary events are not only created and accepted as truth but are vividly experienced as organized, multimodal hallucinations (Hobson, 1988, 1999; Pace-Schott, 2005a). Hirstein (2005) suggests that spontaneous confabulation is the most florid form of a class of neurological syndromes involving expressed false beliefs that are not recognized as such by the patient. Such conditions also include the anosagnosias (denial of illness) and misidentification (mistaken identification of persons, places, or objects) syndromes. A spontaneously confabulating patient recounts events from the past, describes present experiences, or announces future plans that are clearly false or impossible, although usually based upon real autobiographical events sometimes drawn from the patient's remote memory (Hirstein, 2005; Schnider, 2001, 2003). Hirstein (2005) notes two cardinal features of all confabulatory syndromes. First, confabulators recount false events or assert false beliefs that would be readily seen as such by a healthy individual. Second, the confabulator holds an unshakable conviction as to the veracity of his or her claims and is, therefore, not lying.

Hirstein notes that spontaneous confabulation involves both an element of creative storytelling and an inability to verify the truth or falsehood of what is said. While amnesia of diencephalic (thalamus, hypothalamus, and basal forebrain) etiology is often present in confabulators, amnesia alone is insufficient to produce spontaneous confabulation, and executive deficits involving frontal dysfunction must also be present (Hirstein, 2005). Such executive deficits may include failures to distinguish truth from fantasy (impaired "reality monitoring"), verbal disinhibition allowing expression of thoughts without adequate monitoring and verification, or disturbances in temporal labeling of memories such that past events are perceived as current (Hirstein, 2005; Schnider, 2001, 2003).

The syndrome of spontaneous confabulation arises in severe brain disorders such as Korsakoff syndrome and Alzheimer's disease, as well as aneurism rupture of the anterior communicating artery or traumatic brain injury (Hirstein, 2005; Schnider, 2003; Schnider, Bonvallat, Emond, & Leemann, 2005). The most common lesions resulting in spontaneous confabulation involve anterior limbic cortico-subcortical networks that include the caudal orbitofrontal cortex, mammilary bodies, mediodorsal and anterior thalamic nuclei, basal forebrain, and hypothalamus (Hirstein, 2005; Ptak et al., 2001; Schnider, 2001, 2003). Schnider suggests that spontaneous confabulation results from combined mnemonic and executive deficits arising from damage to anterior limbic circuitry including the posterior medial orbitofrontal cortex and its direct and indirect connections with basal forebrain, amygdala, mediodorsal thalamic nucleus, and hypothalamus (Schnider, 2001, 2003).

The location of anterior limbic regions whose damage most commonly leads to spontaneous confabulation provides a striking parallel with regions that show greater activity in REM sleep compared to waking (see Pace-Schott, 2005a). These areas broadly overlap with Nofzinger et al.'s (1997) midline anterior paralimbic REM activation area (septum, ventral striatum, as well as orbitofrontal, anterior cingulate, and insular and subgenual cortices) in which glucose utilization in REM exceeds that of waking. Similarly, areas typically damaged in confabulators overlap with limbic and paralimbic structures that show greater rCBF in REM than in either waking or SWS (anterior hypothalamus, caudal orbital, medial prefrontal and anterior cingulate cortices) or SWS alone (thalamus, insula) (Braun et al., 1997).

Notably, lesions to ventromedial prefrontal area and adjacent subcortical structures have also been associated with wake/dream confusional states (Solms, 1997, 2000). Similarly, early psychosurgical reports of exceptionally vivid daydreams, difficult to differentiate from actual dreams, following anterior cingulate lesions are cited by Hirstein (2005). Notably, in a group of brain lesion patients showing symptoms of increased reality of dreaming and confusion between dreams and reality, two of three with medial frontal/basal forebrain lesions also displayed confabulatory amnesia (Solms, 1997).

Schnider's theory of spontaneous confabulation (Schnider, 2001, 2003) provides a model for certain dream phenomena (Pace-Schott, 2005a). For example, the confabulators certitude in false claims and lack of insight bears striking resemblance to the uncritical acceptance of dream reality in the nonlucid conditions of the vast majority of dreams (Rechtschaffen, 1978). According to Schnider, spontaneous confabulation is a formal thought disorder caused by the failure of a reality monitoring function that normally preconsciously identifies and actively suppresses spontaneously activated memories that do not pertain to the "present" (that is, temporally current facts, plans, and stimuli). As a result, the spontaneous confabulator is necessarily disoriented to time and often to place, a lack of orientation also experienced in dreams (Hobson, 1988, 1999).

In spontaneous confabulation, damage to orbitofrontal regions may release from normal frontally based inhibitory and reality-monitoring constraints innate human tendencies to create explanatory stories and fill amnestic gaps in narratives (Hirstein, 2005). Similar release phenomena may underlie the generation of dream narratives when selective reactivation of limbic midline structures, including the caudo-medial orbital cortex, accompanies continued lateral frontal inactivity in REM sleep (Maquet et al., 2005). The tendency in dreaming to create "ad-hoc explanations" for improbable dream occurrences (Williams, Merritt, Rittenhouse, & Hobson, 1992) has a clear parallel in the tendency of confabulators to create plausible but false explanations for inconsistencies in their stories, or for patients with related syndromes involving denial of paralysis or blindness (anosagnosias) to create explanations for why they are unable to see or to move (Hirstein, 2005). A similar symptom seen in confabulation syndromes, "pathological false recognition" (Hirstein, 2005), also has a clear parallel in deja vu experiences in dreams.

Although, dreaming, unlike spontaneous confabulation, involves the actual hallucinatory experience of an ongoing narrative, dream hallucinations, and particularly their distortion relative to waking counterparts, have been likened to the same neurological syndromes that Hirstein argues are closely related to confabulation (Schwartz & Maquet, 2002; Schwartz, Dang-Vu, Ponz, Duhoux, & Maquet, 2005). In both confabulation syndromes and dreaming, etiological hypotheses invoke a disconnection of perceptual processes subserved by posterior regions from verification and reality monitoring processes subserved by the PFC (Hirstein, 2005; Schwartz & Maquet, 2002). In particular, Schwartz and Maquet (2002) suggest that certain dream phenomena bear formal similarities to waking misidentification disorders such as Fregoli, Capgras, and reduplicative paramnesia syndromes, all waking disorders with confabulatory components (Hirstein, 2005). For example, Schwartz and Maquet (2002) liken ascribing particular identities to dream characters who have perceptual features unlike their waking counterpart to Fregoli syndrome, a hype-identification disorder of waking. These authors hypothesize that a sleep-related disconnection of temporal face recognition areas from prefrontal reality monitoring underlies this dream phenomenon.

Parallels between confabulation and sleep also exist with regard to right hemisphere lateralization of function and dysfunction. Confabulatory syndromes and related syndromes of neglect and anosagnosia are most common following right hemisphere damage (Hirstein, 2005). Similarly, cortical deactivation in NREM sleep is greater in the right hemisphere (Kaufmann et al., 2006). In contrast, in REM, evidence suggests that reactivation is greater in the right hemisphere (Nofzinger et al., 2004). For example, there is greater correlation of REM density with rCBF in the right hemisphere (Hong, Gillin, Dow, Wu, & Buchsbaum, 1995; Peigneux et al., 2001). Similarly, an MEG study of REM sleep reported a predominance of leftward REMs, suggesting stronger right hemisphere activity in REM sleep (Ioannides et al., 2004). In addition, one PET study showed greater activity in REM than in waking in the inferior parietal lobe but only in the right hemisphere (Maquet et al., 1996). Notably, the inferior parietal lobe is also a region where isolated, site-specific damage most often results in global dream cessation and where such dream loss is more severe following right versus left hemisphere damage (Solms, 1997). Therefore, despite the apparent lack of clear overall hemispheric dominance in normal dreaming (Antrobus, 1987; Lavie & Tzischinsky, 1985), evidence exists that certain brain activities necessary for dreaming may be relatively right lateralized.

If indeed both spontaneous confabulation and dream plot generation involve release of normal narrative mechanisms from frontal restraint, the neurophysiology of normal story production may shed light on both phenomena. Mar (2004) has reviewed functional neuroimaging and lesion studies of narrative production and, although sparse in comparison to studies of narrative comprehension, certain parallels exist with both confabulation and dreaming. For example, using PET, Braun et al. (2001), performed conjunction analysis to identify modality-independent regions involved in common by storytelling in both English and American Sign Language. Conjunction analysis showed activity in medial and lateral prefrontal, premotor, superior and middle temporal, inferior and medial parietal, as well as in visual association (extrastriate) cortices. Although functions of the posterior and premotor areas activated in common could be attributed to various steps of language production, imagery, or lexical, semantic, and episodic memory retrieval, these authors suggest that medial prefrontal activation (BA 9 and 10 extending to frontal pole) could be most directly related to the generic production of narrative discourse (Braun et al., 2001). In another study in which subjects generated plans, medial frontal and inferior parietal areas were again activated in addition to cingulate, lateral prefrontal, and temporal regions (Partiot, Grafman, Sadato, Wachs, & Hallett, 1995). Notably, right hemisphere and frontal damage leads to greater impairment in ability to generate normal waking narrative than damage elsewhere in the brain (Mar, 2004). Medial prefrontal activation will be further discussed below when considering sources of thematic content in dream plots.

Despite striking parallels between dreaming and confabulation in terms of the involvement of anterior midline limbic and prefrontal structures, several prominent differences between these phenomena exist. In addition to its hallucinatory, sensory nature, dreaming also differs from spontaneous confabulation in its frequent generation of wholly novel scenes, characters, objects, and scenarios (Hobson, 1988; Pace-Schott, 2005a). For example, a recent study showed that 25 percent of dream characters were wholly novel personages (Kahn, Stickgold, Pace-Schott, & Hobson, 2000) whereas, in another study, only 1.4 percent of elements identified by the dreamer as being caused by a waking event met definitional criteria for a true episodic memory (Fosse, Stickgold, & Hobson, 2003). Such novelty differs from spontaneous confabulation, which invariably relates in some way to patients' past experience (Schnider, 2001, 2003). Another notable difference is the fact that although spontaneous confabulation results from damage to anterior midline limbic and prefrontal structures, REM sleep involves activation of these same regions to levels exceeding those of waking. Absence of exteroceptive input and functional dissociation of prefrontal from posterior regions in sleep may account for the latter differences. Moreover, changes in consciousness can result from abnormal activation of anterior limbic areas (for example, in seizures), as well as from their lesional damage (Devinsky, Morrell, & Vogt, 1995; Servan-Schreiber & Perlstein, 1997; Small et al., 2005; Starkstein & Robinson, 1997).

ALTERED BALANCE BETWEEN MEMORY CONFIRMATION/RECOGNITION AND STRATEGIC SEARCH/RECALL

Sleep-related lateral PFC deactivation and REM-related caudo-ventro-medial PFC activation may alter the interaction of specific mnemonic functions of the PFC. Various executive memory functions are regionally dissociable in the PFC (Fletcher & Henson, 2001; Moscovitch & Winocur, 2002), and alteration in their relative integrity may help explain certain memory features of dreams, such as the paucity of episodic memory (Fosse et al., 2003), weakened WM (Hobson et al., 2000), and bizarrely enhanced recognition memory (Pace-Schott, 2005a; Schwartz & Maquet, 2002). For example, among frontal contributions to memory retrieval, it has been suggested that ventrolateral PFC regions subserve semantically based cue specification, dorsolateral regions provide strategic search strategies, caudal ventromedial regions provide a basic emotional verification of accuracy, while medial frontopolar regions provide more complex, cognitively based verification (Fletcher & Henson, 2001; Moscovitch & Winocur, 2002).

A shift in relative activity favoring caudo-ventro-medial over anterolateral PFC regions in REM may indiscriminatively evoke emotional confirmation of accuracy for any item arising in consciousness, as also appears to occur in spontaneous confabulation. Dream elements arising via ecphory (cued episodic memory retrieval; see Moscovitch & Winocur, 2002) and/or hallucinatory imagery arising in unimodal association cortices may, therefore, be accepted without the benefit of strategic volitional search or cognitive verification. Perhaps reflecting such state-dependent credulity, up to 40 percent of dream characters are identified on the basis of "just knowing" (Kahn et al., 2000).

Schwartz and Maquet (2002) liken such delusional sense of familiarity in dreams to brain-damage induced reduplicative paramnesia in general and to Fregoli syndrome in the case of specific personages. These authors suggest such bizarre recognition results from sleep-induced disconnection of temporal face recognition areas from prefrontal reality monitoring regions. Because false recognition occurs for dream place and objects, as well as characters, one might further hypothesize similar disconnections between multiple ventral stream representations in the inferior temporal cortex (for example, the "parahippocampal place area") and the PFC. Alternatively, experiences of familiarity poorly matched to waking reality in dreams may reflect activity of recognition memory mechanisms in anterior perirhinal cortices (BA 35, 36). Perirhinal neurons show altered responses following a single stimulus exposure, a possible neural basis for familiarity discrimination not present in neurons of the hippocampus proper (Brown & Aggleton, 2001). Double dissociations between recognition and remembering have also been shown in fMRI studies of humans (Brown & Aggleton, 2001). Perirhinal areas are proximal both to the Nofzinger et al. (1997) anterior paralimbic REM activation area and to caudo-ventro-medial PFC. Therefore, in REM there may be a dissociation between episodic recall (hippocampal) and recognition (perirhinal) components of declarative memory.

ASCENDING ACTIVATION OF THE POSTERIOR CORTEX AND DREAM HALLUCINOSIS

In REM, deactivation of lateral PFC along with increased activity in PFC medial-limbic regions may influence the perceptual components of dreams, especially the visual hallucinosis generated by visual association cortices. To hypothesize such changes in frontal influence over sleep imagery in posterior regions, however, begs questions as to the source of activation in posterior perceptual cortices in the absence of retinal input during sleep. Therefore, it is important first to consider neurophysiological conditions that may lead to the complex visual hallucinosis of dreams. Waking hallucinatory syndromes resulting from disruption of primary visual pathways in disorders such as Charles Bonnet syndrome make apparent that activity within visual association cortices at levels seen in waking is alone sufficient to produce complex visual hallucinations (Ffytche et al., 1998; Manford & Andermann, 1998; see discussion in Pace-Schott, 2005a). And in dreaming, of course, primary visual pathways are similarly blocked by the absence of retinal input.

The first comprehensive biological theory of dreaming, the AS hypothesis of Hobson and McCarley (1977), invoked activation of visual cortices by components of the same ascending arousal systems that support cortical arousal in waking. In REM sleep, the forebrain is activated by the brainstem ascending reticular activating system (ARAS) neurons of the pedunculopontine and laterodorsal tegmental nuclei (PPT/LDT) at the pons-midbrain (mesopontine) junction (see Pace-Schott & Hobson 2002a, 2002b, for reviews). Relative to waking, ARAS forebrain activation in REM is heavily biased toward cholinergic neuromodulation because of minimal serotonergic and noradrenergic input resulting from the nadir of activity in dorsal raphe and locus ceruleus nuclei, respectively. Notably, both fluctuating levels of serotonin (Aghajanian & Marek, 1999) and disruption of ARAS neuromo-dulatory pathways (Manford & Andermann, 1998) are conditions leading to waking hallucinosis by hallucinogenic drugs and peduncular hallucinosis, respectively (see Pace-Schott, 2005a).

In REM, cholinergic activation of the cortex via thalamic intermediaries occurs tonically with phasic increases that may be of particular importance to dream hallucinosis (Hobson, 1988; Hobson & McCarley, 1977; Hobson et al., 2000). Among the various measurable EEG and motoric signs of central phasic activity that occur during sleep (reviewed in Pivik, 1991), the rapid eye movements (REMs) that give REM sleep its name have attracted most study. This is because of their association with the ponto-geniculo-occipital (PGO) wave, a transient potential traveling successively from the pons to the lateral geniculate nucleus of the thalamus, and then to the occipital cortex, and which occur just before REMs during REM sleep in cats (see Hobson et al., 2000). The impingement of this PGO wave on the visual cortex provides a putative pseudosensory signal that the brain might interpret as visual input arriving via dedicated visual pathways from the lateral geniculate (Hobson & McCarley, 1977). Therefore, since publication of the AS hypothesis, investigators have sought to demonstrate PGO waves in the human brain during sleep.

After early hints in the scalp EEG (reviewed in Hobson et al., 2000), new neuroimaging technologies have begun to provide more substantial evidence of a human PGO signal. For example, quantitative EEG techniques (dipole tracing) in humans have shown PGO wave-like activity involving the pons, midbrain, thalamus, hippocampus, and visual cortex (Inoue, Saha, & Musha, 1999). In addition, using MEG tomography, Ioannides et al. (2004) have shown that before and correlating with REMs, there is brain activity that is strongest in the pons and is accompanied by simultaneous activity in frontal eye fields (FEFs). These investigators suggest that this pontine/FEF activity represents building excitability in these structures, leading to a threshold at which a REM is generated. Importantly, just before eye movements, limbic activation is also seen in the amygdala, as well as in orbitofrontal and parahippocampal cortices (Ioannides et al., 2004), a phasic pattern these authors link to enhancement of emotional activation and processing during REM. A recent $H_2{}^{15}O$ PET study in humans has shown positive correlations between frequency per unit time of REMs during REM sleep (REM density) and increased rCBF of the midbrain, lateral geniculate nucleus, and primary occipital cortex, in addition to right parahippocampal, precuneus, anterior cingulated, and supplementary motor cortices (Peigneux et al., 2001). Similarly, a combined fMRI and polysomnographic study has shown close correlation of REM sleep REMs, with BOLD signal increases restricted to the lateral geniculate nucleus and to the cuneus in BA 18 of the secondary visual cortex (Wherle et al., 2005).

Phasic thalamo-cortical (that is, from thalamus to cortex) activation by PPT/LDT cholinergic nuclei of the ARAS may be a common feature of mammalian REM sleep (see Pace-Schott & Hobson, 2002a, 2002b, for reviews), but actual pathways may differ between species. For example, in the rat, the pontine P-wave in REM activates the forebrain via a different route than the feline PGO wave and impinges directly on limbic structures such as the amygdalae, hippocampus, and entorhinal cortex, as well as the visual cortex (Datta, Siwek, Patterson, & Cipolloni, 1998). In humans, the thalamo-cortical pathway for ARAS activation in REM might underlie activity in the specific cortical sites observed to be activated in imaging studies of REM sleep. Such pathways might include those to the extrastriate cortex (Braun et al., 1998) via a nonrelay sensory path through the pulvinar nucleus or to limbic prefrontal areas (Nofzinger et al., 1997) via magnocellular portions of the mediodorsal nucleus. In REM sleep, activation of a broad range of thalamic sites and, subsequently, their cortical targets is reasonable given the "desynchronized" wake-like scalp EEG seen in REM. Moreover, ascending cholinergic activation in REM inhibits neurons of the thalamic reticular nucleus, thereby disinhibiting thalamocortical neurons of other thalamic nuclei, whose firing is suppressed by the GABAergic reticular neurons in NREM (Steriade, 2000, 2006). Also of potentially great importance are recent observations that the thalamo-cortical pathway may be less important to cortical arousal than is an extra-thalamic pathway leading directly from mesopontine (junction of pons and midbrain) sites to basal forebrain cholinergic nuclei neurons that, in turn, project to and activate the cortex (Lu, Sherman, & Saper, 2006).

Envisaging the PGO wave as just one example of many pathways for ARAS activation of the cortex via thalamic or basal forebrain intermediaries in REM incorporates PGO waves into a broader view of phasic activity in REM that suggests REM density (and other phasic peripheral activity like muscle twitches) reflects transient elevation of general cortical arousal (Conduit, Crewther, Bruck, & Coleman, 2002; Conduit, Crewther, Coleman, 2004; Germain, Buysse, Wood, & Nofzinger, 2004). It has been suggested that the observed correlations of REM density with activity in cortical areas, including prefrontal regions, reflects phasic activation of attentional networks (Germain et al., 2004; Hong et al., 1995). For example, Hong et al. (1995) reported that during REM sleep, REM density was positively correlated with glucose uptake in right FEFs and dorsolateral prefrontal, bilateral superior parietal, precuneus, occipital, medial prefrontal, and anterior cingulate cortices, areas these authors associate with midline executive and visuospatial attentional systems. Similarly, in depressives, Germain et al. (2004, p. 265) showed that REM density was positively correlated with regional glucose metabolism in the striate, precuneus, posterior cingulate, somatosensory, ventrolateral prefrontal, and medial prefrontal cortices, suggesting that these areas represent a "diffuse cortical system involved in the regulation of emotion-induced arousal and attention." Wherle et al. (2005) specifically link areas correlated with REM density with a model suggested by Braun et al. (1998), suggesting that REM constitutes an active state of internal information processing taking place between extrastriate and limbic cortices in functional isolation from external perceptual input or motor output.

A LIMBIC BIAS IN TOP-DOWN INFLUENCE ON POSTERIOR CORTEX IN REM

Attentional, "top-down" mechanisms originating in multimodal association cortices and influencing unimodal areas (in a direction opposite to "bottom-up" sensory processing) are able to augment sensitivity of primary and secondary perceptual cortices to a particular stimulus type, quality, or location while attenuating cortical sensitivity to competing stimuli (Pessoa, Kastner, & Ungerleider, 2003). Corbetta and Shulman (2002) suggest that, in humans, two dissociable but interacting attentional systems can provide such biasing of perceptual sensitivity. A dorsal, bilateral, cognitively driven (top-down) attentional system with key nodes in superior frontal and intraparietal areas is in dynamic equilibrium with a second "ventral system" whose key nodes are in temporoparietal and inferior frontal cortices and are strongly right-lateralized (Corbetta & Shulman, 2002). When this bottom-up ventral attention system detects unexpected but salient stimuli, it is able to interrupt and override the dorsal cognitively driven system and orient attention to the external event (Corbetta & Shulman, 2002). Despite its reflexive, bottom-up nature, this ventral attentional system may also be modulated by top-down influences, such as motivational salience, and can, like the cognitively driven dorsal system, enhance activation of primary visual cortices (Small et al., 2005).

Another related, bottom-up mechanism can capture attention to fear-eliciting stimuli by preconsciously activating the amygdala via a subcortical route through the superior colliculi and pulvinar nuclei (LeDoux, 1996; Ohman, 2005). This takes place more rapidly than a coactivated conscious mechanism that utilizes the retino-geniculate pathway to the primary and secondary visual cortices and then to the amygdala (LeDoux, 1996; Ohman, 2005). Amygdalar activation by either route can lead to enhanced attending to and more rapid, preferential processing of emotionally salient stimuli (Ohman, 2005). Following amygdalar activation by either route, consciously perceived fear is accompanied by a further increase in amygdala activity, as well as by activation of anterior cingulate, insular, and orbitofrontal limbic cortices and activation of midbrain periaqueductal gray areas associated with behavioral responses (Ohman, 2005). However, dorsolateral prefrontal and lateral orbitofrontal cortices are able to modulate amygdalar activation to potentially fear-eliciting stimuli and attenuate consciously perceived fear (Ohman, 2005). Therefore, top-down influences, such as competing conscious attentional demands, can attenuate even the collicular-pulvinar pathway to emotional activation (Pessoa et al., 2003). Strong projections from the basolateral amygdala to multimodal and unimodal association, as well as some primary sensory cortices, support such bottom-up amygdalar biasing of posterior sensory cortices (Heimer & Van Hoesen, 2006).

In sleep as in waking, limbic activation may underlie augmented sensitivity in areas of posterior unimodal cortices whose activation correlates with REM density (Germain et al., 2004). In REM sleep, such limbic top-down influences, for example from activated limbic medial prefrontal cortices, may be strengthened relative to competing external inputs or endogenous cognitive activity. In the case of external (for example, acoustic) input, Maquet and colleagues note that the temporo-parietal and inferior frontal gyrus areas of Corbetta and Shulman's (2002) ventral attentional system fall within regions consistently hypoactive in REM sleep relative to waking. These authors note further that noradrenergic modulation of this ventral attentional system, that in waking facilitates rapid orientation to salient stimuli, also reaches its nadir in REM. These authors, therefore, suggest that hypoactivity and noradrenergic demodulation of these areas may greatly attenuate the sleeper's sensitivity to external stimuli (Dang-Vu et al., 2005a; Maquet et al., 2005).

Similarly, although dorsal regions of lateral prefrontal cortex are not invariably deactivated in REM relative to waking (Dang-Vu et al., 2005a; Maquet et al., 2005), the DLPFC is deactivated in NREM relative to waking (Braun et al., 1997; Kaufmann et al., 2006; Maquet et al., 1997), has been reported less active than in wake in some REM studies (Braun et al., 1997; Maquet et al., 1996), and, unlike the limbic medial PFC, does not reactivate to levels exceeding waking in REM (Braun et al., 1997; Nofzinger et al., 1997). Therefore, in REM, it is reasonable to suppose that any top-down influences on the sensitivity of unimodal primary and secondary cortices to endogenously activated hallucinatory percepts will be biased toward functions subserved by the relatively active limbic ventromedial cortices. In addition, diminished activity in lateral frontal cortices in REM (Maquet et al., 2005) may weaken the ability of frontal, top-down influence to modulate emotional responses (Ohman, 2005) to dream imagery. Diminished cortical connectivity as reflected in diminished antero-posterior oscillatory coherence (Corsi-Cabrera et al., 2003; Massimini et al., 2005; Perez-Garci et al., 2001) may further attenuate top-down influences during REM.

Therefore, differences in regional activation between waking and REM sleep will alter the manner in which attention, emotion, and expectancy modulate the sensitivity of unimodal primary and secondary cortices to exogenous or endogenous stimuli. REM-associated activity in limbic-related medial PFC may create a *bias* (see Miller & Cohen, 2001; Pessoa et al., 2003) toward the generation of emotionally salient dream imagery in unimodal association cortices. That is, extrastriate regions may be sensitized to attend to emotional imagery, while endogenous nonemotional imagery may fail to persist in the face of weakened WM during sleep that results, in turn, from deactivation of the lateral PFC (Hobson et al., 2000; Pace-Schott, 2005a).

During sleep, ascending activation of visual association cortices may evoke ambiguous visual experiences that resolve into hallucinatory percepts congruent with the ongoing dream plot (Pace-Schott, 2005b). If this is the case, the internal consistency of dream plots may arise because the evolving dream context itself influences which images will be next evoked or attended to. Dreams may evolve by a "boot-strapping" process whereby current images provide the dream context that thereby evokes or prioritizes succeeding dream imagery (Pace-Schott, 2005b). During sleep, the dreamer lacks the full WM capacities that provide a sense of continuity to our waking experience (Hobson et al., 2000). Hence, the evolving plot can be strongly influenced by immediate previous dream experience. In the face of weakened WM, top-down limbic influence may provide an important added measure of plot continuity by biasing association cortices toward generating or attending to mood-congruent imagery. Therefore, in REM, augmented cortical and subcortical limbic activity that is perhaps released from lateral prefrontal modulation may adhere dream plots and imagery to their various emotional themes (see Seligman & Yellen, 1987).

THE DEFAULT MODE IN SLEEP AND THE EXPERIENCE OF SELF AND OTHERS IN DREAMS

Several functional neuroimaging investigators (for example, Czisch et al., 2004; Kaufmann et al., 2006; Laufs et al., 2006) have noted a relationship between sleep-related deactivations and a hypothesized waking "default" or "baseline" mode of brain operation (Gusnard & Raichle, 2001; Raichle, MacLeod, Snyder, Powers, Gusnard, & Shulman, 2001). The concept of a waking default mode of brain operation derives from findings that there are brain regions that characteristically decrease rCBF or BOLD signal in response to a wide variety of goal-directed cognitive tasks (Raichle et al., 2001). Elements of this default-mode network include (1) a posterior medial parietal region that includes posterior cingulate, precuneus, and retrosplenial cortices, (2) a lateral inferior parietal/superior temporal region within BA 39, 40, 22, and 19, (3) vmPFC, and (4) dmPFC. Under default mode conditions, oscillatory activity in these regions shows considerable temporal synchrony that is interpreted as a high "functional connectivity" (Greicius, Krasnow, Reiss, & Menon, 2003).

Raichle and colleagues link the posterior medial parietal region of the waking default mode to a baseline visuospatial, dorsal-stream monitoring of stimuli in a wide circumference of extra-personal space including the periphery—functions that may have evolutionary origins in the need to monitor surroundings for predators (Gusnard & Raichle, 2001; Raichle et al., 2001). These authors similarly ascribe environmental monitoring of novel stimuli and biological motion to lateral temporo-parietal components of the default mode (Gusnard & Raichle, 2001). They ascribe activity in the vmPFC to the processing of multimodal interoceptive and exteroceptive stimuli as well as one's visceromotor and autonomic responses—emotion-related functions shown to be reciprocally related to effortful cognition in neuroimaging studies (Gusnard & Raichle, 2001). Lastly, they suggest dmPFC baseline activity serves to process stimulus-independent, introspective, self-referential cognitive, emotional, and behavioral simulation and rehearsal (Gusnard & Raichle, 2001; Gusnard et al., 2001). Analagously, Northoff et al. (2006) associate the vmPFC with a basic, affective identification of self-related stimuli and the dmPFC with their conscious, cognitive appraisal. Northoff et al. (2006) associate posterior regions of the waking default-mode (posterior cingulate, precuneus, retrosplenial corticesa region known to be associated with a number of higher cognitive functions, see Cavanna & Trimble, 2006) with retrieval of episodic and autobiographical memory via their extensive connections with the hippocampus.

Clearly, during sleep including REM, one is not able to engage in the exteroceptive effortful cognitive activity that Gusnard and Raichle (2001) believe interrupts the brain's waking default mode in order to redirect resources toward the task at hand. In the absence of such effort, activity in the brain's waking default mode might be expected to arise with the reactivation of the brain during REM sleep. However, during NREM, widespread deactivation appears to attenuate even regions that show this waking baseline activity (Kaufmann et al., 2006). This widespread deactivation follows an initial persistence of the waking default mode during diminishing attentiveness (Drummond et al., 2005) and even, possibly, during early light sleep (Fukunaga et al., 2006). Kaufmann et al. (2006) link deactivation relative to waking in posterior, parietal default-mode regions with disengagement from external stimuli in Stages 1 and 2 of NREM, and associate the further deactivation of anterior default-mode regions with the further loss of alertness in SWS.

In functional imaging studies of REM sleep, these posterior, parietal areas of the waking default mode, especially the lateral inferior parietal regions, remain deactivated relative to waking (Maquet et al., 2005). In contrast, portions of the medial prefrontal anterior default networks (for example, anterior cingulate, paracingulate, subgenual, and caudomedial orbitofrontal cortices) reactivate to levels above NREM and can even exceed waking levels as measured by rCBF or glucose metabolism (Braun et al., 1997; Maquet et al., 1996; Nofzinger et al., 1997; reviewed in Hobson et al., 2000). Brain activation in REM relative to NREM appears most clearly in vmPFC regions (Braun et al., 1997; Maquet et al., 1996; Nofzinger et al., 1997, 2004), although increases in dmPFC regions such as paracingulate (BA 32) and BA 10 are also reported (Braun et al., 1997; Maquet et al., 2005).

During reactivation of the brain in REM, there are no external environmental stimuli to which to attend (at least in the visuospatial domain) contributing, perhaps, to the absence of activity in the posterior parietal environmental-monitoring component of the waking default mode. Moreover, if as Northoff et al. (2006) suggest, posterior default-mode regions subserve episodic and autobiographical memory retrieval, the dearth of such memories in REM sleep dreaming (Fosse et al., 2003) may also be further explained (Fosse et al., 2003). There is, however, enhanced activity in those medial prefrontal regions of the default mode that Gusnard et al. (2001) suggest attend to interoceptive stimuli and emotion (vmPFC) and introspective, self-referential behavioral simulation, and rehearsal (dmPFC). Braun et al. (1998) have suggested that REM sleep is accompanied by enhanced emotional processing of endogenous stimuli in the absence of exteroceptive input. Such processing is reflected in selective reactivation of anterior regions of the waking default mode along with localized activity in extrastriate visual cortices (Braun et al., 1997, 1998; Peigneux et al., 2001; Wherle et al., 2005).

In what ways is activity in this anterior midline region of the waking default mode reflected in dreaming? As discussed above, the ubiquity of emotional themes in dreams may be one manifestation of activity in these regions. Activation of somatic markers and their associated memories might also be predicted to occur in dreams, although the relative paucity of viscero-ceptive experience in dreams suggest that somatic markers operate in a hypo-thetical central "as if" mode (Damasio, 1996, 1999) that does not require the re-experience of peripheral sensations (see Pace-Schott, 2001). Memory and emotion linked by somatic markers may be evoked as integrated units similar to what Grafman (2002) terms "structured event complexes," and such experiences may involve both self-referential emotions and feelings involving others. In dreams, "others," of course, are the dream characters and the interactions and feelings of the dreamer toward dream characters recruits "mentalizing" or ToM, a high-level cognitive skill in the social do-main that appears to be well preserved in dreaming (Kahn & Hobson, 2005; McNamara, McLaren, Kowalczyk, & Pace-Schott, 2007; Pace-Schott, 2001).

ToM is mediated by brain networks subserving social cognition that include medial prefrontal and anterior cingulate cortices, temporal poles and amygdala, and the superior temporal sulcus (Blakemore et al., 2003; Castelli, Happe, Frith, & Frith, 2000; Fletcher et al., 1995; Goel, Grafman, Sadato, & Hallett, 1995; Gallagher et al., 2000; Vogeley et al., 2001). ToM skills have been associated with a variety of cortical (Hynes, Baird, & Grafton, 2005; Rilling, Sanfey, Aronson, Nystrom, & Cohen, 2004; Samson, Apperly, Chiavarino, & Humphreys, 2004; Saxe & Kanwisher, 2003; Saxe & Wexler, 2005; Stone, Baron-Cohen, & Knight, 1998; Stuss, Gallup, & Alexander, 2001; Stuss & Anderson, 2004) and subcortical areas (Grezes, Frith, & Pas-singham, 2004; Calarge, Andreason, & O'Leary, 2003; Rilling et al., 2004). However, areas most consistently activated in neuroimaging studies of ToM tasks include the medial prefrontal cortex (especially the paracingulate cortex in BA 32), superior temporal sulcus, and temporal poles including the amyg-dala (Amodio & Frith, 2006; Brune & Brune-Cohrs, 2005; Frith & Frith, 2003, 2006; Gallagher & Frith, 2003; Harris, Todorov, & Fiske, 2005; Sie-gal & Varley, 2002). Therefore, ToM-related brain regions include areas that, in REM, are strongly activated relative to NREM and waking. REM-associated activity in these areas, especially the medial prefrontal cortex, has been suggested as the substrate of mentalizing in dreams, as well as the brain activity that underlies the ubiquity of social interactions and highly salient interpersonal emotions in dream plots (Dang-Vu et al., 2005a; Kahn & Hobson, 2005; Maquet et al., 2005; Pace-Schott 2001, 2003, 2005a).

OUTSTANDING QUESTIONS

Much of the above is necessarily speculative, and many outstanding ques-tions remain. Three of many examples follow. First is the above-discussed association of waking confabulation with medial prefrontal damage, but dream "confabulation" with *enhanced* activity of these same regions. Second NREM dreams, although explicable in terms of Nielsen's 2000 "covert REM" theory (see Pace-Schott, 2005a, for discussion), do not arise from the same sustained limbic-activated, lateral-PFC demodulated, substrate as REM dreams. Because distinct NREM-related deactivation relative to waking occurs in the very medial prefrontal areas that become highly active in REM (Dang-Vu, 2005b; Kaufmann et al., 2006), how can the more transient activational events of NREM produce typical dream-like features? Third, it appears paradoxical that the inferior parietal cortex, the brain area where isolated, site-specific damage most often results in global dream cessation (Solms, 1997), is also a region consistently deactivated in REM (Maquet et al., 2005). Therefore, despite relative inactivity in both NREM and REM sleep, the inferior parietal cortex, especially in the right hemisphere, must participate in key functions of dreaming such as spatial cognition (Hobson et al., 2000; Pace-Schott, 2005a; Solms, 1997). Clearly, many more questions are raised than are answered in the previous discussion, and it is important to remember that far less is known about the brain bases of sleep mentation than of waking cognition. Therefore, new neurobiological discoveries bearing on both states of consciousness may, in the future, dramatically alter our understanding of the cognitive neuroscience of dreams.

SUMMARY AND CONCLUSION

The role of the PFC in dreaming is one of combined release of top-down control by lateral and dorsal regions and enhanced influence of medial limbic regions on posterior association cortices involved in perception and memory. These processes closely interact because, in sleep, medial PFC regions are themselves released from lateral PFC modulation. As a result, dream consciousness is characterized by both diminished cognitive control and reality monitoring and biases toward personally salient emotional and interpersonal themes. Such "limbic bias" may impact not only dream plot and theme but, via top-down effects on posterior cortices, may influence the construction of or attention to actual hallucinated imagery evoked from memory or created de novo. Diminished WM attributable to weakened lateral PFC activity may, in dreams, increase the relative importance of dream context to evoked or attended to imagery that, along with the above limbic influences, may allow the remarkable internal consistency of dream plots. Dream plots may emerge in a manner analogous to spontaneous confabulation with the dreamer's uncritical acceptance of emerging imagery, along with a willingness to accept and explain, however illogically, bizarre occurrences and gaps in knowledge. In both dreaming and confabulation, one may see revealed humans' innate tendency to organize and explain experience in terms of story-like narratives without the constraints of logic and plausibility that exist in normal waking.

REFERENCES

Achermann, P., Finelli, L. A., & Borbely, A. A. (2001). Unihemispheric enhancement of delta power in human frontal sleep EEG by prolonged wakefulness. *Brain Research, 913,* 220–223.

Aghajanian, G. K., & Marek, G. J. (1999). Serotonin and hallucinations. *Neuropsychopharmacology, 21,* 16S–23S.

Amodio, D. M., & Frith, C. D. (2006). Meeting of minds: The medial frontal cortex and social cognition. *Nature Reviews Neuroscience, 7,* 268–277.

Andersson, J., Onoe, H., Hetta, J., Lindstrom, K., Valind, S., Lilja, A., et al. (1998). Brain networks affected by synchronized sleep visualized by positron emission tomography. *Journal of Cerebral Blood Flow & Metabolism, 18,* 701–715.

Antrobus, J. S. (1987). Cortical hemisphere asymmetry and sleep mentation. *Psychological Review, 94,* 359–368.

Antrobus, J. S. (1990) The neurocognition of sleep mentation: Rapid eye movements, visual imagery, and dreaming. In R. Bootzin, J. Kihlstrom, & D. Schacter (Eds.), *Sleep and cognition* (pp. 3–24). Washington, DC: American Psychological Association.

Arnsten, A. F. T. (1997). Catecholamine regulation of the prefrontal cortex. *Journal of Psychopharmacology, 11,* 151–162.

Arnsten, A. F. T., & Robbins, T. W. (2002). Neurochemical modulation of prefrontal cortical function. In D. T. Stuss & R. T. Knight (Eds.), *Principles of frontal lobe function* (pp. 51–84). Oxford: Oxford University Press.

Balkin, T. J., Braun, A. R., Wesensten, N. J., Jeffries, K., Varga, M., Baldwin, P., et al. (2002) The process of awakening: A PET study of regional brain activity patterns mediating the reestablishment of alertness and consciousness. *Brain, 125,* 2308–2319.

Barbas, H. (2000). Complementary roles of prefrontal cortical regions in cognition, memory, and emotion in primates. *Advances in Neurology, 84,* 87–110.

Barbas, H., Saha, S., Rempel-Clower, N., Ghashghaei, T. (2003). Serial pathways from primate prefrontal cortex to autonomic areas may influence emotional expression. *BMC Neuroscience, 4,* 25.

Bechara, A., Damasio, H., & Damasio, A.R. (2000). Emotion, decision-making and the orbitofrontal cortex. *Cerebral Cortex, 10,* 295–307.

Bertini, M., De Gennaro, L., Ferrara, M., Curcio, G., Romei, V., Fratello, F., et al. (2004). Reduction of transcallosal inhibition upon awakening from REM sleep in humans as assessed by transcranial magnetic stimulation. *Sleep, 27,* 875–882.

Blakemore, S. J., Boyer, P., Pachot-Clouard, M., Meltzoff, A., Segebarth, C., & Decety, J. (2003). The detection of contingency and animacy from simple animations in the human brain. *Cerebral Cortex, 13,* 837–844.

Borbely, A. A. (2001). From slow waves to sleep homeostasis: New perspectives. *Archives Italiennes de Biologie, 139,* 53–61.

Born, A. P., Law, I., Lund, T. E., Rostrup, E., Hanson, L. G., Wildschiodtz, G., et al. (2002). Cortical deactivation induced by visual stimulation in human slow-wave sleep. *NeuroImage, 17*, 1325–1335.

Botvinick, M. M., Cohen, J. D., & Carter, C. S. (2004). Conflict monitoring and anterior cingulate cortex: An update. *Trends in Cognitive Sciences, 8*, 539–546.

Braun, A. R., Balkin, T. J., Wesensten, N. J., Carson, R. E., Varga, M., Baldwin, P., et al. (1997). Regional cerebral blood flow throughout the sleep-wake cycle. *Brain, 120*, 1173–1197.

Braun, A. R., Balkin, N. J., Wesensten, F. Gwadry, R. E., Carson, M., Varga, P., et al. (1998). Dissociated pattern of activity in visual cortices and their projections during human rapid eye-movement sleep. *Science, 279*, 91–95.

Braun, A. R., Guillemin, A., Hosey, L., & Varga, M. (2001). The neural organization of discourse: An H2 15O-PET study of narrative production in English and American sign language. *Brain, 124*, 2028–2044.

Brown, M. W., & Aggleton, J. P. (2001). Recognition memory: What are the roles of the perirhinal cortex and hippocampus. *Nature Reviews Neuroscience, 2*, 51–61.

Brune, M., & Brune-Cohrs, U. (2006). Theory of mind-evolution, ontogeny, brain mechanisms and psychopathology. *Neuroscience & Biobehavioral Reviews, 30*, 437–455.

Cajochen, C., Foy, R., & Dijk, D. J. (2000). Frontal predominance of a relative increase in sleep delta and theta EEG activity after sleep loss in humans. *Sleep Research Online, 2*, 65–69.

Calarge, C., Andreasen, N. C., & O'Leary, D. S. (2003). Visualizing how one brain understands another: A PET study of theory of mind. *American Journal of Psychiatry, 160*, 1954–1964.

Cantero, J. L., Atienza, M., Madsen, J. R., & Stickgold, R. (2004). Gamma EEG dynamics in neocortex and hippocampus during human wakefulness and sleep. *NeuroImage, 22*, 1271–1280.

Cantero, J. L., Atienza, M., & Salas, R. M. (2000). State-modulation of cortico-cortical connections underlying normal EEG alpha variants. *Physiology & Behavior, 71*, 107–115.

Cantero, J. L., Atienza, M., Salas, R. M., & Gomez, C. M. (1999). Alpha EEG coherence in different brain states: An electrophysiological index of the arousal level in human subjects. *Neuroscience Letters, 271*, 167–170.

Castelli, F., Happe, F., Frith, U., & Frith, C. (2000). Movement and mind: A functional imaging study of perception and interpretation of complex intentional movement patterns. *NeuroImage, 12*, 314–325.

Cavallero, C., Cicogna, P., Natale, V., Occhionero, M., & Zito, A. (1992). Slow wave sleep dreaming. *Sleep, 15*, 562–566.

Cavanna, A. E., & Trimble, M. R. (2006). The precuneus: A review of its functional anatomy and behavioural correlates. *Brain, 129*, 564–583.

Christoff, K., Ream, J. M., Geddes, L. P., & Gabrieli, J. D. (2003). Evaluating self-generated information: Anterior prefrontal contributions to human cognition. *Behavioral Neuroscience, 117*, 1161–1168.

Collette, F., & Van der Linden, M. (2003). Brain imaging of the central executive component of working memory. *Neuroscience & Biobehavioral Reviews, 26*, 105–125.

Conduit, R., Crewther, S. G., Bruck, D., & Coleman, G. (2002). Spontaneous eyelid movements during human sleep: A possible ponto-geniculo-occipital analogue? *Journal of Sleep Research, 11,* 95–104.

Conduit, R., Crewther, S. G., & Coleman, G. (2004). Spontaneous eyelid movements (ELMS) during sleep are related to dream recall on awakening. *Journal of Sleep Research, 13,* 137–144.

Corbetta, M., & Shulman, G. L. (2002). Control of goal-directed and stimulus-driven attention in the brain. *Nature Reviews Neuroscience, 3,* 201–215.

Corsi-Cabrera, M., Miro, E., del-Rio-Portilla, Y., Perez-Garci, E., Villanueva, Y., & Guevara, M. A. (2003). Rapid eye movement sleep dreaming is characterized by uncoupled EEG activity between frontal and perceptual cortical regions. *Brain & Cognition, 51,* 337–345.

Courtney, S. M., Petit, L., Haxby, J. V., & Ungerleider, L. G. (1998). The role of prefrontal cortex in working memory: Examining the contents of consciousness. *Philosophical Transactions of the Royal Society of London, Series B, Biological Sciences, 353,* 1819–1828.

Czisch, M., Wehrle, R., Kaufmann, C., Wetter, T. C., Holsboer, F., Pollmacher, T., et al. (2004). Functional MRI during sleep: BOLD signal decreases and their electrophysiological correlates. *European Journal of Neuroscience, 20,* 566–574.

Czisch, M., Wetter, T. C., Kaufmann, C., Pollmacher, T., Holsboer, F., & Auer, D. P. (2002). Altered processing of acoustic stimuli during sleep: Reduced auditory activation and visual deactivation detected by a combined fMRI/EEG study. *NeuroImage, 16,* 251–258.

Damasio, A. R. (1996). The somatic marker hypothesis and the possible functions of the prefrontal cortex. *Philosophical Transactions of the Royal Society of London, Series B, Biological Sciences, 351,* 1413–1420.

Damasio, A. (1999). *The feeling of what happens: Body and emotion in the making of consciousness.* San Diego, CA: Harcourt.

Damasio, A. (2003). Feelings of emotion and the self. *Annals of the New York Academy of Science, 1001,* 253–261.

Dang-Vu, T. T., Desseilles, M., Albouy, G., Darsaud, A., Gais, S., Rauchs, S., et al. (2005a). Neuroimaging of dreaming. *Swiss Archives of Neurology & Psychiatry, 156,* 426–439.

Dang-Vu, T. T., Desseilles, M., Laureys, S., Degueldre, C., Perrin, F., Phillips, C., et al. (2005b). Cerebral correlates of delta waves during non-REM sleep revisited. *NeuroImage, 28,* 14–21.

Datta, S., Siwek, D. F., Patterson, E. H., & Cipolloni, P. B. (1998). Localization of pontine PGO wave generation sites and their anatomical projections in the rat. *Synapse, 30,* 409–423.

De Gennaro, L., Vecchio, F., Ferrara, M., Curcio, G., Rossini, P. M., & Babiloni, C. (2004). Changes in fronto-posterior functional coupling at sleep onset in humans. *Journal of Sleep Research, 13,* 209–217.

Derrfuss, J., Brass, M., Neumann, J., & von Cramon, D. Y. (2005). Involvement of the inferior frontal junction in cognitive control: Meta-analyses of switching and stroop studies. *Human Brain Mapping, 25,* 22–34.

D'Esposito, M., Aguirre, G. K., Zarahn, E., Ballard, D., Shin, R. K., & Lease, J. (1998). Functional MRI studies of spatial and nonspatial working memory. *Brain Research. Cognitive Brain Research, 7,* 1–13.

D'Esposito, M., Postle, B. R., & Rypma, B. (2000). Prefrontal cortical contributions to working memory: Evidence from event-related fMRI studies. *Experimental Brain Research, 133*, 3–11.

D'Esposito, M., & Postle, B. R. (2002). The organization of working memory function in lateral prefrontal cortex: Evidence from event-related functional MRI. In D. T. Stuss & R. T. Knight (Eds.), *Principles of frontal lobe function* (pp. 168–187). Oxford: Oxford University Press.

Devinsky, O., Morrell, M. J., & Vogt, B. A. (1995). Contributions of anterior cingulate cortex to behavior. *Brain, 118*, 279–306.

Dietrich, A. (2003). Functional neuroanatomy of altered states of consciousness: The transient hypofrontality hypothesis. *Conscious Cognition, 12*, 231–256.

Drummond, S. P., Bischoff-Grethe, A., Dinges, D. F., Ayalon, L., Mednick, S. C., & Meloy, M. J. (2005). The neural basis of the psychomotor vigilance task. *Sleep, 28*, 1059–1068.

Domhoff, G. W. (2003). *The scientific study of dreams: Neural networks, cognitive development, and content analysis.* Washington, DC: American Psychological Association.

Doricchi, F., & Violani, C. (1992). Dream recall in brain damaged patients: A contribution to the neuropsychology of dreaming through a review of the literature. In J. S. Antrobus & M. Bertini (Eds.), *The neuropsychology of sleep and dreaming* (pp. 99–140). Hillsdale, NJ: Lawrence Erlbaum.

Duncan, J. (2001). An adaptive coding model of neural function in prefrontal cortex. *Nature Reviews Neuroscience, 2*, 820–829.

Duncan, J., & Miller, E. K. (2002). Cognitive focus through adaptive neural coding in the primate prefrontal cortex. In D. T. Stuss & R. T. Knight (Eds.), *Principles of frontal lobe function* (pp. 278–291). Oxford: Oxford University Press.

Duncan J., & Owen, A. M. (2000). Common regions of the human frontal lobe recruited by diverse cognitive demands. *Trends in Neurosciences, 23*, 475–483.

Engel, A. K., Fries, P., & Singer, W. (2001). Dynamic predictions: Oscillations and synchrony in top-down processing. *Nature Reviews Neuroscience, 10*, 704–716.

Ferre S., Fredholm, B. B., Morelli, M., Popoli, P., & Fuxe, K. (1997). Adenosine-dopamine receptor-receptor interactions as an integrative mechanism in the basal ganglia. *Trends in Neurosciences, 20*, 482–487.

Ffytche, D. H., Howard, R. J., Brammer, M. J., David, A., Woodruff, P., & Williams, S. (1998). The anatomy of conscious vision: An fMRI study of visual hallucinations. *Nature Neuroscience, 1*, 738–742.

Finelli, L. A., Borbely, A. A., & Achermann, P. (2001). Functional topography of the human nonREM sleep electroencephalogram. *European Journal of Neuroscience, 13*, 2282–2290.

Finelli, L. A., Landolt, H. P., Buck, A., Roth, C., Berthold, T., Borbely, A. A., et al. (2000). Functional neuroanatomy of human sleep states after zolpidem and placebo: A H215O-PET study. *Journal of Sleep Research, 9*, 161–173.

Fletcher, P. C., Happe, F., Frith, U., Baker, S. C., Dolan, R. J., Frackowiak, R. S. J., et al. (1995). Other minds in the brain: A functional imaging study of "theory of mind" in story comprehension. *Cognition, 57*, 109–128.

Fletcher, P. C., & Henson, R. N. (2001). Frontal lobes and human memory: Insights from functional neuroimaging. *Brain, 124*, 849–881.

Fosse, M., Fosse, R., Hobson, J. A., & Stickgold, R. (2003). Dreaming and episodic memory: A functional dissociation? *Journal of Cognitive Neuroscience, 15,* 1–9.

Foulkes, D. (1962). Dream reports from different stages of sleep. *Journal of Abnormal and Social Psychology, 65,* 14–25.

Foulkes, D. (1996). Dream research: 1953–1993. *Sleep, 19,* 609–624.

Foulkes, D., & Vogel, G. (1965). Mental activity at sleep onset. *Journal of Abnormal Psychology, 70,* 231–243.

Frith, C. D., & Frith, U. (2006). The neural basis of mentalizing. *Neuron, 50,* 531–534.

Frith, U., & Frith, C. D. (2003). Development and neurophysiology of mentalizing. *Philosophical Transactions of the Royal Society of London, Series B, Biological Sciences, 358,* 459–473.

Fukunaga, M., Horovitz, S. G., Jacco, D. A., Peter, V., Susan, F. C., Balkin, T. J., et al. (2006). Spatio-temporal characteristics of fMRI signal fluctuation during light sleep. *Sleep, 29,* A25.

Fuster, J. M. (1997). *The prefrontal cortex: Anatomy, physiology, and neuropsychology of the frontal lobe.* Philadelphia, PA: Lippincott, Williams, & Wilkins.

Gallagher, H. L., & Frith, C. D. (2003). Functional imaging of "theory of mind." *Trends in Cognitive Sciences, 7,* 77–83.

Gallagher, H. L., Happe, F., Brunswick, N., Fletcher, P. C, Frith, U., & Frith, C. D. (2000). Reading the mind in cartoons and stories: An fMRI study of "theory of mind" in verbal and nonverbal tasks. *Neuropsychologia, 38,* 11–21.

Germain, A., Buysse, D. J., Wood, A., & Nofzinger, E. (2004). Functional neuroanatomical correlates of eye movements during rapid eye movement sleep in depressed patients. *Psychiatry Research, 130,* 259–268.

Goel, V., Grafman, J., Sadato, N., & Hallett, M. (1995). Modeling other minds. *NeuroReport, 6,* 1741–1746.

Goldberg, E. (2001). *The executive brain: Frontal lobes and the civilized mind.* Oxford: Oxford University Press.

Goldman-Rakic, P. S. (1996). The prefrontal landscape: Implications of functional architecture for understanding human mentation and the central executive. *Philosophical Transactions of the Royal Society of London, Series B, Biological Sciences, 351,* 1445–1453.

Gottesmann, C. (2002a). The neurochemistry of waking and sleeping mental activity: The disinhibition-dopamine hypothesis. *Psychiatry & Clinical Neurosciences, 56,* 345–354.

Gottesmann, C. (2002b). Dreaming: Monoaminergic disinhibition hypothesis. In E. Perry, H. Ashton, & A. Young (Eds.), *Neurochemistry of consciousness: Transmitters in mind* (pp. 133–146). Amsterdam: John Benjamins Publishing Company.

Gottesmann, C. (2006). The dreaming sleep stage: A new neurobiological model of schizophrenia? *Neuroscience, 140,* 1105–1115.

Grafman, J. (2002). The structured event complex and the human prefrontal cortex. In D. T. Stuss & R. T. Knight (Eds.), *Principles of frontal lobe function* (pp. 292–310). Oxford: Oxford University Press.

Greicius, M. D., Krasnow, B., Reiss, A. L., & Menon, V. (2003). Functional connectivity in the resting brain: A network analysis of the default mode hypothesis. *Proceedings of the National Academy of Sciences of the United States of America, 100,* 253–258.

Grezes, J., Frith, C. D., & Passingham, R. E. (2004). Inferring false beliefs from the actions of oneself and others: An fMRI study. *NeuroImage, 21,* 744–750.

Gross, D. W., & Gotman, J. (1999). Correlation of high-frequency oscillations with the sleep-wake cycle and cognitive activity in humans. *Neuroscience, 94,* 1005–1018.

Guevara, M. A., Lorenzo, I., Arce, C., Ramos, J., & Corsi-Cabrera, M. (1995). Inter- and intrahemispheric EEG correlation during sleep and wakefulness. *Sleep, 18,* 257–265.

Gusnard, D. A., Akbudak, E., Shulman, G. L., & Raichle, M. E. (2001). Medial prefrontal cortex and self-referential mental activity: Relation to a default mode of brain function. *Proceedings of the National Academy of Sciences of the United States of America, 98,* 4259–4264.

Gusnard, D. A., & Raichle, M. E. (2001). Searching for a baseline: Functional imaging and the resting human brain. *Nature Reviews Neuroscience, 2,* 685–694.

Harris, L. T., Todorov, A., & Fiske, S. T. (2005). Attributions on the brain: Neuroimaging dispositional inferences, beyond theory of mind. *NeuroImage, 28,* 763–769.

Heimer, L., & Van Hoesen, G. W. (2006). The limbic lobe and its output channels: Implications for emotional functions and adaptive behavior. *Neuroscience & Biobehavioral Reviews, 30,* 126–147.

Hirstein, W. (2005). *Brain fiction, self deception and the riddle of confabulation.* Cambridge, MA: MIT Press.

Hobson, J. A. (1988). *The dreaming brain.* New York: Basic Books.

Hobson, J. A. (1999). *Dreaming as delirium.* Cambridge, MA: The MIT Press.

Hobson, J. A., & McCarley, R. (1977). The brain as a dream state generator: An activation-synthesis hypothesis of the dream process. *American Journal of Psychiatry, 134,* 1335–1348.

Hobson, J. A., Pace-Schott, E. F. & Stickgold, R. (2000). Dreaming and the brain: Toward a cognitive neuroscience of conscious states. *Behavioral & Brain Sciences, 23,* 793–842.

Hofle, N., Paus, T., Reutens, D., Fiset, P., Gotman, J., Evans, A. C., et al. (1997). Regional cerebral blood flow changes as a function of delta and spindle activity during slow wave sleep in humans. *The Journal of Neuroscience, 17,* 4800–4808.

Hong, C. C. H., Gillin, J. C., Dow, B. M., Wu, J. & Buchsbaum, M. S. (1995). Localized and lateralized cerebral glucose metabolism associated with eye movements during REM sleep and wakefulness: A positron emission tomography (PET) study. *Sleep, 18,* 570–580.

Hynes, C. A., Baird, A. A., & Grafton, S. T. (2005). Differential role of the orbital frontal lobe in emotional versus cognitive perspective-taking. *Neuropsychologia, 44,* 374–383.

Inoue, S., Saha, U. K., & Musha, T. (1999). Spatio-temporal distribution of neuronal activities and REM sleep. In B. N. Mallick & S. Inoue (Eds.), *Rapid eye movement sleep* (pp. 214–220). New York: Marcel Dekker.

Ioannides, A. A., Corsi-Cabrera, M., Fenwick, P. B., del-Rio-Portilla, Y., Laskaris, N. A., Khurshudyan, A., et al. (2004). MEG tomography of human cortex and brainstem activity in waking and REM sleep saccades. *Cerebral Cortex, 14,* 56–72.

Jonides, J., Badre, D., Curtis, C., Thompson-Schill, S. L., & Smith, E. E. (2002). Mechanisms of conflict resolution in prefrontal cortex. In D. T. Stuss, & R. T. Knight

(Eds.), *Principles of frontal lobe function.* (pp. 233–245). Oxford: Oxford University Press.

Kahn, D., & Hobson, J. A. (2005). Theory of mind in dreaming: Awareness of feelings and thoughts of others in dreams. *Dreaming, 15,* 48–57.

Kahn, D., Pace-Schott, E. F., & Hobson, J. A. (1997). Consciousness in waking and dreaming: The roles of neuronal oscillation and neuromodulation in determining similarities and differences. *Neuroscience, 78,* 13–38.

Kahn, D., Stickgold, R., Pace-Schott, E. F., & Hobson, J. A. (2000). Dreaming and waking consciousness: A character recognition study. *Journal of Sleep Research, 9,* 317–325.

Kajimura, N., Uchiyama, M., Takayama, Y., Uchida, S., Uema, S., Uema, T., et al. (1999). Activity of midbrain reticular formation and neocortex during the progression of human non-rapid eye movement sleep. *The Journal of Neuroscience, 19,* 10065–10073.

Kaufmann C., Wehrle, R., Wetter, T. C., Holsboer, F., Auer, D. P., & Pollmacher, T. (2006). Brain activation and hypothalamic functional connectivity during human non-rapid eye movement sleep: An EEG/fMRI study. *Brain, 129,* 655–667.

Kjaer, T. W., Law, I., Wiltschiotz, G., Paulson, O. B., & Madsen, P. L. (2002). Regional cerebral blood flow during light sleep-a H215O-PET study. *Journal of Sleep Research, 11,* 201–207.

Koechlin, E., Ody, C., & Kouneiher, F. (2003). The architecture of cognitive control in the human prefrontal cortex. *Science, 302,* 1181–1185.

Krain, A. L., Wilson, A. M., Arbuckle, R., Castellanos, F. X., & Milham, M. P. (2006). Distinct neural mechanisms of risk and ambiguity: A meta-analysis of decision-making. *NeuroImage, 32,* 477–484.

Kringelbach, M. L. (2005). The human orbitofrontal cortex: Linking reward to hedonic experience. *Nature Reviews Neuroscience, 6,* 691–702.

Kringelbach, M. L., & Rolls, E. T. (2004). The functional neuroanatomy of the human orbitofrontal cortex: Evidence from neuroimaging and neuropsychology. *Progress in Neurobiology, 72,* 341–372.

Laufs, H., Holt, J. L., Elfont, R., Krams, M., Paul, J. S., Krakow K., et al. (2006). Where the BOLD signal goes when alpha EEG leaves. *NeuroImage, 31,* 1408–1418.

Lavie, P., & Tzischinsky, O. (1985). Cognitive asymmetry and dreaming: Lack of relationship. *American Journal of Psychology, 98,* 353–361.

LeDoux, J. (Ed.). (1996). *The emotional brain.* New York: Simon and Schuster.

Levy, R., & Goldman-Rakic, P. S. (2000). Segregation of working memory functions within the dorsolateral prefrontal cortex. *Experimental Brain Research, 133,* 23–32.

Llinas, R. & Ribary, U. (1993). Coherent 40-Hz oscillation characterizes dream state in humans. *Proceedings of the National Academy of Sciences of the United States of America, 90,* 2078–2081.

Lovblad, K. O., Thomas, R., Jakob, P. M., Scammell, T., Bassetti, C., Griswold, M., et al. (1999). Silent functional magnetic resonance imaging demonstrates focal activation in rapid eye movement sleep. *Neurology, 53,* 2193–2195.

Lu, J., Sherman, D., & Saper, C. B. (2006). Neuronal substrates of the ascending reticular activating system (ARAS). *Sleep, 29,* A19.

Madsen, P. C., Holm, S., Vorstup, S., Friberg, L., Lassen, N. A., & Wildschiodtz, L. F. (1991). Human regional cerebral blood flow during rapid eye movement sleep. *Journal of Cerebral Blood Flow & Metabolism, 11,* 502–507.

Manford, M., & Andermann, F. (1998). Complex visual hallucinations: Clinical and neurobiological insights. *Brain, 121,* 1819–1840.

Maquet, P. (1995). [Contribution of positron emission tomography in the study of wakefulness and sleep. Status of the question]. *Neurophysiologie Clinique, 25,* 342–350.

Maquet, P. (2000). Functional neuroimaging of normal human sleep by positron emission tomography. *Journal of Sleep Research, 9,* 207–231.

Maquet, P., Degueldre, C., Delfiore, G., Aerts, J., Peters, J. M., Luxen, A., et al. (1997). Functional neuroanatomy of human slow wave sleep. *The Journal of Neuroscience, 17,* 2807–2812.

Maquet, P., Peters, J. M., Aerts, J., Delfiore, G., Degueldre, C., & Luxen, A. (1996). Functional neuroanatomy of human rapid-eye-movement sleep and dreaming. *Nature, 383,* 163–166.

Maquet, P., Ruby, P., Maudoux, A., Albouy, G., Sterpenich, V., Dang-Vu, T., et al. (2005). Human cognition during REM sleep and the activity profile within frontal and parietal cortices: A reappraisal of functional neuroimaging data. *Progress Brain Research, 150,* 219–227.

Mar, R. A. (2004). The neuropsychology of narrative: Story comprehension, story production and their interrelation. *Neuropsychologia, 42,* 1414–1434.

Massimini, M., Ferrarelli, F., Huber, R., Esser, S. K., Singh, H., & Tononi, G. (2005). Breakdown of cortical effective connectivity during sleep. *Science, 309,* 2228–2232.

McNamara, P., McLaren, D., Kowalczyk, S., & Pace-Schott, E. F. (2007). "Theory of mind" in REM and NREM dreams. In D. L. Barrett, & P. McNamara (Eds.), *The new science of dreaming.* Westport, CT: Praeger Publishers.

Mesulam, M. M. (2002). The human frontal lobes: Transcending the default mode through contingent encoding. In D.T. Stuss, & R.T. Knight (Eds.), *Principles of frontal lobe function* (pp. 8–30). Oxford: Oxford University Press.

Mesulam, M. M., Hersh, L. B., Mash, D. C., & Geula C., (1992). Differential cholinergic innervation within functional subdivisions of the human cerebral cortex: A choline acetyltransferase study. *Journal of Comparative Neurology, 318,* 316–328.

Miller, E. K. (1999). Neurobiology. Straight from the top. *Nature, 401,* 650–651.

Miller, E. K. (2000). The prefrontal cortex and cognitive control. *Nature Reviews Neuroscience, 1,* 59–65.

Miller, E. K., & Cohen, J. D. (2001). An integrative theory of prefrontal cortex function. *Annual Reviews of Neuroscience, 24,* 167–202.

Moscovitch, M., & Winocur, G. (2002). The frontal cortex and working with memory. In D. T. Stuss & R. T. Knight (Eds.), *Principles of frontal lobe function* (pp. 392–407). Oxford: Oxford University Press.

Muzur, A., Pace-Schott, E. F., & Hobson, J. A. (2002). The prefrontal cortex in sleep. *Trends in Cognitive Sciences, 6,* 475–481.

Nielsen, T. A. (1999). Mentation during sleep: The NREM/REM distinction. In R. Lydic, & H. A. Baghdoyan (Eds.), *Handbook of behavioral state control: Molecular and cellular mechanisms* (pp. 101–128). Boca Raton, FL: CRC Press.

Nielsen, T. A. (2000). Mentation in REM and NREM sleep: A review and possible reconciliation of two models. *Behavioral & Brain Sciences, 23,* 851–866.

Nofzinger, E. A., Berman, S., Fasiczka, A., Miewald, J. M., Meltzer, C. C., Price, J. C., et al. (2001). Effects of bupropion SR on anterior paralimbic function during waking and REM sleep in depression: Preliminary findings using [18F] FDG PET. *Psychiatry Research, 106,* 95–111.

Nofzinger, E. A., Buysse, D. J., Germain, A., Carter, C., Luna, B., Price, J. C., et al. (2004). Increased activation of anterior paralimbic and executive cortex from waking to rapid eye movement sleep in depression. *Archives of General Psychiatry, 61,* 695–702.

Nofzinger, E. A., Buysse, D. J., Miewald, J. M., Meltzer, C. C., Price, J. C., Sembrat, R. C., et al. (2002). Human regional cerebral glucose metabolism during non-rapid eye movement sleep in relation to waking. *Brain, 125,* 1105–1115.

Nofzinger, E. A., Mintun, M. A., Wiseman, M. B., Kupfer, D. J., & Moore, R. Y. (1997). Forebrain activation in REM sleep: An FDG PET study. *Brain Research, 770,* 192–201.

Nofzinger, E. A., Nichols, T. E., Meltzer, C. C., Price, J., Steppe, D. A., Miewald, et al. (1999). Changes in forebrain function from waking to REM sleep in depression: Preliminary analysis of [18F] FDG PET studies. *Psychiatry Research: NeuroImaging, 91,* 59–78.

Northoff, G., Heinzel, A., de Greck, M., Bermpohl, F., Dobrowolny, H., & Panksepp, J. (2006). Self-referential processing in our brain—a meta-analysis of imaging studies on the self. *NeuroImage, 31,* 440–457.

Ohman A. (2005). The role of the amygdala in human fear: Automatic detection of threat. *Psychoneuroendocrinology, 30,* 953–958.

Pace-Schott, E. F. (2001). "Theory of mind," social cognition and dreaming. *Sleep Research Society Bulletin, 7,* 33–36.

Pace-Schott, E. F. (2003). Recent findings on the neurobiology of sleep and dreaming. In E. F. Pace-Schott, M. Solms, M. Blagrove, & S. Harnad (Eds.), *Sleep and dreaming: Scientific advances and reconsiderations* (pp. 335–350). Cambridge, MA: Cambridge University Press.

Pace-Schott, E. F. (2005a). The neurobiology of dreaming. In M. H. Kryger, T. Roth, & W. C. Dement (Eds.), *Principles and practice of sleep medicine* (4th ed., pp. 551–564). Philadelphia, PA: Elsevier.

Pace-Schott, E. F. (2005b). Complex hallucinations in waking suggest mechanisms of dream construction. *Behavioral & Brain Sciences, 28,* 771–772.

Pace-Schott, E. F., & Hobson, J. A. (2002a). The neurobiology of sleep: Genetic mechanisms, cellular neurophysiology and subcortical networks. *Nature Reviews Neuroscience, 3,* 591–605.

Pace-Schott, E. F., & Hobson, J. A. (2002b). Basic mechanisms of sleep: New evidence on the neuroanatomy and neuromodulation of the NREM-REM cycle. In D. J. Charney, Coyle, K. Davis, & C. Nemeroff (Eds.), *American College of Neuropsychopharmacology, Fifth Generation of Progress* (pp. 1859–1877). New York: Lippincott, Williams & Wilkins.

Pandya, D. N., & Schmahmann, J. D. (2006). *Fiber pathways of the brain.* Oxford: Oxford University Press.

Pandya, D. N., & Yeterian, E. H. (1996). Comparison of prefrontal architecture and connections. *Philosophical Transactions of the Royal Society of London Series B, Biological Sciences, 351,* 1423–1432.

Partiot, A., Grafman, J., Sadato, N., Wachs, J., & Hallett, M. (1995). Brain activation during the generation of non-emotional and emotional plans. *NeuroReport, 6,* 1397–1400.

Peigneux, P., Laureys, S., Fuchs, S., Delbeuck, X., Delgueldre, C., Aerts, J., et al. (2001). Generation of rapid eye movements during paradoxical sleep in humans. *NeuroImage, 14,* 701–708.

Perez-Garci, E., del-Rio-Portilla, Y., Guevara, M. A., Arce, C., & Corsi-Cabrera, M. (2001). Paradoxical sleep is characterized by uncoupled gamma activity between frontal and perceptual cortical regions. *Sleep, 24,* 118–126.

Perry, E., Ashton, H., & Young, A. (Eds.). (2002). Neurochemistry of consciousness: Transmitters in mind. Amsterdam: John Benjamins Publishing Company.

Pessoa, L., Kastner, S., & Ungerleider, L. G. (2003). Neuroimaging studies of attention: From modulation of sensory processing to top-down control. *Journal of Neuroscience, 23,* 3990–3998.

Petrides, M. (2005). Lateral prefrontal cortex: Architectonic and functional organization. *Philosophical Transactions of the Royal Society of London Series B, Biological Sciences, 360,* 781–795.

Petrides, M., & Pandya, D. N. (2002). Association pathways of the prefrontal cortex and functional observations. In D. T. Stuss, & R. T. Knight (Eds.), *Principles of frontal lobe function* (pp. 31–50). Oxford: Oxford University Press.

Phan, K. L., Wager, T., Taylor, S. F., & Liberzon, I. (2002). Functional neuroanatomy of emotion: A meta-analysis of emotion activation studies in PET and fMRI. *NeuroImage, 16,* 331–348.

Pivik, R. T. (1991). Tonic states and phasic events in relation to sleep mentation. In S. J. Ellman, & J. S. Antrobus (Eds.), *The mind in sleep* (pp. 214–247). New York: Wiley Interscience.

Price, J. L. (1999). Prefrontal cortical networks related to visceral function and mood. *Annals of the New York Academy of Sciences, 877,* 383–396.

Ptak, R., Birtoli, B., Imboden, H., Hauser, C., Weis, J., & Schnider, A. (2001). Hypothalamic amnesia with spontaneous confabulations: A clinicopathologic study. *Neurology, 56,* 1597–1600.

Raichle, M. E., MacLeod, A. M., Snyder, A. Z., Powers, W. J., Gusnard, D. A., & Shulman, G. L. (2001). A default mode of brain function. *Proceedings of the National Academy of Sciences of the United States of America, 98,* 676–682.

Rechtschaffen, A. (1978). The single-mindedness and isolation of dreams. *Sleep, 1,* 97–109.

Ridderinkhof, K. R., Ullsperger, M., Crone, E. A., & Nieuwenhuis, S. (2004). The role of the medial frontal cortex in cognitive control. *Science, 306,* 443–447.

Rilling, J. K., Sanfey, A. G., Aronson, J. A., Nystrom, L. E., & Cohen, J. D. (2004). The neural correlates of theory of mind within interpersonal interactions. *NeuroImage, 22,* 1694–1703.

Robbins, T. W. (2005). Chemistry of the mind: Neurochemical modulation of prefrontal cortical function. *Journal of Comparative Neurology, 493,* 140–146.

Rogers, R. D., Blackshaw, A. J., Middleton, H. C., Matthews, K., Hawtin, K., Crowley C, et al. (1999). Tryptophan depletion impairs stimulus-reward learning while methylphenidate disrupts attentional control in healthy young adults: Implications for the monoaminergic basis of impulsive behaviour. *Psychopharmacology, 146,* 482–491.

Saint-Cyr, J. A. (2003). Frontal-striatal circuit functions: Context, sequence, and consequence. *Journal of the International Neuropsychological Society, 9,* 103–127.

Saint-Cyr, J. A., Bronstein, Y. I., & Cummings, J. L. (2002). Neurobehavioral consequences of neurosurgical treatments and focal lesions of frontal-subcortical circuits. In D. T. Stuss & R. T. Knight (Eds.), *Principles of frontal lobe function* (pp. 408–427). Oxford: Oxford University Press.

Samson D., Apperly, I. A., Chiavarino, C., & Humphreys, G. W. (2004). Left temporo-parietal junction is necessary for representing someone else's belief. *Nature Neuroscience, 7,* 499–500.

Saper, C. B., Cano, G., & Scammell, T. E. (2005). Homeostatic, circadian, and emotional regulation of sleep. *Journal of Comparative Neurology, 493,* 92–98.

Saper, C. B., Chou, T.C., & Scammell, T. E. (2001). The sleep switch: Hypothalamic control of sleep and wakefulness. *Trends in Neurosciences, 24,* 726–731.

Saper, C. B., Scammell, T. E., & Lu, J. (2005). Hypothalamic regulation of sleep and circadian rhythms. *Nature, 437,* 1257–1263.

Saxe, R., & Kanwisher, N. (2003). People thinking about thinking people. The role of the temporo-parietal junction in "theory of mind." *NeuroImage, 19,* 1835–1842.

Saxe, R., & Wexler, A. (2005). Making sense of another mind: The role of the right temporo-parietal junction. *Neuropsychologia, 43,* 1391–1409.

Schmahmann, J. D. (2004). Disorders of the cerebellum: Ataxia, dysmetria of thought, and the cerebellar cognitive affective syndrome. *Journal of Neuropsychiatry & Clinical Neurosciences, 16,* 367–378.

Schnider, A. (2001). Spontaneous confabulation, reality monitoring and the limbic system—a review. *Brain Research Reviews, 36,* 150–160.

Schnider, A. (2003). Spontaneous confabulation and the adaptation of thought to ongoing reality. *Nature Reviews Neuroscience, 4,* 662–671.

Schnider, A., Bonvallat, J., Emond, H., & Leemann, B. (2005). Reality confusion in spontaneous confabulation. *Neurology, 65,* 1117–1119.

Schwartz, S., Dang-Vu, T. T., Ponz, A., Duhoux, S., & Maquet, P. (2005). Dreaming: A neuropsychological view. *Swiss Archives of Neurology & Psychiatry, 156,* 426–439.

Schwartz, S., & Maquet, P. (2002). Sleep imaging and the neuropsychological assessment of dreams. *Trends in Cognitive Sciences, 6,* 23–30.

Selden, N. R., Gitelman D. R., Salamon-Murayama, N., Parrish, T. B., & Mesulam, M. M. (1998). Trajectories of cholinergic pathways within the cerebral hemispheres of the human brain. *Brain, 121,* 2249–2257.

Seligman, M. E. P., & Yellen, A. (1987). What is a dream? *Behavioral Research & Therapy, 25,* 1–24.

Servan-Schreiber, D., & Perlstein, W. M. (1997). Pharmacologic activation of limbic structures and neuroimaging studies of emotions. *Journal of Clinical Psychiatry, Suppl., 58,* 13–15.

Siegal, M., & Varley, R. (2002). Neural systems involved in "theory of mind." *Nature Reviews Neuroscience, 3,* 463–471.

Simon, N. R., Kemp, B., Manshanden, I., & Lopes da Silva, F. H. (2003). Whole-head measures of sleep from MEG signals and the ubiquitous <1 Hz "Slow Oscillation." *Sleep Research Online, 5,* 105–113.

Small, D. M., Gitelman, D., Simmons, K., Bloise, S. M., Parrish, T., & Mesulam, M. M. (2005). Monetary incentives enhance processing in brain regions mediating top-down control of attention. *Cerebral Cortex, 15,* 1855–1865.

Smith, G. S., Reynolds, C. F., Pollock, B., Derbyshire, S., Nofzinger, E., Dew, M. A., et al. (1999). Cerebral glucose metabolic response to combined total sleep deprivation and antidepressant treatment in geriatric depression. *American Journal of Psychiatry, 156*, 683–689.

Solms, M. (1997). *The neuropsychology of dreams: A clinico-anatomical study*. Mahwah, NJ: Lawrence Erlbaum Associates.

Solms, M. (2000). Dreaming and REM sleep are controlled by different brain mechanisms. *Behavioral & Brain Sciences, 23*, 843–850.

Solms, M. (2002). Dreaming: Cholinergic and dopaminergic hypotheses. In E. Perry, H. Ashton & A. Young (Eds.), *Neurochemistry of consciousness: Transmitters in mind* (pp. 123–131). Amsterdam: John Benjamin's Publishing Company.

Starkstein, S. E., & Robinson R. G. (1997). Mechanism of disinhibition after brain lesions. *Journal of Nervous & Mental Disease, 185*, 108–114.

Steriade, M. (2000). Corticothalamic resonance, states of vigilance and mentation. *Neuroscience, 101*, 243–276.

Steriade, M. (2006). Grouping of brain rhythms in corticothalamic systems. *Neuroscience, 137*, 1087–1106.

Stickgold, R., Scott, L., Fosse, R., & Hobson, J. A. (2001). Brain-mind states: I. Longitudinal field study of wake-sleep factors influencing mentation report length. *Sleep, 24*, 171–179.

Stone, V. E., Baron-Cohen, S., & Knight, R. T. (1998). Frontal lobe contributions to theory of mind. *Journal of Cognitive Neuroscience, 10*, 640–656.

Stuss, D. T., Alexander, M. P., Floden D., Binns, M. A., Levine, B., & McIntosh, A. R. (2002). Fractionalization and localization of distinct frontal lobe processes: Evidence from focal lesions in humans. In D. T. Stuss, & R. T. Knight (Eds.), *Principles of frontal lobe function* (pp. 392–407). Oxford: Oxford University Press.

Stuss, D. T., & Anderson, V. (2004). The frontal lobes and theory of mind: Developmental concepts from adult focal lesion research. *Brain & Cognition, 55*, 69–83.

Stuss, D. T., Gallup, G. G., Jr, & Alexander, M. P. (2001). The frontal lobes are necessary for "theory of mind." *Brain, 124*, 279–286.

Takeuchi, T., Ogilvie, R. D., Murphy, T. I., & Ferrelli, A. V. (2003). EEG activities during elicited sleep onset REM and NREM periods reflect different mechanisms of dream generation. *Clinical Neurophysiology, 114*, 210–220.

Tallon-Baudry, C., & Bertrand, O. (1999). Oscillatory gamma activity in humans and its role in object representation. *Trends in Cognitive Sciences, 3*, 151–162.

Vogeley, K., Bussfeld, P., Newen, A., Herrmann, S., Happe, F., Falkai, P., et al. (2001). Mind reading: Neural mechanisms of theory of mind and self-perspective. *NeuroImage, 14*, 170–181.

Wager, T. D., Jonides, J., & Reading, S. (2004). Neuroimaging studies of shifting attention: A meta-analysis. *NeuroImage, 22*, 1679–1693.

Wager, T. D., & Smith, E. E. (2003). Neuroimaging studies of working memory: A meta-analysis. *Cognitive, Affective & Behavioral Neuroscience, 3*, 255–274.

Werth, E., Achermann, P., & Borbely, A. A. (1996). Brain topography of the human sleep EEG: Antero-posterior shifts of spectral power. *NeuroReport, 8*, 123–127.

Werth, E., Achermann, P., & Borbely, A. A. (1997). Fronto-occipital EEG power gradients in human sleep. *Journal of Sleep Research, 6*, 102–112.

Wherle, R., Czisch, M., Kaufmann, C., Wetter, T. C., Holsboer, F., & Auer, D. P. (2005). Rapid eye movement-related brain activation in human sleep: A functional magnetic resonance imaging study. *NeuroReport, 16*, 853–857.

Williams, J., Merritt, J., Rittenhouse, C., & Hobson, J. A. (1992). Bizarreness in dreams and fantasies: Implications for the activation-synthesis hypothesis. *Consciousness & Cognition, 1*, 172–185.

Wittfoth, M., Buck, D., Fahle, M., & Herrmann, M. (2006). Comparison of two Simon tasks: Neuronal correlates of conflict resolution based on coherent motion perception. *NeuroImage, 32*, 921–929.

Wu, J., Buchsbaum, M. S., Gillin, J. C., Tang, C., Cadwell, S., Weigand, M., et al. (1999). Prediction of antidepressant effects of sleep deprivation by metabolic rates in the ventral anterior cingulate and the medial prefrontal cortex. *American Journal of Psychiatry, 156*, 1149–1158.

Seven

Dream Production: A Neural Network Attractor, Dual Rhythm Regional Cortical Activation, Homeostatic Model

Erin J. Wamsley and John S. Antrobus

Throughout history, theories of dreaming have sought to discover the "source" of mental experiences in sleep. Long thought to have an external origin, regarded as messages from gods, demons, and spirits, a more psychological view of these nocturnal experiences began to emerge only relatively recently, within the last few hundred years. One of the first claims for a natural explanation was Freud's (1900) assertion that dreams were expressions of embarrassing, and therefore repressed, biological drives, disguised so as to prevent awakening the sleeper. Although the theory failed to obtain empirical support, it survived because of its alleged ability to provide therapists and patients with information about the pathological effects of unconscious processes. Today, as a new science of the mind/brain emerges, combining psychological, systems neuroscience, computational, and molecular approaches, exponential growth in our understanding of how the brain produces waking cognition, memory, and emotion is enabling a more informed view of the nature of dreaming. Dreams are viewed by cognitive neuroscientists, not as a mysterious vehicle for communicating hidden messages from gods, demons, or the unconscious, but rather as the natural product of our waking perceptual brain systems, as they continue to function when isolated from the sensory world. On this view, no special source of input is required to direct the dream narrative.

During wakefulness, the essential function of our mind/brain is to successfully navigate through the environment. To accomplish this goal, our perceptual brain systems interpret neural activity relayed from peripheral sensory receptors, creating an internal representation of the sensory world, which is then used to mobilize appropriate responses to the stimuli we encounter in our waking lives. However, during sleep, both sensory input from the periphery and motor output from the central nervous system are actively blocked. The brain, now deafferented, functions as an isolated processor of offline information. Yet, despite the inert outward appearance of a sleeping person, sleep is certainly not a state of inactivity. Parts of the perceptual and motor systems of the brain remain active and interactive throughout all stages of sleep, constructing "perceptions" much as they would during wakefulness. The key distinction is that, in sleep, interpretive interactions among these systems are relatively independent of input from sensory receptors and early sensory regions of the brain. The processes by which perceptual systems generate perceptions are also altered as activity within and between different brain regions' changes across stages of sleep. The subjective experiences generated by the sleeping brain, however, retain a remarkable similarity to waking cognition, as our past experiences and motivations continue to constrain the brain's interpretive construction of perception and thought.

We examine here these processes by which dream experiences are generated, relying throughout on insights from "neural network" theory to help us understand how the sleeping mind/brain continues to carry out its waking interpretive functions during various stages of sleep. Ultimately, we will see that there is no need to postulate that the internally generated activity underlying dream experiences originates in some "dream creation center" of the brain with meaning and storyline fully formed and ready to be translated into individual images and sensations. On the contrary, largely coherent and meaningful dream sequences are an emergent phenomenon arising from the combined activity of a number of cortical and subcortical brain structures, which are quite capable of creating complex dream content without the need for meaningful, structured input from any particular input source.

A NOTE ON TERMINOLOGY: DREAMING VERSUS MENTATION

The term "dreaming" is sometimes taken to refer to only mental experiences in sleep that are particularly vivid and story-like. This type of experience is most likely to be reported from rapid eye movement (REM) sleep, as opposed to non-rapid eye movement (NREM) sleep. As such, some early models of dreaming sought to understand only how these particularly vivid dreams are created through the neural mechanisms of REM sleep. However, it is now known that mental experiences are recalled frequently from NREM sleep as well. A broader goal, then, is to understand how cognition is produced throughout all sleep, focusing on processes common to REM and NREM, as well as those that serve to modulate differences between dreams from these two states. In the following chapter, note that we will use the term "sleep mentation" to refer to any mental content during sleep and "dreaming" to refer to the more vivid and story-like mentation it signifies in the vernacular.

MENTATION IN REM AND NREM

Before the 1950s, sleep was widely regarded as a tonic, inactive state characterized by a global decrease in brain activity. Under this view, the phenomenon of dreaming seemed quite mysterious indeed, because it appeared to arise from a completely inactive, "unconscious" brain. However, all-night electroencephalogram (EEG) recordings allowed us to see that sleep is actually an active, dynamic process (Aserinsky & Kleitman, 1953). About 90 minutes after sleep onset, we enter REM sleep, the markedly unique stage of sleep often associated with reports of the most vivid dream experiences. During REM, our EEG becomes strikingly active, resembling that of waking. Our eyes dart back and forth beneath our lids, possibly in response to images generated by the visual system, but our skeletal muscles are paralyzed. By contrast, as a different set of brain systems become active, NREM mentation, matched for time of night, tends to be less visual and more verbal. Although, as we will see, brain activity is overall substantially reduced in NREM sleep, this sleep stage may nonetheless subserve important information processing functions (Buzsáki, 1996, 1998; Steriade & Timofeev, 2003).

The discovery of REM and its strong association with dreaming (Dement & Kleitman, 1957) suggested to many that neuroscience would be able to discover the processes underlying sleep mentation simply by isolating the neural mechanisms of REM mentation. Following this line of thought, Allan Hobson's "activation-synthesis" hypothesis (Hobson & McCarley, 1977) held that the "input" for dreaming is essentially random stimulation of the forebrain originating in the pontine brainstem exclusively during REM. The forebrain then takes this noisy oculo-motor input to the cortex and "synthesizes" it as it is best able, the noisy input ultimately leading to the bizarreness characteristics of dreaming. Activation-synthesis made several invaluable contributions to the study of sleep mentation, especially in its consistent effort to establish a subcortical basis for dreaming and its explanation for what the Europeans have called "paradoxical sleep"—the co-occurrence in REM sleep of active EEG and skeletal atonia.

Because of the strong association of dreaming with REM sleep, many investigators have assumed the association to be perfect and that NREM dream reports must be merely a remembrance of dreaming from a previous REM period. Indeed, matched for time of night, 93 percent of REM reports are more dreamlike than NREM reports (Antrobus, 1983). This strong association has led to the unfortunate de facto position that an explanation of REM sleep is equivalent to an explanation of dreaming, which in turn has generated considerable opposition to the Activation-Synthesis model, and its revised version, the Activation, Input, and Mode of Processing model (AIM; Hobson, 1992). In particular, the models say very little about how the brain actually constructs the features of dreaming and provide no explanation for how NREM mentation is produced, 7 percent of which is more dreamlike than its REM sleep counterpart. On average, subjects recall mentation from REM about 80 percent of the time and from NREM about 50 percent of the time, with recall from slow wave sleep (SWS) being approximately equivalent to recall from Stage 2 NREM (Nielsen, 2000).[1] The primary distinction between REM and NREM reports is that REM reports are typically much longer, more bizarre, vivid, and emotional than NREM mentation. NREM reports, on the other hand, are more likely to be described as "thought-like," lacking the vivid imagery and bizarreness characteristic of more intense dreams.[2]

The key feature of REM relevant to understanding sleep mentation is that, relative to NREM, it represents a state of heightened cortical activation. However, as we propose in our Dual Rhythm model, at least one other source of cortical activation also supports the production of dreaming and may account for some occasionally very long and bizarre dreams reported from NREM sleep (Wamsley, Hirota, Tucker, Smith, & Antrobus, 2007). Solms (2000) has also proposed an alternate cortical activation basis for the production of dream mentation. We describe these models in greater detail below.

A neurophysiological model of sleep mentation, therefore, requires much more than accounting for the differences between REM and NREM reports. It must describe the necessary neural substrate for the generation of cognitive events in any sleep stage, as well as account for the differences in cognitive features between sleep and other states. It must additionally explain how personal goals and motives influence dream content, and importantly, address the issue of whether the production of coherent dream sequences requires structured top-down input from some dream creation center."

APPLYING NEURAL NETWORK MODELS TO DREAMING: WHERE DO DREAMS COME FROM?

Neural Networks and Attractor States

Several common misconceptions about information processing in the brain have limited our understanding of how the brain processes information "offline" in general, and how it constructs dreaming and other forms of sleep mentation in particular. Since our best evidence about information processing comes from input-output perceptual data, dreaming models have assumed that there must be some "input" that constitutes the origin of the dreaming process. Coupled with this perspective is the erroneous assumption that perceptual processing, and by extension, dreaming, move through the brain in a strictly "feed-forward" hierarchical sequence.[3] In fact, all steps in perception also involve feedback of information from later perceptual areas to earlier steps in the processing "sequence" (Delorme, Rousselet, Mace, & Fabre-Thorpe, 2004; Ro, Breitmeyer, Burton, Singhal, & Lane, 2003).

Feedback or "recurrent" processes are equally essential to the processing of external sensory stimuli and offline imagery and thought in daydreaming or dreaming. Consider the recognition of your dog, "Spot." Spot may be described by a large number of features: name, color, gender, age, weight, height, sound of toenails on wooden floor, eye position, tail length, wagging frequency, hair length, curl, bark, and so on. Such features distinguish him from other dogs, and additional features distinguish dogs from other animals, and animals from plants, and so on. In short, Spot, can be described as a vector in multidimensional feature space. But Spot's features also change with his state, such as when he is running, sleeping, eating, and growling, and with the perspective of the viewer, so any of a very large combination of features will accurately identify Spot. For this reason, the vector representing Spot is a large fuzzy ball rather than a point in feature space. Each of Spot's features is also made up of subfeatures. Barking is defined by certain features of pitch, loudness, and duration, to name a few, each of which may be linked to more elementary subfeature representations.

Attractors

A neural network becomes an attractor if it has recurrent connections with other networks. Recurrency allows interconnected networks to modify the state of each other over time. For example, if the Spot network is mildly active, it will send activation out to its defining feature network, effectively lowering its threshold so that less than normal activation from subfeature networks is necessary to fully activate them. Once active, they, in turn, return activation to the Spot network. Of course, if the recurrent process returns information that is incompatible with the Spot vector, such as white hair rather than black, the Spot vector sends out less activation to its defining feature networks. This recurrency continues until the Spot network either falls to the level of residual neural noise or it becomes sufficiently active to constitute recognition.

Recognition and Context

Recognizing Spot is equivalent to activating the feature vector, in the form of interconnected neural networks, that represent Spot's features—or more precisely, activating it to a greater extent than any competing vectors. Recognition is always facilitated by context, which constrains the set of possible objects that are likely to be present. For example, if Spot is the only dog in the house, only one of his many features, for example, the sound of toenails on wooden floor, is sufficient to achieve accurate recognition. But if Spot is in the park with scores of other dogs, accurate recognition of Spot will require the processing of many more features. In this sense, context "attracts" the representations of objects that, on the basis of past experience, have a high probability of occurring and rejects those representations that have a low probability of occurring. The neural basis of this attraction process is that when networks representing context are temporarily active, they send activation to the representations of objects that commonly occur in that context, effectively lowering the threshold for those representations. The lower these thresholds, the less activation is required from the lower level feature networks to activate an object network supported by that context. Thus, only one feature is needed to recognize Spot in a one-dog house, but many features are required in the context of a multi-dog park. Note that the same feature, clicking toenails, in a neighbor's apartment may accurately identify a different dog, for example, Scott. In this sense, the context attractor biases the "interpretation" of features in favor of recognition that is compatible with the context. The greater the contextual constraints, the less feature input is needed to accomplish accurate recognition. In the context of Spot's kitchen, he may be recognized with only a fraction of the full feature set that defines the Spot vector—and with a different set of features each time, and even with features that are somewhat novel.

It is these characteristics of attractors that give them their great advantage over formal recognition processes. If the brain were not a huge landscape of such attractors, dreaming and other forms of "offline" imagery and thought could not occur.

Dreaming and Other Offline States

Just as widespread cortical activation is required in the waking state for the cortex to process sensory stimuli (Moruzzi & Magoun, 1949), so too the different qualities of mentation that characterize different states of sleep require regional and widespread cortical activation. The primary states are the active phase of subcortical REM-NREM and diurnal rhythms, which we describe below. It is the attractor property of the cortex that enables the activated regions to transform ambient neural noise into objects, persons, and events. Once a cortical region becomes active, its attractor networks are subject to several forms of bias that constrain the possible objects and events they will produce.

Note that neural activity is never completely random. When one network is active, its learned synaptic connections to other networks always activate some related networks and inhibit others, while a different active network may support the opposite pattern. Among the most significant sources of bias are familiarity, recency, and personal value/threat. In attractor theory, bias may be represented as a widening and deepening of an attractor, properties that attract noisy input from neighboring attractors. For example, a substantial portion of the cortex is devoted to face recognition, and within it, to eye recognition. One suspects that two random dots in the visual subfeature network might activate "eyes" in the feature network, and then the face of a person, or if Spot is the most recently recognized face/head in the waking state, the head of Spot. Of course, mentation of some form never ceases altogether, and the context of this mentation, for example of an ongoing dream, constitutes a powerful context within which the brain generates the next object in the dream—that is, "interprets" ambient feature neural noise so as to be compatible with that context. For example, the two feature dots that become eyes in the context of a face attractor field will, in the presence of a street or highway context, support the recognition of headlights and a vehicle. As noted earlier, only a small set of features may be sufficient to generate a dream object, person, or event.

Attractors, Discontinuities, and Bizarreness

The ability of attractor networks to make everything "fit," even in sleep, flies in the face of the hallmark of dreams—their essential bizarreness. The attractor model demonstrates why there are limits to the bizarreness of dream images. Dreamed persons do not have three eyes, or inverted noses, because there are no previous learned attractors representing these images. Attractors transform noisy neural activity into relatively familiar features and objects, or else they inhibit it altogether. Random neural activity is not, as many theorists have suggested, the basis of dream bizarreness.

When cortical attractor regions are disconnected, however, they lose their ability to mutually constrain each other, and in this case will produce special classes of bizarre mentation. For example, the REM report, ". . . he was my brother, but he was a girl in my dream" suggests a disconnect between cortical regions that produce visual-face, naming, and relational features. This tendency toward regional disconnect has been supported by positron emission tomography (PET) studies of regional cortical activation and electrophysiological studies of cortical connectivity in sleep (Braun et al., 1997, 1998; Massimini et al., 2005). We discuss these issues later in further detail. For a more technical description of this neural network attractor model of dreaming, described before the term attractor was introduced to psychology, see Antrobus (1991).

The Incorporation of External Stimuli into Sleep Mentation

Although the explanatory value of attractor models has been evaluated in waking perception, data from the early "incorporation" studies of dreaming nicely illustrates the power of attractors during sleep. Although we suggest that most sleep mentation is constructed independent of external stimuli, some features of external stimuli, if they do not awaken the sleeper, are often attracted into a dream image sequence. Sensory input pathways are inhibited in the sleeping brain, and the difficulty of experimentally altering dream content by presenting sensory stimulation to sleeping subjects renders this type of external input unlikely to be a major component in the creation of most dream content. William Dement presented stimuli in various sensory modalities to subjects during REM and found that a spray of water was most effective in eliciting stimulus-related content from subsequent dream reports (Dement & Wolpert, 1958). Yet, little progress has been made in understanding the mechanisms of such "incorporation" effects. An interesting characteristic of these incorporations, helping to elucidate their mechanism, is that the stimuli presented typically appear in the dream in some altered form, apparently having been "interpreted" by the brain in the ongoing context of the dream narrative. For example, in the dreamed context of drinking a glass of water, a spray of water on the sleeper's arm might be interpreted as water spilled out of the glass, or in the dreamed context of sitting in one's house, a bell may be interpreted as a telephone call or doorbell.

If we understand the ongoing dream narrative as emerging from the collective activation of a number of attractors in cortical neural networks, it follows that some features of the sensory input, whether originating in somatosensory cortex in the case of a spray of water, or in visual cortex in the case of a flashing light, will ultimately be drawn to the attractor states active at any given time. In this way, the brain "interprets" the activation patterns presented to it as originating from a source of sensory stimulation that would be appropriate in the current dream context.

This type of interpretive process is not exclusive to the sleeping brain, but is rather an extension of the same general processes that the brain uses to make sense out of waking experience. Even in our daily lives, we interpret sensations in a context-appropriate manner. For example, Schachter and Singer (1962) famously demonstrated that the physiological effects of a dose of adrenaline might be interpreted as having different origins, depending on the contextual information available to subjects. The interpretive nature of our waking neural systems, though, is most dramatically exposed in pathological cases. Michael Gazzaniga's groundbreaking work with split-brain patients demonstrates that a patient's left brain interprets actions initiated by the disconnected right brain as it is best able, given the current context (Gazzaniga, 2000). In one case, a split-brain patient's right brain was shown a snowy scene, and their left brain was shown a chicken foot,[4] while the subject's two hemispheres were asked to select appropriate response images. The right brain chose a shovel (in response to the snow) and the left brain chose a chicken (in response to the chicken foot). Yet, when the patient's left brain, unable to communicate with the right hemisphere, was asked why he selected the shovel, he responded that "you need a shovel to clean out the chicken shed" (Gazzaniga, 2000, p. 1318). The sleeping brain, as in wakefulness, interprets what is presented to it (whether external stimulation or endogenously generated activation) in a manner most consistent with currently active attractor states. In this way, even input devoid of personal meaning for the dreamer may be ultimately experienced in light of their personal experiences and related to the ongoing dream narrative.

EMOTIONS IN REM AND NREM

So far, we have discussed sleep mentation in general terms as emerging from activity in widely distributed cortical attractor networks. Yet, specific subcortical and cortical brain regions modulating emotion and motivation during wakefulness undoubtedly have a powerful influence on dream content, perhaps by biasing attractors associated with personal motives or powerful emotional responses to be those most likely to become strongly active in sleep. Although dreams have a reputation for being highly emotional experiences, descriptions of emotion are actually fairly infrequent in mentation reports, unless subjects are specifically prompted to report them. When emotions are reported, they tend to be primarily negative in tone within spontaneously recalled home dreams (Domhoff, 2001) but contain a relatively equal proportion of positive and negative emotions when collected in the laboratory setting (Fosse, Stickgold, & Hobson, 2001; Strauch & Meier, 1996), where emotions tend to be more prominent in REM rather than NREM reports. One study has additionally reported that emotional intensity increases across the night selectively within REM sleep (Wamsley et al., 2007). Fear, anxiety, and aggression in REM dreaming are likely related to the enhanced amygdala activation characteristic of this stage (Braun et al, 1997; Maquet, Peters, & Aerts, 1996). During wakefulness, the amygdala is the key component in orchestrating emotional responses to threatening or novel stimuli, and in sleep it likely continues to serve this function of evaluating imaged persons and objects, though in this case input to the amygdala is now endogenously generated rather than relayed from the periphery.

Despite prevalent reports of negatively toned dreaming, autonomic components of dreamed emotions seem to be largely inhibited until the dreamer nears awakening. Night terrors, for example, initiated during the deepest stages of NREM, involve some of the most intense emotionality associated with sleep and trigger an autonomic storm (increased heart rate, respiration, and so on). These autonomic responses, however, are not initiated until just at the moment of waking (Fisher et al., 1973). During wakefulness, autonomic fear responses to stimuli are typically mediated by output from the central nucleus of the amygdala. In NREM sleep, although activation of the amygdala is equal to (Braun et al., 1997) or greater than (Nofzinger et al., 2002) in waking, behavioral evidence of inhibited autonomic response suggests that output pathways from the amygdala may be disrupted. Inhibition of amygdala-mediated autonomic responsiveness could contribute to the relatively less intense emotionality characteristic of NREM reports in general, as feedback from autonomic systems is likely an important component of the conscious experience of fear and anxiety.[5]

Conversely, amygdala control of fear responses in REM sleep appears to be to some degree preserved, perhaps contributing to the more intense emotionality characteristic of reports from this stage. Nightmares occurring during REM sleep have been found to be associated with small increases in heart rate and respiration during the last few minutes before waking (Nielsen & Zadra, 2000). However, these autonomic responses are much more pronounced than reactions that would be elicited to fearful stimuli during wakefulness, and occur only as the sleeper moves towards waking. Still, feedback from autonomic responses could contribute to the increased experience of emotion in REM versus NREM sleep.

Intriguingly, a special relationship between REM sleep, emotion, and the amygdala, is also suggested by recent work on the consolidation of memories during sleep. It turns out that the offline processing of emotional memories is facilitated by periods of REM (i.e., Wagner, Gais, & Born, 2001). This suggests that consolidation of amygdala-mediated emotional memories during REM could be a source of the particularly emotional content of REM dreams. However, no direct evidence yet exists tying memory processing in REM to the content of mentation from this stage.

The symptoms of some sleep disorders complement this cognitive evidence that emotional reactions are particularly pronounced in REM sleep. In REM Behavior Disorder (RBD), patients physically act out their REM dreams because of a dysfunction of the mechanism normally inhibiting motor output during this sleep stage. Unlike in episodes of sleepwalking or night terrors originating in NREM sleep, patients typically recall extended, vivid dreams following RBD episodes, often characterized by feelings of highly intense fear or aggression. It is possible that the heightened emotionality of these dreams may serve as a trigger for the RBD episode. In narcolepsy, characteristics of REM sleep (muscle paralysis, hallucinations) pathologically intrude into wakefulness. Cataplexy (a sudden loss of muscle tone) in these patients can be triggered by the experience of intense emotions during wakefulness. Particularly in REM sleep, then, the amygdala may influence ongoing dream content by continuing to perform the same function as it does during wakefulness, evaluating sensory (in this case pseudo-sensory) input and mobilizing emotional responses.

MOTIVATION AND VALUE

Like emotion, motivation also appears to be a key component of the dreaming process that may bias certain cortical attractors to be more likely to participate in dream content. Frontal regions associated with motivation during wakefulness are actually a necessary component of the neural network for dreaming (Solms, 2000). In clinical interviews, patients with damage to a motivation-related area of the medial prefrontal cortex, near the frontal horns of the lateral ventricles, often report a total cessation of dreaming (Solms, 2000). Like emotion, motivational content[6] is also more prominent in REM versus NREM mentation, independent of report length (Smith et al., 2004), indicating that, although motivation may also be influenced by general levels of cortical activation, this dream feature does hold a particular relationship to REM that cannot be accounted for by overall levels of mentation production.[7] The preferential involvement of motivation-related structures during REM sleep in particular is also suggested by studies demonstrating a relationship between electrical stimulation of reward centers in the rat medial frontal cortex and REM sleep (Steiner & Ellman, 1972). In these studies, rats were trained to administer rewarding stimulation to this brain region by pressing a lever. It was found that (a) depriving rats of REM sleep caused them to subsequently seek more of this rewarding stimulation and (b) after allowing rats to self-stimulate, the typical "rebound" increase in REM sleep following REM deprivation was decreased (Steiner & Ellman, 1972). These results, like Solms's (2000) work, suggest that motivation-related medial frontal areas are normally active during sleep and, furthermore, that stimulation of these centers may be associated with some need. Consistent with the former assumption, brain imaging studies confirm that, relative to some other frontal regions, the medial prefrontal cortex remains active as we move from wakefulness into sleep (Braun et al., 1997).

A significant issue for dream theory is whether one cortical-attractor region dominates the mentation process and, if so, whether it is the same over time and in all sleep stages. Dream "interpretation" is based on the implicit assumption that a particular personal concern or emotional conflict dominates the dreaming process, so that the dream sequence is generated to play out the conflict in a visual form. We suggest that the visual representation regions of the cortex may dominate the REM dream process, and that other cortical regions are activated in response to the visual images. For example, the peculiar shape of an imagined table led one dreamer to conclude that "we must have been at the circus." In another dream, the image of a fingernail was flatter than usual, so the dreamer assumed that it must have been hit by an object. Of particular interest in this regard is the strong association between amygdaloid activation and REM sleep and, therefore, vivid dreaming. Amygdala activation is associated with emotional responsivity, particularly negative emotions, but also with novel, that is, unanticipated, events. It is not clear at this time whether amygdala activity in REM sleep imposes a negative emotional bias to the visual images of REM dreams or whether the REM dream images, lacking the strong contextual constraints of waking perception, are sufficiently "unanticipated" to elicit a novelty-fear response in the amygdala. Although dream content is generally continuous with waking experience, mentation reports appear to be biased toward content with motivational and emotional value (that is, socializing with friends) and are less likely to include content from waking life not associated with particular value to the dreamer (that is, using a computer) (Schredl & Hofmann, 2003). This tendency for dreams to include concepts and events holding personal meaning for the dreamer, however, does not need to be explained via the Freudian notion that the essential meaning of the dream exists in some central location and is then translated into individual images constituting the actual dream content. The more parsimonious alternative is that emotional and motivational structures merely create biases in the ongoing dream content already spontaneously emerging in cortical attractors. Such a process could occur in a manner similar to how these same structures influence waking cognition and action through the mobilization of emotional responses and goal-directed behaviors in response to perceptual experience. Future brain imaging work employing techniques with high temporal resolution may answer these questions by demonstrating whether some sequences of regional activation are more common than others.

BIZARRENESS

Dreams have captured the human imagination, in part because they often seem so strange to us—so unusual, otherworldly, and unlike our waking experiences. Two primary classes of dream bizarreness are "discontinuities" across time and "improbable combinations" within a specific time-space frame. A discontinuity occurs in a dream when the scene suddenly undergoes a dramatic change, with little or no transition. Notice, for example, that in the following excerpt from a laboratory dream, the scene changes twice without any apparent transition:

> I was at a waiting area talking to my friend just sitting there talking about people um around the school but then we were inside a building and then the next thing I was in my ex-boyfriend's house.

"Improbable combinations," on the other hand, are instances of content that would be impossible or improbable according to waking experience, frequently manifested through the unlikely combination of two or more dream elements. Notice in this report, for example, the unlikely juxtaposition of the soccer game and coach with the helicopter:

> It was a soccer game uhm I don't know where I was but what was going through my mind was there was this coach in a helicopter and the soccer game came to some sort of time out or something.

Discontinuity

It is often presumed that these bizarre features of dream mentation are unique to the dreaming state and serve to differentiate sleep mentation from waking perceptual and cognitive processes. Following this line of reasoning, Hobson has proposed that dream bizarreness may result from one or more neurological processes unique to the state of REM sleep. In regard to discontinuity in particular, he has proposed that the occurrence of intermittent ponto-geniculo-occipital (PGO)-like activity[8] in humans may be responsible for rapid changes in this imagery (Mamelak & Hobson, 1989). Other explanations offered for bizarreness in dreams have also relied on mechanisms specific to sleep, including the very low level of aminergic neuromodulators (i.e., serotonin, norepinephrine) during REM sleep (Hobson et al., 2000), and the deactivation of the dorsolateral prefrontal cortex[9] characteristic of both REM and NREM (Muzur, Pace-Schott, & Hobson, 2002).

Although discontinuities are clearly present in sleep mentation, this dream feature is not necessarily caused by neural processes specific to the sleep state. In fact, discontinuity/rapidly shifting imagery is present in waking mentation as well as in sleep, perhaps at even greater levels. Waking thought samples obtained from subjects reclining in a darkened room actually exhibit equal or greater amounts of discontinuity than dream reports from REM sleep, particularly when intermittent auditory stimuli are present (Foulkes and Fleisher, 1975; Reinsel, Wollman, & Antrobus, 1992; Wollman & Antrobus, 1986). Studies of mental imagery abilities complement these findings, demonstrating that when subjects are asked to form visual images, these images have a relatively short duration, either disappearing or changing their appearance after about 10 seconds on average (Cocude, Charlot, & Denis, 1996; Cocude & Denis, 1988). A rapid decay process acting on individual mental images such as this could certainly support overall patterns of discontinuity in both waking and sleeping mentation observed in the aforementioned studies.

Other studies of waking cognition also support the general notion that in the absence of an external source of input, any one image is unable to be maintained for an extended period of time. An inability of the visual system to continue perceiving repetitive input can be inferred, for example, by examining the phenomena of fixational eye movements. Even during periods of steady fixation on a point, our eyes are constantly making very fast tiny movements ("microsaccades"). The result of these microsaccades is that any one feature of a visual scene is constantly being coded by different sets of cells in the retina and represented by different sets of neurons in the brain. This process appears to actually be *necessary* for sustaining vision—when a device is employed to artificially hold a person's visual world motionless on the retina, although they at first perceived stimuli normally, after a few seconds the visual stimuli appeared to disappear (Riggs, Ratcliffe, Cornsweet, & Cornsweet, 1953). If the adaptation to steady visual input demonstrated by Riggs et al. (1953) is mediated at least in part by habituation of neurons in the visual system, the mechanism at work here may be similar to that which causes the constant change present in dreams and mental imagery.

In a neural network model of sleep mentation, discontinuity might be represented by using a decay function, simulating a decline in the activation of any particular attractor state following its initial recruitment. Any individual image would, therefore, be supplanted by another competing image representation at the next time step, after activation of the original image decreased below a certain threshold. Such a model could simulate the generation of a string of discontinuous elements, each fading after a certain period of time, apparently an inherent characteristic of both waking and sleeping cognition.

Improbable Combinations

Improbable combinations between dream elements, as in the example above when a helicopter is seen during the ongoing context of a soccer game, could result from a lack of communication between neural networks that normally inhibit each other during waking cognition. In waking thought, for example, the semantic network for the idea of "soccer game" should not be strongly associated with the visual representation of "helicopter." Attractors for the two objects actively *inhibit* each other in the waking brain—that is, when "soccer game" is the active context, "helicopter" will be much less likely to become active than in the context of "airport."

When we fall asleep, however, communication between brain regions is altered as networks that normally cooperate during waking cognition become functionally disconnected. For example, brain imaging studies show us that, during REM, higher-level visual areas are active, while simultaneously, primary visual areas normally supporting the earliest steps of visual processing in waking are inactive (Braun et al., 1998). A "functional dissociation" is also seen between activity in limbic and paralimbic structures during NREM sleep (Braun et al., 1997). Similarly, although a wide array of cognitive and perceptual tasks during wakefulness recruit the activity of frontal association areas, including the dorsolateral prefrontal cortex, some of these structures appear to be conspicuously inactive during sleep mentation (Braun et al., 1997).

During sleep, therefore, networks that would normally mutually inhibit each other are no longer necessarily communicating as they would in wakefulness. Instead, some brain regions, though active, are operating in relative isolation from other cortical and subcortical networks. New studies combining transcranial magnetic stimulation (TMS) and electrophysiological recordings also give us a glimpse of how cortical connectivity is altered during sleep. In wakefulness, when premotor cortex is stimulated by using TMS, the neural response in that area quickly propagates out to connected cortical areas. However, when this same area is stimulated during NREM sleep, although a very large initial response is seen at the stimulation site, this enhanced response does not then spread activation to adjacent cortex (Massimini et al., 2005). A similar technique has been used to demonstrate that communication between hemispheres through the corpus callosum is inhibited in the moments following awakening from REM sleep (Bertini et al., 2004). This altered functional connectivity could allow thoughts and images that would not normally co-occur in waking cognition to now become simultaneously active. Again, this characteristic of dreaming emerges naturally from activity and communication patterns within the isolated sleeping brain, not requiring the postulation of any particular "input source" to generate the bizarreness of dreams.

VISUAL IMAGERY

Visual imagery has long been presumed the key feature of dreaming—more than a hundred years ago, Freud (1900) described dreaming as "think[ing] predominantly in visual images," and today most researchers still describe dreams as being primarily visual in nature. Freud presumed, however, that the individual visual images constituting the dream were translations of an underlying hidden message created in the unconscious mind. The dream, in other words, began with meaning and was subsequently converted into individual visual symbols in a top-down fashion. Solms's (2000) view that the dream "begins" with higher-level meaning created in frontal motivation-related areas and is then disseminated out to the rest of the brain broadly mirrors this assumption, though placing it in a neurophysiological context. As discussed previously, however, an alternative possibility is that the visual imagery of dreaming emerges spontaneously in cortical attractors, once activation in those regions surpasses some threshold, and the influence of motivations and emotions on dream content arises in an ongoing fashion as this imagery is processed by the amygdala and medial prefrontal regions—a process analogous to how we attend and react to stimuli in the context of motivations and emotion during wakefulness.

Visual dream imagery is presumably supported by the visual cortex and is similar in many respects to the neural representations generated by external visual input in our waking lives. Brain imaging studies support this view, showing that endogenously generated imagery does, in fact, activate visual cortex. Imaging studies of mental imagery tasks have consistently shown activation of higher-order visual areas, and sometimes activation of primary visual cortex[10] as well (for a review see Mellet, Petit, Mazoyer, Denis, & Tzourio, 1998). Imaging studies of REM sleep have also shown increased (relative to NREM) activation in visual cortex (Braun et al., 1997, 1998). However, *primary* visual cortex activity may be low in REM sleep relative to NREM or wake (Braun et al., 1998). In this case, higher-level visual cortex would be carrying out the job of representing visual dream images without the help of the early visual areas that normally support the initial processing phases of stimuli from the external world. We must keep in mind, however, that the phenomenon of sleep mentation is neither unique to REM sleep nor guaranteed by it. Therefore, although imaging studies of REM offer intriguing clues to the neural basis of mentation within REM sleep, this data does not directly inform us about the neural substrate of sleep mentation.

The higher-level visual cortex supports the generation of endogenous imagery during REM sleep and may be operating independently of the earliest visual processing areas that normally transmit "bottom-up" information from the perceptual world to higher-level brain areas during wakefulness. We assume, however, that this imagery is constrained to a significant degree by recurrent interaction between extrastriate visual cortex and motivation and emotion-related subcortical and cortical regions.

TOTAL REPORTED INFORMATION

By far, the largest and most consistent distinction between REM and NREM sleep mentation is that reports elicited from REM awakenings tend to be much longer, containing a greater amount of total information. This could be because of generally greater activation of the neural substrate for sleep mentation simply generating more content during REM, or alternatively, to a relatively greater difficulty in recalling dream content that occurs during NREM.

The generally greater recall of content from REM creates a methodologically problematic confounding influence of report length on other comparisons between REM and NREM reports. It is obvious, for example, that a 300-word dream report will likely have a larger raw number of "discontinuities" than a 10-word dream report, merely by virtue of its greater length. The use of scales that count the number of bizarre events, the number of emotions, the number of visual images, and so on, in a dream report is common, clearly presenting the potential for a report-length confound. Indeed, when the influence of report length is statically removed from comparisons of REM and NREM reports, some widely cited differences between REM and NREM sleep mentation disappear (Antrobus, 1983). Nonetheless, other studies have demonstrated persistent stage differences even when controlling for report length (i.e., Casagrande, Violani, Lucidi, Buttinelli, & Bertini, 1996; Smith et al., 2004).

THE DUAL RHYTHM MODEL OF DREAMING SLEEP

The Dual Rhythm model assumes that both the REM-NREM cycle and changes in cortical activation across the 24-hour cycle are sources of nonspecific brain activation supporting mentation during sleep, with widespread cortical activation being in greater in REM than NREM, and greater in the last hours of normal sleep compared to earlier in the night (Wamsley et al., 2007). Many cortical regions are activated by both sources, and the activation effect appears to be additive, such that late morning dream reports are, for example, longer and more bizarre in both REM and NREM. Though the construction of dreamed thought and imagery is dependent on the structure of attractor networks within cortical and subcortical areas, widespread activation in the sleeping brain is a necessary prerequisite for these networks to become active. REM sleep appears to be one important source of this general activation necessary to drive the dreaming process. However, the generation of cognition in sleep may be driven, in addition to activation changes across the ultradian sleep cycle, by *circadian-driven* and *homeostatic-driven* activation changes across the 24-hour cycle.[11] The late morning seems to be the source of most long, bizarre, and dreamlike reports from NREM.

Dreaming is Influenced by Circadian Factors

Circadian-driven changes in brain activity across the night constitute a source of activation to the neural substrate for sleep mentation other than REM. A "circadian rhythm" is any biological function that fluctuates according to an internally driven 24-hour cycle. Body temperature, vigilance, levels of various hormones, and likelihood of experiencing a heart attack, for example, all follow such a 24-hour cycle. These and other circadian rhythms are said to be "internally generated," because their 24-hour periodicity continues to occur even in the absence of external cues, being primarily driven by the circadian pacemaker in the suprachiasmatic nucleus of the hypothalamus.

A circadian rhythm for general levels of cortical activation is revealed through endogenous 24-hour cycles of alertness and cognitive performance, which are roughly correlated with the well-documented rhythm for core body temperature (CBT) (Broughton, 1975; Carrier & Monk, 1999; Monk et al., 1997). These rhythms each reach a low point in the middle of the night and begin to rise in the morning hours, finally peaking in the early evening. Components of the sleep EEG also reveal a circadian modulation of brain activation. Specifically, the peak of spectral power in the fast spindle range (~14 Hz), the nadir of alpha activity in REM, and propensity for REM sleep all coincide with rising CBT during the late morning hours (Benington, 2004; De Gennaro & Ferrara, 2003; Dijk, Shanahan, Duffy, Ronda, & Czeisler, 1997). The mechanism of this activation rhythm could involve hypothalamic control of the ascending reticular activating system, a primary mediator of general brain activity levels (Moruzzi & Magoun, 1949).

These circadian changes in cortical activation appear to modulate the generation of mentation during sleep. For some time now, it has been noted that propensity for sleep mentation changes throughout the night, such that the most mentation is recalled from experimental awakenings made during the late morning hours (Antrobus, Kondo, & Reinsel, 1995; Casagrande et al., 1996; Pivik & Foulkes, 1968; Stickgold, Malia, Fosse, Propper, & Hobson, 2001). Mentation also changes qualitatively across the night, becoming, for example, more bizarre, vivid, or emotional as the night progresses (Antrobus et al., 1995; Casagrande et al., 1996; Wamsley et al., 2007). Lucid dreaming, in addition, is much more likely to be reported during the late morning hours than earlier in the night (LaBerge, 1990).

Importantly, amount of mentation reported increases across the night in both REM and NREM sleep (Antrobus et al., 1995; Wamsley et al., 2007). This suggests that, whatever the precise mechanism of this circadian influence on dreaming turns out to be, this activation source affects the neural substrate for REM and NREM mentation production similarly.

Though these "time of night" cortical activation effects on sleep mentation might be accounted for by circadian factors, most of the above studies could also be explained via homeostatic-driven changes in sleep need across the night, following the general time course of propensity for SWS. Indeed, most studies on dreaming across the night have not controlled for time since sleep onset, which creates an inherent confound in which circadian and homeostatic changes in brain activity are occurring simultaneously with increasing time since sleep onset. One typical approach to isolating circadian rhythms for biological functions is to employ a "forced desynchrony" protocol, in which subjects initiate sleep at various phases of their endogenous circadian rhythm. Two studies have taken a similar approach in order to address the hypothesis that changes in sleep mentation across the night are specifically attributable to an internally generated circadian rhythm, each concluding that circadian phase does have a powerful influence on propensity for mentation reporting, independently of how long subjects have been asleep or the number of previous awakenings (Antrobus et al., 1995; Suzuki et al., 2004).

The precise time course for the circadian rhythm of mentation in sleep, however, remains uncertain. Antrobus et al. (1995) have presumed that the circadian rhythm for dreaming is correlated with the CBT cycle, and their data have been broadly consistent with this assumption. However, Suzuki et al. (2004) present data supporting a circadian time course for dreaming that peaks in the morning at approximately 8:00 AM and declines thereafter.

Dreaming and Homeostatic Discharge of Slow Wave Activity

Although changes in mentation production across the night appear to be at least partially due to circadian factors, it is also quite possible that "time-of-night" effects are influenced by homeostatic (sleep-dependent) factors. Slow wave activity (SWA) in the EEG is prominent in the early night and discharges with increasing time since sleep onset. SWA has often been taken as a physiological indicator of "sleep pressure," which builds up during wakefulness and discharges during sleep. This decreasing propensity for SWA can be conceptualized as a process that leads the EEG to become more "active" across the night and could, therefore, influence mentation production to be greater in the late morning hours, when SWA is virtually absent from the EEG.

In fact, some data on propensity for mentation recall seem highly consistent with an underlying homeostatic process. Both Pivik and Foulkes (1968) and Nielsen and Powell (1989) have described time courses for mentation reporting characterized by a sharp increase in reporting in the early part of the night, remaining constant for the remainder of the sleep episode. This pattern of results mirrors the steep discharge of SWA that occurs early in the evening and then asymptotes as the sleep period wears on towards the morning hours. Recent work from our laboratory (Wamsley et al., 2006) is also consistent with an influence of homeostatic sleep need on propensity for sleep mentation. We anticipated that if sleep mentation is primarily driven by a circadian rhythm approximating the CBT rhythm, more mentation should be reported from a daytime nap than from night reports. On the contrary, within NREM sleep, we found that substantially less mentation was recalled from afternoon nap reports compared to night reports. These results might be explained by postulating that CBT-related circadian activation of cortical attractor networks can be counteracted by the suppression of activation as homeostatic sleep need builds up during the hours of wakefulness before a nap. Alternatively, it may be the case that diurnal variations in mentation production rely primarily on a circadian generator, with peak circadian activation to the dreaming process occurring in the late morning hours.

Though it has long been proposed that the experience of dreaming requires that brain activity reach some minimal threshold, in early neurocognitive models of dreaming the REM cycle was the only source of fluctuations in activation during the night given detailed consideration. Circadian and homeostatic processes are critical to the study of sleep mentation, in part because they provide alternative mechanisms by which cortical activation can reach a sufficient threshold for mentation production, even outside of REM sleep.

EXPLAINING DREAMING VIA THE "ACTIVATION" OF BRAIN STRUCTURES

Not long ago, the very idea of "brain activity in sleep" was thought to be an oxymoron. In fact, in the years following its discovery, REM sleep was often termed "paradoxical" sleep, because the presence of waking-like EEG seemed so incongruous with the longstanding intuition that sleep was most fundamentally a state of inactivity. Subsequent neurophysiological models of dreaming relied on the general strategy of delineating the types of brain "activation" in sleep presumed to create the dream experience. As we have seen, the earliest investigations of sleep mentation primarily focused on differences between sleep stages, stressing the strong relationship between vivid dreaming and increased *global* neural activity in REM, whereas more recent work has also focused on understanding which particular brain regions are active and, therefore, assumed to contribute to cognition across various stages of sleep and wakefulness (i.e., Hobson, Pace-Schott, & Stickgold, 2000; Solms, 2000). The term "activation," however, is a slippery metaphor that can refer to quite disparate concepts depending on the context in which it is being used. Regardless of the precise type of activation being considered, inferences based on observations of activation patterns in the sleeping brain must be made with great care.

"Activation" Is Not a Unitary Concept

The meaning of "activation" varies substantially depending on the context in which it is being discussed. Early studies of the brain basis of dream experiences employed the still widely used technique of EEG, where electrodes are placed on the scalp to record the average activity of a very large number of cells across a wide area of cortex. Both wakefulness and REM sleep are "desynchronized" states, in that the large number of individual brain cells contributing to the EEG recording are on average "firing" in fast, irregular patterns, and this firing is occurring at different times in different small groups of cells. In contrast, during NREM sleep, and particularly during SWS, the EEG is said to be "synchronized" because the recordings indicate that large groups of cells are all firing in concert with each other in a slower, more regular pattern. "Desynchronized" EEG is considered to be the more active state, because this pattern is presumed to reflect many small groups of neurons "working on" individual information processing tasks. In contrast, during the synchronous EEG of SWS, it is presumed that neurons are firing together in a slow rhythm because they are not currently processing information.

Other methods of examining the neurophysiological basis of cognition, however, employ entirely different definitions of activation. In the last decade, dream theorists have increasingly relied on findings from brain imaging studies to help them understand the specific pattern of regional brain activity that underlies mentation in sleep. Studies of sleep using PET brain imaging provide a significant advantage over EEG recordings in that they have greater "spatial resolution"—meaning that imaging studies can tell us not only whether the cortex is generally more or less active, but also provide us with information about which particular areas of the brain are active during a given time period. PET studies use radioactively tagged glucose, oxygen, or other compounds of interest injected into the bloodstream. Activation is then measured by observing where these compounds are transported and used in the brain. In effect, using PET, a particular area of the brain is said to be more active when an increased amount of blood is flowing to the area or an increased amount of glucose is being metabolized there.[12]

Other techniques of looking into the brain that have been applied to understanding sleep and dreaming include functional magnetic resonance imaging (fMRI), near-infrared spectroscopy, and intracranial electrode recordings in humans and animals. Each of these techniques also presumes a different specific definition of activation. Although in some cases, divergent techniques provide converging pictures of how the brain functions across states of consciousness; in other cases, different measures of activation provide quite different perspectives on the activity of the sleeping brain. The problem is that none of these techniques get at the true complexities of how neurons generate experience. Examining only global electrical activity, or equally so examining only localized blood flow, does not provide us with information about the complex communications both within and between neural networks which give rise to cognition. It is therefore necessary to be careful about what we mean when we propose that sleep mentation relies on a certain type of "activation" in the brain. The application of detailed computer neural network models to the study of dreaming could be useful in creating greater specificity in this regard.

Greater "Activation" ≠ More Cognition

It is tempting to jump to the intuitive conclusion that observing greater brain activation by using any one of the above techniques indicates increased cognitive processing (and perhaps increased conscious experience). Conversely, we would like to be able to jump to the conclusion that observing lesser activation is a clear correlate of decreased cognitive content. Unfortunately, this is not necessarily the case. Greater EEG synchrony during sleep does not signify a lack of cognition. Although the likelihood of experiencing vivid dreaming is greater during the desynchronized REM state than during synchronized SWS, sleep mentation *is* also recalled from NREM sleep about half of the time. This substantial likelihood of recalling mentation from NREM is even higher in the late morning hours (Antrobus et al., 1995; Wamsley et al., 2007). Also perplexing, within NREM sleep, we dream just as much in the "deepest," most highly synchronized stages as we do during light sleep, that is, Stage 2, where EEG is much less synchronized (Nielsen, 2000). These observations question the over-simple assumption that more synchronized EEG = less "brain activity" = less cognition. Furthermore, rapidly accumulating evidence from the study of memory consolidation in sleep points to synchronized SWA as presenting the *ideal* conditions for processing recent declarative memories and "consolidating" them into long-term storage in the cortex (Buzsáki, 1996, 1998; Gais & Born, 2004; Steriade & Timofeev, 2003). Whether studies of memory consolidation in sleep have any bearing on understanding dream experiences remains to be seen, but work in this field certainly questions the assumption that synchronized EEG indicates a global state of inactivity incompatible with information processing functions.

Although greater blood flow to a particular brain region as measured in imaging studies generally indicates greater cognitive processing, there are at least two processes that qualify this relationship. Processes that are highly learned are accomplished with less cortical activation compared to the same process when it is novel. To the extent that dream images and sequences tend to be fairly novel, however, this may not be a serious qualification. Secondly, processes that inhibit sub-classes of dream processing may require as much brain resources as those that generate dream events. Although increased activation as measured by PET or fMRI is generally taken to be an indication of neuronal excitation, it is known that, under certain conditions, inhibition of a group of neurons can also lead to increased blood flow (Tagamets & Horwitz, 2001). That is, inhibition in the brain can itself be an active process requiring metabolic resources.

Activation Patterns in Sleep Do Not Necessarily Have the Same Functional Implications as Similar Activation in Wakefulness

Patterns of neural activity observed using PET and EEG do not necessarily have the same functional and cognitive correlates during sleep as they do during wakefulness. Taking a simple example, the appearance of EEG in the alpha frequency during wakefulness is indicative of *decreased* cognitive arousal, whereas the intrusion of a burst of alpha into the sleep EEG is indicative of *increased* arousal.

The activation of the hippocampus also must be interpreted differently in sleep as opposed to waking. Increased blood flow to the hippocampus during wakefulness is associated with the encoding of new declarative memories. However, although blood flow to the hippocampus is high during SWS, hippocampal activation in this dissimilar state has quite different implications. During the state of active wakefulness, information is primarily flowing *into* the hippocampus, facilitating the storage of new information. However, during sleep, information primarily flows *out from* the hippocampus to the cortex— increased blood flow to the hippocampus in this state is thought to reflect the replay of recent memories, subserving offline processes of long-term memory storage. The cognitive correlates of hippocampal activation in sleep are unknown, but we certainly cannot *assume* that "activation" of the hippocampus seen in a PET scan during sleep signifies the presence of the same type of cognition correlated with similar activation during wakefulness.

Another example is that, in sleep, the lateralization of electrical potentials in the cortex (PGO spikes) is highly correlated with the direction of rapid eye movements. Yet similar electrical activity accompanying waking eye movements is completely unrelated to eye movement direction (Monaco, Baghdoyan, Nelson, & Hobson, 1984). Each of these examples powerfully illustrates that superficial similarity between activation patterns in sleep and known activity patterns in wakefulness cannot necessarily inform us of the functional and cognitive meanings of the observed activity in the sleeping brain. Neurophysiological observations must therefore be accompanied by careful, detailed *cognitive* measurements of the dream features in question.

CONCLUSIONS

Here we have presented a more comprehensive description of the attractor model of dreaming first reported in neural network simulations by Antrobus (1991). The model shows how both regional and widespread cortical activation effectively lower the thresholds of local neural networks so that they produce imagery and thought, even in the absence of external sensory input. This "offline" mentation is common to both waking and sleep. Indeed, under matched environments, waking fantasy differs from REM dreaming primarily in that it is not hallucinatory. The absence of the inhibition of sensory input characterizing REM sleep apparently prevents the daydreamer from confusing his/her images or percepts.

Here we also discussed our Dual Rhythm model of dreaming (Wamsley et al., 2007), which states that both the REM-NREM cycle and changes in cortical activation across the 24-hour cycle are sources of nonspecific brain activation supporting mentation during sleep (Wamsley et al., 2007). Many cortical regions are activated by both sources, and the activation effect appears to be additive, such that more content is reported during the late morning from both REM and NREM. There may be some differences in the patterns of regional cortical activation supported by the active phases of these two activation sources. For example, REM may support more visual and amygdalar activation, whereas the 24-hour rhythm may support more conceptual processing and lack the active afferent and skeletal motor inhibition of the REM sleep.

Because of the substantial difficulties inherent in studying dreaming and other forms of sleep mentation, models of dreaming sleep remain heavily dependent on waking cognitive neuroscience research. Although our models have resolved several problems in this field, we hope that they also provide the basis for asking more specific and informative questions in the future about how different classes of mentation are produced and what function, if any, this mentation plays in the well-being of the individual.

NOTES

1. NREM sleep consists of Stages 2, 3, and 4. Stages 3 and 4 are referred to as "slow wave sleep" or "deep sleep," which consists of slow, high amplitude brain waves, relative to Stage 2.

2. However, we will discuss later that some apparent qualitative differences between REM and NREM reports are merely an artifact of the greater length of REM dreams.

3. The processing of visual stimuli has traditionally been viewed as progressing in a hierarchical manner in which simple visual features are processed first and then only later combined into more complex representations. Primary visual cortex (V1) represents an early step in visual processing, in which simple features, such as lines and edges of different orientations, are being processed. In higher-level visual areas, the features being represented become more complex.

4. Stimuli can be selectively presented to one half of the brain by presenting visual stimuli to only one eye.

5. Autonomic indicators in sleep, however, do not always correlate well with the emotionality they signify during wakefulness. For example, galvanic skin response values, correlated with fear and anxiety during wakefulness, are at their highest tonic values during SWS, from which these emotions are least often reported (Johnson, 1970).

6. Defined as attempts by the dreamer to move from one state to another, more desired state.

7. We presume that the amount of mentation content reported by a subject is roughly indicative of the levels of cortical activation prior to awakening.

8. PGO spikes are intermittent bursts of electrical activity that occur during REM sleep. These bursts originate in the pontine brainstem, then travel to the lateral geniculate nucleus of the thalamus (an early processing area in the visual system), and subsequently stimulate the occipital (visual) cortex.

9. The dorsolateral prefrontal cortex is involved in working memory and goal-directed behaviors during wakefulness.

10. The processing of visual stimuli has traditionally been viewed as progressing in a hierarchical manner in which simple visual features are processed first and then only later combined into more complex representations. Primary visual cortex (V1) represents an early step in visual processing, in which simple features, such as lines and edges of different orientations, are being processed. In higher-level visual areas the features being represented become more complex.

11. For an excellent review see Nielsen, 2004.

12. PET imaging is limited, however, in that it is able to show us only average levels of activity over several minutes of time. fMRI (functional magnetic resonance imaging) provides much higher temporal resolution, and so will be better suited to elucidating.

REFERENCES

Antrobus, J. (1983). REM and NREM sleep reports: Comparison of word frequencies by cognitive classes. *Psychophysiology, 20,* 562–567.

Antrobus, J., Kondo, T. & Reinsel, R. (1995). Dreaming in the late morning: Summation of REM and diurnal cortical activation. *Consciousness and Cognition, 4,* 275–299.

Antrobus, J. S. (1991). Dreaming: Cognitive processes during cortical activation and high afferent thresholds. *Psychological Review, 98,* 96–121.

Aserinsky, E., & Kleitman, N. (1953). Regularly occurring periods of eye motility and concomitant phenomenon during sleep. *Science, 188,* 273–274.

Benington, J. (2004). Homeostatic and circadian influences. In C. A. Kushida (Ed.), *Sleep deprivation: Basic science, physiology & behavior* (pp. 481–506). New York: Dekker.

Bertini, M., De Gennaro, L., Ferrara, M., Curcio, G., Romei, V., Fratello, F, et al. (2004). Reduction of transcallosal inhibition upon awakening from REM sleep in humans as assessed by transcranial magnetic stimulation. *Sleep, 27,* 875–882.

Braun, A. R., Balkin, T. J., Wesenten, N. J., Carson, R. E., Varga, M., Baldwin, P., et al. (1997). Regional cerebral blood flow throughout the sleep-wake cycle: An H20-O-15 PET study. *Brain, 120,* 1173–1197.

Braun, A. R., Balkin, T., Wesensten, N., Gwadry, F., Carson, R., Varga, et al. (1998). Dissociated pattern of activity in visual cortices and their projections during human rapid eye movement sleep. *Science, 279,* 91–95.

Broughton, R. (1975). Biorhythmic variations in consciousness and psychological functions. *Canadian Psychological Review, 16,* 217–239.

Buzsáki, G. (1996). The hippocampal-neocortical dialogue. *Cerebral Cortex, 6,* 81–92.

Buzsáki, G. (1998). Memory consolidation during sleep: A neurophysiological perspective. *Journal of Sleep Research, 7* (Suppl 1), 17–23.

Carrier, J., & Monk, T. (1999). Effects of sleep and circadian rhythms on performance. In F. Turek & P. Zee (Eds.), *Regulation of sleep and circadian rhythms.* New York: Marcel Dekker, Inc.

Casagrande, M., Violani, C., Lucidi, F., Buttinelli, E. & Bertini, M. (1996). Variations in sleep mentation as a function of time of night. *International Journal of Neuroscience, 85,* 19–30.

Cocude, M., Charlot, V. & Denis, M. (1996). Latency and duration of visual mental images in normal and depressed subjects. *Journal of Mental Imagery, 21,* 127–142.

Cocude, M., & Denis, M. (1988). Measuring the temporal characteristics of visual mental images. *Journal of Mental Imagery, 12,* 89–102.

Czisch, M., Wehrle, R., Kaufmann, C., Wetter, T. C., Holsboer, F., Pollmacher, et al. (2004). Functional MRI during sleep: BOLD signal decreases and their electrophysiological correlates. *European Journal of Neuroscience, 20,* 566–574.

De Gennaro, L., & Ferrara, M. (2003). Sleep spindles: An overview. *Sleep Medicine Reviews, 7,* 423–440.

Delorme, A., Rousselet, G. A., Mace, M. J., & Fabre-Thorpe, M. (2004). Interaction of top-down and bottom-up processing in the fast visual analysis of natural scenes. *Cognitive Brain Research, 19,* 103–113.

Dement, W., & Kleitman, N. (1957). The relation of eye movements during sleep to dream activity: An objective method for the study of dreaming. *Journal of Experimental Psychology, 53,* 339–346.

Dement, W. & Wolpert, E. A. (1958). The relation of eye movements, body motility, and external stimuli to dream content. *Journal of Experimental Psychology, 55,* 543–53.

Dijk, D., Shanahan, T., Duffy, J., Ronda, J., & Czeisler, C. (1997). Variation of electroencephalographic activity during non-rapid eye movement and rapid eye movement sleep with phase of circadian melatonin rhythm in humans. *Journal of Physiology, 505,* 851–858.

Domhoff, G. W. (2001). A new neurocognitive theory of dreams. *Dreaming, 11,* 13–33.

Fisher, C., Kahn, E., Edwards, A., & Davis, D. M. (1973). A psychophysiological study of nightmares and night terrors, I: Physiological aspects of the stage 4 night terror. *Journal of Nervous and Mental Disease, 157,* 75–98.

Fosse, R., Stickgold, R. & Hobson, J. (2001). The mind in REM sleep: Reports of emotional experience. *Sleep, 24,* 947–953.

Foulkes, D., & Fleisher, S. (1975). Mental activity in relaxed wakefulness. *Journal of Abnormal Psychology, 84,* 66–75.

Freud, S. (1900). *The interpretation of dreams.* New York: Avon Publishers.

Gais, S., & Born, J. (2004). Declarative memory consolidation: Mechanisms acting during human sleep. *Learning and Memory, 11,* 679–685.

Gazzaniga, M. (2000). Cerebral specialization and interhemispheric communication: Does the corpus callosum enable the human condition? *Brain, 12,* 1293–1326.

Hobson, J., & McCarley, R. (1977). The brain as a dream state generator: An activation-synthesis hypothesis of the dream process. *American Journal of Psychiatry, 134,* 1335–1348.

Hobson, J., A. (1992). A new model of brain-mind state: Activation level, input source, and mode of processing (AIM). In J. S. Antrobus & M. Bertini (Eds.), *The neuropsychology of sleep and dreaming.* Hillsdale, NJ: Erlbaum Associates.

Hobson, J. A., Pace-Schott, E., & Stickgold, R. (2000). Dreaming and the brain: Towards a cognitive neuroscience of conscious states. *Behavioral and Brain Sciences, 23,* 793–842.

Johnson, L. C. (1970). A psychophysiology for all states. *Psychophysiology, 6,* 501–516.

Kaufmann, C., Wehrle, R., Wetter, T. C., Holsboer, F., Auer, D. P., Pollmacher, T., et al. (2006). Brain activation and hypothalamic functional connectivity during human non-rapid eye movement sleep: An EEG/fMRI study. *Brain, 129,* 655–667.

LaBerge, S. (1990). Lucid dreaming: Psychophysiological studies of consciousness in REM sleep. In R. R. Bootzin, J. F. Kihlstrom, & D. L. Schacter, (Eds.), *Sleep and cognition* (pp. 109–126). Washington, DC: American Psychological Association.

Mamelak, A., & Hobosn, J. (1989). Dream bizarreness as the cognitive correlate of altered neuronal behavior in REM sleep. *Journal of Cognitive Neuroscience, 1,* 201–222.

Maquet, P., Peters, J., & Aerts, J. (1996). Functional neuroanatomy of human rapid eye movement sleep and dreaming. *Nature, 383,* 163–166.

Massimini, M., Ferrarelli, F., Huber, R., Esser, S. K., Singh H., & Tononi G. (2005). Breakdown of cortical effective connectivity during sleep. *Science, 309,* 2228–32.

Mellet, E., Petit, L., Mazoyer, B., Denis, M., & Tzourio, N. (1998). Reopening the mental imagery debate: Lessons from functional anatomy. *Neuroimage, 8,* 129–139.

Monaco, H., Baghdoyan, H. A., Nelson, J. P., & Hobson, J. A. (1984). Cortical wave amplitude and eye movement direction are correlated in REM sleep but not in waking. *Archives Italiennes de Biologie, 122,* 213–233.

Monk, T., Buysse, D., Reynolds, C., Berga, S., Jarrett, D., Begley, A., et al. (1997). Circadian rhythms in human performance and mood under constant conditions. *Journal of Sleep Research, 6,* 9–18.

Moruzzi, G., & Magoun, H.W. (1949). Brain stem reticular formation and activation of the EEG. *Electroencephalography and Clinical Neuropsychiatry, 1,* 455–473.

Muzur, A., Pace-Schott, E., & Hobson, J.A. (2002). The prefrontal cortex in sleep. *Trends in Cognitive Sciences, 6,* 475–481.

Nielsen, T. (2000). A review of mentation in REM and NREM sleep: "Covert" REM sleep as a possible reconciliation of two opposing models. *Behavioral and Brain Sciences, 23,* 851–866.

Nielsen, T. (2004). Chronobiological features of sleep mentation. *Sleep Medicine Reviews, 8,* 403–424.

Nielsen, T. & Zadra, A. (2000). Dreaming disorders. In M. Kryger, T. Roth, & W. Dement (Eds.), *Principles and practice of sleep medicine.* Philadelphia, PA: W.B. Saunders Company.

Nielsen, T. A., & Powell, R. A. (1989). The "dream-lag" effect: A 6-day temporal delay in dream content incorporation. *Psychiatric Journal of the University of Ottawa, 14,* 561–565.

Nofzinger, E. A., Buysse, D. J., Miewald, J. M., Meltzer, C. C., Price, J. C., Sembrat, R. C., et al. (2002). Human regional cerebral glucose metabolism during non-rapid eye movement sleep in relation to waking. *Brain, 125,* 1105–1115.

Pivik, T., & Foulkes, D. (1968). NREM mentation: Relation to personality, orientation time, and time of night. *Journal of Consulting and Clinical Psychology, 32,* 144–151.

Reinsel, R., Wollman, M., & Antrobus, J. (1992). Bizarreness in dreams and waking fantasy. In J. Antrobus & M. Bertini (Eds.), *The neuropsychology of sleep and dreaming.* Hillsdale, NJ: Lawrence Erlbaum Associates.

Riggs, L., Ratcliff, F., Cornsweet, J., & Cornsweet, T. (1953). The disappearance of steadily fixated visual test objects. *Journal of the Optical Society of America, 43,* 495–501.

Ro, T., Breitmeyer, B., Burton, P., Singhal, N. S., & Lane, D. (2003). Feedback contributions to visual awareness in human occipital cortex. *Current Biology, 13,* 1038–1041.

Schachter, S., & Singer, J. (1962). Cognitive, social, and physiological determinants of emotional state. *Psychological Review, 69,* 379–399.

Schredl, M., & Hoffmann, F. (2003). Continuity between waking activities and dream activities. *Consciousness and Cognition, 12,* 298–308.

Smith, M., Antrobus, J., Gordon, E., Tucker, M., Hirota, Y., Wamsley, E., et al. (2004). Motivation and affect in REM sleep and the mentation reporting process. *Consciousness and Cognition, 13,* 501–511.

Solms, M. (2000). Dreaming and REM sleep are controlled by different mechanisms. *Behavioral and Brain Sciences, 23,* 793–850.

Steiner, S. S., & Ellman, S. J. (1972). Relation between REM sleep and intracranial self-stimulation. *Science, 177,* 1122–1124.

Steriade, M., & Timofeev, I. (2003). Neuronal plasticity in thalamocortical networks during sleep and waking oscillations. *Neuron, 37,* 563–576.

Stickgold, R., Malia, A., Fosse, R., Propper, R., & Hobson, J. (2001). Brain-mind states: I. Longitudinal field study of sleep/wake factors influencing mentation report length. *Sleep, 24,* 171–179.

Strauch, I., & Meier, B. (1996). *In search of dreams: Results of experimental dream research.* New York: State University of New York Press.

Sutton, J. P., Holmes, J., Caplan, J., Rucnick, L., Kwong, K., Breiter, H., et al. (1998). Investigation of human sleep using simultaneous fMRI and polysomnography. *Sleep, 129*(Suppl), 271.

Suzuki, H., Uchiyama, M., Tagaya, H., Ozaki, A., Kuriyama, K., Aritake, S., et al. (2004). Dreaming during non-rapid eye movement sleep in the absence of prior rapid eye movement sleep. *Sleep, 27,* 1486–1490.

Tagamets, M. A., & Horowitz, B. (2001). Interpreting PET and fMRI measures of functional activity: The effects of synaptic inhibition on cortical activation in human imaging studies. *Brain Research Bulletin, 54,* 267–273.

Wagner, U., Gais, S., & Born, J. (2001). Emotional memory formation is enhanced across sleep intervals with high amounts of rapid eye movement sleep. *Learning and Memory, 8,* 112–119.

Wamsley, E. J., Alger, S., Nelson, J., Tucker, M., Hirota, Y., & Antrobus, J. S. (2006). Circadian and homeostatic influences on dreaming: NREM mentation during a short daytime nap. *Sleep, 29*(Suppl), A48.

Wamsley, E. J., Hirota, Y., Tucker, M. A., Smith, M. R., & Antrobus, J. (2007). Circadian and ultradian influences on dreaming: A dual-rhythm model. *Brain Research Bulletin, 71*(4), 347–354.

Wollman, M. C., & Antrobus, J. (1986). Sleeping and waking thought: Effects of external stimulation. *Sleep: Journal of Sleep Research and Sleep Medicine, 9,* 438–448.

Eight

REM-Related Dreams in REM Behavior Disorder

Maria Livia Fantini and Luigi Ferini-Strambi

Parasomnias are abnormal behavioral or physiological events that intrude into the sleep process, disrupting its continuity. They are classified according to the type of sleep in which they occur, namely non-rapid eye movement (NREM) and rapid eye movement (REM) sleep parasomnia (American Academy of Sleep Science, 2005). The latter include recurrent isolated sleep paralysis, nightmare disorders, and REM Behavior Disorder (RBD).

RBD is a fascinating parasomnia in which subjects show complex and often violent motor activities during REM sleep, usually in association with dreams (Mahowald & Schenck, 2000). Common behaviors include screaming, punching, grasping, kicking, and sometimes jumping out from bed, which are potentially harmful for the patients or their bed partner. Indeed, injuries are reported by more than 75 percent of patients (Schenck & Mahowald, 2002), and they may include ecchymoses, lacerations, bone fractures, and even subdural hematomas (Olson, Boeve, & Silber, 2000; Sforza, Krieger, & Petiau, 1997). Arousal from episodes is usually rapid and often accompanied by a dream recall that matches the observed behavior. For instance, one patient may wake up after violently hitting the wall with his feet and recall a dream in which he was being attacked by a dog and kicking him out in self-defense. Video-polysomnographic (PSG) monitoring reveals that these episodes typically occur during REM sleep. In fact, recording of chin or limb activity (electromyography or EMG) shows a complete or intermittent loss of the physiological REM sleep muscle atonia and an excessive EMG phasic activity (for example, sudden and brief burst of activity of the muscles) during this stage.

The prevalence of RBD remains largely unknown. Results of a large telephone survey assessing the prevalence of violent behavior during sleep in the general population aged 15 to 100 years suggested a prevalence of RBD of about 0.5 percent (Ohayon, Caulet, & Priest, 1997). Another study performed among more than a thousand of individuals over 70 years old in the Hong Kong area yielded an estimated prevalence of 0.04 percent (Chiu et al., 2000). RBD affects predominantly men after the age of 50 years (Schenck & Mahowald, 2002). The male to female ratio is about 8:1, and the reason for this male preponderance is unclear. It has been suggested that female subjects may have RBD with less aggressive behaviors that do not call for medical attention. A possible role of sex hormones in mediating violent and aggressive behaviors could explain this gender effect.

RBD in humans was formally identified by Schenck and collaborators in 1986, who described the full clinical and polysomnographic picture of five patients (Schenck, Bundlie, Ettinger, & Mahowald, 1986). However, some earlier cases had been observed by European and Japanese researchers in healthy subjects taking antidepressant drugs (Passouant, Cadilhac, & Ribstein, 1972), as well as in acute psychoses related to alcohol withdrawal or drug abuse (Tachibana, Tanaka, Hishikawa, & Kaneko, 1975). Nonetheless, it was only in 1990 that RBD was included within the *International Classification of Sleep Disorders* as a distinct parasomnia, and diagnostic criteria were established. Recently, diagnostic criteria have been revised (American Academy of Sleep Science, 2005).

PATHOPHYSIOLOGY

The pathogenesis of RBD is still unclear. Multiple neural substrates participate in REM sleep atonia, being potentially involved in the pathogenesis of RBD. They are located mainly in the brainstem, the lower portion of the brain connecting the spinal cord to the brain hemispheres. Indeed, an experimental animal model of RBD has been obtained in cats after lesion in the pons, the middle part of the brainstem (Hendricks, 1982; Jouvet & Delorme, 1965). On the other hand, neurons that utilize dopamine in the meso-striatum pathways might be also implicated, and brain imaging studies performed in small groups of idiopathic patients with RBD using positron emission tomography (PET) or single photon emission computed tomography (SPECT) showed a decreased dopaminergic striatal innervation in patients with idiopathic RBD (Albin et al., 2000; Eisensher et al., 2000). The same type of lesion is encountered in patients with early Parkinson's disease (PD).

CLINICAL FORMS

RBD can occur in two forms, acute and chronic. The acute RBD has been observed in drug abusers (particularly with tricyclic antidepressants, monoamine inhibitors, or serotonin selective reuptake inhibitors), as well as during withdrawal from several substances (namely alcohol, meprobamate, nitrazepam, and pentazocine) (Mahowald & Schenck, 2000).

The chronic form may be either idiopathic or secondary to various neurological disorders. Secondary RBD may be potentially triggered by any lesions involving the brain structures responsible for REM sleep atonia, which are mostly located in the brainstem. RBD has been actually observed in cerebrovascular diseases, brainstem tumors, Guillain-Barré syndrome (Cochen et al., 2005), multiple sclerosis, and Machado-Joseph disease (Friedman, Fernandez, & Sudarsky, 2003; Fukutake et al., 2002; Iranzo et al., 2003). Very recently, RBD has been observed in association with limbic encephalitis (Iranzo et al., 2006) and with Morvan's syndrome (Liguori et al., 2001), two disorders not related to brainstem impairment. However, the most frequent association of RBD is with a group of neurodegenerative diseases called alpha-synuchleinopathies that include PD, dementia with Lewy bodies (DLB), and multiple system atrophy (MSA; Boeve, Silber, Ferman, Lucas, & Parisi, 2001). In PD, muscle tone abnormalities during REM sleep are frequent. The simple loss of muscle atonia, regardless of the history of behavioral manifestations, was found in 58 percent of PD patients, while full RBD is present in approximately one third of patients (Comella, Nardine, Diederich, & Stebbins, 1998; Gagnon et al., 2002). RBD may be also encountered in demented patients who show the clinical and neuropsychological features of DLB (Boeve et al., 1998). Indeed, RBD has been recently included as a suggestive feature within the diagnostic criteria for DLB (McKeith, 2005). RBD is also extremely frequent in patients with MSA, being present in about 90 percent (Plazzi et al., 1997).

IDIOPATHIC RBD

When no neurological signs or central nervous system (CNS) lesions are found, RBD is currently defined as "idiopathic." This form accounts for up to 60 percent of the cases described in the literature. However, one prospective study performed on idiopathic RBD showed that 38 percent of male patients with RBD developed a Parkinsonian syndrome within four years from the RBD diagnosis. The study has been recently updated, showing that up to 65 percent of idiopathic patients with RBD eventually developed a Parkinsonian disorder and/or a dementia without Parkinsonism, about 13 years after the RBD onset (Schenck, Bundlie, & Mahowald, 1996, 2003). On the other hand, in nearly 35 percent of patients, RBD remained idiopathic after a mean of 20 years. Therefore, the condition of idiopathic RBD is receiving increasing attention, as a possible prodrome in the development of a full-blown neurodegenerative disease. Recent studies found several slight abnormalities associated with the motor dyscontrol during REM sleep. The latter include slowing of the electroencephalographic rhythm in both wakefulness and REM sleep (Fantini et al., 2003), neuropsychological abnormalities in specific functions, such as visuo-spatial constructional abilities and visuo-spatial learning (Ferini-Strambi et al., 2004), signs of autonomic impairment (Ferini-Strambi, Oldani, Zucconi, & Smirne, 1996), olfactory deficit (Stiasny-Kolster et al., 2005), subtle motor signs, and decreased color vision discrimination (Gagnon et al., 2006; Postuma, Lang, Massicotte-Marquez, & Montplaisir, 2006). All these observations strengthen the notion of idiopathic RBD as a prodrome of a more pervasive neurodegenerative disease.

ALTERED DREAM CONTENT

An intriguing feature of the disorder is the frequent occurrence of specific dream contents. Indeed, the vast majority of dreams tend to be unpleasant, stereotypical, action filled, and often violent in nature. Patients with RBD very commonly report dreams in which they are attacked by unfamiliar people or animals and they would either fight back in self defense or attempt to flee (Schenck & Mahowald, 2002). Typical dreams may include an unfamiliar person entering the dreamer's house, a stranger threatening the dreamer or his relatives, or being attacked by animals. Fear and anger are the most common associated emotions.

Despite the fact that RBD appears to be a disorder involving both motor behaviors and dream synthesis, dream content has been poorly investigated in RBD. On the clinical ground, it has been observed that the aggressiveness displayed in dreams contrast with the often placid and mild-mannered daytime temperament. One recent study has systematically assessed the dream content and its relationship with the daytime aggressiveness in RBD (Fantini, Corona, Clerici, & Ferini-Strambi, 2005). This study included 49 patients with polysomnographic-confirmed RBD and 71 healthy control volunteers recruited among members of recreational groups for elderly in the same geographical area, matched for age, gender, and education. Subjects were asked to recall one or more recent dreams during an ad hoc visit, according to the Hall and Van de Castle method, using the following words: *We would like you to tell us the last dream(s) you remember having, whether it was last night, last month, or in the last year and the date this dream occurred.* Dreams that occurred within one year from the interview were included. The Hall and Van de Castle method is the most comprehensive and widely used empirical system for dream content analysis, and it has been used by researchers in different countries, showing good reliability, intra-individual consistency over time, and correlation with individual, gender, and cultural differences.

A higher proportion of subjects in the RBD group were able to recall at least one dream compared to same-age healthy subjects. Indeed, 41 of 49 patients with RBD (83.7 percent) and 35 of 71 control subjects (49.3 percent) were able to remember their dreams. The two groups of dreamers were comparable for previous education, present working status, mean duration of retirement, and previous occupation. Ninety-eight patients with RBD and 69 controls dreams were finally collected and analyzed. An average dream report score was calculated in subjects who recalled more than one dream.

Compared with controls, patients with RBD reported a striking frequency of aggression expressed by various indicators, namely a higher percentage of "Dreams with at least one aggression" (66 percent versus 15 percent), an increased Aggression/Friendliness interactions ratio (86 percent versus 44 percent), and an increased Aggressions/Characters (A/C) ratio (0.81 versus 0.12; see Table 8.1).

In both RBD and controls, the dreamer was personally involved in the aggression in about 90 percent of cases, whereas he/she was a witness in about 10 percent of cases. In the RBD group, there was an elevated frequency of all types of aggressive interactions: the dreamer played the role either of aggressor or of victim, and he/she was involved in reciprocal aggressions (for example, when the victim responds with any type of counteraggression), as well as in mutual aggressions (for example, when no aggressor or victim can be clearly identified because the characters are engaging in the same aggressive activity at the same time). On the other hand, any dream with self-aggression was reported by RBD. The characters involved in the aggression were primarily males (96 percent males versus 4 percent females) in the RBD group, whereas they were almost equally represented in the control group (55 percent males versus 45 percent females; see Table 8.2).

Furthermore, among the various types of aggression, physical aggression was far more represented in dreams of patients with RBD than in those of controls (29.3 percent versus 3.8 percent). However, no difference in physical aggression percent (derived by dividing the total number of physical aggression by the total number of aggressions) was observed in RBD and control subjects (71.5 versus 66.7 percent, respectively).

On the other hand, dreams of subjects with RBD expressed the same amount of friendliness as dreams of control subjects, as revealed by various

TABLE 8.1

Dream Characteristics of Patients with RBD and Control Subjects

	RBD	Controls	h	p	N RBD	N Controls
Characters						
Male/Female %	63%	57%	+.11	.49243	83	67
Familiarity %	52%	65%	−.26	.06523	108	93
Friends %	17%	19%	−.04	.77890	108	93
Family %	35%	45%	−.21	.13205	108	93
Dead & Imaginary %	01%	01%	−.04	.76691	129	95
Animal %	19%	04%	+.52	.00013	129	95
Social Interaction Percents						
Aggression/Friendliness %	86%	44%	+.93	.00007	97	23
Befriender %	63%	71%	−.19	.72192	7	7
Aggressor %	29%	00%	+1.14	.00251	61	8
Physical Aggression %	73%	55%	+.40	.19606	94	12
Social Interaction Ratios						
A/C Index	.81	.12	+1.63		129	95
F/C Index	.08	.18	−.22		129	95
S/C Index	.00	.11	−.26		129	95
Dreams with at Least One:						
Aggression	66%	15%	+1.08	.00000	101	69
Friendliness	12%	22%	−.27	.08800	101	69
Sexuality	00%	09%	−.62	.00007	101	69
Misfortune	15%	17%	−.06	.71660	101	69
Good Fortune	00%	01%	−.20	.21069	101	69
Success	03%	10%	−.28	.07673	101	69
Failure	07%	09%	−.08	.59232	101	69
Striving	10%	19%	−.25	.10550	101	69

Source: Neurology, Oct. 11; 65(7):1010–1015. Fantini et al. Reprinted with permission from Lippincott, Williams, & Wilkins.

Notes: Bonferroni correction was applied for multiple testing. Level of significance was set at $\alpha = 0.002$; RBD = REM sleep behavior disorder; N RBD = total number of elements occurring in the category, for the RBD group; N Controls = total number of elements occurring in the category, for the control group.

indicators. When assessing the type of activities, dreams of subjects with RBD showed an overall higher percentage of physical activities and a reduced frequency of visual activity.

An unexpected feature of RBD dreams was the very high frequency of animal characters (19 percent versus 4 percent) that were almost invariably involved in aggressive interactions. Interestingly, none of the patients with RBD had a "dream with at least one element of sexuality," in contrast to what was observed in control subjects (0 percent in RBD versus 9 percent

TABLE 8.2
Subtypes of Aggression in RBD and Controls Dreams

	RBD	%	CTRL	%	P[a]
Total Aggression	41.0	100	5.7	100	
Physical	29.3	71.5	3.8	66.7	<0.0001
Non-physical	11.7	28.5	1.9	33.3	
Dreamer involved	36.9	90.2	5.1	88.4	<0.0001
Dr. as aggressor	9.0	24.2	0.0	0.0	0.01
Dr. as victim	16.9	45.9	4.2	83.6	0.0005
Dr. as reciprocal	8.2	22.3	0.3	6.6	0.01
Dr. as mutual	2.8	7.6	0.0	0.0	NS
Dr. self-aggression	0.0	0.0	0.5	9.8	NS
Witness	4.0	9.8	0.7	11.6	NS
Sex	16.7		2.25		
M	16.1	96.2	1.2	55.6	0.008
F	0.6	3.8	1.0	44.4	NS

Source: Neurology, Oct. 11; 65(7):1010–1015. Fantini et al. Reprinted with permission from Lippincott, Williams, & Wilkins.

[a]Mann-Whitney U Test.

in controls). The latter is concordant with the observation that appetitive behaviors, such as feeding or sexual, have never been observed as a manifestation of RBD, either in humans or in the animal model. Indeed, sexual behaviors during sleep may be the manifestation of a NREM disorder of arousal, but is likely never attributable to RBD.

No correlation was observed between each of the dream characteristics and either age, duration, or frequency of RBD symptoms. Moreover, in both groups, indicators of aggressiveness in dreams did not correlate with years of education, years of retirement, or previous work.

DREAMS IN IDIOPATHIC AND SYMPTOMATIC RBD

The dreams reported by patients with idiopathic RBD (iRBD) seem not to differ with those reported by patients with symptomatic RBD, which are also action-filled and often violent. In the aforementioned study, 14 of 41 were affected by symptomatic RBD (sRBD; 12 men, 2 women; PD, $n = 10$; MSA, $n = 3$; and DLB, $n = 1$). Their dreams shared similar characteristics and same percentages of the majority of indicators with those of iRBD, with the only exception of a lesser frequency of male characters (the percentage of Male/Female characters ratio was lower in sRBD than in iRBD, namely 26 percent versus 78 percent, respectively) and of an absence of "dreams with at least one element of striving" (expressed by the ratio of the sum of dreamer-involved successes and failures divided by the total number of dreams; 0 percent versus 15 percent). However, data were not conclusive, since 10 patients of 14 with sRBD were taking either clonazepam ($n = 4$) and/or dopaminergic drugs in mono- or polytherapy, and an effect of medication could not be excluded. Dopaminergic drugs are actually known to potentially affect dream production (Pagel & Helfter, 1999).

AGGRESSIVE DREAMS AND DAYTIME AGGRESSIVENESS

After dream content collection, subjects completed the Aggression Questionnaire (AQ), a validated test developed to assess different aspect of aggressiveness, namely physical aggression, verbal aggression, anger, and hostility. No between-group differences in daytime aggressiveness, as measured by the total AQ scores, were found (69.9 in patients with RBD versus 73.8 in control subjects). However, when looking at the subtypes of daytime aggressiveness, patients with RBD showed lesser "Physical Aggressiveness" than control subjects (16.5 versus 20.4) and no difference on Verbal Aggressiveness, Anger, and Hostility. This result corroborates early observations of a discrepancy between the aggressiveness displayed in dreams and the frequent placid and mild-mannered temperament in patients with RBD (Schenck et al., 1986).

Interestingly, in patients with RBD, the amount of aggressiveness in dreams inversely correlated with the measures of aggressiveness during the day. Indicators such as the percentage of "dreams with at least one aggression", the Total Aggressions/Total Characters ratio, and the Aggression/Friendliness ratio were inversely correlated to the measures of daytime hostility, meaning that the more patients had dreams with aggression, the less they showed hostility during daytime. Alternatively, it was the frequency of friendliness and family characters in dreams that positively correlated with the levels of daytime hostility. In a similar fashion, the percentage of "dreams with at least one misfortune" correlated inversely with the daytime anger, meaning that those patients with more dreams with misfortune were those showing less anger during daytime. Finally, the percentage of "negative emotions" in dreams were strongly negatively correlated with the measure of daytime total aggression and particularly with physical aggression, so that those patients with RBD having more dreams with negative emotions were those less physically aggressive during the day. Curiously enough, no correlations were found between dreams characteristics and measures of daytime aggressiveness in control subjects.

Although the small size of sample is not suitable for statistical comparison, no gender difference was observed in any dream aggressiveness indicators nor in AQ score.

The inverse correlation found in RBD between aggression in dreams and measures of daytime aggressiveness, in particular the level of hostility, could somewhat corroborate early theories of a compensatory nature of dreams, in which aspects of the personality neglected in waking life would be highlighted in dreams (Jung, 1974). However, these results contrast with the later established principle of continuity between dream content and waking mentation. Indeed, several studies with dream journals showed that wide individual differences in the frequencies of several Hall and Van de Castle dream content indicators are in general continuous with the waking conceptions with past or present emotional preoccupations and interests of the dreamers and with the level of their psychological well-being (Bell & Hall, 1971; Domhoff, 1996; Hall & Nordby, 1972; Pesant & Zadra, 2006). This hypothesis has been also demonstrated by blind analyses of dream journals, where nothing is known about the dreamer until she or he later answers questions developed on the basis of the content analysis (Domhoff, 1996). Furthermore, in several laboratory studies of children's dreams, it was found that children with more violence in their waking fantasies had more aggressive interactions in their dreams (Foulkes, 1967; Foulkes, Larson, Swanson, & Rardin, 1969).

STEREOTYPIC DREAM CONTENT

Although studies of dream content in normal subjects have provided evidence of a link between dreaming and waking cognition, this seems not to be the case in patients with RBD. Indeed, a striking aspect of dreams in RBD is that patients share a highly stereotypic dream content. The elevated occurrence of a human or animal aggressor threatening the dreamer or his entourage, pushing him to engage in a defense activity, and even the similarity of terms used by patients to describe the dream experience are very surprising, considering the variety of their psychological profiles and personal histories. In dreams of patients with RBD, in front of an assortment of settings (such as outdoor settings, houses, work environments, and so on) where continuity with the waking life may be recognized, there are a limited variety of interactions, emotions, and characters.

It has been observed that the repetitive nature of dream content may suggest several potential linkages between dream content and the neural network for dreaming (Domhoff, 2001), and this could be particularly true in the case of patients with RBD.

Several considerations could be made to explain the altered dream content in RBD. (1) *The threat simulation theory and the release of ontogenically early dream patterns.* It has been proposed that the biological function of dreams would be to simulate threatening events and to rehearse threat avoidance (Revonsuo, 2000). Normative data obtained in large samples of the general population, including sporadic and recurrent dreams, as well as nightmares, indicate that aggressions, negative emotions, misfortune, and especially threatening events are overrepresented in dreams compared with positive emotions and peaceful and nonthreatening activities. Furthermore, threats usually coming from the ancestral human environment, namely physical aggression by wild animals or unfamiliar people, mostly of male gender, are more frequent than currently experienced daytime threats. The bias toward ancestral threats seems even greater in children's dream reports. It has been observed that children's dreams are characterized by a higher rate of aggression and a greater number of animal characters compared with adult dreams, and that the frequency of both aggression and animals in dreams decrease as a function of age. In a study about 600 dream reports from children 2 to 12 years of age, animals accounted for 25 to 30 percent of all characters in dreams reported by children 2 to 6 years old and for 15 percent in those reported by children 7 to 12 years old, whereas in adult dreams this percentage declines to 5 percent (Domhoff, 1996). Other studies showed similar age-related decreases of this indicator (Van de Castle, 1983). Interestingly, in their dreams children frequently describe animals that are rarely or never encountered in the waking world (for example, snakes, bears, monsters, spiders, tigers, insects, and so on). Aggression indicators such as the aggression/characters ratio are also high in dreams of children 2 to 12 years old, with most of the aggression consisting of being attacked by animals. Based on these results, it has been hypothesized that dream activity in children, containing wild animals, aggressions, and threats from an ancestral environment to a greater extent than adult dreams, would be useful to the development of threat-avoidance skills and would decrease with age (Revonsuo, 2000). It is intriguing that dreams in RBD share with children similar increased percentages of aggressiveness (expressed also by a higher A/C ratio) and animal characters, compared to same-age and gender controls. It has been suggested that RBD may originate from an inappropriate activation of the threat-simulation system, leading to an intensive threat simulation during dreams and to a behavioral response (mostly adequate) to these threats. On the other hand, increasing evidence indicates that chronic idiopathic RBD is an early manifestation of a more pervasive degenerative process. In light of this, it may be hypothesized that chronic RBD, as a part of a widespread neurodegenerative process involving the brain, would lead to a release of archaic dream patterns.

(2) *Dreams in RBD and the Activation-Synthesis Model.* According to the Activation-Synthesis model of dream generation recently revised into the

Activation, Input, and Modulation model, phasic discharges from brainstem generators activate either motor or perceptual, affective, and cognitive pathways, and these impulses are subsequently synthesized into dreams by the forebrain (Hobson & McCarley, 1977; Hobson, Pace-Schott, & Stickgold, 2000). Thus, in RBD the known increase of phasic EMG activity may be responsible of both motor behaviors and action-filled dreams. Dreams with aggression and vigorous motor behaviors may be two manifestations of hyperactivity of a common neuronal generator. In favor of this hypothesis stands the fact that dream content changes significantly after administration of clonazepam in patients with RBD. Besides a dramatic reduction of the frequency and intensity of behavioral episodes, patients almost invariably report changes in their dreams from stereotyped, violent, and intense to more various, colored, and bizarre, therefore, closer to normal dreams. In the aforementioned study, patients with RBD treated with clonazepam, although less numerous, had higher percentages of familiar and family characters when compared to drug-free patients with RBD and a trend toward both reduced percentages of physical aggression and a lower ratio of Male/Female characters (Fantini et al., 2005). Clonazepam is a benzodiazepine with serotoninergic properties that is highly effective in controlling motor disorder during sleep. In particular, clonazepam was found to significantly reduce the percentage of muscle phasic activity during REM sleep in patients with RBD (Lapierre & Montplaisir, 1992). The effect on dream content might be exerted through a generic anxiolitic effect, but clonazepam was found to be ineffective in treating nightmares in dreams disorder like posttraumatic stress disorder (Cates, Bishop, Davis, Lowe, & Woolley, 2004). Therefore, it seems far reasonable to hypothesize that changes in dream content may be mediated by its inhibiting effect on the sleep motor patterns generator.

Developmental changes in phasic REM sleep parameters have been described as a reflection of the maturation of the brainstem inhibitory systems. From birth to late childhood, both a shortening of REM sleep phasic muscle activity and a decrease of simultaneous occurrence of REMs with phasic muscle activity have been observed (Kohyama, 1996; Kohyama & Iwakawa, 1990; Kohyama, Tachibana, & Taniguchi, 1999). Of interest, the higher frequency of aggression and animal characters in children's dreams compared to adult dreams, as well as their age-related decrease, appear to parallel the developmental reduction in phasic REM sleep motor activity. Furthermore, periodic leg movements during sleep (PLMS, stereotyped and recurring movements of the lower limbs characterized by the extension of the big toe and dorsiflexion of ankle, with occasional flexion of knee and hip) are very frequent in RBD. They are included among phasic motor phenomena, and they are well represented during REM sleep in patients with RBD (Fantini, Michaud, Gosselin, Lavigne, & Montplaisir, 2002). Of interest, in iRBD PLMS index was found to correlate positively with some indicators of aggressiveness in dreams, namely the A/C ratio and the percentage of dreams with at least one aggression (Fantini et al., 2005). Taken together, all these results support the notion of a link between phasic muscle activity during REM sleep and dream content.

A recent very interesting study assessed differences of dream content in dream reports collected after REM and NREM awakening, calculating the number and variety of social interactions (McNamara, McLaren, Smith, Brown, & Stickgold, 2005). These authors found that aggressive interactions were more frequent in REM than NREM dream reports, while dreamer-initiated friendliness was more characteristic of NREM than REM reports. Thus, the authors hypothesized that different representations of social interactions in dreams in the two-sleep state may reflect different neurochemical patterns, with the REM state specialized in simulation of aggressive interaction. On the other hand, it may be postulated that bursts of phasic motor activity, as part of the physiological REM sleep processes (e.g., normal muscle twitches), would be translated by the forebrain in action or movement-filled dreams, and ultimately in dreams with more aggressive interaction compared to dreams in NREM sleep, and that RBD is an accentuation of this physiological phenomenon.

In summary, dreams in patients with RBD appear to be highly stereotyped and characterized by an elevated proportion of aggressiveness. Given the peculiar neurophysiological characteristics of REM sleep in these patients, it is possible that, in RBD, the exaggerated motor phasic discharges prevail over other neurocognitive processes involved in dream synthesis and would shape the dream content toward an increased level of those activities implying abrupt and violent movements of the body, particularly of the limbs. According to the Activation-Synthesis model, it may be hypothesized that such phasic motor activation induced by brainstem locomotor pattern generators would be preferentially translated by the cortical imagery generators in activities such as fighting or running, rather than more static ones.[1] RBD may certainly provide us with a key to improve our understanding about the mechanisms of physiological and pathological dream synthesis.

NOTE

1. Further studies are needed to better explore the causal relationship between the exaggerated muscle activity during REM sleep and the increased aggressive content of dreams in RBD.

REFERENCES

American Academy of Sleep Science. (2005). *International classification of sleep disorders: Diagnostic and coding manual, ICSD-2* (2nd ed.). Westchester, IL: American Academy of Sleep Medicine.

Albin, R. L., Koeppe, R. D., Chervin, R. D., Consens, F. B., Wernette, K., Frey, K. A., et al. (2000). Decreased striatal dopaminergic innervation in REM sleep behavior disorder. *Neurology, 55*, 1410–1412.

Bell, A., & Hall, C. (1971). *The personality of a child molester: An analysis of dreams.* Chicago, IL: Aldine.

Boeve, B. F., Silber, M. H., Ferman, T. J., Lucas, J. A., & Parisi, J. E. (2001). Association of REM sleep behavior disorder and neurodegenerative disease may reflect an underlying synucleinopathy. *Movement Disorders, 16*, 622–630.

Boeve, B. F., Silber, M. H., Ferman, T. J., Kokmen, E., Smith, G. E., Ivnik, R. J., et al. (1998). REM sleep behavior disorder and degenerative dementia: An association likely reflecting Lewy body disease. *Neurology, 51*, 363–370.

Cates, M. E., Bishop, M. H., Davis, L. L., Lowe, J. S., & Woolley, T. W. (2004). Clonazepam for treatment of sleep disturbances associated with combat-related posttraumatic stress disorder. *Annals of Pharmacotherapy, 38*, 1395–1399.

Chiu, H. F., Wing, Y. K., Lam, L. C., Li, S. W., Lum, C. M., Leung, T., et al. (2000). Sleep-related injury in the elderly—an epidemiological study in Hong Kong. *Sleep, 23*, 513–517.

Cochen, V., Arnulf, I., Demeret, S., Neulat, M. L., Gourlet, V., Drouot, X., et al. (2005). Vivid dreams, hallucinations, psychosis, and REM sleep in Guillain-Barre syndrome. *Brain, 128*, 2535–2545.

Comella, C. L., Nardine, T. M., Diederich, N. J., & Stebbins, G. T. (1998). Sleep-related violence, injury, and REM sleep behavior disorder in Parkinson's disease. *Neurology, 51*, 526–529.

Domhoff, G. W. (1996). *Finding meaning in dreams: A quantitative approach.* New York: Plenum Publishing Co.

Domhoff, G. W. (2001). A new neurocognitive theory of dreams. *Dreaming, 11*, 13–33.

Eisensehr, I., Linke, R., Noachtar, S., Schwarz, J., Gildehaus, F. J., & Tatsch, K. (2000). Reduced striatal dopamine transporters in idiopathic rapid eye movement sleep behaviour disorder. Comparison with Parkinson's disease and controls. *Brain, 123*, 1155–1160.

Fantini, M. L., Corona, A., Clerici, S., & Ferini-Strambi, L. (2005). Aggressive dream content without daytime aggressiveness in REM sleep behaviour disorder. *Neurology, 65*, 1010–1015.

Fantini, M. L., Gagnon, J. F., Petit, D., Rompre, S., Decary, A., Carrier, J., et al. (2003). Slowing of electroencephalogram in rapid eye movement sleep behavior disorder. *Annals of Neurology, 53*, 774–780.

Fantini, M. L., Michaud, M., Gosselin, N., Lavigne, G., & Montplaisir, J. (2002). Periodic leg movements in REM sleep behavior disorder and related autonomic and EEG activation. *Neurology, 59*, 1889–1894.

Ferini-Strambi L., Di Gioia, M. S., Castronovo, V., Oldani, A., Zucconi, M., & Cappa, S. F. (2004). Neuropsychological assessment in idiopathic REM sleep behavior disorder (RBD): Does the idiopathic form of RBD really exist? *Neurology, 62*, 41–45.

Ferini-Strambi, L., Oldani, A., Zucconi, M., Smirne, S. (1996). Cardiac autonomic activity during wakefulness and sleep in REM sleep behavior disorder. *Sleep, 19,* 367–369.

Foulkes, D. (1967). Dreams of the male child: Four case studies. *Journal of Child Psychology & Psychiatry, 8,* 81–98.

Foulkes, D., Larson, J., Swanson, E., & Rardin, M. (1969). Two studies of childhood dreaming. *American Journal of Orthopsychiatry, 39,* 627–643.

Friedman J. H., Fernandez, H. H., & Sudarsky, L. R. (2003). REM behavior disorder and excessive daytime somnolence in Machado-Joseph disease (SCA-3). *Movement Disorders,* 18, 1520–1522.

Fukutake, T., Shinotoh, H., Nishino, H., Ichikawa, Y., Kanazawa, I., & Hattori, T. (2002). Homozygous Machado-Joseph disease presenting as REM sleep behaviour disorder and prominent psychiatric symptoms. *European Journal of Neurology, 9,* 97–100.

Gagnon, J. F., Bédard, M. A., Fantini, M. L., Petit, D., Panisset, M., Rompre, S., et al. (2002). REM sleep behavior disorder and REM sleep without atonia in Parkinson's disease. *Neurology, 59,* 585–589.

Gagnon, J. F., Postuma, R. B., Mazza, S., Doyon, J., & Montplaisir, J. (2006). Rapid-eye-movement sleep behaviour disorder and neurodegenerative diseases. *Lancet Neurology, 5,* 424–432.

Hall, C., & Nordby, V. (1972). *The individual and his dreams.* New York: New American Library.

Hendricks, J. C., Morrison, A. R., & Mann, G. L. (1982). Different behaviors during paradoxical sleep without atonia depend on pontine lesion site. *Brain Research, 239,* 81–105.

Hobson, J. A., & McCarley, R. W. (1977). The brain as a dream state generator: An activation-synthesis hypothesis of the dream process. *American Journal of Psychiatry, 134,* 1335–1348.

Hobson, J. A., Pace-Schott, E. F., & Stickgold, R. (2000). Dreaming and the brain: Toward a cognitive neuroscience of conscious states. *Behavioral and Brain Sciences, 23,* 793–1121.

Iranzo, A., Graus, F., Clover, L., Morera, J., Bruna, J., Vilar, C., et al. (2006). Rapid eye movement sleep behavior disorder and potassium channel antibody-associated limbic encephalitis. *Annals of Neurology, 59,* 178–181.

Iranzo, A., Munoz, E., Santamaria, J., Vilaseca, I., Mila, M., & Tolosa, E. (2003). REM sleep behavior disorder and vocal cord paralysis in Machado-Joseph disease. *Movement Disorders, 18,* 1179–1183.

Jouvet, M., & Delorme, F. (1965). Locus coeruleus et sommeil paradoxal [Locus, coeruleus and paradoxical sleep]. *C R Société de Biologie, 159,* 895–899.

Jung, C. (1974). *Dreams.* Princeton, NJ: Princeton University Press.

Kohyama, J. (1996). A quantitative assessment of the maturation of phasic motor inhibition during REM sleep. *Journal of Neurological Sciences, 143,* 150–155.

Kohyama, J., & Iwakawa, Y. (1990). Developmental changes in phasic sleep parameters as reflections of the brain-stem maturation: Polysomnographical examinations of infants, including premature neonates. *Electroencephalography & Clinical Neurophysiology, 76,* 325–330.

Kohyama, J., Tachibana, N., & Taniguchi, M. (1999). Development of REM sleep atonia. *Acta Neurology Scandinavia, 99,* 368–373.

Lapierre, O., & Montplaisir, J. (1992). Polysomnographic features of REM sleep behavior disorder: Development of a scoring method. *Neurology, 42*, 1371–1374.

Liguori, R., Vincent, A., Clover, L., Avoni, P., Plazzi, G., Cortelli, P., et al. (2001). Morvan's syndrome: Peripheral and central nervous system and cardiac involvement with antibodies to voltage-gated potassium channels. *Brain, 124*, 2417–2426.

Mahowald, M. W., & Schenck, C. H. (2000). REM sleep parasomnias. In M. H. Kryger, T. Roth, & C. Dement (Eds.), *Principles and practice of sleep medicine* (3rd ed., pp. 724–741). Philadelphia, PA: W. B. Saunders Company.

McKeith, I. G. (2005). Diagnosis and management of dementia with Lewy bodies: Third report of the DLB Consortium. *Neurology, 65*, 1863–1872.

McNamara, P., McLaren, D., Smith, D., Brown, A., & Stickgold, R. A. (2005). "Jekyll and Hyde" within: Aggressive versus friendly interactions in REM and non-REM dreams. *Psychological Sciences, 16*, 130–136.

Ohayon, M. M., Caulet, M., & Priest, R. G. (1997). Violent behavior during sleep. *Journal of Clinical Psychiatry, 58*, 369–376.

Olson, E. J., Boeve, B. F., & Silber, M. H. (2000). Rapid eye movement sleep behaviour disorder: Demographic, clinical and laboratory findings in 93 cases. *Brain, 123*, 331–339.

Pagel, J. F., & Helfter, P. (1999). Drug induced nightmares: An etiology based review. *Annals of Pharmacotherapy, 33*, 93–98.

Passouant, P., Cadilhac, J., & Ribstein, M. (1972). Les privations de sommeil avec mouvements oculaires par les antidépresseurs [The sleep deprivations with eye movements by the antidepressant drug]. *Revue Neurologique Paris, 127*, 173–192.

Pesant, N. & Zadra, A. 2006). Dream content and psychological well-being: A longitudinal study of the continuity hypothesis. *Journal of Clinical Psychology, 62*, 111–121.

Plazzi, G., Corsini, R., Provini, F., Pierangeli, G., Martinelli, P., Montagna, P., et al. (1997). REM sleep behavior disorders in multiple system atrophy. *Neurology, 48*, 1094–1097.

Postuma, R. B., Lang, A., Massicotte-Marquez, J., & Montplaisir, J. (2006). Potential early markers of Parkinson disease in idiopathic REM sleep behavior disorder. *Neurology, 66*, 845–851.

Revonsuo, A. (2000). The reinterpretation of dreams: An evolutionary hypothesis of the function of dreaming. Discussion 904–1121. *Behavioral & Brain Sciences, 23*, 877–901.

Schenck, C. H., Bundlie, S. R., Ettinger, M. G., & Mahowald, M. W. (1986). Chronic behavioral disorders of human REM sleep: A new category of parasomnia. *Sleep, 9*, 293–308.

Schenck, C. H., Bundlie, S. R., & Mahowald, M. W. (1996). Delayed emergence of a parkinsonian disorder in 38% of 29 older men initially diagnosed with idiopathic rapid eye movement sleep behavior disorder. *Neurology, 46*, 388–393.

Schenck, C. H., Bundlie, S. R., & Mahowald, M. W. (2003). REM behavior disorder (RBD): Delayed emergence of parkinsonism and/or dementia in 65% of older men initially diagnosed with idiopathic RBD, and analysis of the minimum and maximum tonic and/or phasic electromyographic abnormalities found during REM sleep. *Sleep, 26*, 316.

Schenck, C. H., & Mahowald, M. W. (2002). REM sleep behavior disorder: Clinical, developmental, and neuroscience perspectives 16 years after its formal identification in SLEEP. *Sleep, 25*, 120–138.

Sforza, E., Krieger, J., & Petiau, C. (1997). REM sleep behavior disorder: Clinical and physiopathological findings. *Sleep Medicine Reviews, 1*, 57–69.

Stiasny-Kolster, K., Doerr, Y., Moller, J. C., Hoffken, H., Behr, T. M., Oertel, W. H., et al. (2005). Combination of "idiopathic" REM sleep behaviour disorder and olfactory dysfunction as possible indicator for alpha-synucleinopathy demonstrated by dopamine transporter FP-CIT-SPECT. *Brain, 128*, 126–137.

Tachibana, N., Tanaka, K., Hishikawa, Y., & Kaneko, Z. (1975). A sleep study of acute psychotic states due to alcohol and meprobamante addiction. *Advanced Sleep Research, 2*, 177–205.

Van de Castle, R. (1983). Animal figures in fantasy and dreams. In A. Katcher & A. Beck (Eds.), *New perspectives on our lives with companion animals*. Philadelphia, PA: University of Pennsylvania Press.

Nine

"Theory of Mind" in REM and NREM Dreams

Patrick McNamara, Deirdre McLaren, Sara Kowalczyk, and Edward F. Pace-Schott

Many dreams involve the dreamer in interaction with at least one other being or person (Domhoff, 1996; Hall & Van de Castle, 1966). To interact with another often involves attributions or inferences about the other. Most fundamentally, we assume that the other person has a mind and possesses beliefs, desires, and goals just as we do. Therefore, dreaming may involve the attribution of intentionality toward other dream characters. To attribute intentionality to other apparent "agents" is to assume that they have a mind and are motivated by beliefs, desires, intentions, hopes, and fears like our own.

To attribute mind to another is commonly called Theory of Mind (ToM) attributions. Does the dreaming mind perform ToM attributions? Certainly, instances of ToM attributions appear in dreams (Kahn & Hobson, 2005; Pace-Schott, 2001). Presumably, the dreaming mind creates characters and then attributes mind and agency to those characters. Dream memory like wake memory is likely a reconstructive and creative process. Dream elements can be assembled within the dream using knowledge elements from semantic, autobiographical, and episodic memory stores to create characters with motivations (and minds) independent of the dreamer's motivations and desires. This is an extremely important fact that reveals something fundamental about the capacities of the dreaming mind. It is capable of supporting the complex cognitive process called "mind-reading."

Baron-Cohen (1997) has argued that mind-reading involves the interaction of at least four separate cognitive systems. These are an intentionality detector (ID), an eye direction detector (EDD), a shared attention mechanism (SAM), and a theory of mind mechanism (ToMM). The ID is a perceptual device that interprets motion stimuli in terms of the primitive, volitional, and mental states of goal and desire. According to Baron-Cohen, to see anything animate moving, all that is required to interpret its movement is the attribution of goal and desire. X is moving because its goal is to go over there or because it wants something. The EDD detects the presence and the direction of eyes or eyelike stimuli, and it infers that if another organism's eyes are directed at something, then that organism sees that thing. The EDD permits us to attribute perceptual states and, therefore, mind to other organisms. Interestingly, many patients with autism, who are widely believed to be deficient in both dream recall and in key theory of mind skills, do not allow or maintain eye contact with another person.

These two mechanisms, the ID and the EDD, can construct dyadic representations such as Agent wants X, Agent has goal Y (in the case of ID); and Agent sees X, and Agent is looking at Y (in the case of EDD). From Baron-Cohen's point of view, they are not, however, sufficient to account for more complex representations such as Agent A sees that Agent B sees X. For such a representation, Baron-Cohen argues that we need a shared attentional mechanism (SAM).

The SAM builds triadic representations that specify the relations among an Agent, the Self, and a (third) Object, which can be another Agent. Such triadic relations would have the form of "Agent sees that I see X" or "You and I see that we are looking at the same object." The ToMM uses input from the other subcomponents of the system to specialize in detection of specific mental states such as pretending, thinking, knowing, and believing, in which agents are represented as having attitudes toward propositions.

Although the process of mind-reading, as explicated by Baron-Cohen, is clearly complex, the dreaming mind appears to be capable of supporting this cognitive process (Pace-Schott, 2001).

The dreaming brain-mind, however, is composed of at least two distinct substates: rapid eye movement (REM) and non-REM sleep (NREM). The contrasting brain and neurochemical activity patterns of REM and NREM suggest that representation of social interactions, and thus of mind-reading instances in "dreams" associated with the two sleep states may differ. REM sleep involves periodic, significant reductions in forebrain serotoninergic and noradrenergic activity along with selective activation of limbic and paralimbic neuronal circuits, including the lateral hypothalamus, amygdala, parahippocampal and medial and orbitofrontal cortices, but not the dorsolateral prefrontal cortex (Braun et al., 1997, 1998; Maquet et al., 1996; Nofzinger, Mintum, Wiseman, Kupfer, & Moore, 1997). Areas reactivated in REM have been characterized by Nofzinger et al. (1997) as the "anterior paralimbic REM activation area" that they describe as a "bilateral confluent paramedian zone which extends from the septal area into ventral striatum, infralimbic, prelimbic, orbitofrontal and anterior cingulate cortex" (p. 192).

Interestingly, the neuroanatomy of REM may overlap to some extent with the neuroanatomy of ToM. The medial prefrontal (paracingulate) cortex, superior temporal sulcus, and temporal poles including the amygdala are the areas most consistently activated in neuroimaging studies of ToM tasks (Brune & Brune-Cohrs, 2006; Frith & Frith, 2003; Gallagher & Frith, 2003; Harris, Todorov, & Fiske, 2005). It has also been suggested that different anatomical circuits may subserve different elements of theory of mind skills with the orbitofrontal cortex mediating ToMM processes themselves (for example, Hynes, Baird, & Grafton, 2006; Sabbagh, 2004).

Given that the limbic and paralimbic structures implicated in ToM skills include many of the same structures that have been shown to reactivate during REM following relative quiescence in NREM (Braun et al., 1997, 1998; Maquet et al., 1996; Nofzinger et al., 1997), we hypothesized that REM would be able to support forms of mentation that contain frequent instances of mind-reading.

What about NREM? NREM is composed of four progressively deeper substages. While positron emission tomographic (PET) studies of NREM sleep states generally show a global decrease in cerebral energy metabolism relative to REM, this metabolic decline is not as marked in Stage 2 NREM as in deeper NREM Stages (3 and 4 slow wave sleep), and thus Stage 2 NREM sustains relatively higher levels of brain activation compared to Stages 3 and 4 (Maquet, 1995, 2000). Indeed, a recent functional magnetic resonance imaging (fMRI) study found that the frontal cortices were activated in Stage II NREM (Loevblad et al., 1999), although this effect is not as clear in PET studies (Braun et al., 1997). We can, therefore, expect some amount of mentalizing to occur in Stage II NREM as well as in REM; however, the frequency and pattern of ToM instances should differ between the two sleep states reflecting differing brain activation patterns associated with the two sleep states. The differing brain activation profiles for the two sleep states suggest different simulations of social interactions and mentalizing capacity profiles as well. Indeed, in a recent investigation of type and intensity of social interactions in REM and NREM dreams (McNamara, McLaren, Smith, Brown, & Stickgold, 2005), we found that REM dreams were more frequently associated with reports of aggressive social interactions, while NREM dreams favored depictions of friendly social interactions.

For that study and for the present report, we used the "Nightcap," a home-based sleep-wake monitoring system (Ajilore, Stickgold, Rittenhouse, & Hobson, 1995) to collect dream and waking mentation reports from healthy individuals in their home environments. We repeatedly sampled the mental activity associated with REM sleep, NREM sleep, and waking in the same 15 individuals as they behaved and slept naturally over a two-week period. We then used a standardized dream content scoring system (Hall & Van de Castle, 1966) along with a novel scale to identify and quantify ToM in dream reports to analyze the frequency and content of mind-reading instances in the reports collected from these individuals. We predicted greater ToM instances in REM compared to NREM and waking reports. We also predicted differing content-related ToM profiles for REM and NREM. The results are consistent with our predictions and clearly demonstrate more frequent depiction of mind-reading in REM versus wake and NREM reports, as well as dramatically different content profiles for REM and NREM dreams containing ToMs.

METHOD

The data are drawn from a larger database of mentation during wake and sleep states whose overall characteristics have been described in detail elsewhere (Stickgold, Malia, Fosse, Propper, & Hobson, 2001). Dr. Stickgold graciously gave us access to this database of sleep mentation reports for purposes of this report. The study was approved by the local internal review board for protections of the rights of human subjects, and all participants signed an informed consent form. In brief, 15 undergraduate students (18–22 years of age; 8 men, 7 women) carried a pager during the day and wore the Nightcap monitoring system (Ajilore et al., 1995) at night for 14 days and nights. Subjects verbally provided mentation reports via a portable tape recorder four times each day when paged, as well as when they awoke from sleep during the 14 nights. The subjects were instructed to describe in detail their foregoing experiences when paged or awakened, including where they (thought they) were, who else was present, and what they were doing, perceiving, feeling, and thinking. Instrumental awakenings were performed by a Macintosh computer that received continuous input from the Nightcap.

The Nightcap consists of a 25-mm × 8-mm piezoelectric eyelid movement (ELM) sensor and a cylindrical, multiple mercury switch that detects head movements (HMs; Ajilore et al., 1995). The Nightcap samples ELM and HM sensors during each successive 250-ms interval, identifying an ELM interval whenever a voltage in excess of 10mV is detected within an interval. The sensor and associated circuitry are sensitive to REMs and twitches of the *levator palpebrae* and *orbicularis oculi* (eyelid muscles), but not to the slow eye movements (SEMs) characteristic of sleep onset. Sleep onset is normally scored as the start of a period of at least two 30-second epochs of

ELM quiescence following waking or, when hypnogogic reports are collected, after 15 seconds of ELM quiescence. The beginning of an NREM sleep epoch is scored at the start of at least five minutes without ELMs or HMs. NREM periods are characterized by no ELMs and HMs. REM sleep is scored when ELMs occur but with few or no head movements. Nightcap identifications of REM and NREM sleep states have been verified by concomitant electroencephalogram (EEG) studies (Ajilore et al., 1995), thus demonstrating that it can accurately distinguish REM from NREM, although the Nightcap cannot resolve stages within NREM.

Sampling of Sleep and Wake Reports

We used exactly the same sampling procedures as McNamara et al. (2005). Briefly, the 200 sleep mentation reports and 100 wake reports were selected in a semi-random fashion from a database of 1748 sleep and wake mentation reports, provided to us by Dr Stickgold. The full database contained 894 waking (W) reports, 338 sleep onset (SO) reports, 269 REM reports, and 247 NREM reports. In order to approximate the overall normative values for the various Hall/Van de Castle content indicators, Domhoff (1996, pp. 65–66) determined that a minimum sample size of 100 reports is needed. We, therefore, pseudo-randomly selected 100 REM, 100 NREM, and 100 wake reports from the overall Nightcap database and then calculated mean word count per dream for each of the three groups in an attempt to equate mean word length per report across REM, NREM, and wake reports. Because NREM dreams tended to be shorter in length than REM or wake reports, we had to adjust the REM and wake report means to the NREM means by repeated random samplings with replacement of reports from the REM and wake pools until the three means were roughly equated. Using this method, we obtained a dream series from NREM with a mean word count per dream of 64.33 (standard deviation [SD] = 46.63), and dream series from REM of mean 75.39 (SD = 37.85) and a wake report series with a mean word count of 70.13 (SD = 20.20). We were successful in equating report lengths across report types because mean word counts across the three report types were not statistically different from one another, $F(2, 297) = 2.28$; $p = .103$. Word count in all of these reports was calculated by the method of Antrobus (1983), which eliminates fillers, repetitions, and pauses such as "ah," "well," and so on, as well as extraneous descriptions (in dream reports) of waking events.

Given that our sampling procedure for the REM and wake reports was not fully random, we wanted to assess the possibility that the nonselected (eliminated) reports were significantly different from selected (target) reports in terms of key content variables. We, therefore, randomly selected and scored 1 of 3 (33 percent) of the eliminated reports from each category (REM, NREM, and wake). These "eliminated" reports did not differ significantly from the length-matched or "target" reports in terms of character representation or of major social interactions. For example, the Aggressions/Character (A/C) indexes (number of aggressions per character) were 0.16, 0.11, and 0.06 for the target REM, NREM, and wake reports respectively, and 0.17, 0.11, and 0.09 for the eliminated REM, NREM, and wake reports, respectively. In terms of characters, the target and the eliminated reports were also quite similar, with males comprising 47, 53, and 42 percent of the characters in the target REM, NREM, and wake reports, respectively, and 46, 52, and 62 percent in the eliminated reports, respectively. In sum, the target reports and the eliminated reports were reasonably similar in terms of male and female characters and frequencies of aggressive interactions.

On average, subjects contributed about seven reports apiece to each of the report types. After eliminating one subject who contributed only a single report, mean number of reports contributed by each of the 14 remaining subjects to the REM pool was 7.2 (SD = 3.2; range = 3–11); NREM pool was 7.1 (SD = 4.1; range = 3–11), and wake pool was 6.7 (SD = 3.5; range = 6–11).

Content Scoring

Domhoff and Schneider (http://www.dreamresearch.net) provide a spreadsheet program, "DreamSat," which allows for tabulation of dream content scores and automatic computation of derived scales and percents when using the Hall/Van de Castle scoring system. This spreadsheet program greatly increases the reliability of results obtained with use of the system. The Hall/Van de Castle system for scoring dream content (Domhoff, 1996; Hall & Van de Castle, 1966) is a standardized and reliable content scoring system that consists of up to 16 empirical scales and a number of derived scales useful for an analysis of social interactions in dream content (Table 9.1). Three primary types of social interaction are scored: aggressive, friendly, and sexual, with the ability to score subtypes as well (for example, physical versus verbal aggression). Along with identification of the physical settings within which these interactions take place, the character that initiated the social interaction is identified as well as the target or recipient of the interaction. The "characters" scale allows for classification of characters known to the dreamer (for example, family members, friends, and so on), as well as those unknown to the dreamer. Characters (known or unknown) can also be classified as to gender, age, and relation to the dreamer. Our

TABLE 9.1
Dream Variables According to the Hall and Van de Castle Method

Variables	Meaning
Characters (Percent)	
Male/female	Total male characters/(male characters + female characters)
Familiarity	Number of familiar characters/(total familiar characters + total unfamiliar characters)
Friends	Known characters/all human characters
Family	Family + relatives/familiar characters + unfamiliar characters
Dead and imaginary	Number of dead and imaginary/(familiar characters + unfamiliar characters)
Animal	Total animal/total characters
Social interaction	
Aggression/friendliness	Number of aggressive interaction/(total number of aggressive + friendly interaction)
Befriender	Dreamer as befriender/(dreamer as befriender + dreamer as recipient)
Aggressor	Dreamer as aggressor/dreamer as aggressor + dreamer as victim
Physical aggression	Physical aggression/total aggression
Social interaction ratios	
A/C Index	Total number of aggressions/total number of characters
F/C Index	Total number of friendliness interactions/total number of characters
S/C Index	Total number of sex interactions/total number of characters
Settings (percent)	
Indoor	Indoor setting/(indoor + outdoor settings)
Familiar	Familiar settings/(familiar + unfamiliar setting)

primary use of all of these scales was to determine character frequencies and number and types of social interactions while adjusting for various baseline values in order to control for length effects.

Word Count Analyses

We used a computerized word count program known as Linguistic Inquiry and Word Count (LIWC; Pennebaker, Francis, & Booth, 2001) to assess word-related indicators of mind-reading, emotions, and social interactions. For example, if the dreamer says that he thought that another character was angry and planning to attack the dreamer, then the words "thinking," "angry," and "planning" would all indicate at least one instance of mind-reading. The LIWC program is able to tabulate these sorts of words, thus providing an independent check on mind-reading content in dreams. The output from this program consists of a spreadsheet with total number of words in each sample, as well as percentages of words in each of target categories. LIWC 2001 is a well-validated instrument (Pennebaker et al., 2001, and see www.liwc.net). For the purposes of the current study, we had the program tabulate for REM and for NREM dreams the following categories of words: cognitive mechanisms, social processes, and emotion. The emotion category contains 615 words drawn from two subcategories called positive emotions and negative emotions. Positive emotions is further divided into two subcategories of "positive feelings" (for example, "happy," "joy," and "love") and "optimism and energy" (for example, "win" and "excitement"). Examples of negative emotion words include "hate," "worthless," and "enemy." The category of negative emotion also includes three subcategories of anxiety/fear (for example, "nervous"), anger (for example, "hate" and "pissed"), and sadness/depression (for example, "cry"). Note that we focused only on the superordinate categories for this study. The target category, social processes, is made up of social pronouns (first-person plural, second- and third-person pronouns), communication verbs ("talk" and "share"), and references to family, friends, and other humans. The cognitive mechanisms category (cause, know, ought) is made up of subcategories called causation (because, effect), insight (think, know, consider); discrepancy (should, would), inhibition, (block, constrain), tentative (maybe, perhaps), and certainty (always, never). We analyzed the overall indicator cognitive mechanisms and the subcategory of insight because these two cognitive categories seemed to us to best capture potential instances of mind-reading. In addition to the overall social processes category, we analyzed the "references to other people" category because these potentially contain instances of mind-reading. Finally, as a check on overall level of semantic content of REM versus NREM dreams, we had the program also tabulate the number of "unique" words.

As a check on the reliability of the procedure, we compared the word counts we obtained with the LIWC program published norms (available at www.liwc.net). Because the norms are established on discourse passages averaging 353 words per passage, we collapsed all the dreams obtained for each subject into a single "dream passage" per subject per dream state (REM and NREM). Thus, the values obtained for each subject are averaged across all of that subject's REM or NREM dreams (as stated above, that amounted to about 6–7 dreams per subject per state). Thus, the mean word count for this sample of dreams was 511—about 100 words greater than published norms. Inspection of Table 9.2 will show that the means for each of the categories we analyzed here approximate the published norms, thus increasing our confidence in the reliability of the LIWC analyses. We hypothesized that

TABLE 9.2
Mean Word in REM and NREM Dreams and in Published Norms
(www.liwc.net)

	REM	NREM	p Value	Published Norm (Means)
Unique words	42.8 (7.4)	47.7 (17.2)	.36	50.8
Cognitive mechanisms	7.0 (1.8)	8.2 (1.9)	.10	6.4
Insight	1.9 (1.1)	2.8 (1.3)	.09	2.0
Positive emotion	1.0 (.80)	1.4 (1.0)	.26	2.4
Negative emotion	1.2 (.80)	1.2 (.81)	.86	1.6
Social processes	10.24 (2.1)	6.8 (3.0)	.003**	8.8
References to other people	5.4 (1.8)	3.5 (2.1)	.023*	5.0

*$p \leq 0.05$
**$p \leq 0.01$

relative to NREM dreams, REM dreams would evidence higher mean numbers of negative emotion, social process, and cognitive mechanism words.

Scoring of Specific ToM Instances

Instances of ToM activity were categorized as either "definite" or "potential." We defined an instance of definite mind-reading as a situation where the dreamer clearly said or thought what another dream character was thinking or feeling. An example of a definite mind-reading instance is as follows: *she was sort of upset because the french fries had been covered.* Typical examples of potential mind-reading were scored when the scorer had to infer that the dreamer was reading the mind of another dream character, such as when the character was "trying to" or "wanting." An example of a potential mind-reading is as follows: *we're just wasting time trying to make the decision.* After discussion between members of the entire research team, we agreed that no unanimous agreement could be reached concerning the status of these potential instances of mind-reading, thus they were excluded from further analyses. Only definite instances of mind-reading were including in the analyses that follow.

Reliability of Scoring of ToM Content

Two members of our team (S.C. and D.M.) each scored half of the 300 target reports, with each individual scoring 20 percent of the 150 reports originally assigned to the other scorer. Scorers were blind to the status of the reports that they scored (that is, whether they were a REM, NREM, or wake report). By using the "method of perfect agreement" (Domhoff, 1996, p. 28), we calculated interrater reliability (IRR) by dividing the number of agreed upon classifications by the sum of all their classifications and arrived at IRRs above 80 percent for all outcome measures.

With respect to assessing reliability of the scoring of dream content with the Hall/Van de Castle categories, we compared the means of our REM and NREM values for the major Hall/Van de Castle categories to the published norms for these same categories. Our obtained values for REM plus NREM percents are nearly identical with the values of the published norms (Domhoff, 2003, Table 3.2, p. 73).

Statistical Analysis

With respect to analysis of the Hall/Van de Castle categories and content indicators, these are based on nominal rating scales. We, therefore, used tests for the significance of differences between two proportions, as well as χ^2 analyses to compare Hall/Van de Castle content indicators on REM-NREM differences, REM-wake differences, and NREM-wake differences. We used the DreamSat program to compute all of the scales, percent differences, and certain p values we reported. The program also produces Cohen's h statistic, which is an effect size value for samples involving nominal measurement scales. We used Bonferroni-corrected t tests to compare LIWC word count means for REM and NREM dreams.

RESULTS

Word Count Analyses

Table 9.2 summarizes REM and NREM differences on word count categories indicating potential mind-reading processes (cognitive mechanisms), emotions, and social processes. First, it should be noted that no differences were found for a measure of semantic content (a count of "unique" words). The mean unique word count for REM dreams was 42.8 (7.4) and for NREM was 47.7 (17.2). The norm is 50.8 (Table 9.2). Table 9.2 reveals that there were no significant differences between REM and NREM dreams for the categories of cognitive mechanisms or emotion. Consistent, however, with the Hall/Van de Castle analysis, there were significantly greater mean numbers of words indicating social processes in REM (10.2 [2.1]) compared to NREM (6.8 [3.0]; p = .003) dreams. Interestingly, references to other people were significantly more frequent in REM (5.36 [1.8]) than in NREM (3.5 [2.1]; p = .024).

Frequencies of Mind-Reading by State

REM reports were three times as likely to contain instances of mind-reading as were wake reports and 1.3 times as likely as NREM reports. Of 100 reports per state, there were 39 instances of mind-reading in REM reports, 29 in NREM reports, and 12 in wake reports.

Associations of Mind-Reading in REM Dreams

Table 9.3 presents the content profiles of REM dreams with and without instances of ToMs. When REM dreams had at least one instance of a ToM, they were significantly more likely to contain depictions of familiar male characters but types of social interaction (for example, aggressive versus friendly) did not distinguish the two dream types. For example, the male to female ratio for REM dreams with ToMs was 65 percent, whereas the same ratio for dreams without ToMs reached only 31 percent ($h = -0.69$; $p = .001$). Similarly, the "familiarity percent" (a measure of the extent to which characters were familiar to the dreamer) for REM dreams with ToMs was 61 and 47 percent for REM dreams without ToMs ($h = -0.28$; $p = .037$) and the "friends percent" was 46 percent for REM dreams with and 24 percent for REM dreams without ToMs ($h = -0.46$; $p = .001$). There were no significant differences, however, between ToM dreams and non-ToM dreams in the extent to which family characters were depicted in the dream (10 percent versus 16 percent, respectively; $h = 0.19$; $p = .15$).

With respect to the impact of REM dream ToMs on depictions of social interactions, there were no significant differences between ToM and non-ToM dreams in the extent to which social interactions of various types were depicted in the dream (Table 9.3). Only the content indicator "aggressor percent" approached significance with non-ToM dreams tending to depict an aggressor more frequently than did ToM dreams (83 percent versus 40 percent, respectively; $h = 0.93$; $p = .054$). No reliable differences between ToM and non-ToM dreams in depictions of physical settings (in which the dream took place) were detected.

Association of Mind-Reading in NREM Dreams

Unlike the case for REM dreams, virtually no significant content differences emerged between NREM dreams with, and NREM dreams without ToMs (Table 9.4). Animal percent was the sole exception to this rule (7 percent for ToM dreams versus 0 percent for non-ToM dreams; $h = -0.54$; $p = .001$). NREM dreams with and without ToMs evidenced roughly equal

TABLE 9.3
REM Dreams with and without ToMs

Characteristics	REM with ToM	REM without ToM	Cohen's h: REM without ToM versus REM with ToM	p Value: REM without ToM versus REM with ToM
Male/female	65%	31%	−0.69	.001**
Familiarity	61%	47%	−0.28	.037*
Friends	46%	24%	−0.46	.001**
Family	10%	16%	+0.19	.153
Dead and imaginary	0%	.02%	+0.26	.049*
Animal	.02%	.02%	−0.01	.943
Social interaction				
Aggression/friendliness	74%	50%	−0.50	.141
Befriender	33%	71%	+0.78	.159
Aggressor	40%	83%	+0.93	.054
Physical aggression	25%	25%	0	1.000
Social interaction ratios				
A/C Index	.22	.10		
F/C Index	.09	.07		
S/C Index	.00	.02		
Settings				
Indoor	58%	48%	−0.21	.468
Familiar	60%	68%	+0.18	.610

Notes: A/C index = total number of aggressions/total number of characters; F/C index = total number of friendliness interactions/total number of characters; ratios do not use the h statistic.
*$p \leq 0.05$
**$p \leq 0.01$

ratios of male/female characters, familiar characters, friends, and family members. Similarly, no significant differences in profiles of social interactions or of physical settings emerged between the two dream types.

Comparison of REM and NREM ToM Dreams

When we compare content profiles of REM dreams with ToMs to content of NREM dreams with ToMs (Table 9.5), we find that although character profiles do not distinguish REM from NREM dreams, social interactions profiles do. Specifically, indicators of aggressive content are significantly higher among REM than among NREM dreams (74 percent versus 38 percent for the aggression/friendliness percent, $h = -0.73$, $p = .035$; and 40 percent versus 0 percent for the aggressor percent, $h = -1.37$, $p = .008$), while the

TABLE 9.4
NREM Dream Characteristics with and without ToMs

Characteristics	NREM with ToM	NREM without ToM	Cohen's h: NREM without ToM versus NREM with ToM	p Value: NREM without ToM versus NREM with ToM
Male/female	55%	50%	−0.10	.673
Familiarity	51%	46%	−0.10	.553
Friends	38%	39%	+0.01	.934
Family	10%	.03%	−0.31	.061
Dead and imaginary	.00%	.00%	0	1.000
Animal	.07%	.00%	−0.54	.001**
Social interaction				
Aggression/friendliness	38%	20%	−0.41	.435
Befriender	86%	100%	+0.78	.261
Aggressor	.00%	.00%	0	1.000
Physical aggression	20%	14%	−0.15	.758
Social interaction ratios				
A/C Index	.12	.10		
F/C Index	.13	.09		
S/C Index	.00	.00		
Settings				
Indoor	53%	57%	+0.07	.822
Familiar	67%	80%	+0.30	.509

Notes: A/C index = total number of aggressions/total number of characters; F/C index = total number of friendliness interactions/total number of characters; ratios do not use the h statistic.
**$p \leq 0.01$

indicator of friendly social interactions was lower for REM (33 percent) versus NREM dreams (86 percent; $h = 1.14$; $p = .041$).

DISCUSSION

We found that attributions of the mental states of dream characters occur particularly frequently in REM versus non-REM dreams. In addition, REM dreams that contained instances of ToMs were distinguished by greater numbers of dreamer initiated aggressions against male characters who were familiar to the dreamer. Compared with NREM dreams with ToMs, REM dreams with ToMs contained higher amounts of aggressive content and lower amounts of friendly interactions. By contrast, NREM dreams

TABLE 9.5
REM versus NREM Dream Characteristics with ToMs

Characteristics	REM with ToM	NREM with ToM	Cohen's *h*: NREM with ToM versus REM with ToM	*p* Value: NREM with ToM versus REM with TOM
Male/female	65%	55%	−0.20	.360
Familiarity	61%	51%	−0.20	.192
Friends	46%	38%	−0.15	.325
Family	10%	10%	+0.02	.870
Dead and imaginary	0%	0%	0	1.000
Animal	2%	7%	+.26	.068
Social interaction				
Aggression/friendliness	74%	38%	−0.73	.035*
Befriender	33%	86%	+1.14	.041*
Aggressor	40%	0%	−1.37	.008**
Physical aggression	25%	20%	−0.12	.750
Social interaction ratios				
A/C Index	.22	.12		
F/C Index	.09	.13		
S/C Index	.00	.00		
Settings				
Indoor	58%	53%	−0.11	.732
Familiar	60%	67%	+0.14	.743

Notes: A/C index = total number of aggressions/total number of characters; F/C index = total number of friendliness interactions/total number of characters; ratios do not use the *h* statistic.
*$p \leq 0.05$
**$p \leq 0.01$

with ToMs never had the dreamer engaged in aggressive interactions with other dream characters. Instead, NREM dreams with ToMs featured the dreamer engaged in friendly interactions with other dream characters.

Word count analyses confirmed a higher number of social interactions and processes in REM compared to NREM dreams but did not reveal greater numbers of mind-reading-related words in REM versus NREM dreams. The word count analyses suggested a greater number of references to "other" characters in REM versus NREM dreams.

In short, although REM dreams are associated with greater numbers of ToMs, when ToMs appear in REM dreams they are associated with dreamer initiated aggressive interactions with familiar male characters, and when they appear in NREM dreams they are associated with dreamer initiated friendly interactions with both male and female characters.

What might explain this pattern of results? As reviewed in the beginning of this chapter, the brain regions that reactivate during REM are associated with amygdalar, limbic, and paralimbic sites, some of which have been plausibly linked to circuits that mediate aggressive behavioral states/actions in rats and nonhuman primates (Maquet & Franck, 1997). The activation of similar functional circuits in humans may promote emergence of aggressive impulses along with associated mental simulations congruent with those impulses. The lack of activation in these aggression-related circuits in NREM would perhaps explain the lack of dreamer-initiated aggressive social interactions in NREM, but it would not help us explain the relative increase in "befriender" interactions in NREM compared to REM. The dream content data in our view point to an activation of filiative-related brain processes during Stage II NREM sleep. Whatever the functional neuroanatomy of REM and NREM may ultimately turn out to be, we find in our analyses that instances of mind-reading are elicited by differing types of simulations of social processes in the two sleep states, aggression in REM and friendliness in NREM.

It is interesting that REM-related ToMs were preferentially elicited when the dreamer was the aggressor rather than when the dreamer was a victim of an aggression. The dreamer-initiated aggression, furthermore, was typically directed against a familiar male character. According to the Hall/Van de Castle norms, about 50 percent of characters in dreams are familiar to the dreamer. Of course, this fact implies that the other 50 percent of dream characters are strangers or unidentifiable. In an early study of over 1,000 thousand dreams, Hall (1963) reported (1) that strangers in dreams were most often male, (2) that aggressive encounters were more likely to occur in interaction with an unknown male than with an unknown female or a familiar male or female, and (3) that unknown males appeared more frequently in dreams of males than of females. Using the Hall/Van de Castle system, Domhoff (1996) looked at the role of "enemies" in dreams. Enemies were defined as those dream characters who typically interacted (in greater than 60 percent of the cases) with the dreamer in an aggressive manner. Those enemies turned out to be male strangers and animals. Interactions with female strangers are predominantly friendly in the dreams of both males and females. Schredl (2000) reports that almost all murderers and soldiers in dreams are male. Domhoff (2003) has shown that when male strangers appear in a dream, the likelihood that physical aggression will occur in that dream far exceeds what would be expected on the basis of chance. In short, male strangers signal physical aggression against the dreamer.

Yet, we found that although instances of mind-reading were in fact associated with aggressive social interactions, at least in REM dreams, ToMs were not as strongly associated with male strangers as with male familiars. It appears then, that although many dreams involve the dreamer on the receiving end of an aggression, typically from a male stranger, the dreamer does not report that he or she attempted to read the mind of the aggressor. Instead we get mere observations or reports along the lines of "I was being pummeled by some huge man I had never seen before." Nothing is said about the emotions or intentions of the aggressor. Instead, the dreamer uses his/her ToMM capacities to read the mind of a potential victim—a victim moreover who is familiar to the dreamer. REM-related ToMs, in short, occur more often when the dreamer himself or herself is the aggressor and the victim is someone known to the dreamer.

Lest we conclude that ToM capacities are activated only in service to social aggression, the content analyses of NREM dreams revealed a strikingly contrasting picture. Here, we find ToMs occurring most often when the dreamer was befriending someone. No instances of dreamer-initiated aggression occurred in NREM.

What do these findings tell us about ToM capacities more generally? Taken together, the pattern of associations of ToMs in REM and NREM dreams suggests that ToM capacities are used as a tool to facilitate social goals of the dreamer. This, of course, is not too surprising or informative. What is surprising and interesting is that the two sleep states appear to specialize in the types of social goals and the types of ToMs they simulate for the dreamer. Presumably, ToM processes elicit separate neurocognitive networks depending on the goals (aggressive versus friendly) of the agent. Independent neuroimaging and neuropsychologic investigations of ToM processing capacities and processing deficits suggests that ToM capacities are, in fact, mediated by a widely distributed network of contrasting brain sites. Many of these sites are included in what Brothers (1990) has termed the "social brain." This social cognition network minimally involves the medial prefrontal cortex and anterior cingulate, temporal poles, and amygdala and the superior temporal sulcus (for example, Blakemore et al., 2003; Castelli, Happe, Frith, & Frith, 2000; Fletcher et al., 1995; Gallagher et al., 2000; Goel, Grafman, Sadato, & Hallett, 1995; Vogeley et al., 2001). Social cognition and theory of mind skills have also been associated with orbitofrontal cortex (Hynes et al., 2006; Stone, Baron-Cohen, & Knight, 1998), diverse areas in the right frontal lobe (Stuss & Anderson, 2004; Stuss, Gallup, & Alexander, 2001), cerebellum (Calarge, Andreasen, & O'Leary, 2003; Grezes, Frith, & Passingham, 2004), right and left temporo-parietal junction (Saxe & Kanwisher, 2003; Saxe & Wexler, 2005), posterior cingulate/precuneus, and areas in the thalamus, hypothalamus, hippocampus and midbrain. As mentioned earlier, many of the foregoing sites of the "social brain" are also activated during REM and NREM sleep. That is one reason why we expected to find ToMs in dreams. It may be that separate functional circuits can be identified for aggressive and friendly social interactions particularly when ToM capacities are involved.

What might our findings tell us about the nature and function of dreams? First, at a minimum our results suggest that both REM and NREM dreams have the capacity to support very high-level cognitive functions (for example, ToM). More importantly, our results may carry implications for current theoretical models of dreaming. To our knowledge, no current theory of dreaming (with the possible exception of McNamara, 2004) would predict differential ToM representation in REM versus NREM dreams. The finding that dreamers use ToM capacities more often when they are aggressing against male familiars would be particularly hard to accommodate for some theories.

Revonsuo (2000), for example, suggests that the evolutionary purpose of dreaming is to simulate threat so as to practice its detection and avoidance. This author notes that such rehearsal might have had a high selective value in the humans' ancestral environment where both intra- and interspecies aggression against humans was commonplace. Drawing upon the Hall and Van de Castle database, Revonsuo notes both the predominance of unknown males in aggressive encounters in dreams of both men and women, the contrastingly often-friendly nature of encounters with female strangers, as well as a much greater percentage of animals in children's dreams that decreases with age from 4 to 18 years. In addition, many animals in the dreams of young children of a fearsome nature are far out of proportion to children's actual encounters. We assume that the dreamer treats dream characters and male familiars as absolutely real, thus ToM capacities would be predicted to be recruited to deal with what is perceived as a real threat in a presumably aggressive encounter. Such practice would presumably allow one to meet threats more efficiently during waking life. Yet, what we found was that dreamers are not as likely to use ToM capacities when they are being victimized as when they are aggressing against familiar others. If dreaming represents a time when humans simulate threats and how best to deal with them, one would expect that dreamers would call upon one of the most effective tools available to them to deal with the threat (that is, ToM). Yet, they apparently do not do so. This finding, therefore, calls into question basic presuppositions of the threat simulation theory.

We conclude that the study of ToM capacities of REM and NREM sleep demonstrates that dreaming is capable of supporting high-level cognitive capacities, and that the two sleep states specialize in the types of cognitive capacities they support and the social interactions they simulate.

REFERENCES

Ajilore, O. A., Stickgold, R., Rittenhouse, C., & Hobson, J. A. (1995). Nightcap: Laboratory and home-based evaluation of a portable sleep monitor. *Psychophysiology, 32,* 92–98.

Antrobus, J. S. (1983). REM and NREM sleep reports: Comparison of word frequencies by cognitive classes. *Psychophysiology, 20,* 562–568.

Baron-Cohen, S. (1997). *Mindblindness: An essay on autism and theory of mind.* Cambridge, MA: MIT Press.

Blakemore, S. J., Boyer, P., Pachot-Clouard, M., Meltzoff, A., Segebarth, C., & Decety, J. (2003). The detection of contingency and animacy from simple animations in the human brain. *Cerebral Cortex, 13,* 837–844.

Braun, A. R., Balkin, T. J., Wesensten, N. J., Carson, R. E., Varga, M., Baldwin, P., et al. (1997). Regional cerebral blood flow throughout the sleep-wake cycle. *Brain, 120,* 1173–1197.

Braun, A. R., Balkin, T. J., Wesensten, N. J., Gwadry, F., Carson, R. E., Varga, M., et al. (1998). Dissociated pattern of activity in visual cortices and their projections during human rapid eye movement sleep. *Science, 279,* 91–95.

Brothers, L. (1990). The social brain: A project for integrating primate behavior and neurophysiology in a new domain. *Concepts in Neuroscience, 1,* 27–51.

Brune, M., & Brune-Cohrs, U. (2006). Theory of mind-evolution, ontogeny, brain mechanisms and psychopathology. *Neuroscience & Biobehavioral Reviews, 30,* 437–455.

Calarge, C., Andreasen, N. C., & O'Leary, D. S. (2003). Visualizing how one brain understands another: A PET study of theory of mind. *American Journal of Psychiatry, 160,* 1954–1964.

Castelli, F., Happe, F., Frith, U., Frith, C. (2000). Movement and mind: A functional imaging study of perception and interpretation of complex intentional movement patterns. *NeuroImage, 12,* 314–325.

Domhoff, G. W. (1996). *Finding meaning in dreams: A quantitative approach.* New York: Plenum Press.

Domhoff, G. W. (2003). *The scientific study of dreams: Neural networks, cognitive development, and content analysis.* Washington, DC: American Psychological Association.

Fletcher, P. C., Happe, F., Frith, U., Baker, S. C., Dolan, R. J., Frackowiak, R. S., et al. (1995). Other minds in the brain: A functional imaging study of "theory of mind" in story comprehension. *Cognition, 57,* 109–128.

Frith, U., & Frith, C. D. (2003). Development and neurophysiology of mentalizing. *Philosophical Transactions of the Royal Society of London, Series B, Biological Sciences, 358,* 459–473.

Gallagher, H. L., & Frith, C. D. (2003). Functional imaging of "theory of mind." *Trends in Cognitive Sciences, 7,* 77–83.

Gallagher, H. L., Happe, F., Brunswick, N., Fletcher, P. C., Frith, U., & Frith, C. D. (2000). Reading the mind in cartoons and stories: An fMRI study of "theory of mind" in verbal and nonverbal tasks. *Neuropsychologia, 38,* 11–21.

Goel, V., Grafman, J., Sadato, N., & Hallett, M. (1995). Modeling other minds. *Neuro-Report, 6,* 1741–1746.

Grezes, J., Frith, C. D., & Passingham, R. E. (2004) Inferring false beliefs from the actions of oneself and others: An fMRI study. *NeuroImage, 21,* 744–750.

Hall, C. (1963). Strangers in dreams: An empirical confirmation of the Oedipus complex. *Journal of Personality, 31,* 336–345.

Hall, C. S., & Van de Castle, R. (1966). *The content analysis of dreams.* New York: Appleton-Century-Crofts.

Harris, L. T., Todorov, A., & Fiske, S. T. (2005). Attributions on the brain: Neuroimaging dispositional inferences, beyond theory of mind. *NeuroImage, 28,* 763–769.

Hynes, C. A., Baird, A. A., & Grafton, S. T. (2006). Differential role of the orbital frontal lobe in emotional versus cognitive perspective-taking. *Neuropsychologia, 44,* 374–383.

Kahn, D., & Hobson, J. A. (2005). Theory of mind in dreaming: Awareness of feelings and thoughts of others in dreams. *Dreaming, 15,* 48–57.

Loevblad, K. O., Thomas, R., Jakob, P. M., Scammell, T., Bassetti, C., Griswald, M., et al. (1999). Silent function magnetic resonance imaging demonstrates focal activation in rapid eye movement sleep. *Neurology, 53,* 2193–2195.

Maquet, P. (1995). Sleep function(s) and cerebral metabolism. *Behavioral Brain Research, 69,* 75–83.

Maquet, P. (2000). Functional neuroimaging of normal human sleep by positron emission tomography. *Journal of Sleep Research, 9,* 207–231.

Maquet, P., & Franck, G. (1997). REM sleep and amygdala. *Molecular Psychiatry, 2,* 195–196.

Maquet, P., Peters, J., Aerts, J., Delfiore, G., Degueldre, C., Luxen, A., et al. (1996). Functional neuroanatomy of human rapid-eye-movement sleep and dreaming. *Nature, 383,* 163–166.

McNamara, P. (2004). *An evolutionary psychology of sleep and dreams.* New York: Greenwood/Praeger Press.

McNamara, P., McLaren, D., Smith, D., Brown, A., & Stickgold, R. (2005). A "Jekyll and Hyde" within: Aggressive versus friendly social interactions in REM and NREM dreams. *Psychological Science, 16,* 130–136.

Nofzinger, E. A., Mintun, M. A., Wiseman, M. B., Kupfer, D. J., & Moore, R. Y. (1997). Forebrain activation in REM sleep: An FDG PET study. *Brain Research, 770,* 192–201.

Pace-Schott, E. F. (2001). Theory of mind, social cognition and dreaming. *Sleep Research Society Bulletin, 7,* 33–36.

Pennebaker, J. W., Francis, M. E., & Booth, R. J. (2001). *Linguistic inquiry and word count.* Mahwah, NJ: Erlbaum Publishers.

Revonsuo, A. (2000). The reinterpretation of dreams: An evolutionary hypothesis of the function of dreaming. *Behavioral & Brain Sciences, 23,* 877–901.

Sabbagh, M. A. (2004). Understanding orbitofrontal contributions to theory-of-mind reasoning: Implications for autism. *Brain & Cognition, 55,* 209–219.

Saxe, R., & Kanwisher, N. (2003). Other minds in the brain: A functional imaging study of "theory of mind" in story comprehension. *NeuroImage, 19,* 1835–1842.

Saxe, R., & Wexler, A. (2005). Making sense of another mind: The role of the right temporo-parietal junction. *Neuropsychologia, 43,* 1391–1399.

Schredl, M. (2000). Dream research: Integration of physiological and psychological models. *Behavioural Brain Sciences, 23,* 1001–1003.

Stickgold, R., Malia, A., Fosse, R., Propper, R., & Hobson, J. A. (2001). Brain-mind states: I. Longitudinal field study of wake-sleep factors influencing mentation report length. *Sleep, 24,* 171–179.

Stone, V. E., Baron-Cohen, S., & Knight, R. T. (1998). Frontal lobe contributions to theory of mind. *Journal of Cognitive Neuroscience, 10,* 640–656.

Stuss, D. T., & Anderson, V. (2004). The frontal lobes and theory of mind: Developmental concepts from adult focal lesion research. *Brain & Cognition, 55,* 69–83.

Stuss, D. T., Gallup, G. G., Jr., & Alexander, M. P. (2001). The frontal lobes are necessary for "theory of mind." *Brain, 12,* 279–286.

Vogeley, K., Bussfeld, P., Newen, A., Herrmann, S., Happe, F., Falkai, P., et al. (2001). Mind reading: Neural mechanisms of theory of mind and self-perspective. *NeuroImage, 14,* 170–181.

Ten

Dreams and Dreaming
in Disorders of Sleep

Sanford Auerbach

The pursuit to examine the nature of dreams and dreaming in disorders of sleep carries some interesting problems. First, one must confront the issue of definitions. This carries the inherent problem of deciding whether to emphasize the "meaning of content" or simply the general features of dream form, such as changes in duration, intensity, timing, or emotional valence. At the outset, it might be fair to note that an exploration of the impact of sleep disorders on the interpretation of the meaning of dreams will not be addressed in this chapter. Along the same line, it is often tempting to consider rapid eye movement (REM) sleep as being synonymous with the dreaming state. Clearly, this type of definition falls short. It not only fails to recognize that dreaming cannot be considered synonymous with REM sleep, but it also fails to consider the variation in subjective recall that cannot be extracted from a simple analysis of the polysomnogram. The second issue is the need to recognize that disorders that contribute to sleep disorders, such as other medical or neurological conditions may be associated with elements of stress and anxiety. As we shall note, stress and anxiety may have an independent impact on dreams and dreaming. Efforts to sort out these components may often be lacking. The third problem emerges from the facts that although the disciplines of dream research and sleep disorder research have a common origin, they have evolved along distinct lines. Those interested in disorders of hypersomnia or sleep-related breathing disorders rarely address the dreams in their subjects in the same detail as elements of the neurophysiology or neuroanatomy. Similarly, dream researchers tend to emphasize the examination of dreams in otherwise normal individuals. The methodology of these different groups of researchers is quite distinct. These concerns are not intended to discourage the interested reader; they are merely set down as cautions in the exploration of dreams and dreaming in disorders of sleep.

DEFINITIONS

It would be nice to start with a precise definition of dreams and dreaming, a definition that would permit simple quantification and measurement. Although there is agreement that dreams are phenomenological, a precise definition has eluded researchers. Efforts by a joint effort of the Association of Professional Sleep Societies and the Association for the Study of Dreams failed to produce a consensus (Pagel et al., 2001). For the purposes of this review, it is important to keep in mind that any definition will also have to encompass the diverse literature on the topic of dreams in disorders of sleep. This literature spans many decades and researchers with diverse background. Therefore, for the purposes of this chapter, we shall consider mentations or any subjectively experienced cognitive events associated with sleep. This will also include mentations associated with wake-sleep transitions.

METHODS OF DESCRIPTION

Descriptions of dreams can proceed along several lines. Before looking at the impact of sleep disorders on dreams, we must first consider the methods of description. Historically, the focus can be placed either on the detail and meaning of the content or on the form of the content. The former will not be addressed in this review. The "form of the content" refers to features such as quantity, timing, or general intrinsic patterns such as stereotypy or bizarreness. It is possible to develop definitions that will allow one to generalize across populations. Detail of content is often linked to personal experience, cultural background, and so forth. Such an approach has limited value in discussions of disease states.

1. Timing: There is a growing literature that supports the chronobiology of dreaming; certainly, the timing, intensity, and quality of dreams appear to follow patterns that recognize the short ultradian rhythms, the established 24-hour circadian rhythms, a 12-hour circasemidian rhythm, and a gender-based 28-day circatrigintan rhythm (Nielsen, 2005). In this context, it is useful to keep in mind that dreams may vary according to different rhythms. Unfortunately, studies of dreams in sleep disorders have been restricted to disruptions of circadian rhythms.

2. Quantity or intensity. Several descriptions can be found where a recall of dreams has either increased or decreased in quantity. The decreases have been referred to as either a "global cessation" of dreaming (GCD) or a more modest,

"impoverishment" of dreaming. At the other extreme, excessive dreaming has also been described.

3. Quality. Several features or qualitative changes have also been described in the dreams associated with sleep disorders. At times, this may take the form of stereotypy with a repetitive form.

4. Emotional valence. Fear and bizarreness have been described with the changes in dream associated with a variety of disorders. It is quite reasonable to assume that a systematic inventory of dreams associated with disorders of sleep might also include other descriptions.

STRESS AND DREAMS

Disorders of sleep carry stress to the individual. Most of the sleep disorders described in this chapter have evolved in the context of an associated medical or psychiatric disorder. Each of these associated disorders may create additional stress. It is not unreasonable to assume that stress can result in an alteration of dreams. Therefore, before proceeding with a description of dreams in disorders of sleep, it is critical to have some idea of the changes encountered in nonspecific stress.

Several studies have emphasized the impact of stress on the content of dreams. The usual finding is to note that the elements of the stressful experience are incorporated into dream content. Health-related stressors intruding into dream content have been described in patients awaiting surgery (Berger, Hunter, & Lane, 1971), burn patients (Raymond, Nielsen, Lavigne, & Choiniere, 2002), and women with painful menses (Bucci, Creelman, & Severino, 1991). Another study (Duke & Davidson, 2002) suggested that the stress of pending exams led to an increase in dream recall among students, even though the finding was not clearly replicated (Delorme, Lortie-Lussier, & De Koninck, 2002). Similarly, during a particularly stressful period, stockbrokers were found to display a correlation between their stress levels and negative dream features, including recurring nightmares (Kroth, Thompson, Jackson, Pascali, & Ferreira, 2002). This is also consistent with other observations on the impact of stress on the activation of recurring dreams (Brown & Donderi, 1986; Cartwright, 1979; Zadra, O'Brien, & Donderi, 1997-1998). This has been noted to be particularly true for negative recurring dreams (Zadra, 1996).

In addition to naturalistic observations, several experimental studies have supported the observations that stress may influence the content of dreams and activate a tendency to experience recurring dreams. Similar findings have been demonstrated with pain (Nielsen, McGregor, Zadra, Ilnicki, & Ouellet, 1993), fluid deprivation (Bokert, 1967), intellectual stressors (Koulac,

Prevost, & De Koninck, 1985; Stewart & Koulack, 1993), and unpleasant movies (De Koninck & Koulac, 1975).

In addition to nonspecific stress and its impact on dream content and quality, one needs to also consider the impact of depression. Many of the disorders of sleep are associated with chronic illness. Chronic illness, in turn, carries an implicit association with depression and affective disorders. Reviews of the relationship between dreams and depression can be found elsewhere (Benca, 2005). There are two features that need to be highlighted. The first is the association between depression and apparent REM pressure with a shortened REM latency, increased REM density, increased REM activity, and increased REM percentage of total sleep (Kupfer et al., 1984; Kupfer, Reynolds, Ulrich, & Grochocinski, 1986; Nofzinger et al., 1991; Vogel, Buffenstein, Minter, & Hennessey, 1990). This would suggest a shift in dream timing, especially if one places an emphasis on the dreams associated with REM sleep. The observation of increased REM density is curious, but the implication for dreams or other disorders of sleep is still speculative. The second factor is the apparent circadian phase advance that has been proposed as a component of the underlying relationship between depression and sleep (Armitage, Hoffmann, & Rush, 1999; Riemann, Berger, & Voderholzer, 2001; Wehr & Wirz-Justice, 1981). Again, the implication for our discussion is the impact on the timing of dreams and dreaming.

NIGHTMARES

The nightmare is generally considered to be a frightening dream that awakens the sleeper. As with any definition, there is room for controversy. In particular, some argue that a disturbing dream, even in the absence of an awakening, should be considered (Halliday, 1987; Zadra & Donderi, 2000). The argument is based upon several observations. For instance, patients with psychosomatic disorders do not always report awakenings, despite the severity of the nightmare (Levitan, 1976; Van Bork, 1982). Furthermore, in patients with chronic nightmares, the intensity or associated distress of the nightmare does not correlate with the reported awakenings. In fact, it is not uncommon for these patients to report that the nightmare is not associated with an awakening (Zadra & Donderi, 2000). Finally, in those patients reporting both bad dreams and nightmares, the emotional intensity of the bad dream may approach that of the nightmare in almost one-half of the cases (Zadra & Donderi, 2003). As a consequence, the definition has shifted to simply reflect disturbing mental experiences (Hall, 1955).

The lifetime prevalence rate for nightmares is difficult to determine but is considered to be quite high. Pursuit nightmares are fairly common and noted to be 92 percent for women and 85 percent for men (Nielsen & Zadra, 2005). Attack dreams may carry a prevalence ranging between 67 and 90 percent (Harris, 1948; Nielsen & Zadra, 2005). Age is a factor as well. Overall, the prevalence is greater in childhood; increasing through the first decade and then decreasing through young adulthood (Fisher, Pauley, & McGuire, 1989; Salzarulo & Chevalier, 1983). This prevalence then seems to increase gradually over the subsequent decades to the point where 68 percent of older adults may report nightmares at least "sometimes" (Partinen, 1994).

Various surveys indicate that the higher prevalence of nightmares in childhood is matched by a higher frequency in those who did experience nightmares. Surveys suggest that in the 5- to 12- year-old group nightmares occurred at least monthly in 20 to 30 percent (Fisher et al., 1989). Definitions for measuring frequency and intensity vary across studies. For instance, in one study, a problem was identified if the nightmares persisted for more than three months, and the prevalence in children ranged from 22 to 41 percent across the first decade (Salzarulo & Chevalier, 1983). In another study, the prevalence in children was noted to be 5 to 30 percent in cases where the nightmare frequency was described as often or frequent, but 30 to 90 percent when they occurred sometimes (Partinen, 1994).

Gender differences emerge in the reporting of nightmares. These differences have been reported in adolescents (Nielsen et al., 2000), young adults (Coren, 1994; Tan & Hicks, 1995), middle-aged adults (Hublin, Kaprio, Partinen, & Koskenvuo, 1999; Low et al., 2003), and in the general population (Claridge, Clark, & Davis, 1997; Nielsen & Zadra, 2005). Interestingly, these gender differences have not been apparent in studies of children (Fisher et al., 1989; Fisher & Wilson, 1987; Muris, Merckelbach, Gadet, & Moulaert, 2000; Vela-Bueno et al., 1985). A longitudinal study by Nielsen and colleagues (2000) demonstrated a marked divergence between 13 and 16 years of age. In those reporting nightmare frequency as "often," the prevalence in girls almost doubled (2.7 to 4.9 percent), whereas the prevalence in boys dropped from 2.5 to 0.4 percent.

Interpretation of all of these studies must keep in mind that results may vary according to the frequency and intensity of nightmares that are identified. For instance, if one looks at reports of one or more nightmare per month in young adults, several studies indicate a prevalence of 8 to 30 percent (Belicki & Cuddy, 1991; Levin, 1994; Wood & Bootzin, 1990). On the other hand, if one looks at reports of often or always then the prevalence appears to drop to 2 to 5 percent (Partinen, 1994).

It is often assumed that the presence of nightmares carries an increased association with elements of psychopathology (Chivers & Blagrove, 1999; Levin & Fireman, 2002; Nielsen et al,. 2000; Schredl, 2003; Zadra &

Donderi, 2000). Surprisingly, this relationship does not always seem to hold (Belicki, 1992; Wood & Bootzin, 1990). Several factors seem to account for these discrepancies, including the variable nature of the associated psychopathological features, the variability in the distress associated with these nightmares, and the coping style of the individual. For instance, it is generally accepted that if one uses the Minnesota Multiphasic Personality Inventory that lifelong sufferers of frequent nightmares tend to manifest more psychopathological symptoms than matched controls (Berquier & Ashton, 1992; Levin & Raulin, 1991). Hartman, however, emphasized that these affected individuals fell into different subgroups and that personality subtypes were associated with different nightmare prevalence (Hartmann, 1989; Hartmann, Elkin, & Garg, 1991). Distress is another factor that needs to be considered. Frequency and distress have been demonstrated to not be equivalent (Belicki, 1992; Wood & Bootzin, 1990). It appears that it is the distress factor that correlates most closely to extent of psychopathology, especially anxiety and depression (Wood & Bootzin, 1990). Finally, coping style needs to be considered as one examines the relationship between nightmare report and psychopathology. As one might anticipate, a dysfunctional coping style leads to increased distress and associated psychopathology (Agargün et al., 2003).

Syndrome of Recurring Nightmares

This syndrome is associated with recurring or frequent nightmares characterized by a recurrent theme. It is not uncommon that they are associated with increased frequency of dreaming. At least a subset of recurring nightmares has been linked to complex partial seizures (Penfield & Erickson, 1941; Solms, 1997). Some of these recurring nightmares have been considered to be manifestations of these seizures. On the other hand, recurring nightmares may be independent of any obvious epileptic activity. These latter recurrences tend to be less stereotyped and usually depict unpleasant conflicts and stresses that may vary over time (Cartwright, 1979; Zadra, 1996). Although some of these less well-stereotyped recurrences reflect significant trauma or psychopathology, many do not. It is not uncommon to encounter recurrent themes of being chased or threatened in some manner or being confronted with a natural disaster. Dreams with less recurrence and described as recurrent themes or recurrent contents are not so clearly associated with psychopathology and may reflect adaptive functions (Domhoff, 1993).

The Impact of Drugs and Alcohol on Dreams and Nightmares

Several classes of drugs and alcohol have been shown to influence dreams and nightmares (Thompson, 1999). Medications found to most often influence nightmares include: sedative/hypnotics, beta-blockers, and amphetamines. Among catecholaminergic agents, the dopaminergic agents and some of the dopamine-blockers have also been associated with vivid dreams and nightmares. Among the antidepressants, buproprion leads to more vivid dreams and nightmares than most of the others. The selective serotonin reuptake inhibitors are of particular interest since they tend to decrease dream recall, but also increase dream intensity and bizarreness (Pace-Schott et al., 2001). The nocturnal administration of tricyclics and neuroleptics also tend to increase the recall of frightening dreams (Flemenbaum, 1976; Strayhorn & Nash, 1978)

Withdrawal of barbiturates (Firth, 1974; Kales, Bixler, Tan, Scharf, & Kales, 1974) or alcohol (Hershon, 1977) has been associated with the development of vivid dreams and nightmares. In both cases, this phenomenon has been associated with the REM rebound, which occurs from the sudden cessation of a potent REM suppressant. In fact, the vivid and macabre dreaming associated with alcohol withdrawal may be central to the delirium tremens (DTs) of acute alcohol withdrawal (Hishikawa et al., 1981). The underlying pathophysiology for the explanation of the vivid dreams and nightmares encountered in drug withdrawal is not clearly understood (Pace-Schott et al., 2001).

SLEEP-RELATED HALLUCINATIONS

The distinction between dreams and sleep-related hallucinatory phenomena can be challenging. Nevertheless, these dream-like phenomena can be seen as the core of several apparent disorders of sleep.

Terrifying Hypnagogic Hallucinations

Terrifying hypnagogic hallucinations (THHs) are terrifying dreams similar to those in REM sleep. These are thought to be distinct from the vivid dream-like activity that may occur at sleep onset and is thought to be associated with light stages of NREM sleep (Dement & Kleitman, 1957; Foulkes & Vogel, 1965; Gastaut & Broughton, 1967; Vogel, Foulkes, & Trosman, 1966). After a sudden awakening at sleep onset, there is prompt recall of frightening content (American Sleep Disorders Association, 1997). These are generally thought to be correlated to the presence of a sleep onset REM period (SOREMP). In particular, these include narcolepsy-cataplexy syndrome with the incidence of about 4 to 8 percent (Partinen, 1994), but also other factors that might promote the early emergence of REM sleep in a sleep period. These can include sleep deprivation or the sudden withdrawal of agents that may have previously suppressed REM sleep. It has been noted that these may be associated with heightened level of anxiety because of the vivid nature and the fact that they may be associated with a degree of sleep paralysis (Nielsen, 2005). THHs may actually create enough anxiety that they may be associated with sleep-onset insomnia.

Hypnagogic and Hypnopompic Hallucinations of Narcolepsy

Early descriptions of narcolepsy usually reference the sleep-onset (hypnagogic) or awakening (hypnopompic) hallucinations. These are usually associated with a degree of sleep paralysis and usually include vision. These hallucinations may include simple forms changing in size. Images of animals or people may present transiently and may involve color. Auditory features may vary in complexity from simple sounds to elaborate melodies. At times, they may be quite realistic. At times, the individual may experience a variety of unusual somatic sensations including changes in location of body parts or a sense of elevation or floating (Guilleminault & Fromherz, 2005). At any rate, any of these hallucinations may be associated with anxiety and lead to THHs.

Sleep Paralysis Associated With Hallucinations

The discussion of THHs and the hypnagogic/hynopompic hallucinations of narcolepsy noted that these hallucinations may be associated with a degree of sleep paralysis. Sleep paralysis is an inability to move during the transition into or out of sleep. Sleep paralysis likely represents the persistence of REM sleep atonia into wakefulness and is extremely common in nonnarcoleptics, occurring in more than 33 percent of the general population (Partinen, 1994). It may be familial, and it is more common in the setting of sleep deprivation and being in the supine position (Cheyenne, 2002; Ohayon, Zulley, Guilleminault, & Smirne, 1999; Takeuchi, Fukada, & Sasaki, 2002). It is noteworthy that hypnagogic hallucinations are not necessarily accompanied by sleep paralysis. Nevertheless, sleep paralysis is of import in this discussion because it is generally accompanied by vivid hypnagogic hallucinations. In one university sample, it was noted that almost all (98.4 percent) experienced hallucinations in associations with hallucinations (Spanos et al., 1995).

The relationship of sleep paralysis and hypnagogic hallucinations carries an additional historic note. It seems that the original use of the term nightmare was to denote the combination of sleep paralysis and hypnagogic hallucinations (Mahowald & Ettinger, 1990).

Sleep Starts

Sleep starts (hypnic myoclonus, myoclonic jerks, hypnic jerks, hypnagogic jerks) refer to brief, phasic contractions of the limbs or trunk that occur at sleep onset. They may be associated with brief, vivid dream events. A common event is the sensation of falling. Brief sensory flashes, as well as complex hypnagogic images may also accompany sleep starts. Sleep starts are quite common and considered to be a normal phenomenon, with a prevalence of 60 to 70 percent (American Sleep Disorders Association, 1997). Nevertheless, severe starts may interfere with sleep onset (Broughton, 1988). Sleep starts are considered to be similar to the exploding head syndrome, which is associated with a sudden loud auditory sensation with or without a bright flash (Pearce, 1989).

CHANGES IN QUANTITY

GCD

In 1883, Charcot reported a case with a loss of visual imagery and visual dreaming. Over the years, several observations have been made about the general topic of the cessation of dreaming, and these have been reviewed by Solms (1997). When asked, almost a third of patients with "neurological illness" reported a GCD. In general, parietal lobe involvement seemed be particularly implicated in GCD. Unfortunately, 43 percent had nonlocalizing or diffuse pathologies. A total of 42 percent of those reporting GCD also had parietal lobe lesions, and another 7 percent had adjacent lesions (Solms, 1997), a finding consistent with earlier observations (Doricchi & Violani, 1992). Frontal lobe involvement was implicated in about 8 percent of the patients with GCD (Solms, 1997), a finding consistent with a study of schizophrenics with frontal lobotomies (Jus et al., 1973). Additional case studies have provided some clues to the possible lateralization of this effect. Studies of patients with hemisperectomies have implicated the left hemisphere in the recall of dreams. The right hemispherectomy was associated with relative preservation of dream recall, and the left hemispherectomy was associated with a significant impoverishment of dream recall (McCormick et al., 1997; McCormick, Nielsen, & Peito, 1998). Additional neuropsychological studies have been consistent with these findings (Antrobus, 1987; Greenberg & Farah, 1986).

Solms (1997) actually attempted to clarify the nomenclature surrounding the concept of GCD. Historically, GCD was considered as synonymous with the Charcot-Wilbrand syndrome. In fact, he distinguishes two forms. The first is the form attributed to Charcot's initial description and is best referred to as the syndrome of nonvisual dreaming with an associated loss of visual imagery and visual dreaming in the context of normal dreaming. It arises exclusively from damage to the medial occipito-temporal region. Solms also considers four distinct variants.

1. The first is a *complete cessation of visual dream-imagery*, which is actually the variant initially described by Charcot. It is linked to bilateral medial occipito-temporal lesions and an associated visuospatial short-term memory deficit. As one might expect, this variant may be associated with other syndromes linked to similar bilateral lesions such as prosopagnosia, topographical agnosia, or some form of visual agnosia.

2. The second is a *cessation of facial dream-imagery* and was first described by Tzsavara (1967). This variant is associated with similar lesions with involvement of the fusiform gyri bilaterally. As one might expect, it is usually associated with prosopagnosia or the inability to recall familiar faces.

3. The third variant can also be predicted by the location of these bilateral lesions. The cessation of color-dream imagery was described by Sacks and Wasserman (1987). The associated lesions are again bilateral mesial occipito-temporal lesions with involvement of the fusiform gyri bilaterally, but perhaps more posteriorly. As one might anticipate, this syndrome is usually accompanied by cerebral achromatopsia, which is a central impairment in hue discrimination.

4. The fourth variant is a *cessation of kinematic dream-imagery*. Although the lesion is in a similar location to the other variants, only the right hemisphere is implicated. First described by Kerr and Foulkes (1981), it is typically associated with impoverished kinematic imagery and visuospatial short-term memory deficit.

The second form of the Charcot-Wilbrand syndrome actually refers to the more proper GCD. Early descriptions of this syndrome have been attributed to Wilbrand (1887) and Muller (1892). Although this form has been associated with diffuse lesions such as hydrocephalus, there is also an association with focal lesions. It is this form that follows the pattern of parietal lobe involvement as noted above, although Solms emphasizes the inferior parietal localization and notes that it can be seen with either right- or left-sided lesions. Deep, bifrontal lesions have also been implicated and have been noted to be a common occurrence in patients undergoing prefrontal lobotomies (Frank, 1946).

Impoverishment of Dreams

Impoverishment of dreams can be considered in different subgroups. There are several older studies that predate the development of modern criteria for identifying dementia and Alzheimer's disease. As a consequence, some of these observations may be misleading. For instance, a study from 1975 demonstrated a progressive loss of dream recall from REM sleep as the disease progressed from mild to severe (Kramer, Roth, & Trinder, 1975). This seems quite reasonable in view of independent observations that REM sleep decreases with the progression of Alzheimer's disease. In another study of subjects with Korsakoff's psychosis from chronic alcoholism, there was evidence of diminished dream recall, despite near-normal REM sleep time (Greenberg, Pearlman, Brooks, Mayer, & Hartmann, 1968). Obviously, it is somewhat difficult to distinguish a specific dream-recall disorder from a more generalized amnesic disorder. In a similar fashion, patients with amnestic disorders from mild encephalitis were also found to have impoverished recall upon awakening from REM sleep when compared to normal expectations (Torda, 1969). Perhaps it is more reasonable to consider the review of GCD by Solms (1997) where impoverishment is considered as a partial form of global cessation.

There has been an additional attempt to link impoverishment of dreams with alexithymia. Alexithymia refers to a difficulty in verbalizing emotions, literally, to a lack of a lexicon for describing feelings. In general, there had been a tendency to link alexothymia with psychosomatic illness. It was in this population that diminished dream recall and an absence of affect was noted (Apfel & Sifneos, 1979; Levitan, 1978; Sifneos, 1973). In other studies, it was noted that nocturnal asthma patients with a high incidence of alexothymia had an impoverishment of dream recall from REM awakenings (Monday, Montplaisir, & Malo, 1987). In studies of a Finnish population, it was also noted that alexothymic subjects tended to report colorless dreams (Hyyppä, Lindholm, Kronholm, & Lehtinen, 1990) and that nonclinical alexothymics reported less fantastic dreams when compared to controls (Parker, Bauermann, & Smith, 2000). Other studies have suggested a correlation between high alexithymia scores and dreams with macabre or nightmarish content (Levitan & Winkler, 1985). Unfortunately, attempts to delineate the polysomnographic correlates of alexithymia have only produced inconsistent results (Bazydlo, Lumley, & Roehrs, 2001; De Gennaro et al., 2002).

Posttraumatic stress disorder (PTSD) is another disorder with evidence that suggests an impoverishment of dream recall (Lavie, 2001; Pillar, Malhotra, & Lavie, 2000). In a study of PTSD with disturbed dreaming, it was noted that dream recall occurred at a rate of 42 to 54 percent in subjects with PTSD compared to 89 to 96 percent for controls (Kramer, Schoen, & Kinney, 1984). Furthermore, even a "well-adjusted" group of subjects with PTSD had reduced dream recall from REM sleep when compared to either less well-adjusted or control groups (Kaminer & Lavie, 1991). On the other hand, these findings have not always been replicated, and impoverished dreaming has not been recorded (Dow, Kelsoe, & Gillin, 1996; Lavie, Katz, Pillar, & Zinger, 1998). Several explanations have been offered for the possible impoverished dream recall in PTSD. Some have noted the linkage with alexothymia, which has been associated with dream recall impoverishment (Fukunishi, Tsuruta, Hirabayashi, & Asukai, 2001; Hyer, Woods, Summers, Boudewyns, & Harrison, 1990) Hyperarousal and emotional numbing are features common to both groups (Badura, 2003). Another possibility is that suppression of dream recall may be part of a successful coping mechanism (Kaminer & Lavie, 1991).

Other disorders have also been associated with dream recall impoverishment. In particular, patients with temporal lobe epilepsy have demonstrated reductions in dream recall (Epstein, 1979). Furthermore, it was noted that dream recall after awakening from REM sleep was marked by reduced and less varied emotions. Although medication effects need to be considered, it also appears that seizure type may play a role. In particular, patients with generalized seizures have a lower dream recall than patients with complex partial seizures. Lateralization effects were not demonstrated (Bonanni, Cipolli, Iudice, Mazzetti, & Murri, 2002).

Excessive Dreaming

At times, patients may report that their dreams are too abundant, too vivid, or unrelenting. Epic dreaming is the term proposed to describe complaints of both excessive dreaming ("dreaming all night long") and daytime fatigue (Schenck & Mahowald, 1995; Zadra & Nielsen, 1996). These patients describe the sense that they are dreaming continuously through the night. A total of 90 percent of patients report these epic dreams on a nightly basis, and 70 percent of these dreams have been associated with nightmares, although arousals are not a frequent occurrence (Schenck & Mahowald, 1995). Fatigue and feelings of distress are not uncommon features. Although the dreams are usually quite repetitive, they are not rich in detail. The underlying patholophysiology remains uncertain. Reported cases have usually been female. Polysomnographic studies have not revealed any specific disturbances (Schenck & Mahowald, 1995).

Excessive dreaming may also be induced by withdrawal from certain medications. In particular, this has been noted with agents that are considered REM suppressants with relatively short half-lives. For instance, excessive, vivid, and early-onset dreaming have been documented following withdrawal from tricyclic antidepressants (Dilsaver & Greden, 1984) or short half-life serotonin reuptake inhibitors such as paroxetine or fluvoxamine (Belloeuf, Le Jeunne, & Hugues, 2000).

Excessive dreaming has also been described in patients with cerebral lesions (Solms, 1997). Features include an increase in frequency and vividness of imagery. In some cases, the dreaming may become almost continuous as seen in epic dreaming, although there may still be periods of awakening. Cases have been described post cingulotomy (Whitty & Lewin, 1957) and with fatal familial insomnia (Lugaresi et al., 1986). In general, lesions of the anterior limbic system have been implicated in these cases (Solms, 1997).

DREAM STEREOTYPY

Recurrent dream themes are normal in the general population (Nielsen et al., 2003). It is not uncommon to see recurrent themes like pursuit threat and assault. At times, these features may take on a highly repetitive nature and become quite disruptive. Although difficult to quantitate, the degree of stereotypy may become an issue.

Epileptic Dream Stereotypy

Epilepsy may be associated with recurring dreams or disorders of arousal and parasomnias. At times, the distinction between seizure manifestation and primary sleep disorder may be distressful (Boller, Wright, Cavalieri, & Mitsumoto, 1975; Epstein, 1964; Epstein & Hill, 1966; Synder, 1958). Even frontal lobe epilepsy has been noted to mimic nightmares (Scheffer et al., 1995). Nevertheless, the primary issue to be addressed is the stereotypy associated with epilepsy. Obviously, this discussion overlaps with the earlier discussion on recurring nightmares.

The stereotypy associated with epilepsy can be manifest in one of several ways. In some cases, elements of the seizure such as the aura may become a feature of the recurring dream. Another observation is that recurring dream themes may occur in proximity to seizures. Stereotypy may also suggest stereotypy by a linkage between recurring nightmares and seizures. (Epstein, 1964; Epstein, 1979; Reami, Silva, Albuquerque, & Campos, 1991)

Attempts have also been made to assess a lateralizing effect in epileptic dream stereotypy. A recent review of 19 published cases of epileptic patients with dream stereotypy and known epileptic lateralization was performed to assess a possible effect. Of the 19 cases, 12 had a right hemisphere focus, 2 had a left-sided focus, and 5 were bilateral. These findings were suggestive, but not conclusive (Solms, 1997).

Migraine Dream Stereotypy

Migraine disorders are also characterized by stereotypy, and it should not be surprising that migraineurs should experience dream stereotypy. Little has been written on the topic, but an early study suggests recurrence of dreams, often with brilliant colors and at times horrifying (Zadra & Nielsen, 1996).

DREAM-REALITY CONFUSIONS

The syndrome of dream-reality confusion was first described in 1957 by Whitty and Levin. It is characterized by a difficulty in distinguishing dreams from reality (Solms, 1997). It is not uncommon that there is an associated increase in frequency of dreams. Symptoms may overlap with epic or excessive dreaming, with a continuation of dreams across intervening periods of wakefulness. There may also be an increase in nightmares. This syndrome has been associated with lesions of the anterior limbic system (Solms, 1997). It has also been described in association with lesions that may involve the third ventricle, such as a colloid cyst (Solms, 1997). The syndrome may also be seen in association with other disorders of the frontolimbic system, such as executive system dysfunction.

Intensive care unit (ICU) dream delirium can also be considered as another form of dream-reality confusion. This is a well-known syndrome characterized by vivid, sometimes terrifying nightmares, with an inability to clearly separate dream content from reality. Confounding variables such as medication effects and sleep deprivation make it difficult to clearly define the parameters of this syndrome. Bizarre and terrifying nightmares have been noted to be a frequent feature (Schelling et al., 1998). Factors contributing to emergence of the nightmares include length of stay in the ICU (Rundshagen, Schnabel, Wegner, & Schule am Esch, 2002) and exposure to benzodiazepines (Noble et al., 1990). ICU dream delirium is usually considered to be a part of the so-called ICU psychosis or ICU confusional state.

REM BEHAVIOR DISORDER

REM behavior disorder (RBD) is characterized by excessive motor activity during REM sleep. A cardinal feature of normal REM sleep is the relative muscle atonia that is a component of the tonic background. In RBD, the loss of muscle atonia may actually lead to a state where the patient will enact the movements associated with a concurrent dream or nightmare (Mahowald & Schenck, 2005; Schenck & Mahowald, 1996a). The degree of dream enactment may vary across the night. Partial expression of many dreams may be suggested by the presence of elevated levels of muscle tone and phasic electromyographic activity with phasic motor movements. Interestingly, it has also been noted that patients may not always have dream recall on awakening from episodes of executed "dream" behavior. This lack of recall has been attributed to a variety of factors, including the age of the patient and the possibility of a comorbid neurologic disorder. Despite these limitations, most patients will report that their dreams become more vivid, violent, and action filled, and are experienced as nightmares (Schenck & Mahowald, 2002). The associated dreams may be quite varied, but they are usually stereotyped in structure and emotional content (Mahowald & Schenck, 2005; Schenck, Bundlie, Ettinger, & Mahowald, 1986). The most frequent pattern is that of vigorous defense against attack. These may represent defense against attack by people or animals. Sporting themes and friendly social encounters are also not uncommon (Mahowald & Schenck, 2005). Other dreams have included sensations of movement or lack of movement (Schenck & Mahowald, 2002). The latter may be exemplified by a sensation of being stuck and unable to move.

RBD has been associated with a variety of neurodegenerative disorders, most specifically, the alpha synucleinopathies that include Parkinson's disease and Lewy body dementia. It has also been encountered in the context of medication side effect or withdrawal. This includes alcohol withdrawal or caffeine excess (Schenck & Mahowald, 2002). Treatment involves removal of the offending agent, if possible. Otherwise, clonazepam is recommended. Clonazepam is thought to suppress some of the abnormal motor behaviors and, perhaps, reduce some of the recurrence of abnormal behaviors and nightmares (Culebras, 1992; Schenck & Mahowald, 1996b).

REFERENCES

Agargün, M. Y., Kara, H., Ozer, O. A., Selvi, Y., Kiran, U., & Kiran, S. (2003). Nightmares and dissociative experiences: The key role of childhood traumatic events. *Psychiatry & Clinical Neurosciences, 57,* 139–145.

American Sleep Disorders Association. (1997). *International classification of sleep disorders—revised: Diagnostic and coding manual.* Rochester, MN: American Sleep Disorders Association.

Antrobus, J. S. (1987). Cortical hemisphere asymmetry and sleep mentation. *Psychological Review, 94,* 359–368.

Apfel, R. J., & Sifneos, P. E. (1979). Alexithymia: Concept and measurement. *Psychotherapy & Psychosomatics, 32,* 180–190.

Armitage, R., Hoffmann, R. F., & Rush, A. J. (1999). Biological rhythm disturbance in depression: Temporal coherence of ultradian sleep EEG rhythms. *Psychological Medicine, 29,* 1435–1448.

Badura, A. S. (2003). Theoretical and empirical exploration of the similarities between emotional numbing in posttraumatic stress disorder and alexithymia. *Journal of Anxiety Disorders, 17,* 349–360.

Bazydlo, R., Lumley, M. A., & Roehrs, T. (2001). Alexithymia and polysomnographic measures of sleep in healthy adults. *Psychosomatic Medicine, 63,* 56–61.

Belicki, K. (1992). Nightmare frequency versus nightmare distress: Relations to psycho-pathology and cognitive style. *Journal of Abnormal Psychology, 101,* 592–597.

Belicki, K., & Cuddy, M. A. (1991). Nightmares: Facts, fictions and future directions. In J. Gackenbach & A. A. Sheikh (Eds.), *Dream images: A call to mental arms* (pp. 99–115). Amityville, NY: Baywood.

Belloeuf, L., Le Jeunne, C., & Hugues, F. C. (2000). [Paroxetine withdrawal syndrome.] *Ann Med Interne (Paris), 151*(Suppl A), A52–A53.

Benca, R. M. (2005). Mood disorders. In M. Kryger, N. Roth, & W. C. Dement (Eds.), *Principles and practice of sleep medicine* (4th ed., pp. 1311–1326). Philadelphia, PA: WB Saunders.

Berger, L., Hunter, I., & Lane, R. W. (1971). *The effect of stress on dreams.* New York: International University Press.

Berquier, A., & Ashton, R. (1992). Characteristics of the frequent nightmare sufferer. *Journal of Abnormal Psychology, 101,* 246–250.

Bokert, E. (1967). The effects of thirst and a related stimulus on dream reports. *Dissertation Abstracts, 28,* 4753B.

Boller, F., Wright, D. G., Cavalieri, R., & Mitsumoto, H. (1975). Paroxysmal "nightmares." *Neurology, 25,* 1026–1028.

Bonanni, E., Cipolli, C., Iudice, A., Mazzetti, M., & Murri, L. (2002). Dream recall frequency in epilepsy patients with partial and generalized seizures: A dream diary study. *Epilepsia, 43,* 889–895.

Broughton, R. (1988). Pathological fragmentary myoclonus, intensified "hypnic jerks" and hypnagogic foot tremor: Three unusual sleep-related movement disorders. In W. P. Koella, F. Obal F, H. Schulz, & P. Visser (Eds.), *Sleep '86* (pp. 240–243). Stuttgart, Germany: Gustav Fischer Verlag.

Brown, R. J., & Donderi, D. C. (1986). Dream content and self-reported well-being among recurrent dreamers, past recurrent dreamers, and nonrecurrent dreamers. *Journal of Personality & Social Psychology, 50,* 612–623.

Bucci, W., Creelman, M. L., & Severino, S. K. (1991). The effects of menstrual cycle hormones on dreams. *Dreaming, 1,* 263–276.

Cartwright, R. D. (1979). The nature and function of repetitive dreams: A survey and speculation. *Psychiatry, 42,* 131–137.

Charcot, J.-M. (1883). Un cas de suppression brusque et isolée de la vision mentale des signes et des objets (formes et couleurs) [A case of sudden isolated suppression of the mental vision of signs and objects (forms and colors)]. *Progrès Médicale, 11,* 568–571.

Cheyne, J. A. (2002). Situational factors affecting sleep paralysis and associated hallucinations: Position and timing effects. *Journal of Sleep Research, 11,* 169–177.

Chivers, L., & Blagrove, M. (1999). Nightmare frequency, personality, and acute psycho-pathology. *Personality & Individual Differences, 27,* 843–851.

Claridge, G., Clark, K., & Davis, C. (1997). Nightmares, dreams, and schizotypy. *British Journal of Clinical Psychology, 36,* 377–386.

Coren, S. (1994). The prevalence of self-reported sleep disturbances in young adults. *International Journal of Neuroscience, 79,* 67–73.

Culebras, A. (1992). Update on disorders of sleep and the sleep-wake cycle. *Psychiatric Clinics of North America, 15,* 467–489.

De Gennaro, L., Ferrara, M., Curcio, G., Cristiani, R., Lombardo, C., & Bertini, M. (2002). Are polysomnographic measures of sleep correlated to alexithymia? A study on laboratory-adapted sleepers. *Journal of Psychosomatic Research, 53,* 1091–1095.

De Koninck, J. M., & Koulac, D. (1975). Dream content and adaptation to a stressful situation. *Journal of Abnormal Psychology, 84,* 250–260.

Delorme, M., Lortie-Lussier, M., & De Koninck, J. (2002). Stress and coping in the waking and dreaming states during an examination period. *Dreaming, 12,* 171–183.

Dement, W. C., & Kleitman, N. (1957). The relation of eye movements during sleep to dream activity: An objective method for the study of dreaming. *Journal of Experimental Psychology, 53,* 339–346.

Dilsaver, S. C., & Greden, J. F. (1984). Antidepressant withdrawal phenomena. *Biological Psychiatry, 19,* 237–256.

Domhoff, G. W. (1993). The repetition of dreams and dream elements: A possible clue to a function of dreams. In A. Moffitt, M. Kramer, & R. Hoffmann (Eds.), *The functions of dreaming* (pp. 293–320). New York: State University of New York Press.

Doricchi, F., & Violani, C. (1992). Dream recall in brain-damaged patients: A contribution to the neuropsychology of dreaming through a review of the literature. In J. S. Antrobus & M. Bertini (Eds.), *The neuropsychology of sleep and dreaming* (pp. 99–129). Mahwah, NJ: Lawrence Erlbaum.

Dow, B. M., Kelsoe, J. R., Jr., & Gillin, J. C. (1996). Sleep and dreams in Vietnam PTSD and depression. *Biological Psychiatry, 39,* 42–50.

Duke, T., & Davidson, J. (2002). Ordinary and recurrent dream recall of active, past and non-recurrent dreamers during and after academic stress. *Dreaming, 12,* 185–197.

Epstein, A. W. (1964). Recurrent dreams. Their relationship to temporal lobe seizures. *Archives of General Psychiatry, 10,* 49–54.

Epstein, A. W. (1979). Effect of certain cerebral hemispheric diseases on dreaming. *Biological Psychiatry, 14,* 77–93.

Epstein, A. W., & Hill, W. (1966). Ictal phenomena during REM sleep of a temporal lobe epileptic. *Archives of Neurology, 15,* 367–375.

Firth, H. (1974). Sleeping pills and dream content. *British Journal of Psychiatry, 124,* 547–553.

Fisher, B. E., Pauley, C., & McGuire, K. (1989). Children's Sleep Behavior Scale: Normative data on 870 children in grades 1 to 6. *Perceptual & Motor Skills, 68,* 227–236.

Fisher, B. E., & Wilson, A. E. (1987). Selected sleep disturbances in school children reported by parents: Prevalence, interrelationships, behavioral correlates and parental attributions. *Perceptual & Motor Skills, 64,* 1147–1157.

Flemenbaum, A. (1976). Pavor nocturnus: A complication of single daily tricyclic or neuroleptic dosage. *American Journal of Psychiatry, 133,* 570–572.

Foulkes, D., & Vogel, G. (1965). Mental activity at sleep onset. *Journal of Abnormal Psychology, 70,* 231–243.

Frank J. (1946). Clinical survey and results of 200 cases of prefrontal leucotomy. *Journal of Mental Science, 92,* 497–508.

Fukunishi, I., Tsuruta, T., Hirabayashi, N., & Asukai, N. (2001). Association of alexithymic characteristics and posttraumatic stress responses following medical treatment for children with refractory hematological diseases. *Psychological Report, 89,* 527–534.

Gastaut, H., & Broughton, R. (1967). A clinical and polygraphic study of episodic phenomena during sleep. *Recent Advances in Biological Psychiatry, 7,* 197–221.

Greenberg, M. S., & Farah, M. J. (1986). The laterality of dreaming. *Brain & Cognition, 5,* 307–321.

Greenberg, R., Pearlman, C., Brooks, R., Mayer, R., & Hartmann, E. (1968). Dreaming and Korsakoff's psychosis. *Archives of General Psychiatry, 18,* 203–209.

Guilleminault, C., & Fromherz, S. (2005). Narcolepsy: Diagnosis and management. In M. Kryger, N. Roth, & W. L. Dement (Eds.), *Principles and practice of sleep medicine* (4th ed., pp. 780–790). Philadelphia, PA: WB Saunders.

Hall, C. S. (1955). The significance of the dream of being attacked. *Journal of Personality, 24,* 164–180.

Halliday, G. (1987). Direct psychological therapies for nightmares: A review. *Clinical & Psychology Review, 7,* 501–523.

Harris, I. (1948). Observations concerning typical anxiety dreams. *Psychiatry, 11,* 301–309.

Hartmann, E. (1989). Boundaries of dreams, boundaries of dreamers: Thin and thick boundaries as a new personality dimension. *Psychiatric Journal of the University of Ottawa, 14,* 557–560.

Hartmann, E., Elkin, R., & Garg, M. (1991). Personality and dreaming: The dreams of people with very thick or very thin boundaries. *Dreaming, 1,* 311–324.

Hershon, H. I. (1977). Alcohol withdrawal symptoms and drinking behavior. *Journal of Studies on Alcohol, 38,* 953–971.

Hishikawa, Y., Sugita, Y., Teshima, T., Iijima, S., Tanaka, K., & Tachivana, M. (1981). Sleep disorders in alcoholic patients with delirium tremens and transient withdrawal hallucinations: Reevaluation of the REM rebound and intrusion theory. In I. Karacan (Ed.), *Psychophysiological aspects of sleep* (pp. 109–122). Park Ridge, NJ: Noyes Medical.

Hublin, C., Kaprio, J., Partinen, M., & Koskenvuo, M. (1999). Nightmares: Familial aggregation and association with psychiatric disorders in a nationwide twin cohort. *American Journal of Medical Genetics, 88,* 329–336.

Hyer, L., Woods, M. G., Summers, M. N., Boudewyns, P., & Harrison, W. R. (1990). Alexithymia among Vietnam veterans with posttraumatic stress disorder. *Journal of Clinical Psychiatry, 51,* 243–247.

Hyyppä, M. T., Lindholm, T., Kronholm, E., & Lehtinen, V. (1990). Functional insomnia in relation to alexithymic features and cortisol hypersecretion in a community sample. *Stress Medicine, 6,* 6277–6283.

Jus, A., Jus, K., Villeneuve, A., Pires, A, LaChance, R., Fortier, J., et al. (1973). Studies on dream recall in chronic schizophrenic patients after prefrontal lobotomy. *Biological Psychiatry, 6,* 275–293.

Kales, A., Bixler, E. O., Tan, T. L., Scharf, M. B., & Kales, J. D. (1974). Chronic hypnotic use: Ineffectiveness, drug-withdrawal insomnia, and dependence. *Journal of the American Medical Association, 227,* 513–517.

Kaminer, H., & Lavie, P. (1991). Sleep and dreaming in Holocaust survivors: Dramatic decrease in dream recall in well-adjusted survivors. *Journal of Nervous & Mental Disease, 179,* 664–669.

Kerr N., & Foulkes, D. (1981). Right hemispheric mediation of dream visualization: A case study. *Cortex, 17,* 603–610.

Koulac, D., Prevost, F., & De Koninck, J. M. (1985). Sleep, dreaming, and adaptation to a stressful intellectual activity. *Sleep, 8,* 244–253.

Kramer, M., Roth, T., & Trinder, J. (1975). Dreams and dementia: A laboratory exploration of dream recall and dream content in chronic brain syndrome patients. *International Journal of Aging & Human Development, 6,* 169–178.

Kramer, M., Schoen, L. S., & Kinney, L. (1984). Psychological and behavioral features of disturbed dreamers. *Psychiatric Journal of the University of Ottawa, 9,* 102–106.

Kroth, J., Thompson, L., Jackson, J., Pascali, L., & Ferreira, M. (2002). Dream characteristics of stock brokers after a major market downturn. *Psychological Reports, 90,* 1097–1100.

Kupfer, D. J., Reynolds, C. F., III, Ulrich, R. F., & Grochocinski, V. J. (1986). Comparison of automated REM and slow-wave sleep analysis in young and middle-aged depressed subjects. *Biological Psychiatry, 21,* 189–200.

Kupfer, D. J., Ulrich, R. F., Coble, P. A., Jarrett, D. B., Grochocinski, V. J., Doman, J., et al. (1984). Application of automated REM and slow wave sleep analysis: II. Testing the assumption of the two-process model of sleep regulation in normal and depressed subjects. *Psychiatry Research, 13,* 335–343.

Lavie, P. (2001). Sleep disturbances in the wake of traumatic events. *New England Journal of Medicine, 345,* 1825–1832.

Lavie, P., Katz, N., Pillar, G., & Zinger, Y. (1998). Elevated awaking thresholds during sleep: Characteristics of chronic war-related posttraumatic stress disorder patients. *Biological Psychiatry, 44,* 1060–1065.

Levin, R. (1994). Sleep and dreaming characteristics of frequent nightmare subjects in a university population. *Dreaming, 4,* 127–137.

Levin, R., & Fireman, G. (2002). Nightmare prevalence, nightmare distress, and self-reported psychological disturbance. *Sleep, 25,* 205–212.

Levin, R., & Raulin, M. L. (1991). Preliminary evidence for the proposed relationship between frequent nightmares and schizotypal symptomatology. *Journal of Personality Disorders, 5,* 8–14.

Levitan, H. L. (1976). The significance of certain catastrophic dreams. *Psychotherapy & Psychosomatics, 27,* 1–7.

Levitan, H. L. (1978). The significance of certain dreams reported by psychosomatic patients. *Psychotherapy & Psychosomatics, 30,* 137–149.

Levitan, H., & Winkler, P. (1985). Aggressive motifs in the dreams of psychosomatic and psychoneurotic patients. *Interfaces, 12,* 11–19.

Lippman, C. W. (1954). Recurrent dreams in migraine: An aid to diagnosis. *Journal of Nervous & Mental Disease, 120,* 273–276.

Low, J. F., Dyster-Aas, J., Willebrand, M., Kildal, M., Gerin, B., & Ekselius, L. (2003). Chronic nightmares after severe burns: Risk factors and implications for treatment. *Journal of Burn Care Research, 24,* 260–267.

Lugaresi, E., Medori, R., Montagna, P., Baruzzi, A., Cortelli, P., Lugaresi, A., et al. (1986). Fatal familial insomnia and dysautomania with selective degeneration of thalamic nuclei. *New England Journal of Medicine, 315,* 997–1003.

Mahowald, M. W., & Ettinger, M. G. (1990). Things that go bump in the night: The parasomnias revisited. *Journal of Clinical Neurophysiology, 7,* 119–143.

Mahowald, M. W., & Schenck, C. H. (2005). REM sleep parasomnias. In M. Kryger, N. Roth, & W. C. Dement (Eds.), Principles and practice of sleep medicine (4th ed., pp. 897–916). Philadelphia: WB Saunders.

McCormick, L., Nielsen, T. A., Ptito, M., Hassainia, F., Ptito, A., Villemure, J. G., et al. (1997). REM sleep dream mentation in right hemispherectomized patients. *Neuropsychology, 35,* 695–701.

McCormick, L., Nielsen, T. A., Ptito, M., Ptito, A., Villemure, J. G., Vara, C., et al. (1998). Case study of REM sleep dream recall after left hemispherectomy. *Brain & Cognition, 37,* M15.

Monday, J., Montplaisir, J., & Malo, J. L. (1987). Dream process in asthmatic subjects with nocturnal attacks. *American Journal of Psychiatry, 144,* 638–640.

Müller F. (1892). *Ein Beitrag zur Kenntniss der Seelenblindheit* [A contribution to the knowledge of mind-blindness]. *Archiv für Psychiatrie & Nervenkrankheiten, 24,* 856–917.

Muris, P., Merckelbach, H., Gadet, B., & Moulaert, V. (2000). Fears, worries, and scary dreams in 4- to 12-year-old children: Their content, developmental pattern, and origins. *Journal of Clinical Child Psychology, 29,* 43–52.

Nielsen, T. A. (2005). Chronobiology of dreaming. In M. Kryger, N. Roth, & W. C. Dement (Eds.), *Principles and practice of sleep medicine* (4th ed., pp. 535–550). Philadelphia, PA: WB Saunders.

Nielsen, T. A., Laberge, L., Paquet, J., Tremblay, R. E., Vitaro, F., & Montplaisir, J. (2000). Development of disturbing dreams during adolescence and their relationship to anxiety symptoms. *Sleep, 23,* 727–736.

Nielsen, T. A., McGregor, D. L., Zadra, A. L., Ilnicki, D., & Ouellet, L. (1993). Pain in dreams. *Sleep, 16,* 490–498.

Nielsen, T. A., & Zadra, A. L. (2005). Nightmares and other common dream disturbances. In M. Kryger, N. Roth, & W. C. Dement (Eds.), *Principles and practice of sleep medicine* (4th ed., pp. 926–935). Philadelphia, PA: WB Saunders.

Nielsen, T. A., Zadra, A. L., Simard, V., Saucier, S., Kuiken, D., & Smith, C. (2003). The typical dreams of Canadian university students. *Dreaming, 13,* 211–235.

Noble, D. W., Power, I., Spence, A. A., & Weatherill, D. (1990). Sleep and dreams in relation to hospitalization, anaesthesia and surgery: A preliminary analysis of the first 100 patients. In B. Benno, W. Fitch, & K. Millar (Eds.), Memory and awareness in anaesthesia (pp. 219–225). Lisse, The Netherlands: Swets & Zeitlinger.

Nofzinger, E. A., Thase, M. E., Reynolds, C. F., III, Himmelhoch, J. M., Mallinger, A., Houck, P., et al. (1991). Hypersomnia in bipolar depression: A comparison with narcolepsy using the multiple sleep latency test. *American Journal of Psychiatry, 148,* 1177–1181.

Ohayon, M. M., Zulley, J., Guilleminault, C., & Smirne, S. (1999). Prevalence and pathologic associations of sleep paralysis in the general population. *Neurology, 52,* 1194–1200.

Pace-Schott, E. F., Gersh, T., Silvestri, R., Stickgold, R., Salzman, C., & Hobson, J. A. (2001). SSRI treatment suppresses dream recall frequency but increases subjective dream intensity in normal subjects. *Journal of Sleep Research, 10,* 129–142.

Pagel, J. F., Blagrove, M., Levin, R., States, B., Stickgold, R., & White, S. (2001). Definitions of dream: A paradigm for comparing field descriptive specific studies of dream. *Dreaming, 11,* 195–202.

Parker, J. D. A., Bauermann, T. M., & Smith, C. T. (2000). Alexithymia and impoverished dream content: Evidence from rapid eye movement sleep awakenings. *Psychosomatic Medicine, 62,* 486–491.

Partinen, M. Epidemiology of sleep disorders. In M. H. Kryger, T. Roth, & W. C. Dement (Eds.), *Principles and practice of sleep medicine* (2nd ed., pp. 437–452). Philadelphia, PA: WB Saunders.

Pearce, J. M. (1989). Clinical features of the exploding head syndrome. *Journal of Neurology, Neurosurgery & Psychiatry, 52,* 907–910.

Penfield W., & Erickson, T. (1941). *Epilepsy and cerebral localization.* Springfield, IL: Thomas.

Pillar, G., Malhotra, A., & Lavie, P. (2000). Post-traumatic stress disorder and sleep: What a nightmare! *Sleep Medicine Reviews, 4,* 183–200.

Raymond, I., Nielsen, T. A., Lavigne, G., & Choiniere, M. (2002). Incorporation of pain in dreams of hospitalized burn victims. *Sleep, 25,* 765–770.

Reami, D. O., Silva, D. F., Albuquerque, M., & Campos, C. J. (1991). Dreams and epilepsy. *Epilepsia, 32,* 51–53.

Riemann, D., Berger, M., & Voderholzer, U. (2001). Sleep and depression—results from psychobiological studies: An overview. *Biological Psychology, 57,* 67–103.

Rundshagen, I., Schnabel, K., Wegner, C., & Schule am Esch, J. (2002). Incidence of recall, nightmares, and hallucinations during analgosedation in intensive care. *Intensive Care Medicine, 28,* 38–43.

Sacks, O., & Wasserman, R. (1987). The case of the colorblind painter. *New York Review of Books, 34,* 25–34.

Salzarulo, P., & Chevalier, A. (1983). Sleep problems in children and their relationship with early disturbances of the waking-sleeping rhythms. *Sleep, 6,* 47–51.

Scheffer, I. E., Bhatia, K. P., Lopes-Cendes, I., Fish, D. R., Marsden, C. D., Andermann, E. et al. (1995). Autosomal dominant nocturnal frontal lobe epilepsy. A distinctive clinical disorder. *Brain, 118,* 61–73.

Schelling, G., Stoll, C., Haller, M., Briegel, W., Manert, W., Hummel, T., et al. (1998). Health-related quality of life and posttraumatic stress disorder in survivors of the acute respiratory distress syndrome. *Critical Care Medicine, 26,* 651–659.

Schenck, C. H., Bundlie, S. R., Ettinger, M. G., & Mahowald, M. W. (1986). Chronic behavioral disorders of human REM sleep: A new category of parasomnia. *Sleep, 9,* 293–308.

Schenck, C. H., & Mahowald, M. W. (1995). A disorder of epic dreaming with daytime fatigue, usually without polysomnographic abnormalities, that predominantly affects women. *Sleep Research, 24,* 137.

Schenck, C. H., & Mahowald, M. W. (1996a). REM sleep parasomnias. *Neurological Clinics, 14,* 697–720.

Schenck, C. H., & Mahowald, M. W. (1996b). Long-term, nightly benzodiazepine treatment of injurious parasomnias and other disorders of disrupted nocturnal sleep in 170 adults. *American Journal of Medicine, 100,* 333–337.

Schenck, C. H., & Mahowald, M. W. (2002). REM sleep behavior disorder: Clinical, developmental, and neuroscience perspectives 16 years after its formal identification in SLEEP. *Sleep, 25,* 120–138.

Schredl, M. (2003). Effects of state and trait factors on nightmare frequency. *European Archives of Psychiatry & Clinical Neuroscience, 253,* 241–247.

Sifneos, P. E. (1973). The prevalence of "alexithymic" characteristics in psychosomatic patients. *Psychotherapy & Psychosomatics, 22,* 255–262.

Snyder, C. H. (1958). Epileptic equivalents in children. *Pediatrics, 21,* 308–318.

Solms, M. (1997). *The neuropsychology of dreams.* Mahwah, NJ: Lawrence Erlbaum.

Spanos, N. P., DuBreuil, C., McNulty, S. A., DuBreuil, S. C., Pires, M., & Burgess, M. F. (1995). The frequency and correlates of sleep paralysis in a university sample. *Journal of Research in Personality, 29,* 285–305.

Stewart, D. W., & Koulack, D. (1993). The function of dreams in adaptation to stress over time. *Dreaming, 3,* 259–268.

Strayhorn, J. M., & Nash, J. L. (1978). Frightening dreams and dosage schedule of tricyclic and neuroleptic drugs. *Journal of Nervous & Mental Disorder, 166,* 878–880.

Takeuchi, T., Fukada, K., & Sasaki, Y. (2002). Factors related to the occurrence of isolated sleep paralysis elicited during a multi-phasic sleep-wake schedule. *Sleep, 25,* 89–96.

Tan, V. L., & Hicks, R. A. (1995). Type A-B behavior and nightmare types among college students. *Perceptual & Motor Skills, 81,* 15–19.

Thompson, D. F., & Pierce, D. R. (1999). Drug-induced nightmares (review). *Annals of Pharmacotherapy, 33,* 93–98.

Torda, C. (1969). Dreams of subjects with loss of memory for recent events. *Psychophysiology, 6,* 358–365.

Tzavaras, A. (1967). *Contribution à l'étude de l'agnosie des physiognomies [Contribution to the study of agnosia for faces].* Unpublished doctoral dissertaion, Faculté de Médicine de Université de Paris.

Van Bork, J. (1982). An attempt to clarify a dream-mechanism: Why do people wake up out of an anxiety dream? *International Review of Psycho-Analysis, 9,* 273–277.

Vela-Bueno, A., Bixler, E. O., Dobladez-Blanco, B., Rubio, M. E., Mattison, R. E., & Kales, A. (1985). Prevalence of night terrors and nightmares in elementary school children: A pilot study. *Research Communications in Psychology, Psychiatry & Behavior, 10,* 177–188.

Vogel, G. W., Buffenstein, A., Minter, K., & Hennessey, A. (1990). Drug effects on REM sleep and on endogenous depression. *Neuroscience & Biobehavioral Reviews, 14,* 49–63.

Vogel, G., Foulkes, D., & Trosman, H. (1966). Ego functions and dreaming during sleep onset. *Archives of General Psychiatry, 14,* 238–248.

Wehr, T. A., & Wirz-Justice, A. (1981). Internal coincidence model for sleep deprivation and depression. In W. P. Koella (Ed.), *Sleep 1980* (pp. 26–33). Basel, Switzerland: Karger.

Whitty, C. W. M., & Lewin, W. (1957). Vivid daydreaming: An unusual form of confusion following anterior cingulectomy. *Brain, 80,* 72–76.

Wilbrand, H. (1887). *Die Seelenblindheit als Herderscheinung und ihre Beziehung zur Alexie und Agraphie* [Mind-blindness as a focal symptom and its relationship to alexia and agraphia]. Wiesbaden, Germany: Bergmann.

Wood, J. M., & Bootzin, R. R. (1990). The prevalence of nightmares and their independence from anxiety. *Journal of Abnormal Psychology, 99,* 64–68.

Zadra, A. L. (1996). Recurrent dreams: Their relation to life events. In D. Barrett (Ed.), *Trauma and dreams* (pp. 231–247). Cambridge, MA: Harvard University Press.

Zadra, A. L., & Donderi, D. C. (2000). Nightmares and bad dreams: Their prevalence and relationship to well-being. *Journal of Abnormal Psychology, 109,* 273–281.

Zadra, A. L., & Donderi, D. C. (2003). Affective content and intensity of nightmares and bad dreams. *Sleep, 26,* A93-A94.

Zadra, A. L., & Nielsen, T. A. (1996). Epic dreaming: A case report. *Sleep Research, 25,* 148.

Zadra, A. L., O'Brien, S., & Donderi, D. C. (1997–1998). Dream content, dream recurrence, and well-being: A replication with a younger sample. *Imagination Cognition & Personality, 17,* 293–311.

Eleven

Metacognition, Recognition, and Reflection while Dreaming

David Kahn

Consciousness is state dependent. If we want to learn about the brain basis of consciousness, we need to look at how consciousness changes when the state of the brain changes. We learn about the brain basis of consciousness by observing how the mind is affected when the brain changes because of accidents of nature, such as a stroke. We can also learn about the brain basis of consciousness through the normal process of dreaming where anatomical changes do not occur but functional changes do. In dreaming, functional changes in the brain occur naturally without any change to the underlying physical structure. What then are the functional changes that occur in the brain during the dreaming stages of sleep? And how does the mind respond to these functional changes in the brain during dreaming? Research into how the brain-mind changes during dreaming should lead to a better understanding of the brain basis of consciousness.

To do this research, researchers have looked at the phenomenology of dreaming by asking subjects to provide dream reports of their subjective experiences during the dream. And, specifically, if the researchers are interested in a particular aspect of consciousness during dreaming, the researchers may ask the dreamer not only to provide dream reports but to also answer specific questions about what occurred in the dream. For example, if the researcher is interested in characterizing thinking during dreaming, the subject may be asked to pay attention to her thinking during the dream and to describe and compare this thinking during the dream with her wake-state thinking.

The complementary method to obtaining first person reports of dreams is to obtain objective data on the functional changes that occur in the brain during dreaming. This has been done through the use of electroencephalogram (EEG), magnetoencephalograph (MEG), brain imaging techniques such as positron emission tomography (PET) and functional magnetic resonance imaging (fMRI), as well as through the use of methods to uncover changes in the chemistry of the brain during dreaming. Ideally, researchers from both camps work together on the same team. Researchers who have characterized unique aspects of dream reports, and thereby indirectly of the dream itself, will share these findings with researchers who have obtained objective data on changes that have occurred in the brain during dreaming. In this way it is possible to correlate the observed changes in the brain that occurred during dreaming with the subjective experience of dreaming. Doing this would lead to a better understanding of the brain basis of consciousness during dreaming.

This chapter reports on the results of research into the ways we think during dreaming compared to wake-state thinking. We explore the question, how is thinking during dreaming the same and how is it different than thinking when awake? We do this by exploring dream reports and objective data on chemical and functional connectivity changes in the dreaming brain. The correlation between first-person reports of dreams and data on brain changes during dreaming suggests a model for the brain basis of state-dependent thinking as a self-organizing process of cognitive elaboration.

ABILITY TO REFLECT ON IMPLAUSIBILITY DURING DREAMING

If we discover something that seems out of place when we are awake, we are usually aware of a discrepancy between what we expect and what actually is, and we try to make sense of the discrepancy. For example, if we see an old friend who now has blond hair and not the red hair we expected her to have, we assume she changed her hair color. Likewise, if we see a letter on our desk that we do not remember placing there, we try to think of how it got on the desk. Maybe someone else in the household put it there or we just forgot that we put it there ourselves. What is common in these two examples is that the discrepancy is noted and dealt with in some way. We reflect on the unexpected and try to resolve it.

This is often not the case in a dream. A study on reflective consciousness was conducted by Kahn and Hobson (2003) where it was shown that discrepancies and implausibility are often not noticed while dreaming. The study was undertaken to investigate our ability to recognize implausibility while dreaming and to compare this with our ability to recognize implausibility when awake. In this study, participants were asked to write down their dreams immediately upon awakening from a dream. The participants were also instructed to create a dream log to record all characters that appeared in the dream; for example, Mom, Dad, my brother, my friend Joe, a nurse, a girl, my dog Fluffy, and so on. The dreamer was asked to note any and all discrepancies between the character that appeared in the dream and the character it represented in real life, if it did. The participants were asked to distinguish between discrepancies that were noted during the dream and those noticed only upon awakening from the dream. Doing this, the dream acted as its own wake-state control in the comparison between characters as they appeared in the dream and as they actually are in real life. For example, if Mom appeared in the dream in a miniskirt but in real life she always wears below-the-knee skirts, a discrepancy would be recorded in the way Mom appeared in the dream and the way Mom appears in real life. If Dad is screaming and shouting in the dream but never does so in waking life, that would be recorded as a discrepancy with his real-life behavior. If the dreamer's boyfriend has a beard in the dream but does not in real life, that too would be recorded as a discrepancy with his real life appearance. The study investigated the question as to when the dreamer noticed these discrepancies, during the dream or only upon waking from the dream. We hoped to learn more about how we think while dreaming by learning when the discrepancies are noticed and which are more likely to go unnoticed. By comparing the way discrepancies are reported during dreaming to changes in brain connectivity during dreaming, we are able to learn about the brain-mind relationship as well.

In the Kahn and Hobson (2003) study, there were twelve participants, eight women and four men who were graduate students taking a course on the neuropsychology of dreaming at the Harvard University Extension School. They ranged in age from the mid-twenties to the mid-forties. The twelve participants handed in 106 reports over a two-week period, with a mean of almost nine reports per person (standard deviation [SD] = 1.3; median = 8 reports). The mean number of words per report was 257 (SD = 194; median = 199), and the mean number of characters explicitly appearing in a report was four (SD = 2.2; median = 3.4). Incidentally, the large number of dream characters (five when the dreamer is included) reflects the social nature of dreaming. This is in agreement with previous findings on the social nature of dreaming, for example, Domhoff, 1999 and Hall and Van de Castle, 1966.

For dream characters that represented people from real life, the participants were asked to record any discrepancies, illogicality, or inappropriateness of character during the dream narrative compared to the character's real-life counterpart and to note whether these were noticed during the dream. The participants were given choices that ranged from not finding any discernable differences between the dream and real life character to finding major differences. If differences were found, participants were to select from a list of choices. The choices included: the dream character had a different name than the person in real life, the dream character was a blend of two or more known real-life characters, and the dream character engaged in behavior different from that of the person represented in real life. Other choices were: the mortal status of a dream character was different from that of the real person, the appearance of the dream character was different than the real person's appearance, and the gender of the dream character was different than the gender of the person represented. The most common implausibility that was noticed both during the dream and outside the dream was in the character's behavior (30.3 percent relative to other implausibility within the dream, 27.2 percent relative to other implausibility upon awakening). Thus, a dream character's actions and behavior were most likely to deviate from their real life actions and behavior. This result is similar to that found by Revensuo and Tarkko (2002) in their study on dream bizarreness.

Why does the dreamer get the behavior of a person known to him in real life so often wrong in the dream, or at least report a behavior that is not expected from that character's likely wake-state behavior? One approach to this question has to do with dream interpretation, asking what this altered behavior has to teach the dreamer. This is, of course, a valid approach, but one not addressed here. The other approach, which is the focus of this chapter, is to ask what this discrepancy in behavior tells us about the way we think while dreaming. While dreaming there is, in a sense, "freedom" to make up actions and behaviors for ourselves and for our dream characters. This "freedom" is pressed upon us because we cannot accurately access episodic, biographical, and autobiographical memory. The dreaming mind is thus unconstrained by veridical memory data; instead dreams use all sources and combinations of memory data. These often exhibit temporal and spatial order that do not correspond to real life. Dream characters whose real life counterparts are from one era can appear in another era in the dream. Dream characters whose real life counterparts are from one locale can appear in another locale in the dream. Dream characters whose real life counterparts are from one social group or culture can appear in another social group or culture in the dream.

The most striking result of the study was that character implausibility often went unnoticed during the dream. During the dream, almost one character in seven was recognized as having implausibility (43 out of 284 characters). This was during the dream, but what about after waking from the dream? Upon waking from the dream, almost one in two dream characters (133 out of 284 characters) had an implausible feature that was noticed compared to one in seven noticed during dreaming.

TABLE 11.1

Kinds of Implausibility in Character Features per Character Recognized during the Dream and upon Awakening

Kind of Implausibility	Recognized Upon Awakening %	Recognized During the Dream %
Behavior	15.4	7.1
Feelings	10.5	1.2
Age	10.4	2.1
Relationship	4.5	0.2 (Trend)
Appearance	4.7	0.8 (NS)
(Total)	45.5	11.4

Source: Adapted from Kahn & Hobson, 2003.

Table 11.1 provides a summary of different kinds of implausibility of character attributes per character that participants most often reported as having noticed. These included implausibility in a dream character's behavior, feelings, age, relationship, and appearance. It shows how often these discrepancies were noticed during the dream versus outside the dream.

The first three entries, discrepancies in behavior, feelings, and age that were noticed within the dream compared to only outside the dream were statistically highly significant.

In order to illustrate the kinds of dream character implausibility that dreamers recorded, the following excerpts from dream reports and the dreamer's accompanying comments are shown below.

I make the long journey home and run into my sister Joanne, who is worried about Mother. She seems to have disappeared. Elaine Y. will take her apartment. I run into my sister Carol who hugs me, tells me she is worried about Mother and cannot find her. We run into Daddy, who is also worried. He asks where I've been. ... Suddenly we hear "yoohoo, where are you" ... Mimi turns the corner, chattering and pointing.

The dreamer recorded in her dream log that both her mother and father were dead in real life (this mortal status discrepancy was not noticed during the dream). The dreamer also recorded that the behavior of Mimi was implausible, which was, however, noticed both in the dream and after awakening.

A second excerpt from a dream is:

He was very friendly to me and I to him.

The dreamer reported that this was opposite of real life, saying that the character's feelings were implausible. The dreamer reported noticing this implausibility even during the dream.

Another excerpt from a dream is:

> I went outside to play with a group of friends. We were a group of girls in about the fourth grade . . . We formed into two teams. My friend Jenny was on my team.

The dreamer said that the age of the friends and the team members were implausible, but this was not felt to be implausible during the dream. Also the relationship between the dreamer and Jenny was reported as implausible, but it was not felt to be implausible in the dream.

And a final excerpt from a dream is:

> A group of us are in the dining room of my house, which also appears to be a convent. I am there with a group of novices. My mother, the mother superior notices a drip. We are aghast to discover that someone has sabotaged the ceiling by puncturing one of the pipes. We see K walking away, we know she has punctured the pipes.

The dreamer reported that age, relationship, and social role were all implausible attributes of her mother. The subject also reported that the relationship of K to her, as well as K's social role and her behavior were all implausible. The dreamer reported not noticing any of this implausibility during the dream.

The major finding of this study was that implausibility in dream characters often goes unnoticed while dreaming. Not until the dreamer wakes up are the discrepancies between dream characters and their real-life counterparts recognized. The mind during the dreaming state seems not able to reflect on the authenticity of the attributes of dream characters.

One contributing factor for this reduced ability to reflect on the veracity of character attributes is that we are asleep and, therefore, it is not possible to conduct reality checks on the accuracy of dream character portrayal. This absence of reality checking, however, explains only part of the difficulty of being unable to reflect on the accuracy of our dream characters. Dreaming is it's own reality that, in part, is determined by the diminished capacity to call upon one's internal memory for guidance. With no means to call upon external cues while dreaming, the dreamer has to rely upon internal memory for validation of dream character features. But, during dreaming the ability to reflect upon the unfolding events occurs within the context of the dream itself and access to biographical information stored in the dreamer's memory is limited. In fact, it has been shown that episodic memory is almost completely absent during dreaming (Fosse, Stickgold, & Hobson, 2003).

Thus, there is a diminished capacity for reflective consciousness while dreaming, and there is a diminished ability to critically reflect on the accuracy of the attributes the dream assigns to its dream characters. During dreaming we are caught up in the experience of the dream because not only is our ability to utilize external memory sources greatly reduced, but also our access to internal sources is selective.

The brain basis for this may be the functional disconnection of the dorsal lateral prefrontal cortex with most of the rest of the brain, as well as the deactivation of large areas of the parietal cortex (Braun et al., 1997; Maquet, 2000; Maquet et al., 1996, 2000; Nofzinger et al., 2002). A functional disconnection of the prefrontal cortex would make the retrieval of episodic memory difficult (Buckner & Koutstaal, 1998; Cabeza & Nyberg, 2000; Rees, Kreiman, & Koch, 2002). Discrepancies between one's dream and real-life characters would, therefore, often go undetected.

There are also changes in the chemical neuromodulation of the brain from aminergic to cholinergic. The reduction and eventual absence of serotonin and norepinephrine in the forebrain as the subject goes from waking to non-REM (NREM) to REM sleep dreaming may also help explain the difficulty the dreamer has in noticing differences between his dream and real-life characters. Error rates and loose associations increase in the absence of serotonin and norepinephrine (Foote, Bloom, & Aston-Jones, 1983; Mamelak & Hobson, 1989), with the result that discrepancies between dream and real-life characters are likely to occur in the changed chemical environment of the dreaming brain, as was found to be the case from these first person dream report studies.

HOW SIMILAR IS THINKING IN DREAMING AND WAKING?

In the previous section we saw that we often are not aware of differences between dream characters and their real-life counterparts while dreaming. If we are aware, we often accept these differences and the dream goes on. In this section, we want to look at thinking during dreaming more generally (Bosinelli, 1995; Darling, Hoffman, Moffitt, & Purcell, 1993; Fosse, Stickgold, & Hobson, 2001; Fosse et al., 2003; Foulkes, 1962; Hunt, 1982, 1989; Kahn & Hobson, 2005; Rechtschafen, 1978). When we do this, we discover that there are at least two distinct components to cognition during dreaming. One component of cognition is somewhat similar to cognition when awake, the other component is very different. The component that is different is metacognition. By metacognition is meant the capacity to think about our thinking and our behavior. When awake, we generally have little trouble thinking about these. For example, I am now sitting at my computer typing this section. I know that I am doing this, and I know that I know that I am doing this. I can also stop for a moment and indulge myself in a bit of fantasy about my upcoming trip to Maine, and, importantly, I can come back from the fantasy and continue typing on the computer. In the dream-state, by contrast, I am caught up in the dream and cannot control entrances and exits from the unfolding scenes. Furthermore, my capacity to think about the unfolding dream images is limited: as the dream images unfold, I accept them more or less unconditionally; sometimes I completely accept the unfolding narrative, at other times I wonder about incongruities and discontinuities in the narrative. But unless I become lucid, I am not aware that I am dreaming and I cannot think about or remove myself from the hallucinated fantasy being created by the mind-brain during dreaming. During lucidity metacognition returns and may last for the whole dream, though often for just a portion of the dream. Other chapters in this volume address this interesting lucid state of dreaming. Here, we address thinking during the more common nonlucid state of dreaming.

In the Kahn and Hobson (2005) study on thinking while dreaming, twenty-six subjects participated. They were asked to submit dream reports over a two-week period and to submit a dream report log in which they would record whether they were thinking during the dream. In the study, the mean number of dream reports from the 26 participants was 6.8 (SD = 3.2), with a mean number of words per report of 223 (SD = 112). If they reported that they were thinking in the dream, they were asked whether their thinking during the dream was similar to their wake-state thinking. This reliance on the subjects themselves to report about aspects of their dream experience is an example of the affirmative probe methodology. When researchers use this methodology, they must be careful to minimize demand characteristics that could potentially creep in to influence responses. These demand factors were minimized by emphasizing to the participants that there was no expected right answer and that their unbiased participation in this research was important. The advantage of the affirmative probe methodology is that it helps ensure that the subjects pay attention to aspects of the dream that may otherwise go unnoticed or be forgotten upon awakening. In the cited study, researchers asked the dreamer to pay attention to their thinking during the dream. When the subject awoke, he or she was asked to record whether this thinking in the dream was similar to what it would have been had the event of the dream occurred when the subject was awake. The participants were also asked to record whether thinking *about* the occurrence of the dream scene during the dream was similar to what it would have been had the scene occurred when the subject was awake. Thus, the questions were able to probe both thinking *within* the context of given premises and the thinking *about* the premises themselves.

The following is an excerpt from a dream to illustrate what is meant by thinking *within* the context of given premises and thinking *about* the premises.

> I am suddenly in the car with my mother who came to pick me up from school. I was happy. As we drive we end up at the Golden Gate Bridge which was here in Massachusetts. . . . I am now in a store. It looks more like my work at the B. pharmacy. I am looking for my books . . . I search the store wondering where I could have put them. . . . My teacher is now my manager from work.

The dreamer said that had she been awake, she would have thought that the Golden Gate Bridge is not in Massachusetts. This is an example of the dreamer's noncritical thinking about the dream scene while dreaming. During the dream she did not question the premises, in this case, the Golden Gate Bridge being in Massachusetts. The dreamer, on the other hand thought to look for her missing books, as she would have thought to do in the wake state. This is an example of rational thinking while dreaming that is similar to wake-state thinking. Later on in the dream, the dreamer accepted that her teacher was now the manager at the B. pharmacy. This is another example of noncritical thinking about the dream scene itself, the scene in which her teacher is her manager from work.

How often thinking within and about a dream scene was similar to or different than wake-state thinking is illustrated in Figures 11.1 and 11.2. These figures show participants' responses to questions about their thinking while dreaming. The figures show the number of participants who answered yes (Y) or no (N) to the question of whether their thinking during the dream was similar to what their thinking would have been had they been awake.

Figure 11.1 shows the number of yes and no responses as to whether their thinking *within* the dream scene was the same or was different than their wake-state thinking. It shows that most subjects said that their thinking *within* the dream narrative was similar to the way their thinking would have been had the event occurred in real life. The results were statistically significant, ($p < .01$).

Figure 11.2 shows the number of yes and no responses as to whether their thinking *about* the dream scene itself was the same or different than their wake-state thinking. It shows that most subjects said that their thinking *about* the dream event was not the same as it would have been had they been awake. The results were statistically significant, ($p < .01$). Figure 11.2 may be interpreted to mean that metacognition is impaired during dreaming, that is, we

FIGURE 11.1

Thinking while dreaming. The mean number of yes (Y) and no (N) responses per report that thinking within the dream scene was similar to wake-state thinking.

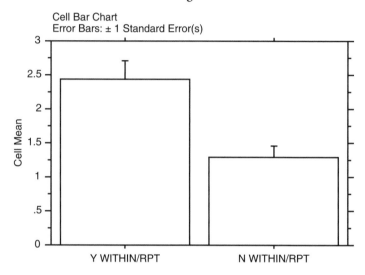

FIGURE 11.2

Thinking while dreaming. The mean number of yes (Y) and no (N) responses per report that thinking about the dream scene was similar to wake-state thinking.

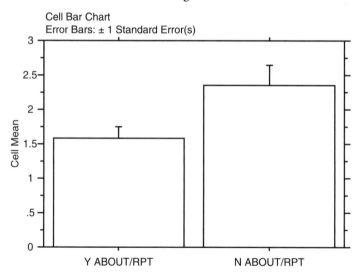

are mostly unable to engage our wake-state critical thinking while dreaming, we do not critically examine the premises within the dream. However, wake-like thinking does occur as we participate in the dream adventure, even if this adventure is bizarre by wake-state standards. Thus, while normal cognition is more or less preserved during some aspects of dreaming, our metacognitive capability is impaired during dreaming. There thus seems to be two components to thinking in dreams, in one our ability to think *within* a dream event is more or less preserved, but our thinking *about* the hallucinatory experience is very different than it is in the wake-state.

However, even though one aspect of cognition (thinking *within* a dream event) seems to be more or less preserved during dreaming, it too is different than wake-state thinking. It is true that the presence of rational thought *within* a dream scenario seems to stand in sharp contrast to the irrational thinking present in the acceptance of irrational behavior. But, in fact, even so-called rational thought is altered during the dream-state because of the cognitive acceptance of irrational situations. Because of this acceptance of irrational situations, even "rational" thinking during dreaming is different than wake-state thinking as the following example of inherently faulty logic during a dream illustrates:

> I am swimming in my bathing suit to a lecture in a very fast moving river. I note how difficult it would be to get back against the current.

Logical thinking seems to be preserved in that the dreamer thinks it would be more difficult to swim back upstream against the rapidly flowing river. This is what the dreamer would think had he been awake. But, the logic is inherently faulty in that he worries about swimming back against the current but does not question swimming to the lecture in the first place.

In contrast, the following is a wake-state excerpt:

> I got off the shuttle bus as usual and walked to the entrance but found the door locked. It never had been locked before. I almost immediately realized that it must be locked because it is the day before July 4 and the building is more than likely celebrating the holiday both days, the day before as well as the actual day itself.

This is an example of logical thinking and deduction that occurred during the wake-state on why the door to my office building was locked the day before the July 4 holiday.

The brain basis for the loss of metacognition is undoubtedly related to the deactivation of both the precuneus and the dorsal lateral prefrontal cortex (DLPFC) during dreaming. The precuneus-DLPFC circuit is activated whenever an episodic or autobiographical memory is retrieved. With only limited access to episodic or autobiographical memory, knowledge about the world and us is limited, as is our history and the history of others in our world. This limitation may very well account for our difficulty in thinking about our thinking and in distinguishing fact from fantasy.

RECOGNITION OF DREAM CHARACTERS WHILE DREAMING

We saw that our ability to reason about our reasoning and our ability to think critically is impaired relative to wake-state thinking during dreaming. Can we learn more about how we think while dreaming by exploring how we recognize our dream characters in the dream? During a dream, we often know characters from our waking life. How we recognize them may shed light on our thought processes during the dream. Do we recognize dream characters while dreaming in the same way as when awake? If not, how do we recognize dream characters while dreaming, and what does this tell us about the way we think during dreaming? It turns out that although we recognize people we know by their face, appearance, and behavior when awake, during a dream we also recognize them by just knowing who they are. Subjects often state "I recognized the person by just knowing who it was." This is true both for known characters (Mother, my friend Joe, my daughter Emily), as well as for generically defined characters (policeman, soldier, doctor) and whether they appear explicitly or only implicitly in the dream. In fact, dream characters are recognized as often by "I just knew who it was" as by their face, their appearance, or their behavior during a dream. The importance of this response is that this "just know" response is a significant way of recognizing characters while dreaming, even when the dreamer does not recognize the character in any other way. This tells us as much about how characters are not recognized as to how they are recognized. This, in turn, informs about the way thinking occurs during dreaming.

In the study on recognition of dream characters by Kahn, Stickgold, Pace-Schott, and Hobson (2000), 320 dream reports were analyzed from 33 participants, 13 men and 20 women. There was an average of 9.7 dream reports per subject having an average word length of 237. The reports contained an average of 3.7 dream characters. These participants ranged in age from the late teens to the elderly who were enrolled in a course on the psychobiology of dreaming at the Harvard University Extension School. The participants were asked to submit dream reports over a two-week period. They were also asked to submit a dream log in which they were to list all the characters that appeared in their dream reports. For these characters, they were to record whether the dream character was known to them from their wake life, whether the dream character was only generically identified in the dream, for example, by their social role in the dream, or whether the dream character was totally unknown (a girl, a man, a woman).

Subjects reported that 48 percent of dream characters were known to the dreamer, 16 percent were unknown to the dreamer, and the dreamer generically identified 35 percent. This result tells us that we mostly dream about people we know, next most often we dream about people that play a role in society (the generically identified dream characters), and least often we dream about people that are unknown to us in our waking life. In addition to this type of identification into known, generic, and unknown categories, participants in the study were asked whether they recognized dream characters from real life, and if so, how. Recognition of people is often related to how we think about them. If recognition is different in dreaming than it is when awake, we should be able to learn how thinking in dreams compares to thinking when awake for character recognition. The choices given to subjects were recognition by a character's face, by the character's appearance, by the character's behavior, or by "just knowing whom it was." The dreamer could report using more than one of these categories. Table 11.2 shows how often characters that were identified as known to the subject were recognized by one of the above recognition categories and how often characters that were only generically identified were recognized by one of the recognition categories.

For characters identified as known to the dreamer, the face category was cited most often (45 percent) as the basis for recognition. This is not terribly surprising. In the wake-state, face recognition is also very often used to identify an individual. By contrast, the percentage of times that face was cited dropped to 9 percent for characters only generically identified by the

TABLE 11.2
How Dream Characters Were Recognized

Recognition Category	Percentage of Times Category Was Cited for Characters Known to the Dreamer	Standard Error %	Percentage of Times Category Was Cited for Characters Generically Identified	Standard Error %
Face	45	5.4	9	3.0
"Just Know"	44	5.0	40	4.3
Appearance	32	5.8	39	4.1
Behavior	21	4.4	38	4.1
Can't Recall	2		3	

Source: Adapted from Kahn et al., 2000.

dreamer, as would be expected since these were not acquaintances of the subject in real life. Also to be expected, dream characters that were generically identified by their social role were very often recognized by their appearance (for example, their uniform) or by their behavior (directing traffic). What is more interesting is the number of times subjects said they recognized a character by a sense of just knowing who they were. This occurred equally often for both known and generically identified dream characters.

Part of the reason for the "just know" response may simply be the fact that we do not actually see our characters or observe their behavior when dreaming as we do when awake. When dreaming, we see dream characters in our "minds eye," which may not be as sharp as physically seeing someone, so we must rely on a sense of just knowing as ways to recognize individuals. While this may be true, as our goal is to investigate the brain basis for consciousness, in general, and for thinking in particular, we suggest that recognition of characters depends upon the prevailing chemistry of the brain, upon the brain's overall activation level, and upon the specific regions of the brain that are preferentially activated or deactivated during a state of consciousness. The "just know" category of recognition of dream characters is as a direct consequence of the diminished accessibility of other ways of recognizing dream characters. And this diminished ability to use wake-state means for character recognition is because of the change in the state of the brain.

One reason facial recognition of dream characters is not used more often during dreaming is because of specific changes in the brain during dreaming that affect facial recognition. There are specific areas in the prefrontal cortex that are needed for face recognition (Scalaidhe, Wilson, & Goldman-Rakic, 1997). Recognition of individuals' faces requires the activation of these prefrontal areas, as well as the activation of areas in the extrastriate cortex specialized for face perception (fusiform gyrus). In addition, there must be neural communication with the heteromodal association areas for face identification. But, activation of prefrontal areas and neural communication with heteromodal areas are reduced during dreaming. Prefrontal and parietal regions of the brain operate at levels that are much lower than wake-state levels during the REM and NREM stages of sleep (Braun et al., 1997, 1998; Maquet et al., 1996; Nofzinger, Mintun, Wiseman, Kupfer, & Moore, 1997). In addition, while dreaming, the brain's chemistry changes from the high wake levels of the neuromodulators serotonin and norepinephrine to levels so small as to be virtually undetectable during the REM stage of dreaming (Hobson, 1988).

And as discussed in the previous section, recognition of individuals requires the activation of areas that allow access to autobiographical memory. In dreaming, some of the areas that allow known associations to be made and autobiographical memory to be accessed are less activated than in waking. These areas include the heteromodal cortices and the dorsolateral prefrontal cortex, as mentioned above. Thus, recognition of a dream character during dreaming must deal with a reduced ability to make associations that relate the character's face, behavior, and appearance with the part the character played in the dreamer's past and present life. Therefore, the dreamer must often rely on just a sense of knowing whom a dream character represents in real life.

FEELING AND THINKING IN DREAMING

There may be a way to tease out the "just knowing" response used as a basis of recognition of a dream character, discussed in the previous section. One way to do this is to offer additional choices as bases for recognition of dream characters. One additional choice, for example, is to use feelings that are evoked in the subject by a dream character as a basis of recognition of that character. We know that feelings are often reported to be present in dreams (Kahn, Pace-Schott, & Hobson, 2002; Merritt, Stickgold, Pace-Schott, Williams, & Hobson, 1994), and we do know that the emotional centers of the brain are activated when dreaming (Braun et al., 1997; Maquet et al., 1996; Nofzinger et al., 1997). In fact, subjects reported that more than 80 percent of their dream characters evoked feelings in them (Kahn et al., 2000). Interestingly, the feelings most often evoked by dream characters in the dreamer were four, namely, affection, joy, anger, and anxiety, the positive emotions being balanced by the negative ones.

Do feelings contribute to the dreamer's ability to identify individuals in the dream? Does the dreamer use his feelings for a dream character as a basis for recognizing that character? And does the dreamer take account of the dream character's feelings for him to identify that character? One hypothesis is that feeling-based reactions to a dream character are used as a basis for character recognition in dreams, and that if dreamers were given that choice they would choose the "just know" basis less often. More broadly, feeling may be important for knowing, in general. We do know that feeling plays an important role in decision-making (Damasio, 1996).

The hypothesis that a feeling-based reaction toward a dream character serves to identify that character even when behavior or appearance is not used or goes unnoticed was tested by Kahn et al. (2002). In that study, there were thirty-five participants, seventeen men and eighteen women, who were enrolled in a Biopsychology of Waking, Sleeping, and Dreaming course at the Harvard University Extension School. The majority of the students were in their 20s and 30s. The students submitted 320 dream reports over a two-week period. The mean number of reports was 9.14 (SD = 6.14). The average word length was 229 (SD = 138). In addition to submitting dream reports, they also submitted a list of all the characters that appeared in their dreams. The mean number of characters per dream report was 3.9 (SD = 2.05). They identified their dream characters as either known to them from their waking life, for example, my friend Susan, as only generically identified, for example, a nun, or as an unknown dream character such as "a boy."

The subjects were asked to record how their dream characters were recognized. The subjects could choose from a list that included "I just know," the character's appearance, the character's behavior, and the social role played by the dream character. Other choices for character recognition could be based on logical deduction, as well as on the relationship between the dream character and the dreamer. Additional choices as bases of recognition included the way the dream character made the subject feel, the way the dream character seemed to feel toward the subject, and the way the character seemed to feel toward another dream character. Subjects could choose from a list of emotions that included no feelings, fear, anxiety, anger, sadness, shame, disgust, joy, affection, erotic, and "other" as a basis for character recognition based on feeling.

In the character recognition study discussed in the previous section, subjects were given only five choices to use as bases for recognition of dream characters, whereas in this study, nine choices were given (appearance, behavior, "just know," feelings, logic, relationship, social role, can't remember, and other). The addition of more choices changed the relative frequency of choices used by subjects as the basis for dream character recognition. The "just know" category of recognition was affected most. The "just know" category chosen 11.9 percent of the time in this study compares with 31 percent in the previous study where less choices were provided as shown in Table 11.3.

Thus, when subjects were given more choices from which to pick as their bases for character recognition, they chose "just know" less often. While other ways of knowing took away from the "just know" response, the one that took most of the responses from the "just know" one was the feeling category (12.7 percent), as hypothesized. The feelings used as a basis for recognizing dream characters included feelings evoked in the dreamer by a dream character (and feelings evoked in dream characters by the dreamer).

Feelings, then, are an important way of knowing. The still not fully understood "just know" category is used when all else fails.

What we learn from this study is that the way individuals are recognized while dreaming is often different than the way they are recognized when

TABLE 11.3
How Known Dream Characters Were Recognized

Recognition Based on	Mean (relative to all others %)	Standard Error %
Appearance (including recognition by facial features)	44.5	3.7
"Just Know"	11.9	2.6
Behavior	11.5	2.0
Logic	7.9	1.7
Feelings evoked in dreamer	7.8	1.3
Relationship	7.1	1.8
Feelings evoked in dream character	4.0	1.0
Social role	0.9	0.4
Feelings evoked in one character by another character	0.9	0.4
Other	1.7	0.8
Can't remember	1.2	0.6

Source: Adapted from Kahn et al., 2002.

awake. The way we think and, in particular, the way we identify individuals depends upon brain activity and brain chemistry. The findings on how dream characters are recognized are consistent with the changed chemical composition of the brain during dreaming (Freeman, 1995; Hobson & Steriade, 1986; Steriade & McCarley, 1990). As discussed in the previous section, there is a reduction of the neuromodulatory influences of serotonin and norepinephrine in NREM dreaming and a complete cessation of their influence during REM dreaming when bursts of cholinergic modulation predominate instead. With just cholinergic and little or no aminergic modulation of the brain during dreaming, attention and volition give way to fictive, illogical, and emotionally charged imagery. This cholinergic predominance and aminergic depletion in dreaming may contribute to the hallucinatory imagery of dreams. And with the emotional limbic centers highly activated and memory systems unable to fully participate during dreaming, it is not surprising then that feelings were often used as a means of identifying dream characters.

SELF-ORGANIZATION AND CONCLUDING REMARKS

The brain is a complex nonlinear system of interacting neurons that are always firing. In the wake mind-brain external sensory input often is enough to override this cacophony of neuronal firing, although, even there, reverie and random thought processes may result from the constant chatter of the neurons. These flights of fancy, however, are often recognized as such when awake. In the aminergically deprived dreaming brain, however, the highly nonlinear connectivity of neurons not subject to the restraints coming from external sensory input are highly sensitive to internal influences. Such internal influences come from short- and long-term memories and from various combinations of these memories, some of which may be illogically connected, which would be dismissed (or enjoyed) as nonsense in the waking mind-brain. With the dreaming brain's susceptibility and sensitivity to internally generated input from its neuronal activity, thought structures are often incongruously woven into the on-going dream narrative, as in the following dream excerpt from the author:

> Dream starts off as a cloak and dagger happening involving me doing things as part of a, perhaps, spy network. Then this guy, a Mr. Vallarian, finds me and is bringing me back to the U.S. where I will be prosecuted or something. I am sad and ask him to go easy on me. Then I am to meet my father, Milton, and Henry at a restaurant called the Office. I and Mr. Vallarian are at a hotel having a drink when my father, Milton, Henry show up. They are in a good expansive mood. I tell Mr. Vallarian to please not tell my father that he is taking me in. Mr. Vallarian is surprised that he knows one or more of them. Mr. Vallarian expresses some surprise that my father is short, and notes how tall Milton is. This is a bit surprising to me, recalling that Henry is the tall one. We are all seated around small tables. My father is dressed in a very nicely cut blue gray suit. I am afraid he will ask Mr. Vallarian what he does for a living. Mr. Vallarian talks to who was Henry but who now looks more like Uncle Storrobin. I am a bit surprised and wonder where he came from.

Upon awakening I commented that in the dream, I accepted three dead people as alive (my father and his brothers Milton and Henry). I am, however, thinking somewhat like I would have had I been awake in my asking Mr. Vallarian not to make my father upset by telling him that he is taking me into custody. Some wake-like logic is preserved (it is logical for me not to want to upset my father). This, however, is superficial compared to the irrational acceptance of the whole scenario. In the dream, I accept the scenario of going out to have a drink and dinner with the government agent (and three relatives who in real life are dead). I also don't question the logic of them just happening to be overseas together and that Mr. Vallarian knows one of them. And, though a bit surprised at the transformation of one person into another during the dream, my logical dream mind does accept the transformation. Some aspects of memory are preserved (for example, my father being the short one) and some aspects of memory are distorted (for example, Milton being the tall one, Henry was the taller one in real life). Other memories seem to just enter into the on-going narrative in an ad hoc way; for example, the sudden appearance of Uncle Storrobin.

As illustrated in the above dream report, we see that thinking in dreams can be very different than thinking when awake, and these differences are consistent with the changed chemistry of the brain and the changed functional circuitry during REM and NREM dreaming sleep as discussed in previous sections. An explanatory model for the production of dreams was suggested in Kahn and Hobson, 1993, and Kahn et al., 2000, 2002, where it was argued that self-organizing neuronal processes through which the firing of neurons become correlated create the imagery and narratives of dreams.

What is self-organization? Self-organization essentially is what the name implies. It is the emergence of structure through dynamic interaction between the elements that make up that structure without an outside agency directing the process. Self-organization often leads to surprising results; for example, the formation of a structure where none existed before, often-called order from chaos. Order from chaos is the creation of an ordered activity or structure from the activity of elements that previously only exhibited chaotic or random behavior. This happens when competition between elements leads to cooperative behavior among the "winners" of the competition and then to their amplification that eventually leads to the emergence of self-organized behavior.

Are special conditions required for self-organization to occur? Under what conditions will chaos lead to order? Certainly, elements may interact without any structure or order emerging from this interaction. This is the case when the elements are completely independent of each other and there is no outside force constraining the elements to behave in a certain way. Molecules of a gas are independent of each other and if no outside force is present, no matter how long they interact with each other, ordered structures will not appear. However, if a force is applied that constrains the molecules to interact in specific ways, an ordered structure can appear. For example, if pressure is applied to a gas so as to cause a phase change, the interacting gas molecules will go over into a liquid state. Another example is when independently moving water molecules are subject to a heat gradient. If the heat gradient is sufficiently strong it will cause the freely moving water molecules to form specific structures. The heat gradient causes long-range forces to appear that connect and correlate activity between the water molecules. Through these long-range forces, the water molecules form a convective cell structure, each cell made up of millions of once independently moving water molecules (Nicolis & Prigogine, 1989).

On the other end of the scale of independently moving molecules are molecules that do not move independently of each other at all. A highly structured crystal is an example of a structure that is not likely to undergo self-organization into another structure without the application of strong forces that are able to break the crystalline structure.

In between these two extremes of very high and very low independence are the regimes of interdependence that allows some degree of coherence to exist within a population of semi-independent elements. This is the regime in which self-organization can most easily take place. This is because in order for self-organization to take place it is necessary that elements have the ability to establish relationships with each other so that they can become integrated into an evolving structure. Elements must have the capacity to develop coherence with their neighbors and they also need a degree of independence that allows them the freedom to explore their environment.

Examples abound both in nature and in the inorganic world. In the inorganic world, the laser is an example of the emergence of structure as a coherent beam of light. This occurs through the cooperative behavior of photons leading to the amplification and self-organization of a narrow frequency of photons, the laser beam (Haken, 1981). In the organic world, the formation of a termite's nest from the interaction of semi-independently acting termites is an example of self-organization. From the initially semi-independent movements of the insects to their eventual cooperation, a termite nest is built. In humans, the emergence of a pattern in a dance in the absence of direction from a choreographer occurs when each randomly moving dancer is constrained by an instruction to keep an eye on one other randomly moving dancer. This instruction almost always leads to the formation of a specific moving spatial pattern among the dancers even though this pattern is not spelled out beforehand.

The brain is also a candidate for a self-organizing system since it consists of very many semi-independently acting neuronal cells. The brain consists of an enormous number of cells (10^{12}), each making on the average 1000 connections with each other. There is competition as to which synapses will form and which will persist within this population of neurons. There is also competition between excitatory and inhibitory neuronal populations. Through this competition, a subset of the winning synapses in various regions of the central nervous system become amplified as both short and long-range coherence become established. This coherence leads to the emergence of ordered activity, such as thought, feelings, and behavior.

Introduction of the concept of self-organization into brain dynamics is important if we are to avoid the infinite regression of a homunculus within a homunculus to explain brain processes. Infinite regression occurs when we postulate an entity (homunculus) that directs other entities to do its bidding. Who directs the first entity? Self-organizing systems do away with this by assuming that entities create their own structure. This is what Haken (1981) calls circular causality, whereby the interacting elements cause their own structure to form, and the structure that is formed by the interacting elements constrains the very elements that caused it to form. For example, the interacting termites form the termite's nest, but once the nest is formed it constrains the behavior of the insects that formed it by changing their subsequent behavior. In the example of the randomly moving dancers, the pattern that is formed by the interacting dancers constrains the dancers that formed the pattern in that they are no longer moving freely as they were before the pattern emerged. In the example of the self-organizing brain, the synapses and neuronal ensembles that formed from the interaction of neurons now constrain those very same neurons' subsequent firing behavior. This is because the neurons that previously had fired more or less independently are now subject to the firing properties of the neuronal ensemble they helped create.

The behaviors, feelings, and thoughts that emerge in us as a result of our previous actions constrain and influence the further emergence of new behaviors, feelings, and thoughts. In the wake-state, behaviors, feelings, and thoughts are also constrained and influenced by input from the outside world, but while dreaming with little input from the outside world, emerging behaviors, feelings, and thoughts are constrained and influenced almost entirely by reference to our own internal milieu. Access to this internal milieu is different than it is when awake. Not all memories are available; for example, episodic memory is almost entirely absent while dreaming. Furthermore, those memories that are available often appear without regard to the temporal, spatial, or logical order in which they were laid down in the wake mind-brain. The result is the diminished capacity to reflect on implausibility, incongruity, discontinuity, and our acceptance (and sometimes enjoyment) of illogical thinking (by wake-state standards) as discussed in this chapter.

REFERENCES

Bosinelli, M. (1995). Mind and consciousness during sleep. *Behavioural Brain Research*, *69*, 195–201.

Braun, A. R., Balkin, T. J., Wesensten, N. J., Carson, R. E., Varga, M., Baldwin, P., et al. (1997). Regional cerebral blood flow throughout the sleep-wake cycle. *Brain, 120*, 1173–1197.

Braun, A. R., Balkin, T. J., Wesensten, N. J., Gwadry, F., Carson, R. E., Varga, M., et al. (1998). Dissociated pattern of activity in visual cortices and their projections during human rapid eye-movement sleep. *Science, 279*, 91–95.

Buckner, R. L., & Koutstaal, W. (1998). Functional neuroimaging studies of encoding, priming, and explicit memory retrieval. *Proceedings of the National Academy of Sciences of the United States of America, 95*, 891–898.

Cabeza, R., & Nyberg, L. (2000). Imaging cognition II: An empirical review of 275 PET and fMRI studies. *Journal of Cognitive Neuroscience, 12,* 1–47.

Damasio, A. R. (1996). The somatic marker hypothesis and the possible functions of the prefrontal cortex. *Philosophical Transactions of the Royal Society of London, Series B, 351,* 1413–1420.

Darling, M., Hoffman, R., Moffitt, A., & Purcell, S. (1993). The pattern of self-reflectiveness in dream reports. *Dreaming, 3,* 9–19.

Domhoff, G. W. (1999). New directions in the study of dream content using the Hall/Van de Castle coding system. *Dreaming, 9,* 115–137.

Foote, S. L., Bloom, F. E., & Aston-Jones, G. (1983). Nucleus locus coeruleus: New evidence of anatomical and physiological specificity. *Physiological Reviews, 63,* 844–914.

Fosse, R., Stickgold, R., & Hobson, J. A. (2001). Reciprocal variation in thoughts and hallucinations. *Psychological Science, 12,* 30–36.

Fosse, R., Stickgold, R., & Hobson, J. A. (2003). Thinking and hallucinating: Reciprocal changes in sleep. *Psychophysiology, 41,* 298–305.

Foulkes, D. (1962). Dream reports from different stages of sleep. *Journal of Abnormal & Social Psychology, 64,* 14–25.

Freeman, W. (1995). *Societies of brains: A study in the neuroscience of love and hate.* Hillsdale, NJ: Lawrence Erlbaum Associates.

Haken H. (1981). *The science of structure: Synergetics.* New York: Van Nostrand Reinhold.

Hall, C., & Van de Castle, R. (1966). *The content analysis of dreams.* New York: Appleton-Century-Crofts.

Hobson, J. A. (1988). *The dreaming brain.* New York: Basic Books, Inc.

Hobson, J. A., & Steriade, M. (1986). Neuronal basis of behavioral state control. In V. B. Mountcastle, F. E. Bloom, & S. R. Geiger (Eds.), *Handbook of physiology: Section I. The nervous system: Vol. IV. Intrinsic regulatory systems of the brain* (pp. 796–800). Bethesda, MD: American Physiological Society.

Hunt, H. T. (1982). Forms of dreaming. *Perceptual & Motor Skills, 54,* 559–633.

Hunt, H. T. (1989). *The multiplicity of dreams: Memory, imagination, and consciousness.* New Haven, CT: Yale University Press.

Kahn, D., & Hobson, J. A. (1993). Self-organization theory of dreaming. *Dreaming, 3,* 151–178.

Kahn, D., & Hobson, J. A. (2003). State dependence of character perception. *Journal of Consciousness Studies, 10,* 57–68.

Kahn, D., & Hobson, J. A. (2005). State-dependent thinking: A comparison of waking and dreaming thought. *Consciousness & Cognition, 14,* 429–438.

Kahn, D., Pace-Schott, E. F., & Hobson, J. A. (2002). Emotion and cognition: Feeling and character identification in dreaming. *Consciousness & Cognition, 11,* 34–50.

Kahn, D., Stickgold, R., Pace-Schott, E. F., & Hobson, J. A. (2000). Dreaming and waking consciousness: A character recognition study. *Journal of Sleep Research, 9,* 317–325.

Mamelak, A. N., & Hobson, J. A. (1989). Dream bizarreness as the cognitive correlate of altered neuronal behavior in REM sleep. *Journal of Cognitive Neuroscience, 1,* 201–222.

Maquet, P. (2000). Functional neuroimaging of normal human sleep by positron emission tomography. *Journal of Sleep Research*, 9, 207–231.

Maquet, P., Laureys, S., Peigneux, P., Fuchs, S., Petiau, C., Phillips, C., et al. (2000). Experience-dependent changes in cerebral activation during human REM sleep. *Nature Neuroscience*, 3, 831–836.

Maquet, P., Peteres, J. M., Aerts, J., Delfiore, G., Degueldre, C., Luxen, A., et al. (1996). Functional neuroanatomy of human rapid-eye-movement sleep and dreaming. *Nature*, 383, 163.

Merritt, J., Stickgold, R., Pace-Schott, E., Williams, J., & Hobson, J. A. (1994). Emotion profiles in the dream reports of men and women. *Consciousness & Cognition*, 3, 46–60.

Nicolis, G., & Prigogine, I. (1989). *Exploring complexity*. New York: W. H. Freeman and Company.

Nofzinger, E. A., Buysse, D. J., Miewald, J. M., Meltzer, C. C., Price, J. C., Sembrat, R. C., et al. (2002). Human regional cerebral glucose metabolism during non-rapid eye movement sleep in relation to waking. *Brain*, 125, 1105–1115.

Nofzinger, E. A., Mintun, M. A., Wiseman, M. B., Kupfer, D. J., & Moore, R. Y. (1997). Forebrain activation in REM sleep: An FDG PET study. *Brain Research*, 770, 192–201.

Rechtschaffen, A. (1978). The single-mindedness and isolation of dreams. *Sleep*, 1, 97–109.

Rees, G., Kreiman, G., & Koch, C. (2002). Neural correlates of consciousness in humans. *Nature Reviews Neuroscience*, 3, 261–270.

Revensuo, A., & Tarkko, K. (2002). Binding in dreams: The bizarreness of dream images and the unity of consciousness. *Journal of Consciousness Studies*, 9, 3–24.

Scalaidhe, S. P. O., Wilson, F. A. W., & Goldman-Rakic, P. S. (1997). Areal segregation of face-processing neurons in prefrontal cortex. *Science*, 278, 1135–1138.

Steriade, M., & McCarley R. W. (1990). *Brainstem control of wakefulness and sleep*. New York: Plenum.

Index

The letters following page numbers in the index refer to tables (*t*) and figures (*f*) in the book.

About the Editors and Contributors

DEIRDRE BARRETT, PhD, is a clinical psychologist and Assistant Professor of Psychology at Harvard Medical School. She is Past President of the Association for the Study of Dreams, author of three trade books including *The Committee of Sleep* (Random House, 2001) and editor of *Trauma and Dreams* (Harvard University Press, 1996). She is Editor-in-Chief of the journal *Dreaming* and a Consulting Editor for *Imagination, Cognition, and Personality* and the *International Journal for Clinical and Experimental Hypnosis.* She is President of American Psychological Association's Division 30, the Society for Psychological Hypnosis. Dr. Barrett has published dozens of academic articles and chapters on dreaming, imagery, and hypnosis.

Dr. Barrett's commentary on dreams has been featured on *Good Morning America*, *The Today Show*, CNN, Fox, The Discovery Channel, and Voice of America. She has been interviewed for dream articles in the *Washington Post*, the *New York Times*, *Life*, *Time*, and *Newsweek*. Her own articles have appeared in *Psychology Today*, and her film review column "The Dream Videophile" is published in the magazine *Dream Time*. Dr. Barrett has lectured on dreams at Esalen, the Smithsonian, and at universities across the United States and in Russia, Kuwait, Israel, England, and Holland.

PATRICK McNAMARA, PhD, is Director of Evolutionary Neurobehavior Laboratory, in the Department of Neurology at the Boston University School of Medicine and the Veterans Administration New England Healthcare System. Upon graduating from the Behavioral Neuroscience Program at Boston University in 1991, he trained at the Aphasia Research Center at the Boston VA Medical Center in neurolinquistics and brain-cognitive correlation techniques. He then began developing an evolutionary approach to problems of brain and behavior and currently is studying the evolution of the frontal lobes, the evolution of the two mammalian sleep states (REM and NREM), and the evolution of religion in human cultures.

John S. Antrobus, PhD, is Emeritus Head of the Cognitive Neuroscience subprogram of the PhD Program in Psychology, City University of New York, located the City College of New York. He has published extensively on dreaming as well as other forms of offline thought and imagery throughout his career, authoring over 100 journal articles and editing two books on these topics.

Sanford Auerbach, MD, is a behavioral neurologist and a board-certified sleep specialist at the Boston Medical Center, where he has been the Director of the Sleep Disorders Center and the Director of Behavioral Neurology. He is also the Medical Director of the Sleep Disorders Center at Quincy Medical Center, an affiliated facility. He is an Associate Professor of Neurology, Psychiatry, and Behavioral Neurosciences in the Boston University School of Medicine. Dr. Auerbach also serves as the Director of the Sleep Fellowship Program at Boston Medical Center. Dr. Auerbach is a board-certified sleep specialist who has been actively involved in the care of patients with narcolepsy and other sleep disorders since he first became Director of the Sleep Disorders Center in 1988. He has also served as the Medical Director for the Electroneurodiagnostics Program at Laboure College. He has worked collaboratively with several investigators in the medical center and has been quite active in promoting sleep medicine education within the medical center and community. Dr. Auerbach has been actively involved in research efforts at the Framingham Study and within the Boston University Alzheimer's Center. His research interests have covered a variety of interests in sleep medicine and behavioral neurology.

Robert Barton, PhD, gained his PhD in primate behavior from St. Andrews University. He is currently Professor of Anthropology and Director of the Evolutionary Anthropology Research Group at the University of Durham, United Kingdom. He uses phylogenetic comparative methods to study the evolution of brains, physiology, and behavior. Recent work has examined the evolution of neocortex size, the role of visual specialization in brain evolution, ecological correlates of neural system evolution, and evolutionary correlates of sleep in mammals.

Dr. Isabella Capellini's research focuses on the evolutionary and behavioral ecology of mammals, particularly ungulates. She graduated in Natural Sciences in 2000 at the University of Milan (Italy) with a research study on roe deer spatial behavior and mating system. She then pursued her interests in evolutionary biology and obtained a PhD in Biology at the University of Newcastle upon Tyne (United Kingdom) in 2004. Her doctoral research project tested the proposed link between environmental variation and the evolution of morphological divergence at low taxonomic level. Specifically, she tested how natural and sexual selection interacted in shaping divergence in body size and sexually selected traits (horns and related fighting structures) in the hartebeest, a group of African antelopes. Since 2005, she has been working as a postdoctoral researcher with Professor Robert Barton on the "Coevolution of sleep, brain, and behavior" in collaboration with Dr. Charles Nunn of Max Planck Institute in Leipzig, Germany, and Dr. Patrick McNamara of the Boston University School of Medicine and VA New England Healthcare System.

Dr. Thien Thanh Dang-Vu graduated at the University of Liège, Belgium. He is currently a research fellow at the Cyclotron Research Center (University of Liège), supported by the FNRS (Belgian National Funds for Scientific Research). He works on sleep physiology, and especially on sleep oscillations, using neuroimaging techniques: PET (positron emission tomography) and mainly combined EEG/fMRI (functional magnetic resonance imaging). His interests also include sleep medicine and pathophysiology of sleep disorders. He pursues his residency in neurology at Liège University Hospital.

Dr. Martin Desseilles graduated at the University of Liège, Belgium, and he currently pursues his residency in psychiatry at Liège University Hospital. He is a research fellow at the Cyclotron Research Center (University of Liège), supported by the FNRS (Belgian National Funds for Scientific Research). He works on mechanisms of visual attention in healthy subjects and in several psychiatric disorders using neuroimaging techniques, including fMRI (functional magnetic resonance imaging). His interests also include sleep physiology (using PET—positron emission tomography), sleep medicine, and pathophysiology of sleep disorders.

Maria Livia Fantini, MD, MSc, is currently Neurologist at the Sleep Disorder Center, Department of Neurology, Università Vita-Salute San Raffaele, Milan, Italy. Upon graduating from the Medical School at the University of Cagliari (Italy) in 1995, and completing the Residency in Neurology at the same university, she was for three years a fellow at the Centre d'Etude du Sommeil et des Rhythmes Biologiques, Department of Psychiatry, at the Université de Montréal, where she earned a Master of Science Degree in Biomedical Sciences under the direction of Professor Jacques Montplaisir. Her main work has focused on movement disorders in sleep, particularly on idiopathic Rapid Eye Movements Sleep Behavior Disorder (RBD) as an early marker of neurodegenerative diseases. She showed that idiopathic RBD is associated with waking EEG, autonomic and olfactory impairment, challenging the notion of a true idiopathic RBD. Most recently, she is studying the relationship between neurophysiological abnormalities and altered dream content in RBD. She has published several articles on RBD and Periodic Leg Movements and Restless Leg Syndrome. She is a certified "Expert of Sleep Medicine" from the Italian Association of Sleep Medicine (AIMS).

Luigi Ferini-Strambi earned his degree in medicine at the State University in Milan, Italy. Dr Ferini-Strambi completed a fellowship in the Sleep Disorders Center at the Baylor College of Medicine in Houston, Texas, in 1984. He is currently Director of the Sleep Disorders Centre, as well as Head of the Sleep Medicine and Paroxysmal Events Unit of the Neurology Department at the Vita-Salute San Raffaele University of Milan. Professor Ferini-Strambi is also Co-Chair of the Department of Neurology at the Scientific Institute H. San Raffaele in Milan. He is Associate Professor of Psychology and Professor of Psychobiology of Sleep. He has authored nearly 170 scientific publications relating to various neurological topics, and is Editor-in-Chief of the *Newsletter of the Italian Association of Sleep Medicine* as well as Field Editor for the journal *Sleep Medicine*. Professor Ferini-Strambi is a member of numerous editorial boards, associations, scientific societies, and research committees in the field of sleep research.

Claude Gottesmann studied at the university of Paris, where he received an education in Psychology, then in Neuroscience and Psychoanalysis. He obtained his PhD in 1967. Since 1968, he has been working at the University of Nice.

Erica Harris completed her BA from the University of Virginia in January 2001, with a major in Psychology and a concentration in neuroscience. After graduation, she worked at Duke University Medical Center on studies involving at-risk youths and how they make successful transitions in school. She then obtained her MPH from Boston University in January 2005, with dual concentrations in Epidemiology and Social and Behavioral Sciences. She is currently a Research Coordinator in the Department of Neurology at the Boston University Medical Center. She works on a variety of projects including sleep, Parkinson's disease, dreams, the concept of the self, the frontal lobes, and the relationship between religion and the brain.

J. Allan Hobson received his MD from Harvard Medical School, where he is currently Professor of Psychiatry. Dr. Hobson has received many honors and awards, including admission to the Boylston Medical Society and the Benjamin Rush Gold Medal for Best Scientific Exhibit, American Psychiatrist Association, 1978, and the 1998 Distinguished Scientist Award of the Sleep Research Society. His major research interests are the neurophysiological basis of the mind and behavior, sleep and dreaming, and the history of neurology and psychiatry. He has contributed numerous articles to scientific journals and chapters to medical textbooks and is the author or coauthor of many books, including *The Dreaming Brain* (1988) and *Sleep*

(1989), *The Chemistry of Conscious States* (1994) and *Consciousness* (1998), *Dreaming as Delirium* (1999), *The Dream Drugstore* (2001), *Out of Its Mind: Psychiatry in Crisis* (2001), *Dreaming: An Introduction to Sleep Science* (2002), *13 Dreams Freud Never Had* (2005), and *Angels to Neurones* (2005). Dr. Hobson is the creator of Dreamstage: An Experimental Portrait of the Dreaming Brain, which toured internationally from 1980-84. Professor Hobson has held many visiting appointments, most recently as Invited Lecturer at the Dipartimento di Psicologia, Universita' di Bologna, Italy. He lives in Brookline, Massachusetts, and Messina, Italy.

David Kahn received his PhD in Physics from Yale University. He is currently on the faculty of Harvard Medical School in the Department of Psychiatry. He is actively engaged in research to understand normal states of the brain while dreaming. One outcome of this research is the further development of a neuropsychology of dreaming that can be used as a solid basis for a brain-based theory of psychiatry and normal mental experience. In his research, he uses the phenomenological approach of asking subjects to report on their experience. He then attempts to see how those results relate to objective measures of the brain during dreaming found through EEG and brain imaging. Dr. Kahn's recent publications include the 2005 papers coauthored with Allan Hobson "State-dependent thinking: A comparison of waking and dreaming thought" in *Consciousness and Cognition, 14,* 429–438, and "Theory of mind in dreaming: Awareness of feelings and thoughts of others in dreams" in *Dreaming, 15,* 48-57. In this latter study, it was found that a theory of mind is state independent, suggesting that being aware of the intentions of others may be crucial for survival of a social species like man. In addition, stepping into the important dialog between brain scientists and theologians, Dr. Kahn wrote a chapter "From Chaos to Self-Organization" in the book *Soul, Psyche, Brain: New Directions in the Study of Religion and Brain-Mind Science* published by Palgrave MacMillan in 2005.

Sara Kowalczyk completed her undergraduate degree at Syracuse University in 1998 with a major in psychology and minor in neuroscience. Her postundergraduate research experiences led her to a variety of institutions including the Montefiore Medical Center where she became familiar with patient registries and Northwestern University where she coordinated a clinical trial for patients with early-stage Alzheimer's disease and studied sleep and circadian rhythms in mice. At Beth Israel Deaconess Medical Center, she studied orexin and melanin concentrating hormone projections in the hypothalamus and the role of these neurons on mouse sleeping patterns. She completed extensive graduate coursework in neuroscience at Northwestern University and medical science at Boston University, where she completed her MA in 2003 with a concentration in mental health and human behavior. After graduating, Kowalczyk became interested in public health while she was working at the Framingham Heart Study as a DNA research coordinator. She will be graduating in 2007 from Boston University with an MPH in biostatistics and epidemiology. Currently, Ms. Kowalczyk is the research coordinator of the Autism Consortium at Boston Medical Center where she is involved in developing a patient registry and has been able to incorporate her passion for clinical research, public health, neuroscience, human behavior, and patient advocacy.

Pierre Maquet received his MD degree from University of Liège, Belgium (1986). He completed Residency Training in Neuropsychiatry in 1991. From 2000 to 2002, he was Research Fellow at the Wellcome Department of Imaging Neuroscience (UCL, London, United Kingdom) where he conducted functional MRI studies on sleep-related learning, in collaboration with Chris Frith and Sophie Schwartz. He is currently Research Director at the FNRS (Belgian National Funds for Scientific Research). He uses multimodal neuroimaging techniques combining EEG with PET and fMRI to better understand the regulation and mechanisms of human sleep and wakefulness.

Deirdre McLaren received her Associates in Liberal Arts from Massachusetts Bay Community College in 2005. After graduation, she began pursuing her BA at Framingham State College. She has been a Research Assistant at the Evolutionary Neurobehavior Lab at the Boston VA Medical Center where she worked on projects involving sleep, dreams, and Parkinson's disease. She is currently a Research Assistant for MAVERIC at the Boston VA Medical Center where she assists with projects concerning veterans' health and prostate cancer.

Charles Nunn is a research scientist at the Max Planck Institute for Evolutionary Anthropology in Leipzig, Germany, and he holds an adjunct position at the University of California at Berkeley. His research interests include infectious disease, behavioral ecology, and phylogenetic comparative methods. Dr. Nunn's research focuses mainly on primates and other mammals, and he is also interested in applying bioinformatics approaches to address ecological questions.

Edward F. Pace-Schott, MS, MA, LMHC, PhD, is Instructor in Psychiatry at Harvard Medical School in the Center for Sleep & Cognition, Department of Psychiatry, Beth Israel Deaconess Medical Center. His current and long-term research interests include: the neurobiological interactions between sleep, higher cognitive function and emotions in the context of psychopathology (especially the addictions), the effects of sleep and sleep deprivation on higher cognitive functions and on declarative and emotional memory, the neuropsychology and brain bases of dreaming and states of consciousness, and sleep and dreaming in neurodevelopmental disorders.

His current research is focused on the acute and long-term effects of psychostimulant abuse on sleep and cognition using techniques of neuropsychology, neurophysiology, and human behavioral pharmacology. He is also a psychotherapist.

Manuel Schabus graduated at the University of Salzburg, Austria, where he was working on attentional and memory processes in the scheme of EEG brain oscillations. Following up on that, Mr. Schabus established a sleep laboratory at the Department of Physiological Psychology where he did extensive research on the sleep and memory consolidation hypotheses. Currently, Mr. Schabus is postdoctoral fellow at the Cyclotron Research Center (University of Liège) using simultaneous recordings of EEG and fMRI to study sleep mechanisms as well as sleep and cognition relationships. Besides this, Mr. Schabus is involved in research on conscious states in comatose patients and is undergoing training in client-centered psychotherapy.

Sophie Schwartz got an MSc (Biology) from the University of Geneva, Switzerland, and a PhD from the University of Lausanne, Switzerland. During her PhD, she spent two years at the University of California–Berkeley (fellowship from the Swiss National Science Foundation, SNF), where she studied cognitive aspects in dreams. She developed a neuropsychological approach to normal dreaming, showing that some bizarre but typical features in the dreams provide important information about cognitive processes and brain functions in sleep. She then completed a three-year postdoctoral fellowship (SNF) in London (Institute of Cognitive Neuroscience & Wellcome Department of Imaging Neurosciences), where she conducted functional MRI studies on sleep-related learning in collaboration with Chris Frith and Pierre Maquet, and on visual attention in collaboration with Jon Driver and Patrik Vuilleumier. She is currently a group leader at the Department of Neurosciences, University of Geneva (Laboratory for Neurology and Imaging of Cognition, http://labnic.unige.ch). Using behavioral and multimodal brain imaging methods, her team investigates how sleep, attention, and emotion can modulate memory and neural plasticity in adult humans.

Erin J. Wamsley, MPhil, is a doctoral candidate in the City University of New York Cognitive Neuroscience program located at the City College of New York. Working with Professor Antrobus, she has actively studied circadian and homeostatic contributions to dreaming and has published several papers on these topics.